COLUMBIA COLLEGE CHICAGO
3 2711 00135 5506

C0-DKM-922

DATE DUE

DISCARD

SEP 1 1 2007

GAYLORD PRINTED IN U.S.A.

A Series from
Southern
Illinois
University
Press
ROBERT A.
SCHANKE
Series Editor

Other Books in the Theater in the Americas Series

The Theatre of Sabina Berman:
The Agony of Ecstasy *and Other Plays*
Translated by Adam Versényi
With an Essay by Jacqueline E. Bixler

Composing Ourselves:
The Little Theatre Movement and the American Audience
Dorothy Chansky

Women in Turmoil: Six Plays by Mercedes de Acosta
Edited and with an Introduction by Robert A. Schanke

Broadway's Bravest Woman:
Selected Writings of Sophie Treadwell
Edited by Jerry Dickey and Miriam López-Rodríguez

Unfinished Show Business: Broadway Musicals as Works-in-Process
Bruce Kirle

Staging America: Cornerstone and Community-Based Theater
Sonja Kuftinec

Words at Play: Creative Writing and Dramaturgy
Felicia Hardison Londré

Stage, Page, Scandals, and Vandals: William E. Burton and Nineteenth-Century American Theatre
David L. Rinear

"That Furious Lesbian": The Story of Mercedes de Acosta
Robert A. Schanke

Caffe Cino: The Birthplace of Off-Off-Broadway
Wendell C. Stone

Teaching Performance Studies
Edited by Nathan Stucky and Cynthia Wimmer
With a Foreword by Richard Schechner

Our Land Is Made of Courage and Glory: Nationalist Performance of Nicaragua and Guatemala
E. J. Westlake

Messiah of the New Technique

COLUMBIA COLLEGE LIBRARY
600 S. MICHIGAN AVENUE
CHICAGO, IL 60605

Messiah of the New Technique

John Howard Lawson, Communism, and American Theatre, 1923–1937

Jonathan L. Chambers

Southern Illinois University Press / Carbondale

Copyright © 2006 by the Board of Trustees,
Southern Illinois University
All rights reserved
Printed in the United States of America
09 08 07 06 4 3 2 1

Cover illustration: Act 3, *Roger Bloomer.* Illustration by Roland Young.
Frontispiece: John Howard Lawson, ca. 1944. Courtesy of Jeffrey Lawson.

Library of Congress Cataloging-in-Publication Data

Chambers, Jonathan L., 1966–

Messiah of the new technique : John Howard Lawson, Communism, and American theatre, 1923–1937 / Jonathan L. Chambers.

p. cm.— (Theater in the Americas)

Includes bibliographical references.

1. Lawson, John Howard, 1894– 2. Politics and literature—United States—History—20th century. 3. Communism and literature—United States—History—20th century. 4. Social problems in literature. 5. Theater—United States—History—20th century. I. Title. II. Series.

PS3523.A954Z63 2006

812'.52—dc22

ISBN-13: 978-0-8093-2699-0 (cloth : alk. paper)

ISBN-10: 0-8093-2699-X (cloth : alk. paper) 2005032796

Printed on recycled paper. ♻

The paper used in this publication meets the minimum requirements of American National Standard for Information Sciences—Permanence of Paper for Printed Library Materials, ANSI Z39.48-1992. ♾

To Sara

Contents

List of Illustrations xi
Acknowledgments xiii

Introduction: Writing and Righting a Revolutionary's Life 1
1. The Awakening 15
2. Break Down the Walls of the Theatre 34
3. To Beat the Drums of Rebellion 82
4. The Thorny Path to Commitment 119
5. Lost like Hamlet in His Inner-Conflict 154
Epilogue: The Rebel Now Revolutionary 200

Appendix: Plays Written by John Howard Lawson and Their Production History, 1923–1937 209
Notes 211
Bibliography 247
Index 259

Illustrations

Frontispiece: John Howard Lawson, ca. 1944

Following page 118

Lawson as a child, ca. 1904

Lawson, ca. 1925

Roger rescued by the Ragged Man in act 2 of the Marguerite Barker production of *Roger Bloomer*

Louise rejecting Mr. Rumsey's marriage proposal in act 3 of the Marguerite Barker production of *Roger Bloomer*

Roger going toward the lighted doorway in act 3 of *Roger Bloomer*

"Jazzin' up the big strike!" in act 1 of the Theatre Guild production of *Processional*

Jim forcing Sadie into the mine in act 3, scene 2 of the Theatre Guild production of *Processional*

Dynamite Jim hung on a fence in act 3, scene 3 of the Theatre Guild production of *Processional*

The chorus girls from the Richard Aldrich and Alfred de Liagre production of *The Pure in Heart*

Annabel sitting in the tenement awaiting her fate in act 2, scene 3 of the Richard Aldrich and Alfred de Liagre production of *The Pure in Heart*

A Stranger with a Beard casting his spell in act 3 of the New Playwrights' production of *Loud Speaker*

The interior of the abandoned factory from the Theatre Union production of *Marching Song*

Acknowledgments

It is my pleasure to recognize the tremendous network of mentors, colleagues, friends, and family that have made this study possible. Sarah Blackstone, who directed the dissertation version of this project, was keenly perceptive in her criticism, exceedingly generous with her time, and exceptionally constant in her encouragement. I am genuinely moved that when given the opportunity she has persistently championed my work and me. My thanks also to Elise Pineau, Robbie Lieberman, Noreen Barnes, and Lori Merrill-Fink, the fine committee that lent their invaluable criticism and support to that earliest version of this study. Thanks as well to Don Wilmeth, who provided detailed, cogent, and enormously useful criticism to an early draft of the book manuscript. Sections of this study benefited greatly from the input of journal editors with whom I had to pleasure to work: Vera Mowry Roberts of the *Journal of American Drama and Theatre*, John Countryman of *Theatre Symposium*, and Robert Schanke of *Theatre History Studies*.

While teaching in the Department of Speech and Theatre at St. Lawrence University, I profited from the sage council of a number of excellent colleagues, Andrea Nouryeh and Rhea Lehman principal among them. Similarly, in my current appointment at Bowling Green State University, I benefit daily from the unvarying support of Cynthia Baron, Lesa Lockford, Ron Shields, and Lisa Wolford Wylam. Additionally, the Department of Theatre and Film at Bowling Green provided much needed institutional support in the form of research grant monies. Outside of the institutions where I have taught, I have had the encouragement of Dorothy Chansky, Anne Fletcher, and Elizabeth Reitz Mullenix. Many of these persons have graciously suffered my written and spoken ramblings on communists, Marxist aesthetics, and near-forgotten American plays. It is my pleasure to count all these individuals as not only professional colleagues but also as friends of the first order.

Quotations from the John Howard Lawson papers are reprinted by permission of Jeffrey Lawson and the Special Collections Research Center, Morris Library, Southern Illinois University Carbondale, copyright Jeffrey Lawson. Credit is due to Katherine Salzmann, Diane Worrell, and Randy Bixby, archivists who curate the John Howard Lawson papers. Harold Clurman's 8 August 1932 letter to Lawson is reprinted by permission of Ellen Adler. The excerpt in the notes to chapter 4 from the review of *Dynamite* by Ron Kerrigan is reprinted, information courtesy of *The Internet Movie Database* (http://www.imdb.com). Used with permission. Thanks as well to editorial staff at Southern Illinois University Press, principally Karl Kageff, Liz Brymer, Carol Burns, Mary Lou Kowaleski, and Ann Youmans.

I extend my deep gratitude to Bob Schanke (again) in his capacity as editor for the Theater in the Americas series. I can state without risk of hyperbole that this study would not have been completed had it not been for his sustained encouragement, significant suggestions, and invaluable criticism. The study is not only stronger because of Bob's contributions; its very existence is owing to his faith in my abilities and his resolute belief in the importance of the story I was compelled to tell.

I have also had the good fortune of acquiring the advice and support from two of John Howard Lawson's children, Jeffrey and Amanda. In many respects, it is their approval above all others that I hope to secure.

In addition to the mentors, colleagues, and friends who directly and indirectly shaped my research, I owe special thanks to my family, who supported me throughout the process. To my mother, Nellie, and my father, Bob, I owe my abiding curiosity as well as my love of reading and writing. Moreover, the countless discussions around the dinner table with them and my three older brothers were vital in my development. It is there that I learned to ask questions and to debate in a manner that was both civil and humane.

Lastly, my deepest gratitude is reserved for my children Baxter and Truman, who have always brought a smile and a laugh when needed, and my wife Sara, who has been unshakable in her support, love, patience, and generosity. Because there are no words to adequately thank Sara for all she has brought to my life, it is to her that I dedicate this book.

Earlier versions of sections of this work were previously published: "'To Break Down the Walls of the Theatre': John Howard Lawson's *Roger Bloomer*," *Journal of American Drama and Theatre* 14 (2002) and "The Dilemma of Commitment: John Howard Lawson's *Marching Song*," *Journal of American Drama and Theatre* 12 (2000), reprinted by permission of the *Journal of American Drama and Theatre*; "At 'Cross-Purposes': John Howard Lawson's *The International*," *Theatre Symposium* 9 (2001), reprinted by permission of *Theatre Symposium*; "How Hollywood Led John Howard Lawson to Embrace Communism and How He Turned Hollywood Red," *Theatre History Studies* 17 (1997), reprinted by permission of *Theatre History Studies*.

Messiah of the New Technique

Introduction: Writing and Righting a Revolutionary's Life

In the years between World War I and World War II in the United States, playwright John Howard Lawson seemed poised on the brink of greatness. During this period, openings of his plays were regularly met with the passionate response reserved for only the most celebrated artists in the theatre. Critic Gilbert Gabriel wrote in a 1925 critique of the emerging playwright that he felt an "awe of genius" after seeing the Theatre Guild production of Lawson's *Processional.*[1] Later that same year, champion of the little theatre Sheldon Cheney offered a similar view, writing that Lawson was one "of the most promising American playwrights."[2] Three years later, in a favorable review for Lawson's *The International*, produced by the much maligned and lauded New Playwrights' Theatre, Gordon M. Leland hailed Lawson as "a writer of modern philosophy" who was afraid neither of revolutionary politics nor of experimental theatrical forms.[3] And in the early thirties, Harold Clurman, codirector of the renowned Group Theatre, held that Lawson was, quite simply, "the hope of our theatre."[4]

Despite these glowing accolades, by mid-century Lawson's once bright star had faded considerably. In the wake of his 1950 conviction for contempt of Congress before the House Committee on Un-American Activities (HUAC), Lawson's career was reevaluated in a number of critiques that placed primacy on his revolutionary politics, not his art. Echoing the right-wing rhetoric imparted by HUAC, one critic in the mid-fifties cavalierly dismissed Lawson as a minor figure who had "long ceased to interest anyone except grave robbers and the House Committee on Un-American Activities [and] that it seem[ed] hard to believe that there were once persons of taste who thought of him as an important American playwright."[5] In 1962, another critic described Lawson as a playwright whose "leftist attitude toward socio-economic issues" tainted his "promising" artistic facility and, consequently, resulted in the writing of dramas that were merely "vehicles of propaganda."[6] Such damning summations of Lawson's theatrical career, though highly contestable, continue to haunt many of the historical narratives and critical evaluations of the twentieth-century United States theatre. Antithetically, in this study I will argue that Lawson, though perhaps not a major figure in the twentieth-century theatre, did make significant contributions and a thorough examination of his career is requisite when considering the complex mosaic that is United States theatre history.

Endemic to this study of Lawson's playwriting career is a consideration of the cultural and political left in the United States during the first decades of the twentieth century. In the broadest of terms, in this study Lawson's work in the theatre is situated within, as Walter Benjamin puts it, "the context of the living social relations" of the leftist community in the United States, and the texts he authored are considered not merely as "rigid, isolated object[s]," but in light of the political and social processes in which they are bound.[7] It is through this process of taking into consideration specifically the effect the numerous leftward-leaning social and cultural formations had on the theatre in the United States broadly and on Lawson's career in it specifically that a more nuanced and balanced view of this particular historical moment begins to emerge. I hope this study will be viewed as another piece in the still emerging field of scholarship that seeks to write and right the history of the artistic and literary left—a group hitherto marginalized, half-hidden, or completely excluded in the vast majority of studies of culture, including, significantly, those focusing on theatre. The words of contemporary Marxist literary and cultural critic Alan Wald endorse this sentiment:

> [T]he very fact that so many of the most extraordinary US writers felt, for longer or shorter amounts of time, that the ideals of Communism and the organized Communist movement held out the best hope for humanity ought to be understood as an augmentation, complication, and enrichment of their literary lives. The choice of Marxist commitment, no matter how ill-founded in inaccurate information about the

> Soviet Union, ought not be perverted into a means of dismissing their cultural contributions.
>
> The additional fact that so many of the Communist writers [. . .] are entirely absent from the extant literary histories, anthologies, and the lists of publishing houses should by no means be taken as a sign of the "inferiority" of their writings. Increasing evidence shows that the authentic history of twentieth-century US literary practice has yet to be written, especially in regard to the Left.[8]

Because of this underrepresentation, it is my hope to encourage not only a reconsideration of Lawson's career and the cultural and political left of the interwar years, but also the larger cultural matrix of that historical moment. In so doing, I do not necessarily seek to devalue the canonical, major works of theatrical art from this era but instead to allow these works to be "jostled . . . by an array of other texts" that have typically been "regarded as too minor to deserve sustained attention."[9] Such an unsettling of hierarchies will undoubtedly lead to a more inclusively democratic, accurately historical, and, perhaps, "authentic" account of the theatre in the United States.

At the beginning of his theatrical career, in the early 1920s, Lawson was a leader among many artistic rebels in the theatre, sworn to the task of revitalizing the American stage. Referred to at one point as the "Messiah of the new technique," Lawson, along with Eugene O'Neill, Susan Glaspell, Edna St. Vincent Millay, Maxwell Anderson, and Elmer Rice, was a quintessential "modern" theatre artist, introducing and/or experimenting with forms of dramatic expression that challenged the conventions of melodrama and sentimentalism as well as the overt puritan morality that dominated playwriting in the United States.[10] By the end of his theatrical career in the late 1930s, Lawson had evolved into a political revolutionary dedicated to writing realistic, proletarian scripts and theoretical texts that overtly promoted a Communist agenda.

In his 1947 survey *A History of Modern Drama* (significantly, written prior to Lawson's interaction with HUAC), noted critic Barrett H. Clark substantiates this view of the progression of Lawson's creative development. In a succinct, one-paragraph account, Clark briefly charts the playwright's career. He notes both the pivotal role Lawson played in the various experiments in dramatic form in the decade of the twenties as well as the playwright's central place in the movement in the thirties that sought to use the stage as a platform from which to challenge the bourgeois/capitalist political and economic hegemonic order by way of the "well-made play" form:

> Probably the most consistent exponent of the left-wing drama is John Howard Lawson, whose first play, *Roger Bloomer* (1923), stems esthetically from the expressionist theatre of Germany. The play was definitely experimental, in parts odd and confused, yet strangely affecting. *Processional* (1925) was a more mature and stageworthy work, and though not completely realized, it did manage to express excitedly a part of the American scene—its tempo, its color and vigor—that had not yet been brought into the theatre. *Nirvana* (1926), *Loudspeaker* (1927), and *The International* (1928), were further proof of Lawson's eagerness to utilize new forms of drama, but it seems that the young rebel of 1923 had realized after ten years' trial that a play need not necessarily be odd or obscure in order to be effective, either as entertainment or propaganda, for in *Success Story* (1932), one of his best plays, he was apparently satisfied with a character set within the framework of a conventionally well-made play. In *Gentlewoman* and *The Pure in Heart* (both of 1934) he moved still further away from the field of experiment and presented the dilemma of the radical in a world not yet ready to welcome The Revolution.[11]

What is possibly most noteworthy in Clark's brief commentary (and, in fact, separates his account from most of the other encyclopedia-type summaries of the playwright's career) is the recognition of the complicacy of Lawson's development as a playwright as well as the positioning of him as a significant player in the evolution of United States drama in the years between the world wars. A more comprehensive consideration of the playwright's own work further corroborates Clark's observation that Lawson's career in the theatre was remarkably varied and his influence was, in no small part, consequential. It may convincingly be argued that four of Lawson's scripts—*Roger Bloomer*, *Processional*, *Success Story*, and *Marching Song*—though seldom read and never produced today, are among the most outstanding and significant dramas of the interwar period in the United States. The relative critical and popular success of these scripts in production during this period, as well as his writings on playwriting technique and Marxist aesthetics that culminated with his groundbreaking book *Theory and Technique of Playwriting*, speak to the central position Lawson held within the community of theatre artists in the 1920s and 1930s who were constantly reshaping dramatic form and content. Thus a central argument of this study is that the direction, shape, and scope of American theatre in the years between the world wars was affected, in some cases profoundly so, by the aesthetic and theoretical/critical texts produced by Lawson during that era.

Despite his noteworthy contributions, Lawson is frequently ignored, misrepresented, or dictatorially dismissed by many contemporary theatre scholars. Typical of the former approach is *The History of North American Theatre* by Felicia Hardison Londré and Donald Watermeier, a sweeping and, without question, invaluable survey of American theatre that, regrettably, does not include any reference to Lawson's career.[12] While a comprehensive examination of Lawson's art is certainly outside the reach of this type of comprehensive study, his complete absence (as well as of other notable leftist playwrights of the period such as John Wexley, Albert Maltz, and George Sklar) is troubling. Comparable studies by Barnard Hewitt and Garff B. Wilson represent another disquieting tendency. In these oft-used and oft-cited surveys of the theatre in the United States, the representation of Lawson, who by turns is described as a "promising" and "angry" playwright who made minor contributions to "expressionism" and the "drama of social protest," is dated due to both authors' reliance on formalist/New Critical notions of aesthetic value, which inevitably marginalize and exclude.[13] As a result, neither Hewitt nor Wilson takes into account the complexity of Lawson's early experimental dramas, or the variance of his later realistic scripts. While the shortcomings in the studies by Hewitt and Wilson may be justified at least in part by the dominant critical methods distinctive to the historical moment in which their narratives were composed, the objectionable view of Lawson's career offered by Ethan Mordden in his more recent survey *The American Theatre*, wherein the balance of Lawson's career following *Processional* is brutally summarized as "rot," is, quite simply, beyond the pale.[14]

Period-specific works, dedicated entirely to the study of United States drama and theatre in the first decades of the twentieth century, though seldom involving reflections akin to the egregious treatment offered by Mordden, nonetheless tend to forward a reductive view of Lawson's career in the theatre. The foundational texts in this area of study, by scholars such as Morgan Himmelstein, Clay Reynolds, Malcolm Goldstein, Jordon Miller and Winifred Frazer, and Sam Smiley, must certainly be commended for bringing attention to the often-ignored political and cultural left of the interwar period, and do, in fact, go well beyond the superficial and narrow treatments of Lawson's scripts offered in the survey texts of Hewitt and Wilson. Even so, many of these studies place undue significance on the most notorious events in Lawson's life: his hearing before HUAC and his subsequent conviction for contempt.[15] Moreover, none of these scholars offer nuanced considerations of the magnitude or progress of the playwright's internal struggle, which pitted his developing aesthetic sensibility against his emerging political ideology. They instead too hastily label all of Lawson's scripts as polemics of "left-wing" or "Marxist" ideologies and forgo an examination of the gradual escalation of these forces in his work.[16]

As with the period-specific studies, those works including Lawson as part of a larger thematic or area study, though valuable in many respects, do not provide the detailed analysis the playwright's career warrants. For example, in his remarkable study *Work and the Work Ethic in American Drama, 1920–1970*, Thomas Allan Greenfield considers the development of the theme of work in American drama. Though Greenfield's analysis is invaluable, his statements regarding Lawson are specific to how his scripts function within the radical, pro-labor theatre tradition initiated by Elmer Rice and built upon by Clifford Odets. Lawson's dramas thus receive a thoughtful but limited analysis, and the playwright is presented as a minor transitional figure in the development of dramas employing the work theme. Correspondingly, in her outstanding book *Staging Strikes: Workers' Theatre and the American Labor Movement*, Colette A. Hyman includes a lucid and moving account of the instrumental role Lawson played as a member of the New Playwrights' Theatre in the rise of the workers' theatre movement. Likewise, Roberta Lynne Lasky's very useful study "The New Playwrights Theatre, 1927–1929" is specific to Lawson's position in the first professional theatre in the United States dedicated to a radical political agenda. As with Greenfield, however, the thoughtful considerations of Lawson's career provided by Hyman and Lasky are narrowly circumscribed by the scope of their larger research agendas.[17]

Similarly, the fine analysis of Lawson's work offered by Ira A. Levine in his study *Left-Wing Dramatic Theory in the American Theatre* explicitly situates the playwright's theoretical writings—and to a limited extent, his scripts—within the expansive phenomena of socialist, radical theatre in the United States and considers how this work was a consequential force in the formulation of revolutionary theory of the stage. Comparable treatments of Lawson are included in the studies by Anne Fletcher and Mark Fearnow. In her cogent dissertation, "The Theory and Practice of Mordecai Gorelik (1925–1935): Emblem for the Changing American Theatre," Fletcher considers Lawson in terms of how he influenced one of the American theatre's premier designers and, to some extent, vice versa. In *The American Stage and the Great Depression: A Cultural History of the Grotesque*, Fearnow offers a brief but thoughtful and convincing analysis of Lawson's *Marching Song*.[18]

Unlike those studies that incorporate considerations of Lawson as part of their larger thematic and area studies, a few scholars have focused on specific periods or aspects in Lawson's career in the theatre. Such is the case with Liliane Claire Randrianarivony-Koziol's "Techniques of Commitment in the Thirties: A Study of the Selected Plays of John Howard Lawson." While Randrianarivony-Koziol includes thoughtful analyses of *Loud Speaker, Success Story, The Pure in Heart*, and *Marching Song*, her claim that Lawson effectively combined the aesthetic and the political in his dramatic texts is debatable. Specifically, she implies that Lawson's commitment to radical politics sprang fully formed in the late 1920s, while he was a member of the New Playwrights' Theatre, and accounts for neither the troubled and complex evolution of his political convictions nor the impact of these ideals on his craft. A much more convincing study on a singular aspect of Lawson's career in the theatre is found in Beverle Rochelle Bloch's "John Howard Lawson's *Processional*: Modernism in American Theatre in the Twenties." Dealing specifically with the Theatre Guild's 1925 production of *Processional*, Bloch deftly considers the innovative nature of the play, which merged the theatrical with the political; the responses it received from left-wing, liberal, and mainstream critics; the role it played in the development of modern American avant-garde theatre; and the ways Lawson's methods and ideas prefigured Brechtian practice and theory.[19]

The investigations of the handful of scholars focusing solely on Lawson and his entire career in the theatre are limited in other respects, concentrating either on formalist literary analysis of the play scripts or "great-man"–style biography.[20] An example of the former approach may be found in the dissertation "John Howard Lawson as an Activist Playwright: 1923–1937" by Richard Peyron Brown. In his preface, Brown rejects the value of biography, history, sociology, and psychology on a charge of "determinism" and claims that Lawson's texts are independent or autonomous creations.[21] Although he touches on Lawson's struggle between form and meaning, and makes "an attempt to relate the published plays [. . .] to the historical context," Brown is largely concerned with substantiating the intrinsic, didactic quality in the scripts as manifest in plot, characterization, and language. Therefore, most of Brown's study is dedicated to a detailed, New Critical analysis of Lawson's published scripts, documenting, by way of his close readings, recurring aesthetic patterns (that is, themes, images, and words) and structures.[22]

Likewise, the limitations of the "great-man"–style biographic method are apparent in "International Rag: The Theatrical Career of John Howard Lawson," a dissertation by Robert Merritt Gardner. Gardner approaches his work with the idea that "the most important, vital, and rewarding study of Lawson would be a biography."[23] The main objective of his sweeping, near-five-hundred-page study is to provide readers with knowledge of Lawson's life so they might understand the playscripts more fully. Adopting a classic and orthodox mode of biographical study, Gardner uses the broader cultural milieu of the interwar years only as a backdrop to Lawson's life. As a result, while Gardner allows for the idea that history can illuminate the texts authored by Lawson (and does, as a result, provide cogent and nuanced readings of the playwright's scripts), he does not fully acknowledge the complex interconnectivity and dynamic interplay of those texts in relation to the larger cultural field.

It is through an aperture in the investigations by the aforementioned scholars that I enter into the study of Lawson. I view *Messiah of the New Technique: John Howard Lawson, Communism, and American Theatre, 1923–1937* not necessarily as a corrective measure but as a matter of filling in certain gaps left open by others and reconsidering some of the conclusions made about the artist and his work. In building upon the contributions of those who have gone before, the specific aim of this study is twofold: to offer (1) a critical and political biography of John Howard Lawson, focusing on his career in the theatre and emphasizing the evolution and interplay of his artistic vision and political ideology, and (2) a new reading of Lawson's written work from the years 1923 through 1937 that considers that work as both documentation of this evolution and interplay and a product and producer of the sociopolitical and cultural matrix of which he was a part in the twenties and thirties. For the sake of clarity in defining this study, I extract and separate these two aims. In practice, however, these objectives are integrated and allowed to overlap and inform one other. The decision to do so is an outgrowth of my resolute conviction that Lawson's texts, and for that matter any text, cannot be understood in isolation. Indeed, the political force or aesthetic value of any given text is impossible to measure without a rigorous consideration of the context in which the text was written and received. It is through the cogency of this approach that *Messiah of the New Technique: John Howard Lawson, Communism, and American Theatre, 1923–1937* functions simultaneously as a critical and political biography, and cultural and social history.

In an effort to support this broadly defined endeavor, I analyze Lawson's career in the theatre via a materialist methodology, theorizing on the one hand the elaborate relations between his composition of these various texts and on the other, society, history, and the material world that surrounded him in the 1920s and 1930s. By mapping the broad cultural connections between these texts and this historical moment, Lawson is thus situated as both a product and producer of the so-called social energy specific to this era.[24] To that end, a significant portion of the study that follows involves charting some of the ways in which the playwright sought to develop and locate his writings for and about the theatre as instruments of aesthetic and/or social change, thoroughly embedded in the doctrine of dialectical materialism and thus imbued with the ethos that the theatre would not merely reflect but instead energetically and radically reshape the larger cultural field. I conclude by suggesting that the various texts authored by Lawson absorbed, carried, and actualized the social energy of their time and that reading them as such affords a modified and arguably more inclusive view of this moment in the history of the theatre in the United States.[25]

In the broadest and most fundamental sense, then, the approach herein is linked to my unyielding belief that the study of art and the study of society are inextricably intertwined. Regarding this interplay, celebrated (and martyred) mid-twentieth-century Marxist literary critic Christopher Caudwell writes, "Art is the product of society, as the pearl is of the oyster, and to stand outside art is to stand inside society. The criticism of art differs from pure enjoyment or creation in that it contains a sociological component [. . . that] reflects the ruthlessness of a society in which capitalist is continually hurling down fellow capitalist into the proletarian abyss."[26] In the tradition of Caudwell, I consider the societal forces operating within and upon texts authored by Lawson, how those forces influenced the playwright, and whether he impeded or impelled the advancement of socialism.

Notwithstanding the force of such classical Marxist methodology within my study, I recognize the limitations and reductive nature of a reading that employs that mode of analysis in an orthodox or fundamentalist manner.[27] By claiming to have discovered the whole or absolute truth in socialism, the classical Marxist critic can limit him or herself to a task of what literary sociologist Jeffrey L. Sammons has termed "illustrative detail." I therefore seek to go beyond a discussion of how Lawson's scripts do or do not merely reflect Marxist truth and, instead, in the manner eloquently articulated by Sammons, "look upon literary sociology as the pursuit of a large number of open questions about the relationship of literature and society."[28] To that end, I am much indebted to the work of neo-Marxist cultural and literary critics, principally Tony Bennett, Frederic Jameson, and Mark Cousins, as well as the New Historians, principally Stephen Greenblatt, John Brannigan, and Catherine Gallagher, who have in the last fifteen years been instrumental in transforming materialist methodology, moving it from ideology critique into discourse analysis. The efforts of these and other scholars to advance materialist methods of analysis in light of poststructuralist and postmodernist theories have played an integral role in how I have come to understand the cultural forces that played upon the production and consumption of texts authored by and about Lawson.

Of particular importance to the structuring of this study has been Bennett's notion of *reading formations*. In his essay "Texts in History," Bennett, taking into account Derrida's claim that "all is text," calls for a "post-structuralist Marxism." Circumscribed as a mode of materialist analysis that accepts some of the theoretical conditions of deconstruction, particularly those that speak to the ways in which all that "is," is discourse and language, Bennett's poststructuralist Marxism is able to "acknowledge and accept the consequences of its own discursivity."[29] In recognizing its own discursive construction, poststructuralist Marxism is able to expand the parameters of materialist analysis and recognize the fluidity, mutability, and mobility of all texts. As such, "the determinations and accretions which bear upon, re-mould and reconfigure texts" in the act of reading (that is, consumption), are shown to have a "consequential bearing on the nature of [those texts'] functioning." This is to say, the very nature and meaning of a text is determined as much by the condition and practice of reading as it is by the originating conditions of production. Thus, by shifting the focus of materialist analysis away from an exclusive consideration of the originating conditions of the production of a text, as the orthodox Marxist critic would, to one that also includes the reading of a text, the poststructuralist Marxist critic seeks to consider the variable nature of reading/consumption, how reading is shaped by other social and political texts, and how the context of reading (or also, in the case of theatre, viewing), in association with context of production, shapes the meaning and political maneuverability of any given text. Bennett persuasively summarizes his view when he writes,

> [T]he actual and variable functioning of texts in history can only be understood if account is taken of the ways in which [. . .] originary relations [. . .] between literary texts, and other ideological phenomena and broader social and political processes [. . .] may be modified through the operation of subsequent determinations—institutional and discursive—which may retrospectively cancel out, modify or

> overdetermine those which marked the originating conditions of a text's production. [. . .] In view of these considerations, then, I want to suggest that the proper object for Marxist literary theory consists not in the study of texts but in the study of reading formations.[30]

Bennett goes on to define *reading formations* as "a set of discursive and inter-textual determinations which organise and animate the practice of reading, connecting texts and readers in specific relations to one another in constituting readers as reading subjects of particular types and texts as objects-to-be-read in particular ways." Key for Bennett, then, is the notion that the very existence of a text is predicated on the presence of reading formations and, moreover, "that there is no place independent of, anterior to or above the varying reading formations through which their historical life is variantly modulated, within which texts can be constituted as objects of knowledge. Texts exist only as always-already organised or activated to be read in certain ways just as readers exist as always-already activated to read in certain ways: neither can be granted a virtual identity that is separable from the determinate ways in which they are gridded onto one another within different reading formations."[31]

Bennett's ideas regarding the interplay of text and reader—between production and consumption in a complex feedback loop—have been influential concepts in the development of my thinking, shaping in profound ways my reading of the various texts (published and unpublished, theoretical and aesthetic) produced by Lawson. In the study that follows, which is in part founded upon Bennett's theoretical rubric, I consider not only the "originating conditions" that were present at the moments of production (that is, composition) and how those conditions determined the content and form of those texts, but also the ways in which meaning and form was "retrospectively cancel[ed] out, modif[ied] or overdetermine[d]" by those that consumed (that is, produced for theatrical production, read and/or observed in performance) those texts. This method has proven fruitful in my endeavor to write a critical and political biography as well as a cultural and social history.

To begin, and on a level of biography, the texts that Lawson produced were, in his view, often misread and his ideas, both aesthetic and theoretical, misrepresented, not only by audience members and critics experiencing the texts both in production and in print, but also by theatre personnel who were responsible for interpreting and staging his scripts for production. What is more, the playwright also held that on many occasions the text he had created lacked sufficient clarity in terms of its form and/or content and was therefore open to misreading and misrepresentation. Lawson thus recognized his own culpability in the misreading and misrepresentation of his texts. Concerning this sometimes contentious and always complex relationship between the text, the author of the text, and the readers of the text, Stephen Greenblatt writes, "It is possible for a playwright to be in tension with his own medium, hostile to its presuppositions and conditions, eager to siphon off its powers and attack its pleasures. [. . .] We can say, perhaps, that an individual play mediates between the mode of the theatre, understood in its historical specificity, and elements of the society out of which the theatre has been differentiated. Through its representational means, each play carries charges of social energy onto the stage, the stage in its turn revises that energy and returns it to the audience."[32] By considering the historical reading formations that, to some degree, determined the meanings of the texts Lawson composed, I have sought to "activate" the historical context that included him, making it not merely a backdrop to his life but "a set of discursive and inter-textual determinations [. . .] which [impinged] upon [his] text[s]."[33] In light of this theoretical construct, I have attempted to situate sections of my analysis in the space between Lawson's production and the public's reading of the text, remain cognizant of and suspend, insofar as I am able, my own reading practices, and, therefore, hear the "hum" and observe the exchange of social energy in the generally contentious historical discourse that existed between Lawson and the consumers of his texts.[34] In place of hermeneutical, linear, and strictly formalist methods of analysis, I, as does Greenblatt, subscribe to the cyclic theory of exchange. Instead of merely reading the social and the political in terms of how they affected Lawson's work, I also consider how his work was seen and understood in social and political arenas. By bearing in mind the circulation of social energy, I provide a reading of Lawson's authored texts that considers how he as an artist introduced and perpetuated ideas into a community, how the community received, interpreted, evaluated, altered, and circulated those same ideas, and how those ideas were then returned to the artist for further consideration. In so doing, I have offered just one of many possible narrative accounts of Lawson's internal conflict that was manifest in his endeavor to find a suitable method of theatrical expression that would satisfy his requisite and ever-evolving convictions concerning dramatic content and form.

In addition to proving instrumental on the level of biography, the methods of the neo-Marxists and the New Historians regarding the complex and dynamic interplay and interconnectivity of text, author, and consumers have also been instrumental in my endeavor to structure a cultural and social history. To pull "historical consideration to the center stage of literary analysis," thereby taking the view that the meaning and form of the text is determined by both the producer and the consumer, is to situate the literary/artistic text at the site of ideological conflict whereby a myriad of social, cultural, and political forces both move (that is, can shape) and are moved by (that is, are shaped by) the material text.[35] Under these conditions, the literary/artistic text no longer has meaning in and of itself. It is neither a "sacred, self-enclosed, and self-justifying miracle" nor is it merely reflexive of the larger social, political, and cultural milieu. Rather, the meaning of that text is categorically historically specific, created in the exchange of discourses that flow in the wake of the material text as social impulses shape and are reshaped in a constant, dizzying, and ever-evolving exchange. To locate the creative outpourings of artists such as Lawson squarely within the dynamic and complex matrix of a culture and, moreover, to read that culture as text is to recognize, as Gallagher and Greenblatt have suggested, that the art and artist "we love did not spring up from nowhere and that their achievements must draw upon a whole life-world and that this life-world has undoubtedly left other traces of itself."[36] Therefore, in the study that follows I look to uncover the traces of the complex cultural matrix of the 1920s and 1930s that continue to linger within Lawson's creative and theoretical texts in a larger endeavor to track the social energies that circulated through the culture of which he was a part.

Application of these various dialectical methodologies seems particularly appropriate to the study of an artist who struggled to find a balance between his aesthetic sensibility and political ideology. By incorporating these various techniques, I am able to provide not only a long-overdue new reading of Lawson scripts for the theatre (that is, the artist's art) but also a much needed study of the context that enveloped him (that is, the revolutionary's ideology). This broader scope informs and reinforms my readings of text and the context and, in turn, has allowed me to present a fresh account of Lawson's theatrical career.

In the end, then, I have striven to write not only a new history of Lawson's career in the theatre and a detailed analysis of his work but also to recount in detail some of the circumstances that propelled him from "artist-rebel" to "political revolutionary."[37] With *Messiah of the New Technique: John Howard Lawson, Communism, and American Theatre, 1923–1937*, I have endeavored to follow the exceptional precedent of scholars such as Rita Barnard, Mark Fearnow, Rena Fraden, and Michael Denning, who have extended an understanding of the era of the twenties and thirties and its people by engaging it with vitality and passion.[38] In so doing, I hope also to have, in the words of Barnard, "help[ed] shape a more inclusive—more properly historical" account of American theatre history.[39]

The Awakening

> We stand today upon the brink of change,
> A moment breathless, fateful, wonderful:
> Here shall burst forth, as fire burst from coals,
> From ashes of our childhood the full flame
> Of life; and from the soil of peacefulness,
> Shall blossom brightly the red rose of strife.
>
> —John Howard Lawson, untitled poem, 1914

John Howard Lawson was born in New York City on 25 September 1894. The last of three children born to Belle and Simeon Lawson, John Howard was named after an eighteenth-century English prison reformer, a name that clearly implied his parents' pre–Progressive Era liberal leanings. Simeon, the son of Polish-Jewish immigrants, rose from poverty and made a great deal of money as a newspaperman in the western United States and Mexico. Following his founding of the *Mexican Financier*, a financial weekly published in English and Spanish in Mexico City in the 1880s, Simeon moved to metropolitan New York City, where he subsequently achieved the rank of executive manager of Reuters News Agency. Belle (Hart), the daughter of an affluent German-Jewish industrialist, was active in the struggle for women's rights, an advocate in the educational reform movement dedicated to the principle that a child learns through self-expression and imagination, and a member of the Ethical Cultural Society. The family lived in New Rochelle, New York, part of a close-knit, progressive neighborhood that advocated communal living and supported an experimental school called the Children's Playhouse.

Underneath this ostensibly idyllic, privileged, and tranquil life was great turmoil, a product of Belle's long and eventually terminal struggle with breast cancer. The anxiety and grief filling the Lawson home during this period was magnified considerably by Belle and Simeon's refusal, as practicing Christian Scientists, of medical treatment throughout the course of Belle's illness. Later in life, John Howard noted that his parents' refusal to seek essential medical care for Belle was significant in the development of his lifelong distrust of religion. However, a more immediate effect of this unfortunate situation came in the months and years following Belle's death in December 1899 when a inconsolable Simeon divided the family, sending the eldest child, Wendell Holmes Lawson, to study music in Germany while daughter Adelaide Jaffery Lawson and John Howard were enrolled as boarding students at the Halstead School in Yonkers. As an adult, Lawson would assert that his father's actions during this difficult time were typical of his parenting. Though "brilliant and gentle," Simeon was also "aloof and distant," never able to meet his children's emotional needs. Thus, unable to understand his own grief, let alone the grief of three young children, he instead lavished them with material things and strove to secure for them "an American identity."[1]

This endeavor to achieve and maintain social stability is also discernible in Simeon's decision to change the family name from Levy, a name that obviously implied their Jewish heritage, to the more innocuous Lawson. Though he did this before any of the children were born and referred to it as a "naïve and convenient compromise," the younger Lawson recounted later in life that this event prompted the family's apathetic rejection of its Jewish identity.[2] After rejecting his cultural heritage, Simeon felt compelled to manufacture or buy one for himself and his children. These tumultuous circumstances and conflicts were to have a lasting effect upon young John Howard who, "starved for emotional and cultural stability," turned to the "sureness of the [. . .] arts."[3]

At the age of eleven, John Howard returned to New York City to live with his father, who now lived in the exclusive Chatsworth apartment building, and he attended the prestigious Cutler School. Later in life, Lawson would remark that the reputable school and the lavish apartment were unimportant trappings, providing "the physical settings of my life and little more."[4] Simeon, who was still grieving for Belle, tried to find solace in religion, first with the Christian Scientists and later with the Unitarians. Though Simeon's faith in religion was not passed onto his youngest child, it was nonetheless in Unitarian meetings where John Howard got his first indication "that there were wrongs to be righted and human needs that were ignored in society."[5]

Following a summer tour of Europe in 1906, John Howard began developing an interest in the arts. He feasted upon many of the cultural opportunities afforded by New York City, attending theatre, opera, lectures, gallery openings, and recitals. Simultaneously, he became a voracious student of Shakespeare. Regarding his affinity for this work, Lawson would later remark, "I found in Shakespeare the most tangible evidence of the culture that had overwhelmed and mesmerized me in Europe. The light that filtered through the stainglass windows on tombs and statues, the life that stirred in ancient buildings, the frayed splendor of tapestries—these things took shape and meaning in Shakespeare's plays."[6] To further his study of the Bard, Lawson adopted the practice of reading a script, seeing it in production, and then reading it again, all the while taking detailed notes. Within a few seasons, he had not only read all of Shakespeare's scripts but had seen a number of now famous productions, including Robert Mantell's *Hamlet* and *Julius Caesar*, Sothern and Marlowe's *Twelfth Night*, Ben Greet's *As You Like It*, and Ermete Novelli's *Othello* and *Hamlet*.[7] His passion for Shakespeare eventually led to an interest in other classical literature, including Greek and Roman drama and poetry, French neoclassical drama, and Indian epic poetry. As with Shakespeare, his readings of these works included detailed, written analyses. In January 1908, he began to translate his fondness for and knowledge of these classical forms into his first script, *Savitri*, a poetic drama based upon an Indian myth.[8]

Lawson would later comment that prior to writing *Savitri*, his "notions of art were naïve and conventional" and that the ten-month period of composition of that text was the genesis of a decade-long process of discovery regarding the mutable nature of aesthetic standards. He continues, "The culture that was offered to upper-class and upper middle class people in New York seemed to me the only culture there was. I could not conceive of any other standards of value."[9] His conventional notions were further challenged when he attended a production of Charpentier's controversial opera *Louise* at the Manhattan Opera House in February 1908 and the Ash Can School exhibition later that spring.[10] By the time he finished *Savitri* in November of that year, Lawson had adopted the view that art was more than a mere imitation of conventional technique and structure. However, his ideas as to what lay beyond those conventions and structures was not yet defined.

In 1910, Lawson entered Williams College as the youngest member of the class of 1914, where he joined the socialist club and became active in the two college literary publications, the *Williams Record* and the *Literary Monthly*. During his four years at Williams, Lawson published numerous essays that by his own assessment were "radical" but decidedly "naïve."[11] In addition to writing, his association with these publications afforded him the opportunity to carry on correspondence with other collegiate would-be radical essayists and news reporters. Through this correspondence, Lawson was exposed to contemporary avant-garde forms of expression, including the works of playwright Frank Wedekind. His education in the avant-garde was furthered in early spring 1913 when he attended the International Exhibition of Modern Art at the Armory in New York. By his own admission, Lawson was both fascinated and puzzled by the works of avant-garde artists such as Van Gogh, Cezanne, and Picasso and did not know what to make of them. In his essay "Art for Cube's Sake" written for the *Literary Monthly* a few months later, Lawson considered the limitations of his traditional, albeit prestigious, education in regard to viewing this new art: "We [that is, traditionalists] base the wildest sublimities of our artistic imagination upon the calculations of science. We go mad according to rule; we see visions and dream dreams by mathematical principles."[12] This recognition of new forms of expression, however, did not lead him to act. Instead, while the battle in the arts gained momentum, Lawson remained a distant and puzzled observer.

During his last year at Williams, Lawson once again tried his hand at playwriting and wrote *A Hindoo Love Drama*, a blank verse script loosely based upon the Indian epic poem *The Mahabharahta*.[13] Intrigued with the idea of a writing career, Lawson sent the script to the Galbraith Welch Literary Agency (later Brant and Brant) who, to the young man's surprise, submitted it to the actors Sothern and Marlowe.[14] Although *A Hindoo Love Drama* was neither produced nor published, Mary Kirkpatrick, head of drama at Galbraith Welch, encouraged Lawson to continue to write play scripts.[15]

Thus, following his graduation from Williams in 1914 and encouraged by his relative success with *Hindoo Love Drama*, Lawson devoted himself to playwriting. Because the commercial stage was where he had seemingly been accepted, he was determined to find his place within that environment.[16] Supporting himself as a cable editor for Reuters, a job given to him by his father, Lawson found that through his daily dealings with the war in Europe his disdain for the atrocities grew and grew. Finding it increasingly difficult to do his job and suppress his antiestablishment feelings, he was much relieved when, in February 1915, his script *Standards*, a well-made farce, was sold to producers George M. Cohan and Sam Harris, allowing him to resign from Reuters.

In the three years that followed, Lawson had few similar successes. Instead, his endeavor to make his way in the commercial theatre was replete with a series of tantalizing possibilities and promising affirmations that, time and again, ended in frustration. To begin, Cohan and Harris, believing *Standards* was unplayable and unmarketable in its original form due to its subtle but biting attack on bourgeois morality, assigned their general manager Sam Forrest to rewrite the script in accordance with the commercial demands of Broadway.[17] Lawson and Forrest worked for months but were unable to modify *Standards* to the satisfaction of Cohan and Harris. As a result, at the end of 1915, the producers dropped their option. While the sting of being released by Cohan and Harris was difficult for the young playwright, it was soothed by other apparent successes. In early 1916, Lawson sold two more scripts, *The Spice of Life* to actor Dorothy Donnelly and *Servant-Master-Lover* to Los Angeles producer Oliver Morosco.[18] While *Spice of Life* was never produced, *Servant-Master-Lover* was staged in Los Angeles in the summer of 1916. The production was disastrous and it received scathing reviews. Nonetheless, feelings of failure were once again briefly offset when producer George Mooser acquired the option on *Standards* and produced it for a run on the upstate New York circuit in the autumn of 1916. Unfortunately, as with *Servant-Master-Lover* earlier that year, the production was, according to Lawson, poorly executed and poorly received.[19] About these early forays into the theatre, Lawson later remarked: "My experience with [. . .] these productions was that I came to them with a passion for the theatre and an assumption that the people in it knew what they were doing. And I found that the people in the theatre didn't have the slightest idea what they were doing and that they hoped desperately that there would be some element of genius in my play that would solve their problems for them."[20] Thus, in June 1917,[21] embittered and confused by his experiences, unsure about the direction of his career, and intent on rethinking his life, Lawson enlisted as a volunteer in the Norton-Harjes Ambulance Corps, serving the highly volatile western front in France, and sailed for Europe.

On the first evening of this trip across the Atlantic, Lawson met another struggling writer named John Dos Passos, and the two became fast friends. While the two young men shared certain ideas and goals—principally the view that the war was immoral and that service in the Ambulance Corps would provide some much-needed clarity—Dos Passos differed from Lawson in two essential ways. First, Dos Passos had a solid grounding and an astute awareness and appreciation of the avant-garde, particularly automatic and impressionistic writing. Conversely, Lawson had only a "cursory" familiarity and knowledge of current experimental trends in the arts.[22] Second, Dos Passos possessed a strong and clearly articulated distaste for all things bourgeois, which was informed by a firm understanding of contemporary radical politics. In contrast, while Lawson did maintain something of a leftist stance and had some familiarity with the works of Marx by way of Karl Kautsky's *The Class Struggle*, his politics were decidedly naïve, firmly grounded in mid- and late-nineteenth-century liberal ideologies that forwarded utopian socialism. Lawson would later recall:

> [Dos Passos and I] were drawn together from our first meeting by our hatred of the war and we both joined the ambulance service solely to escape the draft. But Dos saw our opposition to the war as a function of the sensibility and vocation of the artist. I was intoxicated by the idea that my creative intelligence was pitted against the stupid and criminal plans of the statesmen, and that I was part of a band of artist-brothers united in our scorn for the masters of our botched civilization. [. . .]
>
> Dos gave me my first keen awareness of the aesthetic revolution that had been in progress for more than ten years. He was not a systematic political thinker—he was not systematic about anything—but he took for granted that no intelligent person, and certainly no self-respecting artist, could ignore the stupidities of bourgeois society.[23]

Upon their arrival in France and over the course of the next two months, Dos Passos persuaded Lawson to embark on an earnest study of the current trends in the arts and radical politics. At the same time, he encouraged the would-be "artist-rebel" to begin to identify his art with things other than the commercial stage and conventions of Western dramatic form. The process of reexamining his work and his worldview, coupled with his daily dealings with the death and destruction engendered by the war, shook Lawson to the core. Regarding this time, Lawson would later write, "I could not organize my impressions of the [war]—just like my life. [. . .] Further, my talks with Dos filled me with wonder and fear. [. . .] I was suddenly aware that there was a whole world out there and that I was ill-equipped to deal with it."[24]

One September day in 1917, following a particularly bloody battle, Lawson sat with Dos Passos on a haystack on the outskirts of a small French town.[25] In response to his mounting confusion, and "with a symphony of insect sounds and bombs exploding in the distance," Lawson began to write. On the top of the first page he wrote, "Roger Bloomer."[26] Although it would be six years before *Roger Bloomer* reached the stage, in writing those two words Lawson took the first steps toward joining the artistic rebellion and thus initiated the first phase of his mature playwriting career: "The Metaphysical Phase."[27]

Furthermore, and what is perhaps more intriguing when considering the larger historical frame of Lawson's life, is that at the instant when the words "Roger Bloomer" were first inscribed on the page, consequently standing as the defining moment for the first of Lawson's three phases in the theatre, so too began another course of movement for the young playwright, one of intellectual and spiritual upheaval that would continue and intensify through the middle years of the 1930s, culminating in his exodus from the professional theatre. Regarding the more narrowly defined historical frame, it would be during this so-called Metaphysical Phase, which would span the next eight years, that Lawson would complete and see produced in New York his first three major scripts, *Roger Bloomer, Processional*, and *Nirvana*, and therefore establish himself as one of the premier "artist-rebels" in the American theatre. Regarding the more broadly construed historical frame, it was also during this period that the would-be "political revolutionary" began to develop and express more clearly his distaste for all things associated with capitalism and bourgeois culture.

Although Lawson was not yet ready during this period to offer any serious anticapitalistic solution, the seeds for his commitment to revolutionary politics were sown and nurtured during these years. It may, thus, be posited that while Lawson's rebellion in this early period was primarily centered on aesthetic issues, he, like many in the so-called lost generation, also took as one of his governing credos the socially charged words of Emma Goldman: "The artist being part of life cannot detach himself from the events and occurrences that pass panorama-like before his eyes; impressing themselves upon his emotional and intellectual vision. The modern artist is, in the words of Strindberg, a 'lay preacher, popularizing the pressing questions of his time.' Not necessarily because his aim is to proselyte, but because he can best express himself by being true to life."[28] In summary, then, in the early and mid-1920s Lawson held that the theatre had a dual objective. Not only was it a temple for artistic expression and experimentation with aesthetic form, but it was also a pulpit from which he could communicate radical content, specifically his dissatisfaction with the social status quo. Significantly, these two objectives correspond to and were reinforced by the governing ideals of two communities that held competing views of the theatre: those who believed the theatre to be a "garden," and those who thought it "the cauldron of the Revolution."[29] In the early and mid-1920s, Lawson would frequently find himself simultaneously seeking to comply with the ideals of these two communities and yet, more often than not, failing to satisfy either.

Art Theatre's Garden and Revolution's Cauldron

In the spring of 1925, noted critic Sheldon Cheney, reflecting on the objectives of the "art theatre" in the United States, wrote:

> From the viewpoint of the artist-producer, the art theatre is a place where the arts of the theatre are creatively practiced, free alike from the will of the businessman, from the demands of movie-minded audiences, and from the fetters of superstitious traditionalism; he probably entertains, moreover, a vision of the several contributive arts of the playwright, the actor and the designer brought together in a union or synthesis, and in the final result invariably stamped with the style of brilliance or the quality of his own imagination—this viewpoint implying an aesthetic policy and a lasting association of creative workers under artist-leadership. Theatrically moving plays, plays that widen the horizon of life, plays that stir the emotions and enrich the adult mind; ensemble acting, inspired acting, a standard of speech; reinforcement of the playwright's and the actor's effectiveness by adequate and at times beautiful setting, costuming, and lighting; all these are implications of the "art" theatre name.[30]

Throughout the rest of his study, Cheney, in seeking to define this broadly construed "creative" theatre, situates the "business theatre" as its antithesis. Forasmuch as Cheney's view of the American theatre of the time relies on the existence of these two opposing and antagonistic communities—the commercial stage dedicated to "amusements" and the art theatre dedicated to "beautiful things"—each contingent upon and defined by a mutual animosity for the other, the historical record may be read to reveal a theatrical topography that was decidedly more complex and divergent.[31]

The descriptive and uncomplicated history offered by Cheney implies the emergence and continued existence of a galvanized community of "radical artists," "bedded together—in the garden of [. . . the] 'art theatre,'" forged by the "visionaries who founded an amateurish little theatre" in the years before World War I, dedicated to the advancement of progressive democratic ideals, and committed to the staging of works "mark[ed by] the sense of unity, the subtlety of mood, [and] the attainment of the primary synthetic ideal."[32] Despite the tone of absoluteness and objectivity in Cheney's account, his text should not be accepted as a marker of immutable historical fact. It should, instead, be viewed as a positivist-inflected and, therefore, fictive narrative, affirming his politicized vision of noncommercial art theatre in the middle years of the 1920s. Cheney's text may be examined as a site of ideological conflict and, therefore, read for traces of the discursive instabilities in the theatre at that historical moment.

When Cheney first published *The Art Theatre* in 1917, the little theatre movement was in need of a champion, one who could both define the parameters and ideals of the new theatre by citing and praising those who had succeeded as well as encourage that largely grassroots, community, and amateur movement toward professionalism and, ultimately, the establishment of a national theatre. By the time Cheney's text was revised and reissued in 1925, the little theatre movement had taken some decisive steps toward realizing his vision of 1917. This progress in part was manifested in the emergence of professional art theatre companies such as the American Laboratory Theatre, the Theatre Guild, and the Actor's Theatre as well as in the newfound professionalism of prewar companies such as the Provincetown Players and its offshoot Experimental Theatre, Inc. It follows, then, that the objectives, both overt and covert, expressed in the text reissued in 1925 were markedly different from those set forth in the 1917 text. Simply put, Cheney's task in the mid-twenties was less about definition and encouragement and more about fortifying and defending the parameters and ideals established in the years immediately preceding World War I. His charge at that time was to codify and guard the set of strictures and concerns that had given rise to the aforementioned professional art theatre companies. The 1925 version of Cheney's text seems haunted by his narrow conception of the noncommercial theatre forged in the years before World War I. To that end, as was standard for the community of progressive democratic theatre critics of which he was a prominent member, Cheney makes no direct mention of the social function of the theatre or its potential to serve political ends in an overt manner. His prose, instead, is peppered with abstract and ethereal terms such as "beautiful," "creative," and "intuitive" and sentiments that might well be described as "precious" and "naïve."

Juxtaposed against Cheney's ethereal and idealistic vision—and seemingly apolitical tone—was a strikingly different view of the theatre espoused by an emerging community of outspoken revolutionary (that is, socialist and Marxist) critics. Included in this camp were Walter Long, Floyd Dell, V. F. Calverton, and Michael Gold, all of whom had written and published polemical treatises by mid-1925 advocating for the development of a new, socially conscious art created by and dedicated to the American working class.[33] The conceptions of the theatre rendered by this community of critics stood in stark contrast to the views expressed by Cheney.

Arguably, the critic most central to this movement in the theatre was Gold.[34] In his essay "Towards Proletarian Art," published in the *Liberator* in 1921, Gold calls for the creation of a literature and art distinctly by, for, and about the American proletariat. The essay, which is often cited as one of the pivotal documents in defining radical critical theory in the United States, is, nonetheless, a strangely poetic, mystical, Whitmanesque manifesto that is somewhat naïve and, in many ways, decidedly un-Marxist. Despite this Romantic tone, as well as its broadly inclusive focus on "the arts" in general, with the publication of "Towards Proletarian Art" Gold not only coined the term "proletarian literature" but also established himself as the chief purveyor in the United States of that new genre. Moreover, the tenets set forth in this essay most certainly inform all subsequent English-language Marxist theorizing and criticism regarding the theatre.[35]

Gold opens "Towards Proletarian Art" lauding the "artistic spirit." Significantly, he does not directly berate bourgeois artists, who unknowingly "fight for [capitalism] against [them]selves" and thus hesitate to "sink . . . the old culture" in a "maelstrom" of revolution. Instead, sounding very much like his idols Whitman and Nietzsche, Gold claims that all "[a]rtists are bitter lovers of life," all art is sacred, capable of "stifl[ing] the meanest of Life's moods," and that he, for one, would not wish "to speak a word against their [that is, the artists'] holy passion." Gold then calls for the creation of a "new art," one that will express the experiences of the poor—his own experience:

> I was born in a tenement. That tall sombre mass, holding its freight of obscure human destinies, is the pattern in which my being has been cast. It was in the tenement that I first heard the sad music of humanity rise to the stars. The sky above the airshaft was all my sky; and the voices of all my world. There, in suffering youth, I feverishly sought God and found Man. In the tenement Man was revealed to me, Man, who is Life speaking. [. . .]
>
> All that I know of Life I learned in the tenement [. . .] The tenement is in my blood. When I think it is the tenement thinking. When I hope it is the tenement hoping. I am not an individual; I am all that

> the tenement group poured into me during those early years of my spiritual travail. [. . .]
>
> What is art? Art is the tenement pouring out its soul through us, its most articulate sons and daughters. What is life? Life for us has been the tenement that bore and moulded us through years of meaningful pain.

After Gold foretells the advent of the new artists who will be "sprung from the workers" and shall "express in art that manifestation of Life which is so exclusively ours [that is, the proletariat's], the life of the toilers," he contrasts these "spawn" of Whitman to the "proud and baffled solitaires" of capitalist society, bound to "be lonely beasts of prey—competitive and unsocial." The latter, lacking faith and will, "spiritually sterile," and cultivating a "sick aestheticism," have "lost everything in the vacuum of logic where they dwell." Conversely, the former have found sanity and salvation through "solidarity with the people." The artists of the tenement therefore must cling to the masses and "create a new and truer" art that derives from and advances the social revolution.[36]

As the decade of the 1920s progressed and his political convictions became more pronounced and well defined, Gold's ideas concerning proletarian art became undeniably more dogmatic and forceful. This shift is reflected in many of his essays penned in the first half of the decade. By the time Gold made an impassioned call for the "development of a revolutionary, working-class [. . .] drama," in a February 1925 editorial, there was little hint of Romanticism in his prose.[37] Further, upon assuming the editorship of *New Masses* in 1928, Gold's ideas concerning proletariat literature began to reflect not only an astute understanding of Marxist ideology and an ability to cogently express that view without excessive sentiment but also an intense will to advance that ideology from a hard-line, sectarian stance. Communism, Gold wrote in his 1929 landmark essay "Go Left Young Writers," did not impose a "barracks of discipline" upon the writer but induced a "creative self-discipline." Whereas Fascism required its supporters to refurbish decadent institutions, "to rewrite the stale hymns to the fatherland," Communism demanded that the writer be a "life-bringing Prometheus, a daring experimenter, a smasher of idols." Communist writers avoided rhetorical flourishes and "embraced unshrinkingly" the hard facts of their times and culture.[38]

Given the presence of this emerging community of revolutionary critics that included Gold as well as the fledgling attempts by left-wing and politically assertive theatre companies housed in northeast labor colleges including the Brookwood Labor Players,[39] Cheney's galvanized "art theatre" community circa 1925 may well be regarded as something of a mythical community. Created and narrated by Cheney in concert with other progressive democratic theatre artists and critics in the postwar years, Cheney's narrative of the mythical art theatre community performed two functions. On the one hand, it served ostensibly to represent, produce, and advance the myriad of like-minded theatre professionals (Cheney principal among them) working against and/or outside the commercial or "business theatre." On the other hand, it served a more furtive purpose: to protect and contain that same community from the then-emerging population of noncommercial theatre artists, both amateur and professional, and arts advocates who sought the advancement of political and social ideals deemed subversive and dangerous within the United States culture at large. While it would be imprudent to suggest a conscious conspiracy on the part of Cheney to limit the domain of noncommercial theatre in the mid-1920s, his totalizing definition and record, which continues to act upon contemporary narratives of this historical moment, nonetheless collapses and generalizes the numerous widely contrasting conceptions regarding the shape and scope of theatre expressed by various members of the noncommercial theatre community generating work during this period. The lives and works existing within that larger community of artists, but running counter to the ideals of the collective, albeit fictive, community narrated by Cheney, are marginalized, harshly denounced, or, in some cases, erased. Specifically, those such as Gold who sought to promote revolutionary left-wing political agendas are, to all intents and purposes, cleaved from Cheney's art theatre community or, to extend the latter's own garden metaphor, "weeded out."[40]

A thorough consideration of the social and political forces in the pre- and postwar years, which in part produced and maintained this division within the noncommercial theatre community in the United States, reveals the emergence and presence of two formidable reading formations: the first progressive in name but conservative in agenda (à la Cheney), and the second, revolutionary in name but doctrinaire in agenda (à la Gold). Working in tandem, these reading formations acted, in no small way, as competing sets of discursive and intertextual determinations, which not only affected the critical and commercial success of any play produced in the noncommercial theatre but also exerted considerable force upon texts generated for and about that theatre, shaping those texts from the outside in and from the inside out.

Near the beginning of his study *Left-Wing Dramatic Theory in the American Theatre*, Ira Levine notes how, over the course of the first fifteen years of the twentieth century, there arose within the larger liberal/leftist community of artists and intellectuals in the United States a new attitude regarding the social function of art. Levine succinctly summarizes four "common characteristics" defining this new attitude:

> The first of these was an insistence on the independence of political and artistic practice. While politics was not considered to be the subordinate to art, neither was art deemed to be subservient to political matters. The art-for-art's-sake approach to aesthetics was viewed as neglecting the economic and social world, and was therefore dismissed as a violation of art's claim to be a reflection of life. But conversely, artistic works were held to be nondogmatic and nondidactic; while they might expose shortcomings of society they were not expected to offer specific solutions. A second characteristic was that, stimulated by the prevalent tenets of Progressivism and Pragmatism, the left-wing thinkers believed that ideas and artistic perception had power in themselves to hasten the momentum and affect the direction of social change. Thus, engagement for the artist did not necessitate his taking to the streets. Instead, despite the inspiring political exploits of a writer like John Reed, it could be satisfied simply by the socially enlightened pursuit of his own craft; no party of ideological ties were required. Thirdly, among all the arts the theatre tended to be singled out specifically as the best artistic medium for the presentation of social ills and discontents. Fourth and finally, realism was sometimes overtly but more often obliquely adopted as the preferable style for a leftist drama, and little attention was given to a possible correspondence between radical political beliefs and avant-garde experiments in form.

The balance of Levine's study is devoted to mapping the evolution of this "loose conglomerate of principals" in the rise of "the revolutionary dramatic theory that would be formulated in the 1920s and 1930s."[41]

Although outside his predominate aims of identifying central principles in a revolutionary aesthetic and tracing the dialectical development of left-wing dramatic theory, with his identification of these "common characteristics," Levine also suggests the emergence and existence of a discernible reading formation in the United States in the years immediately preceding World War I. This reading formation was a dominating, albeit expansive and often "oblique," force that determined, in no small way, not only the material content and form of texts but also the way those texts were perceived. The substantial force of this formation is evident in many theatrical scripts and critical texts on the theatre produced in this period. Representative are the popular and/or critically lauded social melodramas of William Vaughn Moody, Edward Sheldon, Eugene Walter, and Rachel Crothers, all of which might well be viewed as initial attempts by American playwrights to adopt the late-nineteenth-century European realist/thesis-play method; and the critical texts of Cheney, Oliver Sayler, and Emma Goldman, all of which echoed and reinforced this same Modernist conceit by championing the new social spirit and formal advances in European drama and calling for their application by theatre practitioners in the United States. Though all these playwrights and critics envisioned, reordered, and articulated the principles Levine identifies in ways specific to their variant individual passions and agendas, all also were, in ways, reliant on, conditioned by, and authors of the overarching, determinant social discourse. Each of these authors' works may be read as more than merely a reflexive relic of the larger social, political, and cultural milieu: indeed, the dramatic form and social content employed and/or espoused is an articulation in the exchange of discourse within the reading formation identified by Levine.

While this reading formation was, in some respects, dynamic, it nonetheless functioned as a dominant and determining force in the years it was most politically, socially, and culturally assertive, roughly 1900 through 1915. Nevertheless, its capacity to affect the shape, scope, and reception of texts created in the years immediately following this historical frame was substantial and, in some cases, profound. An analysis of a representative polemic by one the leading contributors to and proponents of this reading formation, George Jean Nathan, will serve to illustrate the influence it exerted. The method of analysis of Nathan's essay—who, it is significant to note, was without exception hostile to the work of Lawson—will be drawn principally from the theory espoused by Thomas S. Kuhn. Kuhn's notions of *anomaly, crisis,* and *emergence* in relation to the theory of *paradigm shift* in science prove very useful when discussing the advent and entrenchment of a reading formation.[42] To that end, his vocabulary and concepts will help demonstrate the ways in which the ideals of dramatic content and form expressed, practiced, and valued in this historical reading formation haunted theatrical practice and critical discourse beyond the historical moment when they were most ubiquitous.

In his 1922 essay "Drama as an Art," Nathan, hailed as "the first modern American critic," succinctly summarized the view of those who had been instrumental in the development of new theatrical forms in the United States in the years immediately preceding World War I, thus echoing the fundamental vocabulary and ethos of that paradigm.[43] Nathan writes:

> Drama has been strictly defined by the ritualists in a dozen different ways. "Drama," says one, "must be based on character and the action proceed from character." "Drama," stipulates another, "is not an imitation of men, but of an action and of life: character is subsidiary to action." "Drama," promulgates still another, "is the struggle of will against obstacles." And so on, so on. Rules, rules and more rules. Pigeon-holes upon pigeon-holes. Good drama is anything that interests an intelligently emotional group of persons assembled together in an illuminated hall. Moliere, wise among dramatists, said as much, though in somewhat more, and doubtless too, sweeping words. Throughout the ages of drama there will be always Romanticists of one sort or another, brave and splendid spirits, who will free themselves from the definitions and limitations imposed upon them by neo-Bossus and Boileaus, and the small portion Voltaires, Le Harpes and Marmontels. Drama is struggle, a conflict of wills? Then what of *Ghosts*? Drama is action? Then what of *Nachtasyl* [the title given to Reinhardt's Berlin production of Gorky's *The Lower Depths*]? Drama is character? Then what of *The Dream Play*?[44]

Nathan's ardent endorsement of the "new theatre," envisioned and manifested by "brave and splendid spirits," had begun in the first decade of the twentieth century during his tenure as theatre critic for *Outing*, *The Bohemian*, and *The Smart Set*, whose coeditorship he assumed in 1914 with H. L. Mencken. Noted for his unabashed and unapologetic condemnation of the popular, commercial theatre of the day along with his passionate support of European playwrights Ibsen, Strindberg, and Shaw, Nathan's criticism was initially an "anomaly" espoused by a marginal and modest "preparadigmatic school" situated within and against the larger province of dramatic criticism in the United States, which was governed by "anonymous puffsters and scholarly genteel types."[45] Eventually, the anomaly of Nathan's criticism was taken as credo by the emerging and fast-growing community of critics[46] committed to questioning and challenging the fundamental generalizations of the dominant paradigm, and it thus evoked a "crisis" within that aforementioned province of dramatic criticism. The response to that crisis was the emergence of a new paradigm, one that reconstituted the foundational ideals of the previously dominant paradigm. In short, then, Nathan's criticism became a touchstone for an emerging paradigm, offering new vocabulary and concepts. This new paradigm of dramatic criticism went hand in hand with the ethos of libertinism, the doctrine of individual creative genius, and the nonpartisan, though radical, sociopolitical objectives espoused by the also-emerging, so-called lyrical left.[47]

Based in Greenwich Village, this loosely organized and carefree community of youthful and optimistic artists and intellectuals welcomed anyone who self-identified as "radical"[48]—social or progressive democrats, revolutionary socialists, suffragists, and anarchists—regardless of specific party affiliations and political convictions. Relatively free from the constraints of party politics, the devotees of the lyrical left sought to refashion the world by way of individual introspection, which, in turn, would lead to the "integration of conflicting values."[49] This loosely defined community of liberals and leftists not only allowed but celebrated subjective contemplation of the world and, thus, encouraged each individual's compulsion to displace in his or her own life Yeats's claim that art and politics, fantasy and fact, and individual belief and civic life were diametrically opposed.[50] In short, then, the thoroughly modern lyrical left sought to move beyond the conservative, bourgeois traditions of puritanism, capitalism, and nationalism and, to appropriate the words of Nathan, "free themselves from the definitions and limitations imposed upon them." Theirs was a progressive movement, emerging from and breaking with one set of traditions perceived to have gone badly astray and introducing a new set of traditions, conducted under different rules and within a different universe of discourse.

With the onset of World War I in 1914, however, the optimism, ardent individualism, and carefree attitude that oriented and constituted the lyrical left began to dissipate quickly. Soon after the American Socialist Party's (SP) official condemnation of the war in December 1914, the various leftist communities in the United States, the lyrical left among them, splintered into right-wing, or pro-war, and left-wing, or anti-war, camps. While the left wing's anti-war stance was fortified further by the presence in the American SP of leaders such as Louis Fraina, an unabashed Marxist revolutionary, and the seemingly constant and, very often, violent protests of the Industrial Workers of the World (IWW or Wobblies), the right wing found support with many of the moderate organizers of the American SP, such as Morris Hillquit, as well as leading members of the socialist intelligentsia. Accordingly, by the time the United States entered the war in April 1917, the lyrical left, like the larger leftist community, was divided. Some participants in the movement, such as Isadora Duncan and Walter Lippman, threw their full support behind the war effort, while others, such as Max Eastman and Randolph Bourne, were highly critical of the government and its decision to intervene.[51] It follows, then, that members of the lyrical left who identified with the left-wing faction at last felt a kinship with and connection to the working-class, socialist laborers (for example, the IWW), a community that typically looked askance at the liberal intelligentsia. Conversely, those "workers of the brain" who supported the war were further isolated from that community of laborers and were accused by its leaders with "carry[ing] into the ranks of the workers the ideology and enthusiasm of Imperialism."[52]

Regardless of the side with which any one member of the lyrical left identified, the war prompted a transformation in intellectual and aesthetic life in the leftist community in the United States, with the aspiration for individual introspection giving way to need for concrete praxis. On the right, many members embraced and were embraced by President Woodrow Wilson's administration and were used by the government in its pro-war efforts. Antithetically, for those committed to the left, the entry of the United States into the war in the spring of 1917 and the signing of the Espionage Act of 1917 two months later meant that the lyrical left's doctrines of antipuritanism, anticapitalism, and antinationalism, theorized and idealized on an ethereal level by their community in the years immediately preceding the war, were now criminalized within the larger cultural field when identified as subversive and potentially dangerous. Moreover, these issues in their own community became grounded in the material world and, therefore, requiring of concrete and specific action. That is to say, for those identifying with the revolutionary politics of the left-wing faction, ethereal contemplation of these doctrines seemed woefully inappropriate in the face of the all-too-real atrocities of war and violations of civil liberties. As anti-war demonstrators were tried, jailed, and/or tortured and as the numbers of dead and wounded from the war mounted, there arose within the left-wing faction of the disintegrating lyrical left a new fervency for collective action that reflected the burgeoning revolutionary ideology.

The notion that these now "revolutionary" leftists could forge a new world order was reinforced further with the advent of the Bolshevik-led Communist International, or Comintern, in March 1919. Instituting Marx's term "communism" to distance themselves from the centrist social democrats, the Comintern ordered every socialist party in the world to separate itself from right-wing socialist factions. Within months, the American SP, shackled with a name and, in part, leadership that was no longer in favor, was decimated as two-thirds of its membership deserted, most finding new homes in either the Communist Party (CP) or the Communist Labor Party (CLP), both of which were decidedly Marxist. Ultimately, it could be argued the capitulation of revolutionary leaders in the United States to the Comintern thwarted the development of an indigenous communist party that could truly address the needs in the United States. For all intents and purposes, from this moment forward the communist movement in the United States entered into a deeply dependent and symbiotic relationship with Moscow, thus setting in motion a series of decisions and actions on both sides that would result in the movement being tethered to the political agendas of Lenin and, eventually, Stalin. This resolution of the American left to function as an affiliate of the Comintern thus may be viewed as a central force in another paradigmatic shift, this one in the sociopolitical sphere, in that it would lead irrevocably to the death of the ideal of socialism in the United States, which would, in turn, eventually produce "Stalinization."[53]

This divisive moment may also be characterized as a moment of paradigmatic shift in the history of left-wing aesthetics in the United States. In the wake of World War I and all it brought, the artists who identified with the left-wing faction of what had been the lyrical left set aside subjective contemplation and carried into the 1920s a determination to find in one's self, and inspire in others, revolutionary ideological clarity. For these artists and critics on the left, it was acceptable neither to view artistic works as nondogmatic and nondidactic nor create or praise work that failed to offer specific solutions.

In view of these shifts within the sociopolitical and aesthetic realms of the leftist community, it is ever so apparent that Nathan's views expressed in the early 1920s no longer corresponded in any way whatsoever with the governing ethos, ideals, and objectives of the revolutionary left-wing community. His musings of 1922, as well as those of Cheney reinscribed three years later, reflected, supported, and continued to produce the paradigmatic belief system of the lyrical left, as constituted in the years prior to World War I and the Bolshevik Revolution. The left-wing faction of what had been the lyrical left, conversely, looked to critics such as Gold, whose initial writings in the years immediately following the war may be identified as preparadigmatic "anomalies," representing an emerging belief system. By the mid-1920s, this left-wing faction had constituted an equally forceful reading formation that reflected, supported, and produced revolutionary ideology. It was therefore a world ruled by these two sharply defined, powerful, and sectarian reading formations that awaited John Howard Lawson in the early 1920s. Therefore, the texts he generated in the early and mid-1920s might well be read for traces of the intertextual and discursive formations and determinations born from the clash between these opposing ideological forces.

2

Break Down the Walls of the Theatre

> I can't stay here, I need to move. . . . I know this place, I know the streets, faces: I want what I don't know.
>
> —John Howard Lawson, *Roger Bloomer*, 1923

> I am a man—bankrupt before the stars.
>
> —John Howard Lawson, *Nirvana*, 1926

In the fall of 1917, the French army discontinued its association with the Norton-Harjes Ambulance Corps. Refusing transfers to United States military ambulance units, Lawson and Dos Passos were sent to Paris with instructions to proceed to the United States.[1] Ignoring this directive, the young men instead stayed in Paris illegally. For the next three months, they took advantage of the cultural opportunities of that city, seeing early surrealist productions of Apollinaire's *The Breasts of Tiresias* and the Cocteau-Picasso-Satie ballet *Parade* as performed by Diaghilev's visiting Ballets Russe as well as numerous productions at Copeau's Théâtre du Vieux Colombier and Lugné-Poë's Théâtre de l'Oeuvre. Lawson later wrote, "The theatre in Paris was as new to me as if I had arrived from another planet. While I was mesmerized by it, I could not think of it in any coherent way as art."[2] After three months, Lawson's time in Paris came to an abrupt end when he was offered and accepted a salaried position with the American Red Cross in Rome. Thus, at the end of 1917, Lawson left Dos Passos and Paris behind and spent the better part of the next two years in Italy.

While in Italy, Lawson met Kathryn Drain, a scene and costume designer who was serving as a Red Cross volunteer. In November 1918, he and Kate married. When the war ended in the early summer of 1919, they returned to the United States. The birth of their son Alan in July and financial concerns dictated they remain in the States, living in New York, for the remainder of 1919. Making his living in real estate and struggling with his writing, Lawson was nevertheless buoyed by his continued study of the avant-garde, radical politics, and his ongoing correspondence with Dos Passos.[3] Disturbed by the conservative, puritanical, and isolationist turn in New Era American society and politics following the war, which was manifest in the presidencies of Harding, Coolidge, and Hoover as well as the rise of isolationist patriot groups such as the Ku Klux Klan, and dismayed by the Palmer raids,[4] the Lawsons used the proceeds from the sale of *Spice of Life* (renamed *The Butterfly Lady*) to Paramount Studios and returned to Europe in March 1920 where they took up residence in a working-class neighborhood in Paris. There, among the other literary expatriates, the playwright found a dynamic and tolerant literary and artistic community supportive of his developing ideas and methods.[5]

The direction of Lawson's exploration during this period was largely determined by his desire to find new forms of drama that would, in his words, "accurately and theatrically reflect the reality of [the] time."[6] Lawson therefore embarked on an in-depth study of current, nonrealistic theatrical forms, specifically expressionism, surrealism, and Dada. Significant to the composition of *Roger Bloomer*, it was during that late spring of 1920 that he had his first, direct exposure to expressionism when he attended Georges and Ludmilla Pitoëff's production of Lenormand's *Failures* and Copeau's production of Vildrac's *The Steamship Tenacity*.[7] These plays led him to seek out the works of the German forerunners who, the previous decade, had developed the expressionistic dramatic mode—Kaiser, Kokoschka, and Toller—and to study Freud and Jung, the theorists/philosophers whose work focused on the unconscious mind and had inspired the expressionists.[8] While immersed in this study, Lawson again began to work on *Roger Bloomer*, the script he had started on the haystack in France three years before. Upon returning to that text in April 1920, Lawson entered into a five-month period of intense work that would culminate in the first finished draft of *Roger Bloomer*—completed in June 1920—and the first manifestation of what would become *Processional*.[9]

Roger Bloomer

The first complete draft of *Roger Bloomer* stands as a significant milestone in Lawson's journey to find that new form of drama. While the fluidity of movement and the rejection of the conventions of drawing-room drama in this draft of the script were the results of years of experimentation dating back to the episodic form employed in *Standards* and *Servant-Master-Lover*, the earliest complete incarnation of *Roger Bloomer* differs from those endeavors in the inclusion of techniques adopted from expressionism—specifically juxtaposition, character as symbol, and multiple focus—and the cinema, the attempt to incorporate Freudian theory, and the effort to "crystallize [these] ideas in terms of a personal statement."[10]

In the autumn of 1920, Lawson learned that both the Theatre Guild and Provincetown Players had decided not to produce *Roger Bloomer*. In reaction to these rejections, Lawson put aside his writing and began once again to reconsider his art and the necessary philosophy behind it, looking this time to Freud's recently published *Totem and Taboo*. This study led him to anthropologist James G. Frazer's landmark work *The Golden Bough*, which initiated an in-depth study of Cambridge structuralism and "cult of the primitive" artists Picasso, Matisse, and Stravinsky, who were interested in uncovering, reclaiming, and reinterpreting the so-called primitive impulse in art. The consideration of the cult of the primitive fed Lawson's desire to unearth the roots of American entertainment, and that prompted another reworking of *Roger Bloomer* and *Processional* in the spring and summer of 1921.[11] This rewriting was cut short in late 1921 when word reached him that the newly formed Equity Players (aka the Actor's Theatre) was interested in *Roger Bloomer* and he was needed in New York. This encouraging news was offset, however, by his separation from Kate in January 1922. Thus, when Lawson returned to New York in the early spring of that year to continue his revising of *Roger Bloomer* and prepare for the production, he brought both the hope engendered by the promise of success in the theatre as well as no small amount of despair caused by the turmoil in his personal life. The final draft of *Roger Bloomer*, completed in late 1922, embodies this tension. It demonstrates moreover Lawson's desire to employ the techniques and ideas gleaned through the study of various artistic and philosophical movements that consumed him while in Paris in 1920 and 1921.

In act 1 of *Roger Bloomer*, the restless eighteen-year-old Roger is disturbed by the business practices and, by extension, moral principles of his father Everett Bloomer, a well-to-do merchant in Excelsior, Iowa, because he privileges profits over human dignity. In the first scene, as the Bloomers eat dinner, Everett sets forth his point of view:

> BLOOMER. [. . .] There's no poor in America. [. . .] This is the U.S.A., isn't it? (*They [that is, Roger and Mrs. Bloomer] all nod sheepily*). This is Iowa, isn't it. Little old Iowa! Down to the store, the poor come in and buy aluminum pans and silk stockings that you wouldn't afford yourself, mother. [. . .] Over-pay the poor and you cheat the rich. [. . .] Why should I, who built the store out of my sweat, I did, why should I be bullied into paying inefficient people more than they deserve? [. . .] I need every penny, I'm thinking of spreading, spreading . . . opening stores in other cities . . . my stores, spreading.[12]

Concerned that Roger spends too much time alone in his room with his books, Everett attempts to spark a friendship between the young man and Eugene, the son of a business associate, Poppin. A student at Yale, Eugene looks askance at Roger, who is five years his junior. Roger, in turn, finds Eugene boorish and stupid, but is nonetheless both mesmerized and terrified by the older boy's talk of "skirts" and "loving in a strictly technical sense" (49). When Roger turns their conversation toward an abstract discussion of "women's souls" and "passion," a bewildered Eugene declares as he exits, "Fool! Fool! Where will you end, on what ashheap? I've done what I could, stay alone with your passion" (54). Everett, determined Roger will follow Eugene to Yale and then one day inherit the business, takes Roger to his office. Looking over the sales floor and overtly echoing Satan's temptation of Jesus, Everett proclaims:

> BLOOMER. [. . .] some day it's going to be yours. [. . .] Have a look over the store. . . . Want you to take an interest! Enlargements all the time. . . . Spread! That's been my motto: spread! (29)

Thus, pressured by his father to succeed in the world, Roger arrives to take his college entrance exams, but gets in a fight with the College Examiner:

> ROGER. I've been writing, writing . . . Latin . . . French and Geometry—I don't know what's true and what's false.
>
> EXAMINER. That happens: put your head in cold water and then go on.
>
> ROGER. I can't, I won't!
>
> EXAMINER. (*Rising majestically.*) Are you a man? (*He waves long ruler at map of the United States.*) All over the United States today boys are sitting at desks, answering, getting on, into college and on . . .
>
> ROGER. Lies! They're telling lies—

EXAMINER. I'm the authority here: as a Supreme Court Judge sits at his desk, I sit at mine! This is the climax of your youth and you flunk it, you come to me in a state of nerves: haven't you any Will? Haven't you any Manhood?

ROGER. What is the Will of Man?

EXAMINER. Obedience and competitive ambition. Stop and think: College is your first step into the United States and you begin by defying authority. Take the examination and write it like a man. (*Roger stands stiff, looking fixedly at the Examiner and shakes his head.*)

ROGER. I can refuse, I am able to refuse!

EXAMINER. Where will you end your life if you start like this?

ROGER. How do I know? There are so many people in black sitting on thrones, so many judges! They crammed my head full of lies to write an examination—I can't do it! I can't remember the lies. (*He turns away.*)

EXAMINER. (*In magisterial fashion.*) This is definitive: leave this room and your chance at college ends: Never again. (*Roger turns and tears his paper into bits.*)

ROGER. There, then: it's lies, full of lies! (61)

Leaving the exam and returning to his father's office, Roger meets Louise, another restless youth and his father's clerk. When Louise quits her job, protesting, "A dollar a week raise and consumption . . . I'm too proud. You and your store ain't worth it" (69), and flees to New York, Roger, sensing he has found a kindred soul, someone else "wanting something just out of sight, just around the corner" (72), follows after her, "chasing destinies" (78).

In act 2, Roger, devoid of his money and idealism, seeks refuge in a seedy boarding house in New York. With Louise he has an affair and through her influence eventually secures a position in an office on Wall Street. However, his boss, Mr. Rumsey, recognizes that Roger lacks the "money-making manner" and fires him (110). Roger conveys his antipathy in a monologue laden with apocalyptic images:

ROGER. The air is full of gasoline and perfume and the smell of it is poison! I sweat with fear hurrying in tall streets among gray windows. What do those windows hide, what people laughing among treasures? To be home, just to be home! Oh, City, oh, City of stone and steel. . . . I belong to you now! Beaten and afraid I take my way hungrily among the living dead. . . . Give me bread, only bread! What are dreams? I came looking for golden women, I came from wide prairies. . . . Why does your stone splendor touch the sky? Oh, City, do you mock the

> stars with your brightness? . . . In the gray pit of the streets pass the gray millions—and all these that pass are hungry . . . starving men and women, hungry . . . like me! like me! What doom will come on this place, what doom, oh, hungry City? Your thrones will fall and your buildings will crash together, Singer and Woolworth will go to dust. . . . Death will come in a whirlwind breaking your sky towers—and the hungry will shout for joy! Are these dead, these that pass with white faces? Will these men rise from their graves in the streets and the subways, will they rise laughing to destroy the city of their shame? . . . I am yours, oh, City of slaves. . . . I am one of the millions, servants of death and time, hungry, moaning for bread! I pray before you, New York. . . . I, Roger Bloomer, pray and curse you, oh, City, mother of my fear . . . like my own mother, my flesh mother, to whom I curse and pray. . . . (116–18)

In turn, Roger, distraught, attempts to poison himself only to be rescued by the mystical Ragged Man and nursed back to life by Louise. The act ends with Roger declaring boldly, "No more nonsense; I'll find something, then I'll come to you, tell you all about it. [. . .] Better wait, the battle's just beginning" (125).

The final act opens with Eugene and Roger visiting a gentlemen's club. In due course, it is revealed that Eugene, at the prompting of Roger's father, agreed to find Roger and encourage him to return to Iowa. Roger, however, responds forcefully, "Can't go backward, I must go on, find myself" (135). Meanwhile, Louise becomes increasingly baffled by the inhumaneness in the world, turns down a marriage proposal from Mr. Rumsey, steals three thousand dollars in bonds from his office, professes "for me there will never be any freedom," and eventually kills herself by taking rat poison (179). The play ends with Roger in prison on suspicion of having aided in Louise's death. In the cell, he has a nightmare in which eroticism and death are recurring motifs. Just when he is about to yield to the visions in his dream, Louise appears and encourages him: "Go it alone, Roger; are you ready now? I've given you yourself, take it. . . . Face the music; what music, falling about you like rain; what splendor of broken chords, brass trumpets braying in the morning and whisper of harps in the dusk . . . and far off, listen, the tread of marching people singing a new song . . . Goodbye. . . . A man's luck, Roger" (224–25).

In many ways, *Roger Bloomer* is a simple retelling of a well-known story: the youngster goes to the city to become an adult.[13] However, a close reading of the final stage direction in the script, "Roger rises and goes toward the lighted doorway," indicates that Lawson went well beyond the traditional boundaries of this narrative pattern (225).

Conventional dramatic manifestations of this storyline, such as George Lillo's *The London Merchant* (1731) and Tom Taylor's *The Ticket-of-Leave Man* (1863), show a young person entering a urban space, suffering at the hands of city life, and longing for or returning to the safety of home (that is, usually small-town or country life) and its traditions. All attempts made by these youthful protagonists to secure agency and exercise free will in the world are met with hostility. Lawson radically modifies this story by creating in Roger a protagonist who, despite the obvious risks and unforeseen dangers, is persistently moving forward, never dreaming of returning to his previous life, and fervently committed to the notion that his choices will create a new world. By reshaping this traditional rendering of the "youngster going to the city" storyline, Lawson took his place alongside other members of the American literary community such as Edgar Lee Masters (that is, *Spoon River Anthology*, 1915), Willa Cather (*My Antonia*, 1918), and Sherwood Anderson (*Winesburg, Ohio*, 1919), who were metaphorically saying farewell to the past and facing an unsure future.

Reading the text on something of a more autobiographical level, Lawson's reshaping of the "youngster going to the city" storyline might also be read as a thinly veiled allegory for the playwright's own monumental sojourn to which he had dedicated six years of his life.[14] Indeed, Roger's journey from small-town Iowa to standing on the threshold of a lighted doorway parallels, in striking ways, Lawson's own journey from naïveté to recognition. In this light, Roger's flight from Iowa may be read as analogous to Lawson's flight to Europe in early 1917, in that both suffered alienation and confusion imparted and supported by their respective material environments. As the disgruntled and directionless Roger idealistically seeks solace in the skyscrapers of New York, so too did Lawson innocently seek a sense of purpose, direction, and clarity in the ambulance service. Ultimately, the war for Lawson, as the city for Roger, offered neither clarity nor understanding but, instead, indecipherable, overwhelming horror. To continue this line of analysis, Roger's time in prison might be regarded as a metaphor for Lawson's brief return to America in 1919 wherein the awakening experimental artist and political revolutionary found, as did many in the lost generation, that America's "emotional sterility, [. . .] cultural hegemony, and [. . .] puritanical morality" was counterproductive to his development.[15] Alienated in his own world, Lawson, like his protagonist, chose to "listen, the tread of marching people singing a new song," and fled America again for a two-year, self-imposed exile in Paris, where the desire to identify a dramatic form that would "accurately and theatrically reflect the reality of [his] time" fed his quest for personal liberation and was manifest in his study of Freud, his belief in the power of abstract forms of expression, and his desire to free himself from the restraints of bourgeois morality. Thus, by the end of 1922, with the completion of the final draft of *Roger Bloomer*, Lawson, like the title character at the end of the play, was poised on the brink of a frightening and tantalizing new world, ready to demand life on his own terms. Considered in this light, Roger, and by extension Lawson, is comparable to Ibsen's unyielding Reverend Brand (*Brand*, 1866), whose journey also ends in a nightmare. But unlike Ibsen's hero, whose vision leads him to death, Roger is determined to "ride the nightmare free and awake." He stands alone against the furies who pursue him in his dream and shout, "Fill his mouth with straw . . . stuff his mouth with sand!," and he triumphs as he screams, "I alone against these bloody generations" (217).[16]

Lawson's move beyond the confines of the traditional "youngster going to the city" storyline may be further analyzed by considering his employment of expressionistic methods and Freudian theory. A cursory analysis of *Roger Bloomer* reveals that Lawson managed to include most of the recognized techniques of expressionism. The structure is episodic (for example, there are over forty scenes efficiently packed into three acts), the scenes are disconnected, and the spiritual sojourner theme is utilized. The characters are either types or symbols: for example, Roger, in many ways, is the stereotypical American young man off to find his destiny in the city, Everett Bloomer is a typical business man consumed with making a profit, and Mrs. Bloomer is the stereotypical housewife and mother intent on providing for her family; whereas the Ragged Man symbolizes death and the College Examiner and the Judge symbolize the abuse of authority. Some of the language is telegraphic and distorted, and the suggested music, lights, and settings are abstract.[17]

In many ways, however, the text goes well beyond the limits of the expressionistic mode as it had been recognized and practiced in the United States. Prior to Lawson's experimentation with the Germanic technique, American expressionists had remained true to the pre–World War I mode of the form that focused on the idea that spiritual sojourns end in defeat, defiled by material wants and greeds. A brief historical recounting of the course of German expressionism will help to clarify how Lawson broke the shell of this traditional form and, thus, advanced the practice of expressionism in the United States.

Germanic expressionistic drama is typically divided into two basic eras or strategies.[18] "Mysticism," popularized in the years leading up to World War I, highlights the spiritual journey of a stereotypical hero who holds the stage from beginning to end while the rest of the world fades into symbols. In scripts such as Oskar Kokoschka's *Murderer, Hope of Womankind* (1907), Reinhard Sorge's *The Beggar* (1911), Georg Kaiser's *From Morn to Midnight* (1912), and Walter Hasenclever's *Humanity* (1918), the protagonist—hero, universal citizen, or everyperson—constantly battles bitterness and frustration but is ultimately doomed to sacrifice to internal pressures. Thus, by its very nature, the mystic strategy is pessimistic. Furthermore, because of the focus upon the individual, mystic expressionism bears the stamp of extreme subjectivity. Conversely, "activism," popularized in the years 1918 through 1923, underscores the stereotypical hero's conflict with a social problem or institution. In scripts such as Yvon Goll's *The Immortal One* (1918), Rolf Lauckner's *Cry in the Streets* (1922), and Ernst Toller's *Transfiguration* (1918) and *Man and the Masses* (1920), the protagonist strives to impress his or her message upon the world and, through that struggle, transforms society. It follows that, with its focus on social change as opposed to an individual's doomed spiritual journey, the activist strategy separates itself from the mystic strategy by being optimistic and overtly revolutionary in tone.[19]

The expressionistic dramas of American playwrights Elmer Rice and Eugene O'Neill are in the tradition of German mystic expressionists whose characters lament and struggle with internal forces but ultimately accept their defeats. In Rice's *The Adding Machine* (1923), Mr. Zero cannot escape his destiny. As is Kaiser's bank clerk in *From Morn to Midnight,* who has stolen a large amount of money and spends fourteen hours in the dizzying excitement of the city but is doomed from the start, Rice's hero is condemned, even in heaven, to work on a huge adding machine. O'Neill's expressionistic heroes, Brutus Jones in *The Emperor Jones* (1921) and Yank in *The Hairy Ape* (1922), are more aggressive and self-assertive than Mr. Zero, but they too are destined, despite their struggles, to die trapped and unrewarded in the jungle and the zoo. Although they incorporated uniquely American subject matter, O'Neill and Rice wrote expressionistic dramas that were subjective in nature (that is, dealing with an individual's internal struggle) and pessimistic in tone and, thus, never ventured outside the parameters of the mystic strategy.[20]

In his first completed draft of *Roger Bloomer* (June 1920), Lawson, as were O'Neill and Rice, was indebted to the mystic strategy. Indeed, later in life Lawson recalled that "*Roger Bloomer,* as it emerged in Paris, was mainly influenced by German expressionism," and this influence was manifest in his (that is, Lawson's) "inability to move Roger into action."[21] By the time the playwright completed the final draft three years later, he had allied himself firmly with the activist strategy. Lawson himself suggests such a shift when he writes, "Roger's attempt to express hiself, to *be* himself, leads to a confrontation with society—which is still experienced subjectively, as a dream. Yet this implies a further step—to confront the reality projected in the nightmare."[22] A comparison of the two drafts illustrates Lawson's move beyond the subjective nature and pessimistic tone associated with the mystic strategy and reveals how the playwright's thinking evolved between 1920 and 1922.

The most obvious difference in the two drafts is found at the end of the script. In the early draft, Roger's spiritual journey has left him forlorn. Passively (indeed, almost catatonically) sitting beside the coffin holding the body of Louise, he quietly muses, "Those who watch by the unlight dead . . . the truth . . . if they live to tell."[23] Conversely, in the final draft, Roger's nightmarish, almost Dada-esque, confrontation with the shadows, involving staccato pantomime, modern dance, and thunderous music, culminates in his defiance of and victory over the shadows: "If I die, then I die like a man . . . laughing . . . I'm ready to shake the roof of the world with laughing" (220).[24] Thus, the dream, in all its violence and ugliness, ends in success.

As the pessimistic and passive ending in the first draft of the play is clearly evidence of an artist working within the mystic mode, the more optimistic and aggressive ending of the final draft is evidence of an artist committed to the activist strategy.[25] Louise's encouragement for Roger to "face the music" and "listen [to] the tread of marching people singing a new song" is strikingly similar to the revolutionary call of Frederich, the protagonist in Ernst Toller's activist script *Transfiguration*:

> FREDERICH. Now, brothers, now I bid you march! March now in the light of day! Go to your rulers and proclaim to them with the organ tones of a million voices that their power is but an illusion. Go to the soldiers and tell them to beat their swords into ploughshares. Go to the rich and show them your heart, your heart that was buried alive beneath their rubbish. But be kind to them, for they too are poor, poor and straying. But the castles—those you must destroy; destroy them laughing, the false castles of illusion. Now march! March forward in the light of day![26]

Other notable differences in the two drafts further illustrate Lawson's commitment to the activist mode and the progression of his thinking. In the early draft of the text, Lawson relied upon a naïve and narrow interpretation of Freud. Roger in this version is concerned almost exclusively with being freed from the conventions of bourgeois morality. His struggle is internal, a product of his suppressed sexual desires. In the first act Roger has a sprawling (that is, three-page, single-spaced), nearly incoherent monologue in which he quotes an extended passage from Shelley's poem "To a Skylark," attempts to liken his pain to that of the Romantic poet, denounces the internal forces binding him, and calls for sexual release:

ROGER. Life like a curtain before me, a curtain figured with breasts.
You shake the cloth and they squirm strangely behind it, but behind the curtain what mystical things? [. . .]
Then just supposing I believe, believe hard, believe all over, that behind that curtain there stands a maiden with dulcimer, rubies in her gold hair, her face pink, her arms pink, pink breasts bared to me . . .
(bitterly)
she too knowing just where to draw the line—Come out to me then, come out, wherever you are . . magic girl, melting girl—[. . .]
. . . you and I, Shelley, you and I . . . To a Skylark!
[He reads from a book of Shelley.]

"Higher still and higher
From the earth thou springest
Like a cloud of fire,
The blue deep thou wingest,
And singing still dost soar
And soaring over singest
In the golden lightning
Of the sunken sun
O'er which clouds are brightening
Thou dost float and run
Like an unbodied joy whose race is just begun"
"Like an unbodied joy whose race has just begun"—but I have a body!
If I could "wing the deep blue"

(He almost tears the book in a feeling of revulsion and throws it violently away.)
What's the use of Shelley when I feel myself going insane? . . . Why not? . . .
I've got my health. Away with ghosts . . . away . . .
I'm a man. It's poetry that gets me into trouble. Shelley knew nothing, Shelley was pure spirit, Shelley never read the *Police Gazette*!
(He draws out a copy of the Police Gazette.)
The *Police Gazette*! That's healthy anyway: it's full of prize fighters and girls.
(He turns over the pages eagerly.)

Girls waving their legs and sticking out their stomachs, and fat strong naked men, prize fighters and girls [. . .]

What else? It's full of advertisements about vile diseases. So that's all Sex is, one long disease! . . . And then girls, waving their legs and sticking out their stomachs . . .

(He throws it away violently.)

Go to the corner there with Shelley!

(He sits, clenched hands, his voice choked with sobs.)

If I could wing the deep blue! . . . I wish it were dawn. Birds sing and you breath [*sic*] the air, and for just a moment, just a breath, you're free from the hideous weight of the body . . .

But at night among books and ghosts, everywhere you turn, flesh, flesh . . . And yet not just flesh . . . something with lights in it, something mystical, beckoning eyes, with limbs leading me where . . . My God! Take the Bible for help! What? "Mahalallel begat Jared, Jared begat Enoch, Enoch begat Methuselah, Methuselah lived nine hundred and sixty-three years, he begat sons and daughters and he died"—Huh? Isn't there any religion? Just begetting and begetting till weariness brings a long sleep. Am I to beget in my turn? Did my father and mother beget me? My father and mother like that?

(a grim bitter smile)

Surely there was not hot flesh, no fevered reaching in that . . . but like at the dinner-table, with a little talk of the weather and the high cost of living, calmly . . . calmly.

I . . . I against all those generations, I mocking, alone, I asking . . . I red with fever tossing in the night . . . I fighting my body, denying my body, alone till the dawn brings laughter that I may go out on tiptoe reaching for golden apples . . . [27]

In the 1922 version, the quotation from Shelley is reduced to a single line and the rebellious sentiment includes a pointed, albeit symbolic, denunciation of bourgeois social structures:

ROGER. . . . nothing but books, old books! I ask life for its secret and old books come to me grinning! Then help me, help me now when I need you. . . . Shelley . . . . "Like an unbodied joy whose race is just begun." . . . But I have a body—I've got my health—away with ghosts—away. I'm a man. It's poetry that gets me into trouble. Shelley knew nothing. Shelley was pure spirit. Shelley never read the *Police Gazette*! That's healthy anyway; it's full of prize fighters and girls—. Girls waving their legs and sticking out their stomachs, and fat, strong, naked men—Maybe I could be a prize fighter—(*Finding something in the magazine*). "Loss of Will!" What is the will of man? "Loss of Manhood." My God, what is manhood, how do you lose it? . . . Manhood—That's me, that's me—

> [. . .] Myself against all these generations, I mocking, asking . . . red with fever tossing in the night . . . alone till dawn brings laughter. . . . I myself, fighting my body, denying my body . . . a man is made out of flesh and passion! All right. . . . Come on, you damned ghosts, come on, you laughing shadows, I'm strong and alone, and somehow . . . I'll beat you yet! (56–57)

While the longing for sexual freedom remains central, in the 1922 edition Roger's rebellion has been expanded to include other concerns. This change clearly demonstrates the progression and deepening of Lawson's understanding of Freudian theory. In the final draft, the playwright moved beyond a mere telling of Roger's internal struggle to find sexual freedom in a stifling environment and, instead, used the protagonist's external struggle to warn against many of the evils—that is, "old books"—inherent in puritanical society. In so doing, Lawson allied himself with the more revolutionary activist strategy and, in turn, moved the American expressionistic mode away from the mystic strategy.

With *Roger Bloomer*, Lawson had hoped to "break down the walls of the theatre."[28] The Equity Players company was apparently unprepared and unwilling to stage the theatrical rebellion Lawson envisioned. Offended by the "vulgar" language, sexual references, and revolutionary themes, director Shelley Hull cut many lines and focused on the lyricism in the play.[29] Designer Woodman Thompson, befuddled by the expressionistic devices and episodic structure, created elaborate and realistic sets for every scene and, thus, worked against the fluidity of the play. Opening on 1 March 1923, the poor quality of the production was not lost on critic Kenneth Macgowan.[30] In his short review, Macgowan praised the playwright and the script but described the Equity Players as "home-folk from Peoria, lost in a modern 'art' gallery."[31] Following a number of other highly unfavorable notices, the Equity production of *Roger Bloomer* closed after a ten-day run.

Skirting an unceremonious end, independent producer Marguerite Barker acquired the rights to the production and moved it to the Greenwich Village Theatre where it reopened on 15 March. Barker, along with Lawson who codirected, focused on the subverted themes, restored the cut lines, and eliminated the elaborate sets. For example, the detailed and realistic judge's chamber built for the Equity production was abandoned in Baker's remounted production, substituted with a stepladder placed in the center of an empty stage. The degree to which this reworked production differed from the Equity Players production was significant enough for Hull to write a letter to Lawson that reads, in part:

> I'm going to ask you [Lawson], if you don't mind, to please not have my name on the programs when your next edition is printed—for two reasons, because really it isn't my work anymore (nor is it W. Thompson's!), and second because I do feel so badly about the lines you restored. You had every right to do so, and more than every right, a justification of your own beliefs and ideals [. . .] but I do not want even to seem to have directed these speeches! [. . .] You have been so understanding in everything that I feel you won't misunderstand now.[32]

Not surprisingly, Lawson's reaction to these changes was wholly different. For him, the "effect" of this reworking and minimizing process "was electric."[33] He later recalled, "I was concerned largely with economy, but I also wanted to restore the theatrical quality of the play. Without the cumbersome scenery, the fluidity of the play was restored; the bare stage restored life to the actors, and gave them contact with the audience that had been obstructed by the 'picture frame' realism of the earlier production. [Still, t]here was too little time to develop values; the visual poetry, the pantomime and changing images that should have accompanied the rhythms of speech could not be imaginatively developed."[34] The changes were apparently enough for Macgowan. In a review of the remounted production, he was again brief and to the point: "*Roger Bloomer* is thoroughly redirected, somewhat recast, and considerably improved."[35]

Other critics were not as taken with the play in either production. Most of those writing in the mainstream presses railed against Lawson.[36] Representative are the reviews of Alan Dale and John Corbin. In a short critique in the *Hartford Times*, Dale cavalierly dismissed the play as "freakish, disagreeable, and nerve-racking."[37] John Corbin had taken a similar stance a week before in his lengthy review for the *New York Times*:

> Doubtless Mr. John Howard Lawson and his friends will insist that he has written a real play. Certainly it is a resolute and sustained example of the art of the younger generation knocking at the door. Except in momentary lapses, nobody on stage speaks like a human being. Strenuously and insistently they all speak what can only be explained as the language of John Howard Lawson, handing themselves out to the audience with as little realism as possible. They philosophize and lyrically expatiate in quite a Russian manner. They are ironic and sardonic, very cynical and very, very impassioned. They mock us with fantastic nightmares and shock us with psychologic disquisitions upon sex. It is, in fact, free verse applied to the theatre—the poetic drama of expressionism. [. . .] For those who like free verse,

> sex talk, expressionism, philanthropic cynicism that is funnier than it is meant to be, together with general futility, this is just the sort of play they like.[38]

By the next week, Corbin's distaste for the play had grown considerably. Referring to the production as "callow nonsense" and encouraging Lawson to look to Shaw's *Candida* for aid in characterization, Corbin concluded by chiding the Equity Players for staging a play full of "puppy whining."[39]

Some audience members wrote letters to editors in Lawson's defense. One spectator wrote, "One has here that experience, rare in the theatre, of looking on at a birth. [. . .] One feels in Lawson's play that here is an organism struggling into existence. Here is life, pushing and straining against a static, or comparatively static, environment."[40] Another, who thought the play was "terrible," praised Lawson for endeavoring to create "a striking [. . .] method for the purposes of modern drama."[41] A third pondered the seeming intellectual limitations of the New York audiences and likened the shortsightedness of the conservative newspaper critics to the attitude of the noisy man seated next to her at a production of the play "who seemed restless and greatly annoyed because there was 'no scenery,' and finally exclaimed in a rather loud tone: 'Oh, anyhow, what is it all about?'"[42]

A number of members of the liberal literati defended the play as well. The most passionate of these statements came from Lawson's friend Edna St. Vincent Millay. In a letter she sent to a number of newspaper editors, Millay pondered, "It is apparently not enough, even for intelligent people, that a piece of work would be interesting, thoughtful, stimulating, humorous, tender, passionate, and sincere. [. . . I]t is refreshing that somebody should be driving at something."[43]

The more liberal critics in the press echoed these supportive sentiments. Writing for *The Nation*, Ludwig Lewisohn admitted that "[d]efinite and simple things are to be said against the play," but, unlike the reviewers in the daily press who "performed a can-can of derision," he believed the young playwright showed promise and hailed the message in the play:

> There is youth in it and passion and rebellion and irony and observation and the color of dreams. There is astonishment in the face of life and woe at its inadequacy and a desire to dig deep to the roots or soar to the peaks of ecstasy. Clarity and ecstasy are the criteria of this seeker and dreamer, no efficiency or prosperity or rubber-stamped happiness. The lawn, the Buick, and the business are not enough. The church and the school are not enough. [. . . W]hat I heard at every

> moment was the cry for a cleaner and more passionate world, a world less cluttered and corrupted by law and greed and irrational isolation, a world in which men and women can tread the path of their salvation unafraid.[44]

Stark Young took a similar stance in his penetrating analysis published in the *New Republic*:

> The play has poetry often and often and such a young, pressing, pitiful and reckless, insolent beauty as you seldom see in the theatre. [. . . I]nstead of the usual simplicities of our theatre, [. . .] we get in this play of *Roger Bloomer* some freedom to talk about the bewildered dreams of the mind and flesh, about society and education and family. [. . .] At this rate our theatre will begin to vibrate with new life.
>
> If there were nothing else to be said for it, *Roger Bloomer* would be worth doing as a sheer extension of the possibility of content in our theatre. Any play that does that does much. For if the business of art is to express life, it must follow that one of the chief needs in any art is to stretch the limits of its expression, to include and to force into its own terms more of our life, to seek a perpetual dilation of form and idea, which are in the end inseparable.[45]

The most passionate defense of the play came from Anita Block, writing for the socialist *New York Call*. In urging *Call* readers concerned with "the problems of America—to its idolatry of business, its bourgeois smugness, its moral hypocrisy and its false 'Americanism,'" to attend a benefit for the play, Block praised Lawson for his willingness to show "America prostrate before the false gods of Wealth and Success, and, more terrible and soul killing than these, the great god Conformity" and claimed that *Roger Bloomer* was "one of the most penetrating, courageously outspoken presentations of American life our stage has produced."[46]

Despite the many earnest pleas and affirming critiques, the remounted *Roger Bloomer* ran for a relatively modest fifty performances. The writing and subsequent theatrical productions of that text in the spring of 1923, nonetheless, stand as significant events in the history of the theatre in the United States in that they highlight Lawson's notable contribution to the development of a theatrical idiom: expressionism. By eliminating the tone of pessimism and overarching subjectivity inherent in mystical expressionism and employing instead the method of activist expressionism, Lawson advanced not only his own writing toward a more overt presentation of pressing social issues but that of drama in the United States as a whole. The techniques incorporated and the issues addressed would echo in many popular American dramas in the years between the wars, from *Beggar on Horseback* (1924) to *Machinal* (1928) to *Our Town* (1938). Later in life, Lawson himself noted how he was keenly aware of the advances he had made. He recalled, "*Roger Bloomer* carries the expressionistic mode further than any other play of the time. It carries the mode so far that it exceeds the limits of the form and overflows it. [. . . Prior to *Roger Bloomer*, American] Expressionism had remained within the ideology of the status quo; it was subjective and frustrated."[47]

Furthermore, and on a more personal level, *Roger Bloomer* is significant because it contains the first explicit—albeit nascent—expression of the ideas, both artistic and political, that would torment, evade, and, eventually, become the foundation to Lawson's thought and worldview. *Roger Bloomer* thus would be, as Dos Passos prophetically wrote in the foreword to the published script, "only a beginning."[48] Lawson's own critique of the script, written three days following the opening of the remounted production, offers perhaps the best summation of the script as well as the playwright's goals for the future: "I think I am pretty familiar with the Broadway Book of Etiquette. I have broken from it intentionally, and shall continue to do so."[49]

Processional

When Lawson finished the first draft of *Roger Bloomer* in June 1920, he immediately began working on *Processional*. As he did so, the progression of his ideas regarding the shape and direction of dramatic form and content were determined, in large part, by the question "Now that Roger had awakened from the dream of adolescence, what would he face in reality?"[50] A close analysis of this question, as well as the scripted response provided in the early drafts of *Processional*, reveals that Lawson's worldview and, by extension, his theatrical vision were rapidly evolving. Specifically, while a Freudian-inspired concern for internal, psychological forces (that is, "the dream of adolescence") was still a controlling determinant, his thoughts regarding the power of external, material forces (that is, "reality"), and the individual's status within and response to that setting, were germinating and becoming increasingly evident in the texts Lawson generated.

Evidence of this evolution of thought may be found in Lawson's initial answer to the question posed as manifest in the stark opening passages from the early version of *Processional*, circa summer 1920:

> In the desolate outdistricts of a city in Western Pennsylvania. The feel and color of coal smoke heavy like a pall. Across the front of the stage a huge iron fence, taller than a man, severely formal, the bars of it grotesquely big and foreboding, each bar ending in a spike. Center a

> big iron gate thrown wide. Just inside the gate, facing out toward the audience, a very new shiny white marble monument, a war monument obviously, showing a dying soldier being comforted by Victory with a sword in her hand. An uglier use of the same amount of stone could hardly be invented. Behind a mass of factory windows and chimneys against the leaden sky. Evidently the iron wall rims the courtyard of a factory, the statue triumphantly to guard the entrance.

As the curtain rises on this bleak scene, a group of five men in silk hats and suits, "rather grotesque figures of the pork barrel," stand with their backs to the audience and listen to another man who, with "mock gentleness," makes a speech dedicating the statue:

> In times of social disturbance . . . In times, I might say, of social stress, when the masses rise like an ocean at full tide . . . and subside like the tide . . . We and others, the good citizens, the religious men, the thinkers, stand firm in the flood of anarchy and Bolshevism, we stand firm above the flood on the rock of tradition, the American tradition, the tradition that made the dollar the world's standard coin and the stars and stripes the world's noblest flag. The ship of Democracy will navigate the flood, the winds of freedom shall fill its sails and the dollar shall be its compass in distress.[51]

The oppressive and overwhelming milieu suggested in the description of this scene and the playwright's explicit sarcasm underpinning the monologue imply a growing recognition on the part of Lawson regarding the force of material conditions, specifically the deadening force of the increasingly conservative sociopolitical environment in the United States in the early 1920s. Nevertheless, the acidity and sarcasm implied should not be taken as evidence of clearly defined political convictions on the part of the playwright or as proof of a commitment to "materialist aesthetics."[52] Instead, they are read more appropriately as an indication of Lawson's still narrowly subjective, internalized view of the world, albeit one that is somewhat socially progressive.

In this early draft, composed while living as an expatriate in Paris, Lawson was responding to the past three years of his life and the events that had dominated it: the unspeakable violence and destruction of the war, the adoption of isolationist ideology on the part of many United States citizens and the government, as well as the moral and political conservatism that consumed the United States following the war.[53] In a manner similar to the early manifestations of the internalized and mystic character of Roger Bloomer, condemned to sacrifice himself to the pressures of the world, the hint at angry social satire in the early draft of *Processional* is a subjective, pessimistic view of an individual's futile struggle against the escalating force of the hegemonic, machinelike, bourgeois society. Unlike *Roger Bloomer*, however, which deals almost exclusively with Roger's internal struggle against traditional conventions, *Processional*, even in this early draft, attempts to comprehend and counter, by way of the externalized actions of the protagonist, those same conventions and "to tell the raw, brutal truth of American life, [seen] as an orgy of violence and sex."[54] This embryonic concern with the individual's actions in and against an external society is clearly a shift away from the internalized Freudian nightmare that remains at the core of all manifestations of *Roger Bloomer*. Lawson later commented on this change of focus: "As I sat at my dormer window overlooking the Seine, I felt threatened, by forces in myself as well as in society. In endeavoring to move from Roger Bloomer's nightmare to the reality that lay behind it, I experienced horror that darkened my mind."[55]

The overwhelming task of processing these weighty philosophical and psychological issues left Lawson exhausted. Consequently, following the completion of the first act in July and August 1920, Lawson stopped work on *Processional*. Later in life, Lawson offered a summation of this earliest draft: "I had not found the main elements that enter into the later versions of the play. What I wrote in August 1920, is crudely theatrical and there are hints of a new use of American language; snatches of popular songs foreshadow the development of a 'jazz symphony.'"[56] Dissatisfied with the text and yet not sure how to proceed, it was a full year later, in July 1921, when the playwright at last found new background material for the developing script in newspaper accounts of labor strife in Mingo County, West Virginia. Inspired once again by a manifestation of an externalized struggle (that is, capital versus labor), Lawson returned to the script, working through the early spring 1922. At that point, consumed by the preparations for the forthcoming Equity Players' production of *Roger Bloomer*, Lawson again set aside the developing script. However, once *Roger Bloomer* closed, and in the wake of the critical excitement surrounding Lawson prompted by Barker's remounting of the production at the Greenwich Village Theatre, the Theatre Guild secured the option on *Processional*. For Lawson, this promise of production by arguably the premier art theatre company in the United States was enough to spur him on toward the final round of rewrites, beginning in the summer of 1923.[57] Even so, the excitement of this period was quelled significantly by his continued separation from Kate and the suicide of his brother, Wendell, in the fall of 1922.[58] In response to these events, late in the summer of 1923 Lawson returned to Europe—living with

Dos Passos and e. e. cummings in the south of France—to continue to rework the play and rethink his life.

While there, Lawson was witness to the last days of the conflict between those involved in the waning Paris Dada movement, led by Tristan Tzara, and those involved in the emerging surrealism movement, led by Tzara's maverick disciple André Breton.[59] The fervent discussions and debate instrumental in defining these modes of artistic expression (and, in the case of Dada, serving as eulogy) would prove influential in Lawson's composition of *Processional*, as well as his next two scripts, *Nirvana* and *Loud Speaker*. In early 1924, the playwright arrived back in the States with what was, for all practical purposes, the final edit of *Processional*. He spent April and May of that year in Pittsburgh, in search of "an American reality that was not visible in New York," working on early drafts of *Nirvana* and *Loud Speaker*, and making minor changes to *Processional* as determined by his correspondence with the Theatre Guild's literary office.[60] Thus, by the late summer of 1924, the script for *Processional* was ready for production.

While the 1920 draft of the script contains, in embryo, many of the elements found in the final draft, an analysis of changes made by the time the script was produced and published in 1925 demonstrates the profound development of the playwright's ideas and methods. In terms of form, central to the earliest draft of the script is the mystic, expressionistic strategy shared by the early drafts of *Roger Bloomer*. In turn, the worldview implied throughout that early draft of *Processional* is irrevocably linked to the governing ethos of the lyrical left, in its somewhat indirect and vague plea to contest and transcend the conservative, bourgeois traditions of puritanism, capitalism, and nationalism. At its core are the one-dimensional, cartoonlike, silk-hatted men, "grotesque figures of the pork barrel," who—as do their counterparts in *Roger Bloomer*, the Judge and the College Examiner—represent the violence and hypocrisy of the authoritative bourgeois and capitalist world order and who had, in part, forced Lawson to flee his homeland. In later editions, these bourgeois-inspired men in silk hats become a singular and subordinate character who is at the end of the play dwarfed and conquered by the masses. Thus, as with *Roger Bloomer*, the pessimism in the early draft of *Processional* is, by 1925, transformed. Indeed, the marching masses who had been heard as a distant sound at the end of *Roger Bloomer* poured onto the stage and out into the house of the theatre in the final draft of *Processional*, bringing with them an even more optimistic view of the future, albeit one that was excessively violent.[61]

The final draft of *Processional* is set in a West Virginia coal-mining town. The play opens on a city street with the newsboy, Boob, shouting that a strike is on against the coal company: "Extry! Extry! Trouble in West Virginia! Charleston paper! Jazzin' up the big strike! Extry! Extry! . . . . Extry! Soldiers an' miners clash! Threats thrill throngs!"[62] Isaac Cohen, the proprietor of the local general store, and his daughter Sadie enter discussing the governor's recent edict establishing martial law in the town. As they speak, the strikers enter, represented by a band of would-be jazz musicians, playing "Yankee Doodle Blues." Jake Psinski, a highly educated Polish immigrant and Marxist agitator who is attempting to organize the miners and instruct them in the ways of class struggle, leads them. In between crudely played jazz numbers, the strikers talk of Dynamite Jim Flimmins, a coal miner who has been jailed for fighting with the soldiers brought in to crush the strike. Various soldiers come and go, led by Connor, "the [town] Sheriff [who] carries two large pistols, [and] dresse[s] in half Buffalo Bill style, high boots, black whiskers, [and] a very big badge on his chest" (32) and an abstract figure referred to only as the Man in the Silk Hat, who holds the title of "President a' the Law an' Order League" (35). In addition to the miners and soldiers, other figures enter and exit the scene including Pop Pratt, a Civil War veteran; Phillpots, "a very George M. Cohan sort of newspaper man"; and Old Maggie, Dynamite Jim's prophesying grandmother (26). The act ends with Old Maggie reflecting, "There's a black time comin' . . ." (48).

In act 2, scene 1, Jim's mother, Mrs. Flimmins, and Old Maggie visit him in jail. In the course of the conversation, it is revealed that the two women have been evicted from their company-owned house and have sought refuge in an abandoned barn. Mrs. Flimmins cryptically suggests she will prostitute herself to the soldiers in an effort to earn enough money to send Jim away from West Virginia once he is set free. After Old Maggie and Mrs. Flimmins exit, and with the assistance of Psinski and another striking minor, Rastus, an African American, Jim breaks out and is carried in a coffin to the safety of the labor temple.

Act 2, scene 2 takes place in front of the labor temple, which the military has seized. Soldiers come and go as they search for Jim. Eventually satisfied Jim is not hiding in or around the temple, the soldiers leave and Sadie and Phillpots enter. Sadie attempts to seduce Phillpots and, when he at last shows some interest, she flirtatiously runs off. As Phillpots follows, Psinski and Rastus arrive carrying the coffin. Hearing the sound of approaching soldiers, they exit quickly, leaving the coffin with Jim in it behind. Soldiers once again arrive, most of whom enter the temple. As the ranks of the soldiers increase, sounds of drunken laughter and raucous singing begin to emanate from the temple. The few soldiers remaining in front of the temple talk with those who continue to arrive, revealing the presence of a woman in the temple who is selling herself to those willing to pay. When all but one of the soldiers has entered the temple, Phillpots returns still searching for Sadie. As he speaks with the lone soldier, the sounds from inside the temple intensify. Sickened and yet inspired that a story of drunken soldiers whoring will make good news copy, Phillpots quickly leaves for the telegraph office. Left with no one to talk to, the remaining soldier too exits, leaving Jim alone in his coffin. Emerging, Jim indicates that all the talk of women and alcohol has whetted his appetite. Just as Jim calls out, "Gawd send me a woman!," Sadie enters looking for Phillpots (95). Jim grabs her savagely and tries to rape her. As Sadie fights back, the soldier returns, and, in the course of a fight, Jim kills him. The act ends with Sadie, hysterical with fright, running off and Jim contemplating his actions and his future:

> JIM. . . . they'll hang me now s'all right to talk but I never kilt a guy before. . . .
>
> *(From the rear comes a sound of drunken laughter)*
>
> That's for me, they're comin' for me . . . "hands up or I knock you down" was the last words he said. What curse makes a feller do them things? Gettin' cold, his soul's gone up in the sky, his soul's asittin' in the moon; he had a mother too. . . . I want my mammy's arms 'cause I done a black thing, oh, mammy, help me now! (99)

With that, Jim flees to the barn where his mother is living.

Act 3, scene 1 takes place the next morning in the fallen-in barn where Mrs. Flimmins and Old Maggie are living. As the women sleep, Jim and Psinski arrive. Once she is awakened, Mrs. Flimmins grows increasingly distressed with Jim and Psinski's talk of violent class struggle. With the sound of marching soldiers drawing ever nearer, Mrs. Flimmins hides Jim and Psinski in a crawl space beneath the floor. When the Man in the Silk Hat and the sheriff arrive, with Phillpots in tow, they interrogate Mrs. Flimmins and Old Maggie. Skeptical but unable to prove any connection to Jim's escape, the men exit to search the area around the barn but not before stationing a garrison of soldiers at all the doors. When they have gone, Sadie enters and tries to tell Mrs. Flimmins about the murder and attempted rape the previous evening. Before she can finish, however, the Man in the Silk Hat, the sheriff, and Phillpots return and begin a second round of interrogation. They, in turn, are interrupted by the entrance of Boob being chased by Cohen, who accuses the newsboy of stealing from him. Then, turning to Sadie, Cohen accuses his daughter of spending the night with Boob. Sadie neither denies nor confirms this charge but does reveal that she and Boob plan to run away to New York where they will make their way as a vaudeville team. To show their skill, they perform a short jazz dance routine only to be stopped by the Man in the Silk Hat, who is scandalized by the youngsters' behavior. Charging that Boob and Sadie's behavior is "disgraceful," the Man in the Silk Hat exits and Phillpots follows. Satisfied that he has caught one criminal, the sheriff turns Boob over to a soldier and exits. Cohen, in turn, is encouraged by Mrs. Flimmins to leave on the promise that she will talk some sense into Sadie. Left alone, Mrs. Flimmins tries to convince Sadie to return home only to be interrupted by the return of the sheriff who announces he will not leave until he catches Jim. Sensing no other way out, Mrs. Flimmins attempts to entice the sheriff, and they exit the barn to work out the details beyond the earshot of Sadie.

Emerging from his hiding place beneath the floor, Jim finds Sadie standing alone. Afraid of what awaits him, Jim flies into a rage, warning Sadie, "I don' wanna hurt you an' I feel like layin' my hands on somethin'" (135). Terrified, Sadie runs away. Jim starts to leave as well but, hearing voices from outside, hides beneath the stairs. Mrs. Flimmins and the sheriff reenter and continue bartering. Just as they are about the reach an agreement, a soldier arrives, recognizes Mrs. Flimmins, and reveals to the sheriff that she had spent the previous night with the drunken soldiers. His interest quelled by this revelation, the sheriff turns angrily to Mrs. Flimmins, who instinctively moves and stands over the hatch leading to the crawl space. As the sheriff and the soldier throw her aside and open the crawl space, Mrs. Flimmins screams, "Listen . . . listen, it's true, I'll give you anythin', it was me with them soldiers, I got money hid away, I done it for my son, I'm a bad woman!" (144). Finding only Psinski, the sheriff and the soldier exit, taking the "Bolshevik rat" with them and leaving Mrs. Flimmins on the floor (145). Enraged, Jim emerges from his hiding place under the stairs, reveals he heard all, and rushes out to face the men who have defiled his mother.

In the final two short scenes that close the act, Jim meets Sadie once again. Afraid but excited by the violence surrounding her, and seeking trust, Sadie tries to calm Jim. Jim responds and relaxes momentarily. Then, as the sound of soldiers approaching grows louder, Jim violently turns on Sadie, repaying her trust by taking her into a mine and raping her. The act ends with soldiers, aided by the Ku Klux Klan, chasing, catching, and blinding Jim, who becomes caught on a fence.

The final act takes place six months later. The soldiers have left and the Ku Klux Klan has taken over the town. The Klan, led by the Man in the Silk Hat (now referred to as King Kleagle), tries Sadie, who is carrying Jim's child, as well as Mrs. Flimmins, and prepares to exercise "holy judgment, moral judgment" for the women's moral transgressions (183). As the trial commences, Mrs. Flimmins attempts to defend Sadie and is removed. Phillpots arrives, and he too attempts to defend Sadie. To drown out Phillpots's pleas, King Kleagle and the rest of the Klan engage in a highly ritualized call-and-response deliberation of the evidence:

KING KLEAGLE. We gather this night to protect morals. Native-born Americans, Patriotic Protestants, regular citizens.

RESPONSIVE CHANT. Glory . . . Glory . . .

KING KLEAGLE. Have you taken the oath to exterminate foreigners?

RESPONSIVE CHANT. God's will be done!

KING KLEAGLE. Are the tar and feathers ready?

RESPONSIVE CHANT. God's will be done!

KING KLEAGLE. Are the guns and knives on hand?

RESPONSIVE CHANT. (*very loud*) God's will be done!

KING KLEAGLE. Clean up the dirty foreigners, make 'em kiss the flag! Skin the Jews, lynch the niggers, make 'em kiss the flag!

RESPONSIVE CHANT. (*quite breathless and with a good deal of grunting*) Halleluliah . . . Halleluliah . . .

KING KLEAGLE. Order. (*Silence*) I wish to announce, the entire Congress of the United States joined the Ku Klux Klan last night.

RESPONSIVE CHANT. (*The whole crowd points fingers directly at the audience and shouts*) Halleluliah! (182–83)

As they chant, Sadie sways violently like a "Jazz bug" to the rhythm of the statement and response (184). Outraged by her behavior, King Kleagle judges she will be given "Christian punishment [. . .] following which we will ride her out of town" (186–88). King Kleagle and the Klan slowly exit, taking Sadie with them. Immediately, however, one member of the Klan returns, dragging Sadie behind him. When Phillpots confronts him, the Klansman removes his mask, revealing he is Cohen. Into this confusion enters another Klansman, who also removes his mask, revealing he is Rastus. In the midst of this mounting chaos, Jim enters in tattered clothes, feeling his way with a cane. Jim and Sadie speak and, slowly, one by one, the striking miners gather on the stage, still led by Psinski, who is now drunk and in despair. The miners reveal that the Klan has all but put down the strike. Abruptly, the Man in the Silk Hat returns, without Klan garb, and announces the strike is over and a pact will be signed without recrimination on either side. However, in an aside to the audience and the sheriff, he confesses that the strike leaders will soon be murdered. The play ends with Sadie marrying Jim in a shotgun "jazz wedding" with the sheriff presiding. The miners' jazz band and others march out into the audience in a noisy procession, leaving Jim and Sadie alone. As the curtain falls Sadie sings quietly, "I'm agonna raise my kid, sing to him soft . . ." (218).[63]

Structurally, *Processional* is a fascinating hybrid, involving the fusion of numerous elements drawn from American vaudeville—owing in part to the playwright's interest in the cult of the primitive and a desire to parlay that interest into an exploration of the roots of American theatre—with other rudiments drawn from the European avant-garde. In terms of its connection to American vaudeville, the plot is almost nonexistent and in many instances contrived and forced, the scenes are loosely related and convey a feeling that the play could end at any time, most of the characters are stereotypes, there is a feeling that the characters are always on the verge of breaking into song, and there is constant intrusion of music into the action.[64] Nonetheless, while Lawson held that vaudevillian method was valuable in large part because it offered a "partial reflection," albeit "distorted," on the state of the common worker, matrimony, class relations, and violence, he was also vehement in his affirmation that he held little interest in honoring the practices and procedures of that method by merely moving them from the vaudeville house to stage of the art theatre. Lawson commented upon his use of vaudeville in the preface to the published script:

> I have endeavored to create a method which shall express the American scene in native idiom, a method as far removed from the older realism as from the facile mood of Expressionism. It is apparent that this new technique is essentially vaudevillesque in character—a development, a moulding to my own uses, of the rich vitality of the two-a-day and the musical extravaganza.
>
> This is not an abstract theory. I have built upon this ground for very practical reasons that it seems to me the only ground on which to build. The legitimate theatre seems without warmth or richness of method. It is only in the field of vaudeville and revue that a native craftsmanship exists. Here at least a shining if somewhat distorted

mirror is held up to our American nature. Here the national consciousness finds at least a partial reflection of itself in the mammy melody, the song and dance act, the curtain of real pearls. Here the concern is with direct contact, an immediate emotional response across the footlights. [. . .]

The reality of America spiritually and materially is a movement, a rhythm of which the inner meaning has not been found. Buried under the hokum of advertisements, headlines, radio speeches, there is a genuine inner necessity, a sense of direction. What is this key and meaning? What does the future hold beside the indefinite prolongation of human life by glandular treatment and the total annihilation of it in the eagerly expected Next-World-War?

I am not offering solutions. I am not even stating concise questions. My concern is with the theatre. But the blood and bones of a living stage must be the blood and bones of the actuality stirring around us. As yet not a whisper of this actuality has been heard across the footlights. While the Twentieth Century is exciting to the point of chaos, no deeper emotions stir the drama than those based on superficial risibilities, or the tear that comes at the sound of an old song. One can imagine a violence of meaning and feeling breaking upon a Broadway playhouse, something like hysteria spreading from row to row, melting the fixed pleasantness of the faces, a contagion of excitement. [. . .]

On the one hand we have what is somewhat ironically termed the commercial theatre, given over to the unbelievable repetition of the same plot, the same joke, the same characters, dished up each year with a pitiful lack of showmanship. . . . On the other hand, we have an art theatre existing in a feeble trance totally removed from the rush and roar of things as they are, a sanctuary with doors barred against the world. This idea of pure beauty as something quite removed from the brutal forms of reality is of course completely uncreative in its results. Art as an escape from life is no better than morphine, rotary clubs, murder, speech-making, or any of the other methods used by hundred-per-cent Americans to escape from actuality.

I have endeavored in the present play, to lay the foundations of some sort of native technique, to reflect to some extent the color and movement of the American processional as it streams about us. The rhythm is staccato, burlesque, carried out by a formalized arrangement of jazz music. A point of attack so far removed from the usual theatre method naturally requires a new vision of directing, acting, and scenic design. (v–ix)

Clearly, then, Lawson's interest in vaudeville extended beyond a mere commodification of that popular entertainment form for the benefit of the art theatre. In choosing to montage the ostensibly low-art, vaudevillian methods with elements borrowed from other forms of artistic expression (including those from the perceived high arts of the European avant-garde), Lawson was endeavoring to find a wholesale, new method suitable for expressing his vision of an ever-more dynamic, violent, and emerging nation. While elements from diverse forms such as expressionism and burlesque occasionally surface and merge with vaudeville, the most substantial form used in combination with it is Dada.[65]

As were the young German and French artists who forged the Dada and surrealist movements, Lawson was profoundly disturbed and disgusted by a world that could produce a global war; was, in no small measure, troubled by the absurdity and incongruity of life; and, most importantly, saw the superficial values that dominated the empowered middle class as grotesque, absurd, and inherently violent. His twofold want to destroy what he believed were outmoded and mistaken ideas and conventions and replace them with spontaneity and freedom were closely akin to those expressed by Tzara in his "Dada Manifesto, 1918."

> Morals have an atrophying effect, like every other pestilential product of intelligence. Being governed by morals and logic has made it impossible for us to be anything other than impassive toward policemen—the cause of slavery—putrid rats with whom the bourgeois are fed up to the teeth, and who have infected the only corridors of clear and clean glass that remained open to artists.
>
> Every man must shout: there is great destructive, negative work to be done. To sweep, to clean. The cleanliness of the individual materializes after we've gone through folly, the aggressive, complete folly of a world left in the hands of bandits who have demolished and destroyed the centuries.[66]

From Dada, then, Lawson integrated into *Processional* his aspiration to lay bare the violence, hypocrisy, and stultifying influence of bourgeois culture by way of the grotesque and the absurd, believing these elements would endow his vision of the American scene in a new and colorful way.

Lawson's description of the first scene in *Processional* illustrates how he merged the broadness and stereotypical milieu typical to vaudeville with absurd and grotesque tones characteristic of Dada:

> A drop curtain like those used in the older vaudeville theatres, repre-

> sents a town street painted with brick buildings, signs of CENTRAL HOTEL, PALACE MOVIE, QUICK LUNCH, etc. In center of curtain is the door of Cohen's General Store, with show window painted on curtain and this sign: ISAAC COHEN THE CUT-RATE STORE, GREEN-GROCER, ANTISEPTIC BARBER, KOSHER DELICATESSEN, MINING TOOLS. Above the door a small practical window in the curtain. *The tone is that of the usual vaudeville drop, except that it is more startlingly crude, vigorous in color, blaringly American.* (8; emphasis added)[67]

While Lawson called for a stereotypical vaudeville setting, he also wanted one that was "startlingly" different. Lawson's vision of the milieu was influenced undoubtedly by Picasso's surreal settings for *Parade*, which took the stereotypical to an absurd extreme. Nevertheless, unlike Picasso's images that made light fun of the French bourgeoisie's detached manner, Lawson's milieu was tantamount to an embittered denunciation of bourgeois values. Thus, in his merging of the stereotypical with the absurd, Lawson made an angry comment on the state of the American spirit and scene.[68]

Some of the characters in *Processional* are also montages, born of the conflation of vaudeville and Dada. The majority of the minor characters are broad stereotypes who represent different personas found within the uninhibited, driven masses and are never taken beyond their vaudevillian prototypes—for example, Phillpots is a stereotypical brash newspaper man, Cohen is a "vaudeville-type of Jewish" merchant with an exaggerated Yiddish dialect and "absurd" clothing, Dago Joe is "a sleek greasy Italian [who] plays an accordion," and Rastus is a stereotypical vaudevillian "Negro [. . . who] plays a banjo and sings most of the time" (4–6). However, the main characters, Jim, Mrs. Flimmins, and Sadie, are pushed to an extreme, break the mold of the stereotype, and become Dada-inspired grotesques. To further analyze this extraordinary range of characters in the text, it may be argued that the aforementioned minor characters are all imbued with an overwhelming and tragic sense of immobility and inevitability. Each, in various ways, seems to lack the will to live. This sense is particularly troubling for characters such as Rastus and Cohen, who represent marginalized segments of the American population. In the final act, when Cohen—the "Jewish" type—and Rastus—the "Negro" type—are revealed wearing Klan garb, Lawson seems to be offering a barbed critique of the treatment of dispossessed persons and marginalized populations in the United States, doomed to suffer at the hands of their exploiters and yet forced, albeit indirectly, to participate in their own exploitation in the struggle to live.

Conversely, those characters that become Dada-inspired grotesques face another set of challenges. Typical of this treatment is the character Sadie. Lawson's initial description of Sadie gives no indication that she is anything other than a stereotypical, vaudevillian ingénue:

> SADIE COHEN, a sallow-faced girl of seventeen, all dressed up in white with short skirts and frills calculated to fill out her childish figure. Her hair in two neat pigtails. Sometimes she sticks her finger in her mouth. She often stands on one leg and giggles. (4–5)

By the end of the play, the stereotypical Sadie has changed. As the Klan circles around her to drive her from the town, she can only sway wildly like a "Jazz bug" and giggle as she sings, "I'm awalkin' in the dark, I ain't goin' home no more, my father cried an' swore. . . . He sighed an' he cried an' he pretty near died" (184–85). She is, in short, a grotesque, an absurd extreme of her former stereotyped self.

Jim is also introduced as a vaudevillian stereotype, who through the course of the first two acts is taken to a ridiculous and violent extreme and becomes a grotesque. Reminiscent of O'Neill's Yank from *The Hairy Ape* (1922), Jim is a brutish antihero who has been plucked from the fringes of society, thrust into the midst of an excessively violent civilization, and forced to commit acts of irrational cruelty and unimaginable violence in order to exist. The acts of cruelty and violence Jim commits, despite being his only means of securing a better future, become more and more brutal and demonstrate his (d)evolution from vaudevillian stereotype to Dada grotesque.[69] However, following the murder of the soldier at the end of the second act, something in Jim is sparked. Unlike the other central characters in *Processional* who never progress beyond their grotesque designation, Jim breaks through this limiting characterization by his need to be himself, by his resolve to live a life of liberty, and by his desire to transcend the violent culture (albeit through violent means) of which he is a part. Throughout the course of the third act, Jim struggles, vacillating between grotesqueness and individuality. This struggle reaches a violent and disturbing climax in the second scene of the act, when Jim rapes Sadie.

At the beginning of this scene, there is a sense Jim has evolved successfully and completely to individuality. The one-dimensional, restraining, and violence-laden moniker "Dynamite" no longer seems an accurate characterization of the now three-dimensional individual.[70] The scene opens with a tender expression of love between Jim and Sadie. As Jim lifts Sadie in his arms he whispers, "I raise you high to the moon, I steal a barrel full a' diamonds for you, reach up an' pick a bunch a' stars" (167). Yet as the scene progresses, the brutality of the grotesque emerges one last time. As the soldiers approach to take him away, the grotesque impulse within Jim is provoked. He quickly becomes brutal, carries the young woman into the dark pit, and rapes her:

JIM. . . . you're comin' with me.

SADIE. Where?

JIM. (*indicating the mine entrance*) Down there.

SADIE. Bluffin', that's all you are; ev'rybuddy kids me!

JIM. I don' bluff, not me, I'll fix you, I will . . .

SADIE. No, no, I don't wanna, lemme go—

JIM. Let them soldiers come, I'll have my way first. (168–69)

In the mine, Jim commits the last in a series of brutal, violent actions that have marked him as a grotesque. In many respects, this descent into the mine and the actions therein recall the narrative of virgin sacrifice and thus connotes Lawson's association with the cult of the primitive. Lawson writes that the descent into the mine "is derived from [Stravinsky's] *Le Sacre du Printemps*; it is related to the death of Louise in *Roger Bloomer*; and the ritual dream in which Louise appears as the life force [when she] tells Roger, 'I have given you yourself.'"[71] Thus, when he emerges from the darkness and horrors of the mine, the grotesque Jim is fittingly prepared for his symbolic death and resurrection as individual. He is first chased, then caught on a fence, "a figure of grotesque defeat," captured by the soldiers, and at last blinded (172). As he is being chased by the soldiers, the Man in the Silk Hat lists Jim's transgressions: "This man is an enemy of society; a beast, he killed men, he attacked a woman, sinner, moral leper, Society must be justified" (171). Only with his capture and blinding does Jim realize his complete evolution from grotesque to individual. His violent, grotesque temperament imparted to him by a violent and grotesque society, which leads to the murder of the soldier and the rape of Sadie, is counteracted through his redemption, which is symbolized in his crucifixion on the fence and his blinding. Therefore, when he returns to the mounting chaos and violence in the fourth act, Jim, messiah-like, may redeem the "sins" of Sadie and Mrs. Flimmins.

Lawson's drawing of Jim in the 1920 version of the script, while similar to the final manifestation in many respects, is, in other ways, strikingly different. An analysis of the two renderings of Jim further reveals the progression of the playwright's thinking. In the first draft of the play, Jim is described as a "savagely primitive man."[72] His actions (or lack thereof), however, do not support this description. Instead of murdering the soldier, he merely gets into a fight with him; when he discovers that his mother has exchanged sex with the soldiers for money, he takes no action; and there is absolutely no suggestion he will rape Sadie. Jim thus remains a passive and one-dimensional character, one who does not commit any of the violent acts that occur in the final draft. As a result, there is neither motive nor cause for his subsequent redemption, and he remains constrained by convention and tradition and unable to change the world. Conversely, the chain of events Lawson creates in the final draft lead logically to Jim's ability to at last act and remove himself from the limiting confines of his predetermined, stereotypical self, and instead become an individual capable of creative action and free will. While a similar chain of events occurs in *Roger Bloomer* (that is, Louise commits suicide and Roger is forced into a dream-like state wherein he can confront and, eventually, conquer his fears), Roger never breaks through his expressionistic-inspired stereotype (that is, everyman) to achieve individuality. Instead, Roger at the end of that play stands poised on the threshold separating the "dream of adolescence" from the world of "reality." Conversely, Jim steps over the threshold into reality and embarks on the journey that will take him from stereotype to grotesque to individual. *Processional* therefore advances beyond the internalized Freudian nightmare that remains at the heart of *Roger Bloomer* and, instead, considers external reality by placing its protagonist in the material world resting beyond that dream. In short, then, that reality, which is only alluded to at the end of that earlier script as Roger "goes toward the lighted doorway," is presented in vivid and violent detail in *Processional.*

The Theatre Guild production of *Processional* opened on 12 January 1925. Directed by Phillip Moeller and designed by Mordecai Gorelik, the production received mixed notices.[73] As with *Roger Bloomer*, most of the critics writing for the mainstream press were thoroughly unimpressed with the playwright's groundbreaking efforts. Percy Hammond found the script "as interesting as a colic";[74] Alan Dale dismissed it as "an oleaginous mess of tommyrot";[75] Burns Mantle could not detect a story within the "discordant jumble";[76] and Alexander Woollcott pronounced it "pretentious" and "boring," and asserted that Lawson had "nothing to say."[77]

While the brutal analyses of these critics writing for the mainstream daily presses were, no doubt, expected, the acidic review in *American Mercury* by George Jean Nathan surely came as a shock to those in the Theatre Guild who had grown accustomed to his ardent support. Charging that Lawson was merely "[t]he latest young playwright to parade the Rialto in his underdrawers with his Hemdschweif hanging out," Nathan declared that *Processional* was "the Guild's embarrassment." He continued,

> Mr. Lawson's manner of walking down Broadway minus trousers takes the form of what he calls "a jazz symphony of American life." [. . .] Unlike many of his accomplished elders who have been content to attract attention to themselves merely by excellent work in more or less time honored and approved dramatic form, Mr. Lawson has stalked sensational attention with indifferent work in what might be called a hoochie-coochie form. This frantic struggle to find new forms is the most amusing of twentieth century artistic phenomena. Engaged in for the major part by the young—and often lazy—of the aesthetic species, it has resulted in a welter of eye-catching but often intrinsically nonsensical methods and manner of expression which are generally found to contain nothing worth expression. [. . .]
>
> Mr. Lawson's trouble lies in his having hit upon a theme for a jazz orchestra in what appears to be his personal dramatic inability to play any other instrument than a tin can. Some of his humor is penetrating and admirable; some of his observation is sharp and sure; certain details of his imagination are excellent; but the job he set himself is apparently far beyond his present talents. His play goes to pieces the moment he abjures the burlesque note; when drama crosses the scene, the back of the play breaks.[78]

The only favorable evaluations of the play came from more liberal critics who typically celebrated advances in dramatic content and form: Stark Young, Heywood Broun, and Gilbert Gabriel.[79] Young, writing for the *New York Times*, found the production of the play "uneven" but, as with *Roger Bloomer* two years before, looked beyond these problems and saw a drama "rich in possibilities and not to be forgotten." In a series of probing articles written during the course of the Theatre Guild's production, Young defended the unique dramatic technique on the grounds that the playwright had "written some astonishing lines for wit, poetry and satire and some scenes that are extraordinary for originality and dramatic truth."[80] "[I]t is a feather in the Theatre Guild's cap. As a drama it throws off astonishing suggestions of living stuff; it is full of strong, wounded, indomitable life. However unequal it may be, it is always creative and streaked with genius. It has thrusts of poetic power. It has [. . .] a remarkable [. . .] pathos, a strange, fresh, young, robust, half brutal pathos unique to our drama. And whatever else it is, it is never anything but theatre."[81] In his two reviews for the *World*, Broun echoed these sentiments and saw a time when Lawson's methods would be widespread: "Mr. Lawson is on no bypath. One or two ingredients in his mixture may be changed, but he will not be compelled to discard his formula. *Processional* alienated its audience because its techniques were strange. There will come a day within our own lifetime when this technique will be wholly familiar."[82] While Young and Broun mainly focused upon Lawson's formal methods, Gabriel grappled with the ideas in the script:

> [Lawson] stood a little way apart from the merry-go-rounding mass and asked himself:—"What's wrong with this picture?"
>
> Mr. Lawson does not answer his own question, though. He shows you the cheap, brassy, tragical, comical, cruel, persevering carnival of life in a West Virginia mining town. It is your own affair to drain away the blare of it and then to find the warm throb of a living race. It is your part to strain your eyes at his gauze sheets of burlesque diorama, awkward and lurid daubs of a small-town nightmare, and discern behind each of them Man in all his nakedness, wretchedness and bravery. The author himself is magnificently contemptuous about what you see and hear. His *Processional* must pass. He must keep it thumping. If the whip in his hands flicks your own face, too, he is equally unsentimental about it.[83]

As with *Roger Bloomer*, *Processional* was a topic of much discussion among other members of the American literary community. Edna St. Vincent Millay, along with other leading members of the New York intelligentsia, sent Lawson a letter on 21 January 1925 that in part reads, "We, the undersigned, after due deliberation but in a state of great excitement, hereby testify that your show is a hum-dinger; and that we are crazy about it; and that it's about the best show we have seen in the last sixty years; and that we shall not sleep a wink tonight; and that we think you have a right to be slightly stuck up."[84] Some, like Thornton Wilder, while intrigued with the method, were more measured. In his piece for *Theatre Arts Monthly*, Wilder questioned what they had seen and wondered what message the playwright was attempting to convey:

> What could be more attractive than a play that intermingles strips of vaudevillian patter, exciting drama and burlesque, a Klux Klan ballet and a Negro song and dance; in which a man in a silk hat steps to the footlights and announces tenderly that it is Mother's Day; in which the stage is framed by famous American advertisements and yet contains a pathetic love story and a fine sober climax? The play

> promised to be as attractive as that, but the author has not been equal to it. His ironies are shallow; his strophes after Whitman were unexhilarating, and the exquisite sense of selection that should gauge the transitions from screaming to laughter was missing. Only the last act approached greatness.[85]

Still, Wilder's own works, from *The Trumpet Will Sound* (1927) to *The Skin of Our Teeth* (1943), show that Lawson's method had an immediate and lasting impact.

Many others in the literary community were more forthright in their praise and saw *Processional* as a landmark play. In an interview with Alexander Woollcott for the *New York Sun*, Elmer Rice challenged those critics, Woollcott principal among them, who charged that Lawson had "nothing to say":

> I'm impelled to challenge your [Woollcott's] rather debonair assertion that John Howard Lawson has nothing to say. In my not very humble opinion he has a lot to say, and *Processional* says it, on the whole, with brilliant effectiveness. [. . .] I hasten to continue, he has had the courage and the imagination to say a few things that are not often heard in our theatre (and incidentally the Theatre Guild has had the courage and the imagination to give them a hearing). He says, this Lawson, that the noble cult of social justice is largely bunk; he says that the noble cult of patriotism is largely bunk; he says that the noble cult of motherhood (noblest of all the noble cults!) is largely bunk.
>
> [. . .]Lawson says these things [. . .] not didactically nor solemnly, but vividly, graphically, in terms of the media from which the free and enlightened citizens of the free and enlightened commonwealth draw their daily mental and aesthetic fare: jazz, vaudeville, soap box oratory, jazz, vaudeville, the newspaper, the movies, jazz. And through and beneath it all that he shows you, struggling to express itself, an indomitable will to live, and elan vital: like a virile and dogged swimmer making imperceptible headway against the tide—almost, but not quite, engulfed in a sea of banality, mediocrity, sentimentality and cruelty.
>
> I see in *Processional* a psychograph of America. I like it.[86]

Processional became the standard by which all of Lawson's other plays would be measured. From the time of the Theatre Guild's production in 1925 until Lawson left the New York theatre in 1937, it was rare to read a review of his plays that did not refer to the "promise" displayed in *Processional*. Urged on by the critics' vying expectations and his own desire to improve, Lawson was forever haunted by the script. Commenting on why he left the theatre in 1937, Lawson wrote, "Regardless of barriers or traps, I could have fought my way to some sort of creative expression in the theatre if I could have fulfilled the search for a theatrical form that was launched with *Processional*."[87] "The search for a theatrical form" that could outdo what he had done with *Processional* would be complicated, first by the playwright's never-ceasing desire to "break down the walls of the theatre" and then by his burgeoning and increasingly revolutionary political beliefs. The next step in that long and progressively more torturous journey came the following year in the form of *Nirvana*.

Nirvana

In the summer of 1925, following on the relative critical and popular success of *Processional*, Lawson remarried, to Susan Edmund, rented a house in Mt. Sinai on Long Island, and settled in to finish his next script, *Nirvana*. Lawson had begun work on what would eventually become that script more than a year before, in the spring of 1924. At that point, *Roger Bloomer*, though still hailed by some as an example of where American theatre was heading, was for most others a fast-fading memory. Further, *Processional*, albeit essentially finished, would not be produced for almost another year. Within this lull, Lawson turned his attention to a piece whose working title was *A New England Fantasy*, completing a first draft in mid-1924 while residing in Pittsburgh. The script began, in Lawson's words, as an attempt to "write the crazy epic of this day."[88] In the end, it became, by his own admission, "the most confused play I ever wrote."[89]

A New England Fantasy is derived, fractionally, from an earlier script entitled *The Mad Moon*, "a mild, little comical whimsy" employing a well-made play form written during Lawson's brief return to the States in 1919 following the war. Many of the names of the characters, the conventional dramatic structure, and the central idea of "a moral conflict between a young poet and stodgy Puritanism" were imported into *A New England Fantasy*. However, the sentimental warmth of the first script of 1919 is completely eradicated in the latter, resulting in a piece that the author later in life summarized as a "bitter display of moral anguish which dissolves into madness."[90] Further, an analysis of *A New England Fantasy* suggests that by the middle of 1924, Lawson had all but abandoned the inward probing of Freudian psychoanalysis as the primary theoretical conceit informing his work and instead turned his attention toward contemporary metaphysics, proposed in the wake of Einstein's scientific discoveries and, thus, imbued by the theory of relativity and quantum physics.[91] *A New England Fantasy*, and by extension *Nirvana*, seems to embody the psychology-or-physics schism that served as a determinate and divisive force in much early-twentieth-century philosophy.

In *A New England Fantasy*, Tommy Weed, a successful author who has led a bohemian lifestyle, returns home for Christmas. Accompanying him is Janet Gold, whom, to everyone's utter surprise, Tommy introduces as his wife. Dr. Alanzo Weed, Tommy's brother, and Aunt Bertha Emerson, the stodgy family matriarch, are pleased, as they perceive the marriage as the end of Tommy's unconventional lifestyle. However, Priscilla Emerson, Tommy's cousin and childhood sweetheart, is distressed by his marriage. When they are alone, Tommy tells Priscilla that Janet is not his wife but is carrying his child. Tommy also admits to Priscilla that he wants to abandon Janet for her but, in the end, cannot. The thematic core of the script is Tommy's failure to choose, his inability to act or exercise his will, and his debilitating sense of guilt.[92]

In his writing of *Nirvana*, Lawson transferred much in the way of subject matter, character, and story from *A New England Fantasy*. Act 1 of *Nirvana* is set in the apartment and medical office of Alanzo Weed. The decor and architecture of the office resemble a church. This temple to the cult of science is equipped with state-of-the-art medical instruments. During the course of the act, Alanzo is visited by Bill Weed, his artist brother; Holz, a millionaire-philanthropist who has financed the building of a manned rocket to Mars; Janet, Alanzo's neighbor and Bill's lover; Priscilla, Alanzo and Bill's cousin; and Bertha, Alanzo and Bill's puritanical aunt. When they are alone, Bill confesses to Priscilla that he is torn between his long-held affection for her and his responsibility to Janet. At the end of the first act, it is discovered that Janet's husband has just committed suicide and that she is carrying Bill's child. Aware of Bill's feelings for Priscilla, Janet turns on him furiously:

> JANET. You don't know whether death has parted us or brought us together . . . do I love you? If I dance on an open grave for you tonight, you'll know what I mean dressed in gaiety of despair till I stand naked in the land of no man's imagination.[93]

Act 2 occurs later that evening in the rooftop garden of Alanzo's apartment and office. Numerous guests, many of them drunk, come and go. The Reverend Dr. Gulick, "spiritual advisor" to Janet's late husband, arrives to console the widow. Disapproving of the drunken activity on the roof, Dr. Gulick warns "'God is not mocked!' There is a moral order. No man has enough imagination to create a new one" (act 2, scene 1, p. 36). Holz arrives and offers Bill the opportunity to pilot his experimental rocket to the stars. Meanwhile, a despondent Janet is questioned by detectives concerning her husband's suicide. The scene ends with Bill and Priscilla alone on the roof. Suddenly and without warning, Priscilla jumps onto the cornice of the roof and proclaims, "I have no choice, I am drunk with something, I look at the sky and the amount of it gives me falling sickness, but sooner or later I must look at the dizzy world . . . spinning so far below" (2.1, p. 39). The short scene that concludes act 2 finds Bill and Priscilla both perched on the cornice. As they try to make their way down, Priscilla stumbles, grabs the electric wires that illuminate a huge sign reading "GOD IS NOT MOCKED," and falls to the rooftop far below.

Act 3 takes place in Dr. Weed's office. It is revealed that Priscilla was not killed by her fall but lies badly injured in a coma. Dr. Weed attends to her and engages in an emergency operation involving electroshock treatment in an attempt to save her life. Bill and Dr. Gulick discuss religion and Bertha prays until Alanzo announces that there is no hope for Priscilla. Janet, wracked with guilt due to her husband's death and her infidelity, makes a false confession that she killed him. The play comes to a climax when Bill abruptly agrees to pilot Hotz's rocket into space, where he will die and wander alone forever in the heavens. This pessimistic mysticism is counterbalanced by a miracle at the final curtain. Aunt Bertha's prayers for Priscilla are seemingly answered. The young woman rises from her bed and sings:

> PRISCILLA. "If there's anybody here like weeping Mary,
> Call upon your Jesus and he'll draw nigh . . .
> Glory . . . Glory . . ."
>
> I've seen such strange things . . . electricity flamed in my path. [. . .] I'm all right, I'm cured now, I know it. [. . .] I can't speak, but I could even dance a little. Because it's so pretty. (act 3, p. 29)

With that, Bertha screams, "No, no, I can't bear it" (3, p. 29). Priscilla, who has faltered through a few awkward dance steps, falls to the floor. The play ends with Alanzo examining the body and announcing Priscilla has been dead for nearly an hour.

While *Nirvana* is indeed very similar to *A New England Fantasy* in character, story, and theme, it goes well beyond that earlier play's portrayal of an individual's internal struggle by way of the well-made play plot structure. Lawson instead grapples with a more expansive issue: the degradation and anguish of the modern individual, within a surrealist-inspired method. Lawson commented upon his lofty intent in the program for the production:

> *Nirvana* is a comedy—of uncertainties and aspirations of the thinking man as he confronts the enlargening universe. Of people doing their

> stuff, if they only knew it, on the dizzy brink of disaster. In fact a good many of them topple over. Yet these people continue to face forces as old as time with the grotesque and humorous half-assurance of the modern mind. It is the delicate convolutions of this mind which the author has desired to probe and consider—a task which he realizes to be so difficult and so ungrateful that the tide of laughter in the last analysis sweeps back upon himself. [. . .]
>
> The word "*Nirvana*" is not used in the specific Buddhist sense, but simply to denote the state of impossible peace which is the goal of our striving. [. . .] Viewing the mental uncertainty of today, I am convinced that there is a religious need, not satisfied by any of the current forms of worship. [. . .] Suppose that even now a faith were stirring in the depths of the crowd's subconscious?[94]

Lawson's want to view "the mental uncertainty of today" resulted in the writing of a fascinating script that is nonetheless weighed down by the ideas the author was seeking to examine. Centered on the exploration of the subconscious by way of post-Einstein metaphysics, *Nirvana* is decidedly more complex and obscure than *Roger Bloomer* or *Processional.* Gone is the pointed and effective, albeit superficial, Dada-inspired grotesque, objective violence of *Processional.* In its place there is a subjective, internal struggle. However, the internal struggle presented in *Nirvana* is more frightening, pessimistic, and complex than what was displayed in *Roger Bloomer.* Instead of a youngster battling through internal turmoil in a Freudian-inspired spiritual journey towards a transcendental truth, the internal struggle in *Nirvana* is an account of moral and emotional depravity and internal violence caused by the protagonist's slow and perhaps unconscious compromise with the material forces in society that continually bombard him. Thus we see in this script a radical departure from the optimism (albeit frightening) of a young man standing at the threshold of a new world (be it Roger or Lawson), to the young artist (be it Bill or Lawson) turning away from a decadent society and accepting instead a suicidal journey into an unknown infinity.

Lawson later commented on the cultural developments and personal events that led to this thematic exploration:

> *Nirvana* was a reflection of the temper of the time, of reports of the advancement of science, and it was also a turn in my personal experience, from the objective burlesque violence of *Processional*, to an inner violence, a convulsion of the psyche, which arose from my alienation from the world of *Processional* and my recognition of myself as a person without the moral and emotional freedom I proclaimed

> in [that] play. [. . .] It was a reflection of the situation of the artist [in this post-Einstein world, and of] my ambitions and actual situation, socially and economically, [that] made me turn from the material riches of New York to a spiritual quest among the stars.[95]

Thus, Lawson and his artist-protagonist, Bill, share a belief that life's mysteries may only be answered in a suicidal mission into an unexplored realm. The playwright's mystical solution for his protagonist and himself bears a strong resemblance to ideas of leading French surrealist André Breton.[96]

As had the Dadaists with whom he had apprenticed, Breton rejected any commitment to bourgeois society on the grounds that it was absurd and grotesque. However, unlike the often-nihilistic Dadaists who graphically and satirically displayed their displeasure with the disastrous bumblings of the bourgeoisie, Breton believed the social status quo was unworthy of a response. The surrealist individual, instead, was encouraged, like the expressionists, to look inward for a truth that existed outside and above the mundane rational existence privileged in the West. However, unlike the expressionists, who held that an outward expression of the internal spirit could reshape the individual and/or society, surrealists looked to internal probing of the unconscious mind for aid in achieving these goals. In short, then, the surrealist was committed to the exploration of the unconscious, believing it held keys that could unlock the doors on the way to a deeper reality. Thus, just as Einstein had introduced novel and, in some respects, terrifying insights regarding the possibilities and uncertainties of the scientific realm, Breton and other surrealists, championed new ways of using Freudian theory. In his *Surrealist Manifestos* (1924, 1930, and 1934), Breton defined the methods and goal of the surrealist artist. No longer was Freudian method reserved for external analysis and mere explanation of the internal; rather, Freudian techniques were creative and powerful tools available to the artist interested in exploring and bringing back the images found within the primordial depths of the mind. Or, in the words of Breton, images brought up from the unconscious could "spark" and "appear like the only guideposts of the mind" on the "night" of reason, thus helping the artist capture and portray a deeper truth.[97]

In part, then, *Nirvana* seems to document the change in Lawson's method and thought from Dada to surrealism.[98] The Dada-inspired grotesque stereotypes in *Processional* are replaced in *Nirvana* with characters that are fully drawn individuals. These characters are not one-dimensional stick figures that ridicule problems through their absurd actions as stereotypes. Rather, they are three-dimensional individualized characters who, because of the deadening effects of rationalized socialization, are forced to explore the depths of their minds. Thus the individualized Bill turns from a corrupt society that had promised moral and emotional freedom but left him empty and confused and tries his luck in an unknown infinity. The realization that his moral and emotional degeneration has caused suffering and death prompts Bill to seek this solution. Blaming neither original sin (as an expressionist would) nor society (as the Dadaist would), Bill takes full responsibility for his present state. His journey into the unknown realm of outer space, a striking a metaphor for the unknown realm of the unconscious, is a final attempt to cope with the moral and emotional struggles consuming him. While his struggles with inner forces harken back to the inner turmoil *Roger Bloomer* faces, unlike Roger, who steps boldly into the "light" and faces the world, Bill chooses to seek freedom alone and in the great unknown of space, a journey that will lead to certain death. Thus Bill's choice to explore the unknown may be read as a manifestation of surrealist thought. Indeed, by denying in himself the rational reaction (that is, to avoid an endeavor that will end in death), Bill breaks the chains of reason imposed by civilization.

While it may be argued that Lawson's worldview was parallel and/or informed by the surrealist movement, this fatalistic choice underscores a sobering pessimism in *Nirvana* that is not in line with surrealism such as it was envisioned by Breton. Certainly, Lawson shared with Breton the belief that bourgeois socialization had led to a numbing of the imaginative capacities. Still, they parted ways in their visions of the future. Breton held great faith in the surrealist method, saw it as a tool for expanding the ways of knowing, and believed that the world was on the verge of a greater tomorrow (a view that was closely tied to his joining of the Communist Party in 1925). Lawson in 1925 held no such faith. Indeed, the action of *Nirvana* suggests Lawson believed the only answer to the moral and emotional degradation of society was in a suicidal mission to the stars.

In terms of Lawson's development as a playwright and cultural critic, *Nirvana* is chiefly notable because of the light it sheds on the rise of these ideas in Lawson's writing and, moreover, its demonstration of how Lawson was actively participating in and responding to a discourse within the larger cultural field. Like many western intellectuals in the 1920s, Lawson was increasingly confused by the temper of the time. While the so-called death of God, announced by Nietzsche thirty years prior, had been readily acknowledged and mourned by modernist intellectuals and artists on a rational level, nothing had been done to answer any lingering emotional and spiritual needs. Albert Einstein's theory of relativity, which had been postulated in 1914 and proved in 1919, at last gave to science the indeterminate, mystical element it needed to deal with humankind's emotional needs. The modernist arts immediately began to reflect the newfound mystery and uncertainty, or crisis, of science. *Nirvana* is Lawson's attempt to address the new religion of science. He does so by posing three questions: Do prevailing religious doctrines serve a purpose in the contemporary world? Do these doctrines appease the dynamic needs of the modern individual? Moreover, do these doctrines have value beyond tethering the modern individual to disabling and anachronistic conventions? Lawson answers these questions with an emphatic "No!" The established, monotheistic religions cannot bring truth or peace to the modern soul. Priscilla's fleeting and failed triumph over death at the end of the script is a poetization of this view that a new system of faith must be forged, a new religion must arise on the foundation of that faith, and a new messiah must be found who will author new gospels. This new messiah will not be flesh and blood. Rather it will arise from the atom or the eon, and it will solve the riddles humanity faces on its earthly journey by offering insight through a wholesale new synthesis of science and religion.[99]

Lawson supports this contention by filling *Nirvana* with characters illustrating the disastrous results of old monotheistic creeds. They are morally depraved people who, despite their vanity and material gains, have failed to achieve happiness. Every character demonstrates some sort of emotional disturbance brought about by trying to rectify modern life within the confines of moral standards that are no longer viable. Some, such as Janet and Bill, are emotionally crippled while others, such as Aunt Bertha, enforce and yet still suffer under the deadening influence of the bourgeois moral code. All harbor fears and misgivings as a product of their belief systems, and all, not unlike Pirandello's surreal protagonist in *Henry IV* (1922), who is forced by his environment to feign madness, are involved in a constant charade wherein they attempt to establish concrete boundaries in a society of ever-changing dynamics.

When he completed the script for *Nirvana* in late 1925, Lawson submitted it to the Theatre Guild, which, following the success of *Processional*, had secured first rights on Lawson's next three scripts. The Guild waived its right to production. Later in life, Lawson commented that the rejection of *Nirvana* by the Guild "was expected and accorded with my growing sense of political issues which separated me from the so-called avant-garde in the [American] theatre."[100] At the time, however, Lawson was convinced the script deserved an immediate production. He quickly agreed to have the play produced by a struggling production firm, Noble, Ryan, and Livy. *Nirvana* opened at the Greenwich Village Theatre on Wednesday 3 March and closed Saturday 7 March 1926. It was an enormous commercial and critical failure. In his autobiography, Lawson recalls that the power of the play and the complex ideas in it were all but lost in the Noble, Ryan, and Livy production. Despite the "stunning" scene designs by Mordecai Gorelik, the production faltered under the direction of Robert Peel Noble, who was, in the words of Lawson, "incompetent," "allergic to theory," and made the play a "complete mess."[101] So poor was Noble's work that with less than a week until opening, Lawson replaced him with George Abbott, who would later beome a noted Broadway director. It was to no avail. While the critics, both conservative and liberal, found fault with the production values, they also generally concurred that the script was problematic.

Many of the critics writing for the mainstream press were brutal. Brooks Atkinson found Lawson's "conception of modern society" to be "sophomoric."[102] The usually reasonable and measured Burns Mantle sarcastically wrote, "Eventually the mind of John Howard Lawson may be cleared of its fungi and something of worth to the audience he hopes to interest will come out of it."[103] Other mainstream critics, though similarly perplexed, were more sympathetic to the difficult task Lawson had set for himself. Alexander Woollcott commented, "The play is largely lacking in the curious quality and excitement and beauty which possess the same young playwright's *Processional*. [. . .] I am troubled by the sense that whereas Lawson has thought and thought till his head ached with all the implications of Freud and Einstein, his own thinking remained too unresolved a jumble for any beauty in play or poem to take form out of it."[104] Likewise, while Percy Hammond acknowledged in his postproduction critique that Lawson would "doubtless be a big man in the theatre someday" and admitted that the quick closing of *Nirvana* was a "dampening influence on those who write plays for the strong minded," he also found the playwright's "expression [. . .] marred by awkward vertigoes."[105] Arthur Pollack offered a similar analysis in the *Brooklyn Eagle*:

> [Lawson] is not the sort of playwright who can be explained away in terms of ridicule. He is too fiercely searching and acquisitive for that. One must admire him even if he does appear to take the things that happen in his head too seriously.

> Lawson has a gift for words. And he uses words vigorously to express thoughts that occur to him. It may be, however, that he hasn't great gifts of thought. On the present occasion he is more determined than ever to say something surprising. He is determined, too, to say his say in the most elaborate manner discoverable, eschewing always the lucid and the simple. He makes the world and the theatre terribly hard for himself.[106]

Gilbert Gabriel observed that while there was "much keen, muscular, vivid writing," the "clutter of scores of quarreling moods, a loud wastage of incidents awry, of expositions out of focus and personalities out of tune" confused the issue.[107] Joseph Wood Krutch offered a similar, albeit more straightforward, analysis: "Mr. Lawson has succumbed, himself a victim of one of the tricks of the mind which he should be analyzing, and one leaves the theatre with a sense of keen disappointment. A great play has slipped through the author's grasp."[108]

Lawson responded to these critiques in an open letter to the press.[109] In it he admitted that while he was "still feeling [his] way toward some sort of form," he "could not rest upon the spectacular and uncertain method of *Processional*, without experimenting in another and even more difficult direction. And I feel that the method of *Nirvana*, dramatizing states of mind and mental stress, is a definite contribution. The method requires some sort of intensity on the part of the actors that is impossible to realize. Being far from pure realism (a sort of ritualistic technique, if I may say so), it runs the risk of being mistaken for just a horribly bad realistic play." Lawson concluded by declaring his aim for the future: "[I] wish to create something new, find a guiding rhythm in our brash and bungling twentieth century—oh, not jazz, it's too flimsy-noisy [. . .] but the deep flow of faith, a philosopher's dream."[110]

With *Nirvana*, as with *Roger Bloomer* and *Processional*, Lawson's central concern was not to offer any serious solution to the problems of bourgeois society. Rather, it was to find some way of representing the reality of American life that was not wholly negative. Within this objective, however, the seeds of his commitment to revolutionary politics were being nurtured. By eliminating the constraints of realism and employing instead nonrealistic styles and allegorical expression through symbolism in plot, characterization, language, and setting, Lawson advanced the American drama and his own writing toward a more overt presentation of pressing social issues.

Still, when the curtain closed on *Nirvana* for the last time, any glimmer of optimism Lawson held was extinguished. The hope he had held for surreal mysticism as a method for representing the reality of life in the United States had ended in frustration and defeat. Unsure of direction, Lawson turned to his writing, the one thing that could bring peace and comfort. The script Lawson began indicates the tortured state of his mind. It opens with a man attempting suicide by jumping through a plate glass window on the top floor of a skyscraper. The rest of the play is the man's ether dream. The stage directions for this untitled working draft read:

> As he lies somewhere between life and death in a hospital bed, he tests his ideas of a future life and finds that his religious beliefs are just as insane as his social beliefs—life lies in a future of which he has never dreamed. He didn't jump through a window, he jumped through a calendar. The reality of the future strikes him like lightening strikes a hollow tree.[111]

Thus, like the protagonists in his first three plays, the man hovering "somewhere between life and death" may be seen to represent Lawson's own personal dilemma. Roger could not act at all, except in a dream; Jim acts, but with an appalling moral cost; and Bill, the middle-class writer in *Nirvana* who wanted to confront the moral and emotional conflicts in himself, found it only in an abstract and mystical realm, beyond the boundaries of what was known and experienced as materially real.[112] Conversely, the man in the hospital is asked to act within reality, and moreover to accept that his continued neglect of responsibility was a criminal act that would lead to suffering and death. The stage directions continue:

> *(An inner voice speaks)* "You're not really in Heaven, there's no such place. You're dying in a hospital . . . You're full of broken glass but you're not dead. You couldn't be dead because there is no such thing. You're going to stay half-alive and see what you're running away from—war, fascism, revolution . . . Do you want to live or die?"

Lawson never finished the script. Instead, he turned over the page and scrawled, "I want to live."[113] With that commitment to life and to responsibility, Lawson's "metaphysical phase" ended.

Social Energy and the Making(s) of Lawson

In his essay on the method of New Historicism, "Towards a Poetics of Culture," Stephen Greenblatt argues that all acts of expression (for example, literary and nonliterary texts), as part of the specific cultures in which they originate, are deeply embedded in a complex and dynamic social fabric of that particular historical moment and are moreover constantly evaluated, modified, and made anew as they continuously and vigorously circulate with other social currencies. He writes,

> [T]he work of art is the product of negotiations between the creator or class of creators, equipped with a complex, communally shared repertoire of conventions, and the institutions and practices of society. In order to achieve the negotiation, artists need to create currency that is valid for a meaningful, mutually profitable exchange. It is important to emphasize that the process involves not simply appropriation but exchange, since the existence of art always implies a return [. . .] The terms "currency" and "negotiation" are signs of our manipulation and adjustment of the relative systems.[114]

The texts examined in this chapter—both those authored by as well as those aimed at Lawson—were social currencies. They therefore may be read for echoes of the negotiations, both supportive and contentious, that persisted between the playwright and various sociopolitical and cultural institutions in the first years of the 1920s in the United States. These social currencies were both produced by and, successively, became powerful forces in the larger cultural field and thus were operational in the creation of systems of value, which determined the very shape and scope of dramatic construction, theatrical expression, and critical assumptions during this period. Thus, imbued with an historically specific social energy, these various texts may be read to reveal the traces of the aforementioned expansive, increasingly quarrelsome, and ever-evolving ideological conflict on the American left, one that would, by the middle and latter years of the decade, pit those who reflected, supported, and produced the paradigmatic belief system of the lyrical left and, by extension, progressive democracy, against those who, following in the wake of Gold's "Towards Proletarian Art," reflected, supported, and produced revolutionary ideology via artistic expression. In charting the compositional history of Lawson's texts and the critiques written in response to those texts, it is clear that the expansiveness and evolution of this conflict had an acute impact on Lawson as he strove "to create currency that [was] valid for a meaningful, mutually profitable exchange."

In the first years of the decade, as is evidenced in the preceding analysis of *Roger Bloomer* and the critical responses written in reply to the two 1923 productions, there still existed something of a united front, albeit one that was waning, on the part of most noncommercial theatre artists and producing companies—such as Lawson, some persons within the Equity Players, and Marguerite Barker—and sympathetic theatre critics—such as Macgowan, Lewisohn, Young, and Block. While the former were committed to radical dramaturgical and theatrical experimentation (and often, by extension, radical, though not revolutionary, causes and politics), the latter championed the whole of noncommercial theatre despite their competing and, oftentimes, adversarial ideologies (that is, radical or progressive democracy on the part of Macgowan, Lewisohn, and Young, and socialism on the part of Block). Significantly, despite these disparate worldviews, these critics in the first years of the 1920s were largely consistent in their praise of Lawson's experimentation with form. In their various critiques of *Roger Bloomer*, for example, these ideologically dissimilar critics were united in their praise of Lawson's work, finding it "promising" and exemplary of the then-emerging and notable dramaturgical approaches (that is, expressionism, Dadaism, and so on) in the theatre in the United States. These critics, thus, stood collectively and in stark contrast against the stalwart conservative critics such as Dale and Corbin, who were hostile toward theatre artists seeking to advance the mode and scope of theatre beyond the now-institutionalized European playwriting and stagecraft practices of the late nineteenth century.

Notwithstanding the argument that there was something of a conciliatory ambience conjoining many within the noncommercial theatre community during the early years of the decade, it seems clear that there were a growing number within this same community who were in no small way troubled by even the most abstract and subtle suggestion of revolutionary politics. With the larger American left split into right-wing and left-wing factions (a construct that was residually linked to the pro-war/anti-war split, circa December 1914) came a division within the community of noncommercial theatre artists and critics. Accordingly, in the spirit of Cheney's seemingly apolitical (that is, right-wing/progressive democratic) musings, Shelley Hull, director of the short-lived Equity Theatre production of *Roger Bloomer*, found Lawson's abstract but biting denunciations of the American bourgeoisie and puritanical morality so disquieting, she chose to cut them from her production and, instead, focus on the lyricism of the script. It is important to note that Hull and Cheney were not alone in holding this rather moderate view.

By the time *Processional* was produced two years later, the gap within the noncommercial theatre community separating those who were radical, in a largely artistic sense, from those who were revolutionary, in a largely political sense, was widening. George Jean Nathan's acidic dismissal of Lawson's script and the Theatre Guild's production may be viewed as not only a response chiefly aimed at

Lawson and the Guild but as a reactionary polemic charged with the critic's resolute desire to forward an aesthetic-centered theatre and, thus, protect the/his "new theatre" (aka Cheney's art theatre) from being tainted by what he perceived as revolutionary precepts practiced by the likes of Lawson and advocated for by critics such as Walter Long, Floyd Dell, V. F. Calverton, and Michael Gold. For Nathan, the production of a play such as *Processional* by the premier noncommercial theatre company in the United States was considerably more than an "embarrassment" for the Guild. It was, as well, an unsettling bellwether, indicative of an emerging but potent system of belief that threatened to shake the ground on which Nathan and other progressive democrats stood. For the noncommercial theatre community, this emerging system of belief prompted a heated debate regarding the purpose of theatrical expression: Should it be, as Cheney envisioned, a "garden" dedicated to the staging of "beautiful things" or, as Gold professed, a "cauldron of the Revolution"? Additionally, who within the noncommercial theatre community would be granted the authority and power to determine the "communally shared repertoire of conventions" regarding theatre?

Ironically, as the preceding analysis of *Processional* demonstrates, the politics implied in that script are more indebted to a radical brand of Wilsonian, progressive democracy than to revolutionary Marxism. While Lawson's critique of the bourgeoisie and capitalism is far from ambiguous, his script is, nonetheless, in want of the ideological explicitness requisite with the revolutionary, working-class drama that Gold et al. were envisioning. Moreover, its critique of the exploitation of the individual (as opposed to class) marks it as a text still deeply entrenched in the ethos of libertinism of the lyrical left. It follows, then, that this lack of explicit revolutionary zeal and dogma might well explain why liberal critics such as Young and Broun were able to forego any discussion of the issues explored in the script and production and instead focus entirely on Lawson's and the Theatre Guild's formal achievements. For them, these accomplishments in technique were enough to warrant praise. Even Gabriel, who did address the issues in the play, did so in a manner typical of "liberal" criticism of this era. That is to say, for Gabriel—as it was for Elmer Rice, a quintessential progressive democrat if ever there was one—it was enough that Lawson and the Guild were "contemptuous" of society, willing to ask "what's wrong with this picture," and, thus, expose societal shortcomings.[115] The fact that neither the playwright nor the producing company felt compelled to offer specific solutions was considered not a defect but an asset.

Regardless of what some such as Nathan might have believed, in the early and mid-1920s Lawson too deemed as suitable for the creation of his art this "communally shared repertoire of conventions," including the aforementioned notions concerning the relation of art to society. Writing in the preface to the published script of *Processional*, the playwright stated in explicit terms, "I am not offering solutions. I am not even stating concise questions. My concern is with the theatre" (viii). Therefore, in a spirit akin to those critics who were supportive of both *Roger Bloomer* and *Processional*, Lawson's primary aim during this period was the production of theatre that was novel, exciting, and radical in an aesthetic sense. These scripts, while including embryonic denunciations of bourgeois social structures, maintained their value with noncommercial companies such as the Theatre Guild as well as with many in liberal critical circles precisely because those texts were essentially nondogmatic and nondidactic.

Lawson's support from this community, of course, would begin to disintegrate with the production of *Nirvana* in 1926. Arguably, the dissolution of support for Lawson may be linked to the playwright's recognition that the goals of the noncommercial theatre community à la Cheney, Nathan, and the Theatre Guild were no longer his own. As Lawson ventured beyond the parameters of the "communally shared repertoire of conventions" common to the paradigmatic noncommercial theatre community that continued to reflect, support, and produce a belief system that was relational to the ethos of the lyrical left, and, instead, shifted toward an acceptance of a worldview that reflected, supported, and produced revolutionary ideology, the material effects of that modification on the playwright's career were swift and definitive: the rejection by the Guild and an onslaught of harsh criticism from those in the critical community who had just a few years prior praised and valued his work. The consequences of Lawson's choice to forgo the support of the "art theatre" community, based at least in part on his "own growing sense of political issues which separated me from the so-called avant-garde in the theatre" would be profound.[116] Moreover, as will be discussed in chapter 3, his initial attempts, in the final years of the 1920s, to secure a position within the emerging community of revolutionary artists and win approval from the already resolute and increasingly powerful community of left-wing critics would prove more difficult and torturous than he could have possibly imagined.

3

To Beat the Drums of Rebellion

> So everything's just the same as it was before, driven along by what I don't understand . . .
>
> —John Howard Lawson, *Loud Speaker*, 1927

In his study of the American left, John Patrick Diggins writes, "Beginning with the Romance of Greenwich Village, America's first Left [that is, the Lyrical Left] ended in the despair of the tragedy of the Charlestown [Massachusetts] prison."[1] Diggins is alluding to the August 1927 execution of Nicola Sacco and Bartolomeo Vanzetti, the two working-class Italian immigrants and avowed anarchists whose case had been the cause célèbre for the American left throughout most of the 1920s.[2]

The ordeal of Sacco and Vanzetti began in late February 1920 in the wake of the second series of Palmer raids, when another Italian immigrant and anarchist by the name of Andrea Salsedo was taken into custody by the Department of Justice and accused of aiding those who had in June 1919 planted a bomb in front of Attorney General A. Mitchell Palmer's home. More remotely, however, the plight of these two Italian immigrants was closely linked to the problematic history of the anarchy movement in the United States.

The decision of Attorney General Palmer and his aide J. Edgar Hoover to target anarchists in the years immediately following World War I was an outgrowth of a decades-old campaign on behalf of the

U.S. federal government. Suspicion of the anarchy movement (and by extension the xenophobia aimed at many of the immigrant peoples living in the United States that may or may not have been members or supporters of the movement) had grown steadily over the course of the last decades of the nineteenth century and first two decades of the twentieth. This growing suspicion was rooted, in part, in the Haymarket Riots of 1886, during which there had been a bombing attributed to Italian anarchists. It gained momentum through events such as the assassination of President McKinley in 1901 by avowed anarchist (and immigrant) Leon Czolgosz and the murder of King Umberto I of Italy in 1900, an act committed by Gaetano Bresci, an Italian who had immigrated to New Jersey in the 1870s where he discovered anarchism, and returned to his native land to avenge the 1898 massacre of workers in Milan. The U.S. government responded to this perceived growing threat of anarchy by passing anti-anarchist legislation, including the Immigration Act of 1903, which barred alien anarchist entry into the United States, and Teddy Roosevelt's federal law of 1908, which allowed stringent governmental regulation of the anarchist press. Salsedo was a known supporter (and sometime editor) of one such publication, *Cronaca Sovversiva*, the foremost Italian-language anarchist journal edited by Luigi Galleani. Galleani had been forced by the federal government to halt publication of *Cronaca Sovversiva* immediately upon the United States' entry into World War I in 1917. Eventually Galleani and a number of supporters of *Cronaca Sovversiva* were deported in late June 1919, on the grounds that the publication, its editors, and its supporters were connected to the May Day Riots of 1919 as well as a series of bombings in June 1919, including the one at the Attorney General's home. Thus, at the beginning of the 1920s, the larger cultural field in the United State was inculcated with a deep-seeded distrust of avowed and suspected anarchists.

On 25 April 1920, two months following Salsedo's arrest, Vanzetti, a friend of Salsedo, traveled from his home in Plymouth, Massachusetts, to New York City, where the accused was being held. After consulting with Salsedo and well-known anarchist militant Carlo Tresca, Vanzetti returned to Plymouth on 29 April. Four days later, on 3 May, Salsedo's lifeless body was found on the pavement below the Department of Justice building in New York. It was widely held within the leftist communities in the United States that Salsedo had been thrown out of a window; however, the Department of Justice asserted their suspect had gone insane during questioning and jumped when left unguarded.

Two days later, on 5 May, Vanzetti and his friend Sacco were arrested in a police trap set to capture Mike Boda, a known anarchist agitator.

The authorities believed Boda had been involved in an attempted holdup of a factory paymaster that had occurred on 24 December 1919 in Bridgewater, Massachusetts. While the trap had been set for Boda, authorities found among the possessions of Sacco and Vanzetti guns and flyers announcing a protest in tribute to Salsedo scheduled for 9 May that was to include Vanzetti as the main speaker. Boda was released and, in due course, Vanzetti was accused of participating in the attempted holdup in Bridgewater. Following his indictment on 11 June, the case moved quickly to trial later that month. Despite a strong alibi supported by many witnesses (most of whom spoke only Italian), Vanzetti was found guilty and sentenced to ten to fifteen years in prison, an exceedingly harsh sentence for a first-time offense in which no person was harmed. At the time, many on the left believed the severity of the sentence was linked to the federal government's desire to exhibit for would-be anarchists the consequences of radical and subversive behavior. Judge Webster Thayer's remarks to the jury before deliberation suggest that this view was well founded: "This man [Vanzetti], although he may not have actually committed the crime attributed to him is nevertheless morally culpable, because he is an enemy of our existing institutions."[3]

Over two months later, in September 1920, Sacco and Vanzetti were indicted for a brutal crime that had occurred on 15 April 1920 in South Braintree, Massachusetts. In this incident, a payroll of over $15,000 was stolen and a paymaster and a guard were murdered. Beginning on 31 May 1921, over a full year after their arrests, Sacco and Vanzetti were tried for the South Braintree crime with Judge Thayer once again presiding. Over the course of a seven-week trial, the defense produced witness after witness who provided alibis and evidence that seemed to prove unquestionably the innocence of the accused. Furthermore, they repeatedly discredited the prosecution's often-confused witnesses who claimed they had seen the accused at the crime scene, presented powerful evidence linking the notorious Morelli gang to the crime, and offered compelling and well-grounded theories that suggested perjury by prosecution witnesses and illegal actions on the part of local and federal authorities. It was, however, to no avail. At one point during the trial, Judge Thayer, with no small amount of hostility, remarked that the political activities of the defendants had included involvement in labor strikes, political agitation, and anti-war propaganda. Thayer went on to state that the two anarchists were either "conscious of guilt as murderers or as slackers and radicals," and he urged the jury to think of "the American boy [. . .] giving up his life on the battlefield of France."[4] When the case at last went to the jury, it responded with a verdict of guilty on 14 June 1921.

Over the next six years, despite numerous appeals, the convictions were upheld. On 9 April 1927, after all recourse in the Massachusetts courts had failed, Sacco and Vanzetti were sentenced to death. As the day of execution drew near, millions of people throughout the world who were convinced of the innocence of the two Italian anarchists held demonstrations and strikes. At the urging of Dos Passos, who had been involved with the Sacco and Vanzetti Defense Committee for a number of years, Lawson went to Boston to participate in the protests. In the first minutes of 23 August, as two hundred and fifty thousand people walked the streets of Boston in silent protest, Sacco and Vanzetti were electrocuted. Diggins writes of that moment, "When the signal went out that Sacco and Vanzetti had been executed, American intellectuals were traumatized, shaken by the thought that the state can kill the innocent and force society into class warfare."[5] In recalling his own reaction to that night years later, Lawson seems the embodiment of Diggins's summation of the condition of the larger leftist community: "I felt fear and pessimism. We had failed; 'the people,' in America and all over the world, had failed, and I had to reexamine what I meant by 'the people,' for I had no specific idea."[6]

Clearly, as it did for so many on the left, the execution of Sacco and Vanzetti stood as a moment of personal crisis, in Kuhn's sense, for Lawson and would operate as a forceful cultural intertext to his writing in the years to follow.[7] To suggest, however, that this moment of personal crisis found its genesis and fulfillment entirely in those first minutes of 23 August 1927, without substantial and dynamic prefigurement or sequela, would be to disregard the complex and arduous evolution of thought—as most clearly manifest in his ever-changing approach to dramatic form—that Lawson had undergone over the first seven years of the decade and would continue to endure in the first years of the 1930s. Furthermore, Lawson's moment of personal crisis in the streets of Boston and by extension the case of Sacco and Vanzetti may both be viewed as microcosmic events contained by and within a macrocosmic phenomenon in the larger cultural field. This more expansive occurrence pitted the hegemony of the puritanical and conservative right against the increasingly dogmatic and leftward-leaning (that is, Stalinist) left—albeit one that was fractured and shrinking—in the United States in the 1920s.[8]

As early as the first months of 1920, this macrocosmic conflict of ideologies (that is, manifest most obviously in the form of the Palmer raids) both entangled Sacco and Vanzetti and inspired the Lawsons' flight to Paris, thus spurring on the playwright's commitment to experiment with and develop forms that could "accurately and theatrically reflect the reality of [the] time."[9] Over the course of the next seven years, as the two Italian anarchists struggled for justice through appeal after appeal, Lawson struggled "toward some sort of form" adequate for expressing his vision of the "brash and bungling twentieth century."[10] The events in Boston in August 1927 merely served as a transformative incident within that more expansive conflict of ideologies taking place in the broader cultural field: Sacco and Vanzetti were, in the eyes of the left, martyred to justice and galvanized the fractured American left, and Lawson, stunned by the events, was consumed by a resolute desire to achieve clarity. Following his "midnight in Boston," Lawson would spend the next six years "reexamin[ing] what [he] meant by 'the people,'" and, subsequently, undergo what he would later describe as "my slow awakening of consciousness."[11]

While Lawson's discontent reached the point of crisis in the streets of suburban Boston in August 1927, the penultimate prelude to that moment was initiated rather unceremoniously in April 1926. At that time, one month following the disastrous production of *Nirvana*, Lawson, in league with Michael Gold, Jasper Deeter, and Ida Rauh, the latter two members of the Provincetown Players, announced the formation of the Workers' Drama League, an amateur troupe that claimed to be the first theatre in the United States to seek a working-class audience and address working-class concerns. In addition to the aforementioned founding members, the Workers' Drama League included in its ranks socialist writer Nathan Fine, graphic artist Louis Lozowick, scene designer Hugo Gellert, and director Alexander Artokov, a member of the Proletariat Theatre in Russia who had come to visit the United States and participate in the 1926 New York Theatre Exposition. While Lawson's association with the Workers' Drama League was entirely superficial—he never even attended any of the organizational meetings—his desire to be associated with this group of artists committed to working-class issues and revolutionary politics suggests he was beginning to feel his way toward some sort of serious political commitment.[12] Even so, an explicit expression of any such dedication was completely absent from his essay "Debunking the Art Theatre," published two months later in the June 1926 issue of *New Masses*.

Despite the promise of revolutionary insurrection indicated in the title of the essay, the tone and message therein is thoroughly grounded in the mores of the "art theatre," circa the mid-1920s. Other than curtly dismissing those "hoity-toity [. . .] playwrights, scenic designers and directors" who, by way of their "slightly muddled statements," established a "complicated and meaningless terminology" in the theatre, the whole of the essay is an ostensibly apolitical celebration of formalism or what Lawson termed "the new showmanship":

> [L]et us agree that the point in concocting a play is to tell a story, to make an emotional contact. This is the age-old function of the theatre—by no means a new innovation. There are those who think that this contact can be made more vigorously and simply by means of a freer method than the restrained and comparatively recent technique of the drawing room play. It is my own opinion that the picture-frame technique, so-called *realism* (in the sense of the supposedly realistic well-made play) is impracticable and dull. Far from regarding this as a startling innovation, I am merely basing my opinion on the whole tradition of the theatre. [. . .]
>
> My point then, is a very simple one: that it is a mistake to think of the New Art of the theatre in terms which are either new or artistic. It is an attempt to apply very ancient forms of showmanship to the needs of current and vital entertainment. It is true that this has not been accomplished. It is true that such accomplishment requires change in the current conventions of the theatre.
>
> We require clarification. It is important to consider in simple untechnical terms, how to develop methods of writing, acting, setting, which carry out these ideas of richer story value, emotional connection; to create a theatre which touches some electrical crowd nerve.[13]

Clearly, Lawson was still largely beholden (despite some vehement protestations) to the discursive operations and intertextual determinations of the "art theatre" as envisioned by critics such as Cheney and practiced by companies such as the Theatre Guild. Indeed, the tone and ideals expressed by Lawson in "Debunking the Art Theatre" are strikingly similar to Cheney's 1925 celebration of "radical artists," "bedded together—in the garden of [. . . the] 'art theatre,'" working collectively to create theatre pieces "stamped with the style of brilliance or the quality of [. . .] imagination," and imbued with the aspiration that such work would "widen the horizon of life, [. . .] stir the emotions and enrich the adult mind."[14] These progressive democratic ideals continued to bear upon and shape the texts Lawson was generating, determining in profound ways his conception of and praxis within the theatre.

Ironically, juxtaposed against the last page of Lawson's June 1926 essay forwarding a formalist, aesthetic-centered view of the theatre was a small notice announcing the continuance of weekly organizational meetings for the "Workers' Dramatic League." The anonymous writer of this notice (perhaps Gold?) calls on all "working men and women who wish to see a Workers' Theatre in America" to attend meetings led by the "extremely able modernist [. . .] Dr. Alexander Artokov." Beyond the plea for participation, this notice also infers a view of theatre that stands in complete contrast to the one advanced by Lawson in his adjacent essay. The writer of the notice suggests that theatre should be used as a tool for social revolution, not as a forum for formal "experiment in the minor esthetic cults."[15]

The enthusiastic call for participation apparently fell on deaf ears. In the end, the Workers' Drama League existed only a few months, produced just one show, Gold's one-act *Strike!*, and was all but ignored in the press. It nevertheless proved to be an influential endeavor, initiating the workers' theatre movement popular in the United States in the early 1930s and establishing in the minds of Lawson, Gold, and Dos Passos the idea of a professional company dedicated to new theatrical forms and radical (if not revolutionary) politics. To that end, in January 1927, following the dissolution of the Workers' Drama League, Lawson, Gold, and Dos Passos joined with playwrights Francis Faragoh and Emanuel (Em Jo) Basshe to form the New Playwrights' Theatre.[16]

Supported by a series of grants from financier Otto Kahn,[17] who had also provided substantial funding for the Provincetown Players and the Theatre Guild, the New Playwrights hoped to establish an independent theatre that produced, on a repertory basis, avant-garde plays that would be committed to working-class issues and audiences. Despite their commendable goals, the New Playwrights' vision of a workers' theatre proved to be "totally impractical" in the United States of the late 1920s.[18] While the group did sometimes appeal to trade unions, intermittently selling the whole house to a union chapter, they found that the unconventional, recondite style of most of their scripts and productions failed to attract the laborers toward whom they had directed their message.[19] Regarding this issue, Lawson later recalled:

> We of the New Playwrights' were trying to educate a "mass audience," before we ourselves were educated—and the audience was conspicuously absent. We endeavored to organize audiences, selling blocks of tickets for reduced prices to organizations, with special inducements to trade unions. But only a few unions could be persuaded to come en masse and there was no massive enthusiasm in their response. I recall an evening when the Union of Window Cleaners occupied most of the

> house to hear and see *The International.* I moved to strategic points around the theatre, studying their faces. They were good people; they wanted to enjoy themselves; but they would have been happier at a movie. I knew that evening that we had failed. Those faces of the workers were the measure of our failure.[20]

In addition to the ever-present struggle to attract their projected audience, the New Playwrights' three-year existence was troubled for a number of other reasons. To begin with, no single person was ever appointed or elected to unify the similar but various artistic visions and political positions into a single purpose.[21] The members were apparently aware of the problems inherent in communal work from the beginning, as is evidenced by their attempts to obtain the services of director Edward Massey, a close friend of Dos Passos and Lawson, as artistic director. In the end, Massey's other commitments prevented him from assuming this role. With Massey unavailable, the playwrights then tried to secure the services of Deeter. He, however, wanted "too much control" and left before the first season began. With their opening dates quickly approaching, the playwrights resigned themselves to bring in "Broadway or Broadway-like directors" to stage the first season.[22] This proved to be a crucial mistake. Harry Wagstaff Gribble directed Lawson's *Loud Speaker* but, according to the playwright, "failed to realize the intention." Similarly, Earl Browne directed a "visually stunning" production of Basshe's *Earth* but had "no sense of the play's meaning."[23]

As a result of these half-realized productions, Lawson and Basshe decided to direct their own plays during the second season, which included Basshe's *The Centuries* and Lawson's *The International,* as well as Gold's *Hoboken Blues* and nonmember Paul Sifton's *The Belt.*[24] The results were just as disastrous, and by the end of the season, three of the original five members had committed to other projects. Gold became increasingly consumed by his duties as editor of *New Masses,*[25] Dos Passos left for an extended visit to the Soviet Union, and Lawson accepted a contract from MGM to write screenplays. Only Basshe and Faragoh, along with new members Sifton and Massey, remained to struggle through a third season of commercial and critical failures.[26] On 26 April 1929, the *New York Times* at last announced the dissolution of the New Playwrights' Theatre with the headline, "New Playwrights Abandon Productions."[27]

Notwithstanding their many failures, the New Playwrights were an enormously influential theatre group, greatly affecting the shape and practice of theatre in the United States in the 1930s. The company may count among its many accomplishments being one of the first theatre groups outside of Russia to incorporate constructivist scenery into its productions with *Loud Speaker.* Additionally, it was one of the first companies in the United States to present serious plays about working-class life with *Singing Jailbirds* and *The Belt*, to explore unsympathetically life in the Jewish ghetto with *The Centuries*, and to give serious treatment to the African American situation using an all-black cast with *Earth*.[28] In her study on the New Playwrights, Roberta Lasky summarizes the group's contributions thusly:

> Perhaps the theatre's greatest contribution was providing an outlet for experimentation in both the subject matter of the plays and in their scene design, costumes, lighting, and staging. All productions were linked by themes of social justice, yet each drama treated the subject differently. Lawson's *Loud Speaker*, Sifton's *The Belt*, Basshe's *The Centuries* and Dos Passos's *Airways, Inc.* center on the disintegration of the American family. Yet, *Loud Speaker* also surveys aspects of political corruption; *The Belt* and *Airways Inc.* deal with themes of labor against big business. *The Centuries* revolves around problems of organized crime and the assimilation of ethnic minorities. Lawson's *The International* treats political corruption on a world scale, while Sinclair's *Singing Jailbirds* illustrates a personal struggle against social injustice. Basshe's *Earth* and Gold's *Hoboken Blues* also handle problems of assimilation.[29]

Aside from the advances made by the group as a whole, a critical reading of the scripts and essays composed by Lawson while a New Playwright supports the view that this period in his life may be viewed as one of aggrandizing intellectual upheaval, leading to the moment of personal crisis in the streets of Boston, wherein the playwright's internal struggle, pitting his aesthetic sensibility against his burgeoning political commitment, became decidedly more pronounced. Lawson later remarked that his time with the New Playwrights served as an "introduction to *praxis*, to the world of action, involving an understanding of working people."[30] Still, when Lawson wrote "The New Showmanship," the first in a number of unofficial manifestos he penned for the New Playwrights, he stated in explicit terms that the theatre's central commitment was not to political revolution but artistic rebellion by way of the avant-garde.

The essay, which first appeared in the program of the Neighborhood Playhouse production of Faragoh's *Pinwheel* in February 1927, opened with the bold declarative claim that "the theatre of the future [. . .] is, here and now, an actuality." Lawson went on to assert that "the sole aim of the younger playwrights is to return to [the] honorable principles [. . .] of telling a story" that is both "pictorial and dynamic," and attack the "flesh marts and somber commercial temples" (that is, Broadway), charging, "The walls of these playhouses seem to have grown damp and musty with the gradual rot of stale sentiments, old jokes and dead repetitions." He concluded by asserting that while the expressionist movement had awakened the American theatre to the idea of a "story-play," it was just one "certain stage in the growth of native drama" leading to an "American type of show." This new method "utilizes [. . .] jazz, [. . .] sentiment and buffoonery," "is rich in plot," and "is concerned with real events which happen in the lives and hearts of people about us." Above all else, however, it abandons "realism" for "theatricalism."[31]

"The New Showmanship" is the statement of an artist whose main concern is aesthetics. Nonetheless, while this essay forwards a view of the theatre quite similar to the one expressed one year prior in "Debunking the Art Theatre," there is in "The New Showmanship" a heightened sense, albeit tacit, of fervency and desire to connect with "the live and hearts of people about us."

By the autumn of 1927, following the lackluster first season and the events in Boston that summer, Lawson and the other playwrights' central objective of returning to the "honorable principles [. . . of] pictorial and dynamic" theatre was broadened to allow for revolutionary political overtures that were increasingly overt. This shift in the theatre's policy is expressed in Lawson's second unofficial manifesto for the New Playwrights, "What Is a Workers' Theatre?," which appeared in the *New York Sun* on 12 November 1927. With this essay, the playwright demonstrated how far he had traveled in a matter of months from the aesthetic-centered view of the New Showmanship. Now Lawson, writing in a manner and tone that is decidedly more self-reflexive and inquisitive, claims that the New Playwrights' Theatre's ultimate aim is:

> to find and coordinate [. . .] the presentation of mass plays, people's plays, done for workers at prices that workers can afford. [. . .] Why introduce the killing wind of controversy into the greenhouses where flowers of pure art ought to be delicately nurtured? Because you cannot separate art from social problems without getting a pasty anemic byproduct without integrity or vitality. A writer for the stage who doesn't face America industrially and physically is shirking his whole duty as an artist. He can't conceal his lack of contact by handing out a thin knowledge of psychoanalysis and a few notions about love.

> And if he does his duty as an artist he has got to appeal to the people who constitute his real audience; not the stuffed shirts who come to the playhouse for a few hours of mild diversion between dinner and dancing, not the few thousand spirits hungry for soul-fodder who will patronize any theatre that labels itself "Culture."

Still, since "[t]he purpose of the stage is not to argue or convince, but to report—to see passionately and fully," and because it was "not the business of theatre to be controlled by any class or theory," the New Playwrights would not use their stage as a "soap box" for propaganda. They would instead seek to augment their earlier goal of aesthetic rebellion by bringing to the stage a "revolutionary tone" and a "passionate vision of the current scene" that would reflect who they were as radicals.[32]

The subtle adjustment in focus that is at the heart of "What Is a Workers Theatre?" was counterpart to international movements and events in both theatrical and political arenas. This more overtly leftist political slant positioned the New Playwrights as part of an international group of theatre artists, led by Meyerhold and Mayakovsky in Russia and Piscator and Brecht in Germany, who were calling for the creation of independent theatres where representation, illusion, and the picture-frame stage would be discarded in exchange for demonstration, anti-illusion, and the view that the theatre might be used to ferment social and political change. The shift of intent in Lawson's essay also parallels the emergence of an increasingly unified and revolutionary political left in the United States, energized in part by the case of Sacco and Vanzetti and further galvanized by the stock market crash of 1929. This unifying and radicalizing of the left in the United States in the latter years of the 1920s is perhaps most evident in the Communist movement proper.

As discussed in chapter 1, at the beginning of the 1920s the Communist movement in the United States was haunted by pervasive factionalism and continual infighting, as manifest in the presence of two competing and, often, adversarial camps: the Communist Party or CP (a group that broke away from the Socialist Party, was led by Louis Fraina and Charles Ruthenberg, and whose membership was largely composed of non-English-speaking immigrant citizens) and the Communist Labor Party or CLP (a group with ties to the IWW, led by John Reed and Benjamin Glitow, whose membership was largely composed of native-born citizens and would eventually absorb a breakaway group from the CP led by Ruthenberg and change its name to the United Communist Party or UCP). Under order from the Comintern, the two parties (that is, the CP and the UCP) were officially unified in May 1921 as the Communist Party of America (CPA), which quickly absorbed the militant, William Z. Foster–led Trade Union Educational League (TUEL) and was renamed the Workers (Communist) Party (WP or WCP) in December 1921. From late 1921 through 1928, the WP followed the dictates of the Comintern and eschewed revolutionary militancy in favor of working through established labor organizations and developing a mass following.

In spite of the official unification, the factionalism and infighting continued. Indeed, throughout its convoluted history in the mid-1920s, there persisted two opposing sides in the WP. Very broadly speaking, on the one side were the leftist, doctrinal Marxists who sought to promote revolutionary sectarian orthodoxy, balked at the notion of working within unions (principally the AFL) as opposed to destroying them, and therefore mirrored the Bolshevik-revolutionary ideals being espoused by Trotsky. On the other side were the electoral politics Communists who sought to create a legitimate/legalized party, engage in electoral activity, and eventually forge "united fronts" with other progressive organizations. In short, this group sought to promote political activism that would slowly lead to a broad mass following, a mirror of Lenin's own move to the right as was reflected in his New Economic Policy of 1921. It follows, then, that in the first years of the decade it was this second group that, by and large, had the support of the Soviet-controlled Comintern. So adverse were the ideals of these two camps that one chronicler of the movement characterized the middle years of the 1920s as a time of "political gang warfare." During this period, the electoral politics Communists, led by Ruthenberg, who served as the party secretary until his death in March 1927, and his successor Jay Lovestone, clashed again and again with more militant trade unionists, led by Foster and James P. Cannon. This clash grew more violent during the Lovestone era.

Beginning in 1927, the Lovestone administration forwarded a right-wing agenda (relative to the larger Communist movement) advocating class collaboration. Further, these so-called Lovestoneites held the view that the United States operated under "exceptional circumstances" and was, therefore, immune from the operation of capitalist economic laws. While these policies certainly would have found favor with Lenin-era Comintern in the early years of the decade, in the latter years of the decade these right-wing issues were increasingly contested, both within the leftist ranks of the WP in the United States and, more importantly, in the Soviet CP in Moscow. It seems paradoxical that the shift to the left in the Communist movement in the United States had its genesis in Stalin's successful endeavor to stamp out the leftist insurrection of Zinoviev and Trotsky in 1927, resulting in the capitulation of Zinoviev and the expulsion of Trotsky and other members of the left opposition from the Soviet CP in 1928, which led to the expulsion of Trotsky's supporters in the United States, Cannon principal among them. This paradox is rectified, however, in light of what happened next. With his rivals on the left contained and/or expelled, Stalin moved to and occupied the now-vacant left and set his sights on destroying all opposition on the right, specifically Bukharin in Moscow and by extension his proxy in the United States, Lovestone. So began the so-called Third Period in Soviet politics, a period marked by its ultraleft policies. Thus by the end of 1928, the rightward-leaning WP under the leadership of Lovestone now stood in stark opposition to the now-leftward-leaning, Stalin-controlled Comintern. As a result, in June 1929 the rightist Lovestone and 200 of his fellow Lovestoneites were expelled from the party. Soon after, the WP changed its name to the Communist Party USA (CP-USA), and a secretariat of four was created to oversee the party: Robert Minor, William Weinstone, Max Bedacht, and William Foster. This group of four, with Bedacht as acting secretary, served until the following summer (June 1930). At that point, Bedacht and Minor both stepped down, Weinstone went to Moscow to serve as representative to the Comintern, Foster was in jail for his involvement in unemployment demonstrations, and Earl Browder, finding himself head of the CP-USA, slowly began to institute policies that would serve the interests of Stalin.[33]

Thus, in the latter years of the 1920s powerful alliances were forged, both within the Soviet Union and, by extension, the United States, which laid the foundation for a more unified and revolutionary left at the turn of the decade, both nationally and internationally. This complicated process of unification would profoundly influence leftward-leaning intellectuals like Lawson. Regarding this process of unification, Lawson writes, "A process of radicalization and alliance was taking place among American intellectuals; it was not solely due to the events in Boston; the mobilization there was an effect as well as a cause; it happened because artists and writers were motivated by manifold discontents, which could no longer find an outlet in eccentricity or metaphysics. It is a mistake to suppose that the economic breakdown in 1929 created an unexpected turn to the left. The leftward movement had been gaining momentum throughout the twenties."[34]

Lawson's view that the emergence of a newly construed ("radicalized") and unified American left in the latter years of the 1920s may well be read as an indication of the presence of a social energy circulating through the ranks of leftward-leaning intellectuals at this historical moment. The presence of such a social energy—one that included historically and culturally specific aural, visual, and verbal traces that, in turn, produced, organized, and shaped the mental and, in some cases, physical experiences of this segment of the population—is also identified by Michael Denning in his study, *The Cultural Front*. In his discussion of the "political sea change" affecting those on the cultural left in the United States in the last years of the 1920s, Denning notes,

> Though a few had had ties to the Greenwich Village radicalism of the *Masses*, most of the [radical] moderns were apolitical. If they were critical of the commercialism and Babbittry of US culture, their alienation was expressed in expatriation to Europe and avant-garde formal experiment. The turning point came in the 1920s: for some [. . .] it was the execution of Sacco and Vanzetti; for others it was the crash of 1929 and the depression that ensued. "It would be three years," Josephine Herbst wrote in her memoir of 1927, "before we took down the volume of *Kunstgechichte* [literally "Art Stories" by Otto Fischer] from our shelves, to be replaced by a thin narrow book in red entitled *What Is to Be Done?*, by V. I. Lenin." [. . .T]he turn to the left by American modernists was not simply a shift in political opinion, nor was it a retreat from modernism to a Victorian realism. [. . . I]n almost every case, writers and artists of the modernist generation attempted to reconstruct modernism, to tie their formal experimentation to a new social and historical vision, to invent a "social modernism," a "revolutionary symbolism."[35]

Over the course of the final three years of the 1920s, those in the United States who had once identified as progressive liberals, particularly intellectuals and artists, were, time and again, creating and responding to a social energy that was reconceiving revolutionary politics and aesthetics. As many on the cultural left began to embrace unshrinkingly the view that art should enable the proletarian revolution, there arose within that same loosely organized community of radical moderns a willingness to forgo the operations and determinations that had produced and defined the discourse and methods central to the maintenance of the procedures and practices of the lyrical left. This same group of culture makers instead chose to accept and, in turn, participate in generating new modes and methods of ideological discourse. As such, they sought to advance revolutionary politics, not aesthetic rebellion.

For Lawson, while his focus in 1927 and 1928 would still be on the aesthetic and not the political, the struggle to find an intermediary position between these two objectives became resolutely more pronounced. The dramatic and theoretical texts he produced during his tenure with the New Playwrights contain overt and covert traces of this burgeoning personal struggle, which was inevitably coupled to "political sea change" occurring within the cultural left and, by extension, the transformations taking place in the larger cultural field. As such, the differing conceptions regarding the essence of "revolutionary" theatre—as theorized in "The New Showmanship" and "What Is a Workers Theatre?"—are necessarily more than just reflexive records of the playwright's ever-evolving personal struggle. These theoretical texts, endowed with the dynamic social energy of the American left circa 1927–1928, illuminate the ways in which Lawson's personal struggle was deeply ingrained within the cultural field as well as the vibrant community of "radicals" and "revolutionaries" of which he was a part. The content and form of these texts, imbued with the aforementioned social energy, may thus be read for vestiges of the discursive operations that created and underpinned that community's interests, pleasures, and anxieties.

Loud Speaker

As were the first three scripts of his mature playwriting career, Lawson's *Loud Speaker* was the result of a developmental process spanning a number of years. In the late summer of 1924, the playwright compiled notes and a rudimentary outline for a script with the working title *A Jazz Tragedy.*[36] Set in New York, this script in nascent form centers on socialite and businessman Harry U. Collins. Suggesting a sprawling, contrived, and forced dramatic structure akin to the vaudeville-like *Processional*, and including once again the use of jazz to make a satiric comment on the absurdity of modern American society (specifically class relations, the puritanical hegemony, and yellow journalism), the outline and notes for *A Jazz Tragedy* also entail character descriptions that echo the Dada-inspired grotesque stereotypes of that earlier script. Additionally, there is a sense in these notes that Lawson is trying desperately to move beyond the soul-searching metaphysical labyrinth he had constructed in *Nirvana* (then *A New England Fantasy*) earlier that year and instead embrace and chart through his art his emerging notion of "The New Showmanship." By December 1924, *A Jazz Tragedy* had evolved into *X Plus Y*, an even more absurd and satiric comment on the modern American scene, which situates his Dada-inspired grotesques—described by the playwright as "stiff with nervous rapidity, as if they were marionettes very tense and uncomfortable on their jangling strings"—within a farcical well-made play structure.[37] In the summer of 1925, *X Plus Y* became *The Invisible Mob*, wherein Collins, no longer just a businessman, is running for the governorship of New York and is described as "a machine."[38] This character description, as well as the call for a set using "platforms," "stairs," and "slides," suggests that Lawson had a growing familiarity with the constructivist movement and, specifically, the work of Meyerhold.[39]

As does *The Invisible Mob*, *Loud Speaker*, completed in the spring of 1927, tells the story of Harry U. Collins's run for governor of New York. Act 1 opens on the night before the election. Through a series of contradictory speeches and meetings, it becomes clear Collins has no platform and is willing to do anything to win the election, including buying votes. He speaks first to a group of "Hebrews" and then "The Irish," praising the diversity that has made America great and promising economic prosperity and continued respect for their respective traditions.[40] He then immediately turns to address a gathering of white Anglo-Saxon Protestants (represented by the "audience actually in the theatre") and refutes his earlier claims:

> COLLINS. Ladies and Gentlemen . . . a plain business man, running for governor on a business man ticket, one hundred per cent for law and order and Americanism . . . Law and order, and a return to decency: Could I promise more? No . . . not to you real Americans. And let me tell you, if any of these so-called racial groups think they can get away with anything by pointing to their alleged foreign tradition, you'll see how an American stands . . . (18)

Following his speeches, Collins steadies himself with liquor from a flask and then "confers" with his "committee": "two dummies with wax business faces," where his self-serving attitude is furthered revealed in a stream-of-conscious monologue:

> COLLINS. [. . .] Confidentially I wish I'd never gone into this political game; why should a man who's cleaned up a few million dollars want to be Governor as well? Yet I don't mind telling you boys it's the dream of my life . . . and I'll make it good too; I always get what I want. [. . .] Tomorrow I'll be elected, go up to Albany and be called His Excellency. [. . .] I guess I understand the public; all a matter of advertising technique, bunk of course, but give a slogan, repeat it enough and you're safe; a man with a genius for slogans can rule the world today, provided he's got the machines to spread 'em, newspapers and radio. (19–21)

In the balance of the first act, it is revealed that Collins's run for the governorship is threatened by various dilemmas and secrets that if exposed could destroy his "Law and order, and a return to decency" campaign. His home life, apparently a paragon of virtue, righteousness, and decency, is in reality dangerously dysfunctional. In addition to Collins's incessant and clandestine drinking, it is revealed that Emma Collins, his wife, wants "something that money can't buy" (34), has betrayed the traditions of the Methodist church, and has succumbed the hypnotic charms of the unidentified "A Stranger with a Beard," a mystical figure who cryptically foretells the advent of a new religion, speaks only Armenian, and has shown Emma what is only referred to as "the spark in the dark" (30). Clare, the Collins' charismatic flapper daughter, drinks bathtub gin throughout the day, frankly discusses the implications of Freud and free love, threatens to have an illegitimate child, and dances to jazz with Josephus, the Collins' African American butler. The intrusion of Johnnie, a young, optimistic, health-conscious, socialist reporter who writes for a tabloid and suspects that Collins is guilty of "corruption, lust, and indecency," is met with contempt. He is thrown unceremoniously out of the house when he asks who paid for the gaudy, electric sign hanging in Central Park that reads "Harry U. Collins is a good man" (50). Collins himself is haunted by images of Floradora, the winner of an Atlantic City bathing suit contest, with whom he had an affair.

The first act closes in standard farce style, with eavesdropping, miscommunication, multiple entrances and exits, and slamming doors. Johnnie breaks into the darkened house in search of documents to prove Collins's true motives and is discovered by Josephus. Josephus, wanting to arrest the interloper, asks him to wait while he goes for help. Johnnie retreats to a closet. Thinking the room vacant, Emma enters with the Stranger with a Beard. In the dark she speaks of her spiritual awakening in a language laden with sexual innuendo and professes her desire to find a "Love that quite engulfs the universe." Collins enters, overhears and misconstrues his wife's statement, "Love is all, all is love," and turns on the lights (68). As the Stranger with a Beard flees, Collins accuses his wife of indiscretion and threatens to divorce her. Emma, exasperated, retreats to her bedroom. Johnnie, who has overheard everything, phones his editor to report the scandalous happenings. He is interrupted by Josephus, who arrives with "the combined political clubs of Harlem, [. . .] six negro politicians of exaggerated type [. . .] with wax faces, each carrying an enormous floral wreath in the shape of horseshoes, stars, etc., each piece with the words, 'Harry U. Collins is a good man'" (75). As the curtain falls, the strains of a newsboy's voice are heard offstage, "Collins' divorce . . . sensational divorce . . . all about the Collins' divorce," and the "six politicians break into a wild jazz rhythm, laughing as they dance" (76).

In the second act, each move Collins makes to rectify his precarious position seems to bring him closer to destruction. The infamous Dorothy Dunne, a seemingly sympathetic journalist with a "motherly pathos" (and Johnnie's mother) tries to unearth Emma's side of the story through trickery and passive-aggressive mediation (86). Johnnie and Clare are hypnotized by the Stranger with a Beard, are locked in a closet, and strike up a romance. Meanwhile, Peterson, Collins's chief advisor, schemes to smooth over the stories of unfaithfulness and corruption and "lick the tabloids yet" (133), and Collins begs Emma "to put up a united front" (116). Further complications arise when Collins's personal papers, including his autobiography that describes "the true story of my life, my rise to power," are stolen from his safe, and Floradora arrives announcing to all her affair with Collins (122). The act closes as reporters besiege the Collins' home. In the mounting chaos, a photographer snaps a photo of the Stranger with a Beard kissing the hand of Emma. Befuddled by all that has happened, Collins makes a speech over the radio and inadvertently tells the truth:

> COLLINS. I greet this great invisible audience . . . to justify myself as a man whose sole interest is the public; the tongue of slander is afoot, the tabloids are cracking, and rightly . . . rightly that is, because they are trying to take you in, make fools of the great American public, and they can do it too. . . . Why? Because the newspapers are blah . . . the Government is blah, you folks are fed on pap that wouldn't deceive an infant in diapers—I'm here to give it to you straight, are you listening, you gang out there? . . . to hear me slobber about honesty and good government! Suppose they tell you I'm a man of sinful life. . . . Well, most of you are. . . . So am I! (*He realizes that his speech is going utterly astray, sways uncertainly, then pulls himself to his full height and lets himself go.*) I'm a man standing here now with the truth coming out of my mouth instead of drool, but for the first time in my life I'm a man! I've done a lot of crooked things and I've enjoyed them, I'm too good to be governor, I get more satisfaction out of telling the American public to go to hell . . . (139)

The final act opens with the discovery that Collins has disappeared and is feared dead. His secret papers revealing all, as well as the incriminating photo of Emma and the Stranger with a Beard, have been published. Regardless, it appears that Collins will win the election, and the citizens of New York will accept enthusiastically their "tabloid governor" (146). As Emma and Clare read the newspapers, which have published Collins's autobiography that includes the admission, "Everyone, including my wife and daughter, are stepping stones to be tread on" (144), Emma muses, "[O]f course they'll elect him—that's American sentiment—vote for a dead man every time" (143). Floradora arrives abruptly and claims that Collins is alive, has gone to election headquarters to resign, and will be taking her to the South Seas. Her dreams of romance are frustrated, however, when Collins returns and announces that he will accept the results of the election and that his promise to take his mistress away was a foolish and alcohol-induced fantasy. As Floradora exits crying, the Stranger with a Beard enters. Emma convinces Collins to accept the mystical man's council, claiming, "He can save us Harry, he can even make you a good governor, he can lead us all into a sunlit future with starry eyes" (174). Despite Johnnie's protestations that "He just wants to get money out of you," Collins agrees to accept the stranger's advice (176). A Stranger with a Beard casts a hypnotic spell and "the kaleidoscope of the future" floods the stages, illuminating the impending corruption of the Collins administration (177). Visions of the future governor in league with big business melt into others that show him paying hush money to Floradora. The dream sequence ends with Collins walking out on a high platform to address a group of people, his arms spread wide. He complains of his failing eyesight and says, "I don't see anything but a multitude of stars" (181). With that, he falls with a crash into the crowd.

The scene suddenly shifts to Johnnie and Clare, who are married and on their honeymoon. "[A]gainst a blue drop, a love boat floats on a Chinese river" and a voice sings "Dreamy moon . . . Creamy moon" as the youngsters talk of life and their future.

JOHNNIE. There's no tragedy to it, except there's no sense in it. Anything's possible nowadays; look at the theatre, jumps around till you're dizzy—if you want to be in China, there you are!

CLARE. (*With a sigh.*) Here we are.

JOHNNIE. What a honeymoon! Just you and I in a love boat, on the most beautiful of China's sacred rivers.

CLARE. (*Yawns.*) Coney Island is better.

JOHNNIE. You said it . . . lying on a smelly river, listening to bad music, I think these cushions are wet—and where the devil is that Chinese moon?

CLARE. Honeymoon! Dear old moon!

(*The moon very large, yellow and artificial, rises behind them, with romantic tootling of Chinese horns.*)

JOHNNIE. I don't think so much of that. Clare, love is a failure.

CLARE. I knew that before I married you.

JOHNNIE. Then why?

CLARE. I thought it over and decided you were a terrible fool but I could probably make a millionaire of you.

JOHNNIE. Money, so that's it? I'll make some money when we get back to New York.

CLARE. The newspapers are still coming out every hour.

JOHNNIE. It's a crazy town, but it rules the earth—I'm going into politics and clean up a million.

CLARE. And be just like father—

JOHNNIE. And you'll be like your mother. (182–84)

Thus, as the curtain falls, it is clear Johnnie and Clare will return to New York and begin the cycle again.

In writing *Loud Speaker*, Lawson once again borrowed heavily from the various avant-garde forms of expression he had been experimenting with throughout the decade—expressionism, Dada, surrealism—as well as one that was for him wholly new, constructivism. He combined these with elements drawn from farce and burlesque and imbued this hybrid form with subject matter resembling a tabloid journalistic view of big business and American politics. The text that emerged disregards all conventional expectations inherent to the myriad popular and high art forms on which it draws and, instead, seeks to simultaneously raze and radically remake the practice of theatre such as it existed in the United States in the late 1920s. In some respects, Lawson succeeded in this endeavor to chart a new course for the theatre in that *Loud Speaker* seems an apposite attempt to move the theory of the New Showmanship into script form and then onto the stage of the theatre. More often than not, however, the script falters under the weight of the playwright's increasingly cynical view of life in the United States.

In his autobiography, Lawson suggested that in a quest "to escape" the confused "soul-searching" that is central to *Nirvana*, he "had gone too far in the other direction" and adopted a highly fatalistic and hostile tone that rests at the center of *Loud Speaker*.[41] This assessment is borne out in an analysis of the text. In place of the surreal, languishing, tragic, and morally bankrupt characters who struggle with metaphysical problems in *Nirvana*, in *Loud Speaker* there are stereotypical character types, stripped entirely of anything approximating individualism, who voice humorous and pious admonitions as well as utterly distasteful views of the world: for example, Collins's

"Just tell me what you want, and I'll write you out a check" (30) and "If X is money and Y is bunk, the answer to X plus Y is the great American public" (32). Still, in *Loud Speaker* Lawson's humorous warnings to the world—significantly beginning with the use of a banal quotation by Calvin Coolidge as an epigraph to the published text, "Look well to the hearthstone, therein all hope for America lies" (v)—as well as the outrageous and chaotic happenings in a millionaire and would-be governor's household, are all too obvious and simplistic affronts on life in the United States that, in the end, offer little hope or guidance.

Unlike their counterparts in *Processional*, the stereotypes in *Loud Speaker* never emerge from the limiting confines of their assigned types. They are, instead, doomed to exist within their narrowly drawn, one-dimensional lives, unable to enjoy triumph, suffer defeat, or even experience true emotion. They are beings without souls, doomed to a life of servitude and unable to challenge, or even recognize, the hostile environment and exploitative conditions they are forced to suffer. Only Collins shows signs of advancing beyond his type and achieving cognizance. During his campaign speech at the end of act 2, he inadvertently tells the truth and speaks with a passion suggesting he has a soul and individual will. Still, unlike Dynamite Jim who explodes full-force into life from his stereotype, Collins is unaware of his growth, and by the time he returns in act 3, he has regressed to embody yet again his shallow type and willingly accepts the mystical teachings of a prophet speaking a language he does not understand.

At the end of *Loud Speaker*, contented (or perhaps condemned) to play the puppet for big business, Collins loses his sight and becomes the embodiment of the idiomatic expression "the blind leading the blind." This loss of sight, which brings with it no apparent benefit for Collins, his family, or the people he was elected to serve, is a shockingly pessimistic symbol when juxtaposed against the similar event in *Processional*. In that earlier script, Dynamite Jim's blinding while hanging on a fence is situated as an event that cements the triumph of his individual will, leads to the emergence of his second sight, and thus positions him as one who is able to guide those around him toward salvation. There is no such hope for salvation in *Loud Speaker*. Johnnie and Clare, who in the early part of the script contest the hegemony represented by Collins, Emma, and Dorothy Dunne, are by the end devoured by that force. The youths of the world are destined to repeat the mistakes of their elders.

Pessimism is likewise apparent in the "kaleidoscope of the future" scene. When contrasted against the dream sequence at the end of *Roger Bloomer*—an assemblage of sights, sounds, and actions that suggests profound optimism and hope in the future—the visions of deepening and deadening corruption and deceit in "the kaleidoscope of the future" at the end of *Loud Speaker* suggest increasing cynicism and despair. In *Roger Bloomer*, the young man's triumph over the violent and ugly shadows, the promise of a new world shimmering just beyond the "lighted doorway," and the inspiring call to listen to "the tread of marching people singing a new song" are visual and verbal traces connecting that text, and by extension Lawson, to the value systems of the cultural left such as they were constituted in the early 1920s. Conversely, the visions flooding the stage at the end of *Loud Speaker* are symbols of Lawson's view that the promise of progressive democracy and of the emancipatory ethos of the lyrical left had led not to a triumph over the violent and ugly shadows but to moral and creative failure.

Moreover, it may be argued that Lawson's attempt to critique through laughter led him to confuse satire with flippancy.[42] In the wake of this flippancy comes a script full of characters that evoke laughter but thwart sympathy. The critical reception of the New Playwrights' March 1927 production of the script illustrates this response.[43] The left-wing press, the only critics the New Playwrights had any respect for, were unified in their ridicule. Representative is Bernard Smith's essay "Machines and Mobs" in *New Masses* in which he praised "Mr. Lawson's attempt to write a farce of modern metropolitan life for a constructivist stage" but found that, on the whole, "it lack[ed] the very harmony and composition that is essential to any art."[44]

A few of the critics writing for the mainstream press saw promise in Lawson's new method. Surprisingly supportive, the typically conservative Percy Hammond claimed that the playwright had fired off a "naughty blunderbuss at the follies of our time, including the tabloids, love among debutantes, married life, politics, the radio and occult religions."[45] Most critics writing for the doctrinal press, however, did not care for the play. Burton Davis found that he was "laughing at" not "laughing with Mr. Lawson."[46] George Winchell described the play as "self-conscious sophistication, and so childish it will either drive you plumb cuckoo wondering where all the gall comes from to present such attractions, or you'll grow long hair."[47] Brooks Atkinson, while admitting that it was "sometimes amusing by the sheer excess of its farcical spirits," found the play on the whole lacked "distinction."[48] Not surprisingly, George Jean Nathan was unreservedly hostile, opening his acidic review by claiming that the play was "written by [a man] who can't write drama" and concluding with assertion that "*Loud Speaker* is just plain, ordinary, obvious hooie that brazenly tries to palm itself off as something important."[49]

Lawson later remarked that he wrote *Loud Speaker* as "a model" of the aesthetic-centered New Showmanship: an "American type of show," employing "jazz, [. . .] sentiment and buffoonery" and abandoning "realism" for "theatricalism." In other words, the play can be seen as another in a long line of attempts by Lawson to indict the corruption and shallowness of American bourgeois society via nonrealistic methods, all the while never offering a specific solution. Even so, while the final product clearly documents further movement of Lawson's thought from an optimistic to a highly pessimistic worldview, it had only echoes of the passion that surfaced in *Roger Bloomer*, *Processional*, and even *Nirvana*. Perhaps the playwright's own words offered the best evaluation of the play: "In trying to come closer to the American world that I knew, the New York world of sex and money, I had been content to show only the surface, and even the surface impression was too negative and mannered to provide any real insight."[50] That sense of negativity would become even more pronounced in *The International*.

The International

The idea for Lawson's next script, *The International*, was derived directly from newspaper headlines in the spring and summer of 1927. In the first days of March of that year, troops from the Chinese National Revolutionary Army, the military arm of the moderate Kuomintang (KMT or Chinese Nationalist Party), followed the command of military leader Chiang Kai-shek and entered the warlord-controlled city of Nanjing.[51] Rioters supporting the KMT takeover attacked foreign missions and consulates, ransacked foreign-owned buildings and dwellings, and robbed and killed several resident aliens. The United States Navy, an ever-present foreign military force in China during the 1920s and 1930s, attempted to quell the rioting and protect the resident alien population and their investments by firing shells into the city from their gunboats posted on the Yangtze River. On 5 March, roughly 1,000 U.S. Marines landed in China on orders to "protect American property." Chiang was incensed over the rioting. Clearly seeking to quell the raising ire of foreign powers, the commander promised safety for alien residents and their concessions.

Meanwhile two hundred miles east of Nanjing in the city of Shanghai, various labor unions operating under the direction of the Chinese Communist Party (CCP), a body that was an ally to the KMT, rose up in support of the advancing National Revolutionary Army, disarming the police and dispelling that city's warlord troops. On 12 March, KMT troops began to enter the city. European and U.S. naval forces, fearing a recurrence of the violence in Nanjing, poised warships on the banks of the Yangtze near Shanghai and readied themselves for action. At the same time, foreign businesses leaders in Shanghai, concerned with what the rise of the Communists would mean for their capitalist ventures and investments, obtained the services of an international expeditionary force that included military troops from the United States, England, France, and Japan. Despite such apprehensions, the advance of the National Revolutionary Army into Shanghai was completed without a single resident alien harmed or killed.

Over the course of the next week, the relieved foreigners living in Shanghai, as well as the city's resident propertied classes, relaxed and began congratulating and praising Chiang for the control that he held over his forces. Believing Chiang was the best alternative to Communist upheaval and confiscations, these foreign business leaders and propertied Chinese citizens began to negotiate with the KMT, promising Chiang money and loyalty in exchange for security. The CCP and the Shanghai General Labor Union—in no small way troubled by the developing agreements between Chiang and Chinese and foreign capitalists—called a general strike on 21 March, an action involving some 600,000 workers. Three days later, members of the Chinese Communist Party seized Nanjing and announced a break with Chiang, claiming the commander's recent actions constituted an ideological shift to the right. A few weeks of tense calm followed before Chiang responded to these events.

On 12 April, members of the Green Gang, Shanghai's most notorious mobsters, attacked the offices of all the major unions in that city, aided by the National Revolutionary Army on orders from Chiang. Numerous workers were murdered in these attacks. The next day, protests in various cities, including Shanghai, Nanjing, and Canton, led to many brutal killings in the streets. In more than one instance, it was reported that Chiang's troops machine-gunned peaceful demonstrators. On 18 April, Chiang, who ironically had received military training in the Soviet Union, formally led the rightist members of the KMT in a revolt against the left-wing faction of the party (a division that was comprised almost entirely by members of the Comintern-controlled CCP). The CCP responded the next day by declaring war on Chiang. These were merely the first volleys in what would prove to be a lengthy and bloody civil war between the Nationalist forces led by Chiang and the Communist forces led by Mao Tse-Tung.[52]

Lawson, provoked and impassioned by the events in Asia, worked quickly through the early part of the summer. By the end of July he had completed the first two acts of what would become *The Interna-*

tional. Although his worldview was already pessimistic, the executions of Sacco and Vanzetti in August only intensified that feeling in the playwright. Thus, upon returning to New York in September 1927, he was poised to write the third and fourth acts, in which war and revolution take over the world.[53]

The International opens with two American businessmen, Edward Elliott Spunk and Simeon Silas Fitch, talking of the possibility of war in front of a gigantic map of the world on which "special attention is given to the great oil centers":[54]

FITCH. Sometimes I wonder if money is any good. [. . .] To me money means responsibility.

SPUNK. To me it means power to do as I please.

FITCH. In all parts of the world vast interests are at stake.

SPUNK. My ethics about that are simple: make sure of our share and leave the rest of the problems to Washington.

FITCH. I am not impugning the wisdom of our government. Men of high integrity are sailing the ship of state, but it comes down to a question of finance. If England forces our hand in the East, if lawless elements make trouble in Mexico and South America, we might be embroiled.

SPUNK. I believe in peace as much as you do, but we can't stand still . . . spread . . . that's the big game.

FITCH. Exactly, it's international: in my youth, a railroad, a steamship line, a mine, they were independent entities; now the world is involved.

SPUNK. That's why we must spread, take the map for a garden, cultivate it—

FITCH. And war—

SPUNK. Then if war comes, our country will be impregnable at least.

FITCH. That's what they say in London, they say it in Berlin and Moscow. To be impregnable is a pretty dream, but I wonder where it leads?

SPUNK. Dollars, and more dollars. (17–20)

Into this scene enters Fitch's son, David, a recent college graduate who is full of radical notions and dreams. David rejects his father's offer to work with the company, claiming that his map of the world "is painted in blood" (28). Instead, he longs for one of two things: "to see the working-class, be it . . . or see the world" (30). When Fitch and Spunk's business partner T. Jerome Henley enters with news of an expedition to see the mysterious Grand Lama of Thibet concerning newly discovered oil fields, Fitch recognizes an opportunity for David to "see the world."

The play suddenly changes from the realist representation of Wall Street to a highly symbolic style, incorporating statement and choral response, which recalls the stasimon structure of Greek tragedy. A chorus of eight stenographers, notebooks in hand, enters dancing and offers a "prayer" to "the machine" (46). The scene ends and the play reverts to a realist, representational mode. David, now in Thibet, meets Karneski, a general in the Soviet army, who has been sent to Thibet to initiate a revolution for the Thibetan peasants who will then overthrow the feudal regime of the Grand Lama. Armed only with an antiquated cannon, Karneski is about to fire when David enters. Despite David's pleas to wait, the cannon inadvertently goes off and the revolution begins.

As the explosion reverberates, the scene suddenly shifts to an office in Moscow. Rubeloff, a cynical and heartless Soviet official, and Alise, a refugee from Fascist Italy who has dedicated her life to the freedom of the masses, discuss her next assignment and the Soviet-induced revolution in Thibet. Alise longs to go to America, "the country of the Ford and the skyscraper," to aid in the revolution there, but Rubeloff refuses and, instead, sends her to Thibet to deliver a message to Karneski.

In Thibet, Alise meets Karneski and David. Henley's attempts to buy off the Grand Lama have failed in the wake of the revolution. The first act ends with Alise, Karneski, David, Henley, and Tim, the "strapping American youth" who piloted David and Henley's plane, accused of aiding in the revolution against the Grand Lama and being bound by a dancing chorus of robed women and soldiers (97). From this point, the rest of *The International* is comprised of brief realistic scenes alternating with or augmented by choral odes that paint a picture of the revolution as it moves from Thibet, to China, to the Soviet Union, and finally to the western world.

Henley, who is tortured to the point of insanity, kills the Grand Lama. The rest of the captives escape in Tim's plane to China where they crash in the desert, are saved by the British Indian army (who are later massacred by the "hordes of Asia"), and witness the introduction of United States troops into the conflict. While Karneski, following the orders of Rubeloff, chooses to lead the Russian army as it helps to "defend China against the greedy world of militarism," David commits to the revolution and with Alise returns to New York (192).

In New York, David and Alise visit Fitch's office where they instill in the stenographers the revolutionary spirit. The chorus of women sing the blues, in which they equate sexual freedom with the revolutionary cause, and dance off to Madam Miau's brothel, leaving Fitch "utterly alone" (220). In the brothel, the prostitutes, led by Gussie who counts Spunk among her clients, join in the revolution. In the scene that follows, Gussie, the blues-singing servant-prostitute, intuitively responds to the revolutionary call by strangling her master, Spunk.

At the beginning of the final act, the war has consumed New York, left it in shambles, and workers have left their jobs. Still, it is clear that the revolution will fail because of the money and resources on the side of capitalism. Alise accuses David of being in love with her and not the revolutionary cause. In a flashback montage, she remembers the events that led to her commitment to revolution. Suddenly, she is a young girl working in the fields of Italy:

ALISE. The vines are rich on the hills, twining embracing the hills.

CHORUS. Peace on our hills, peace . . .

ALISE. What do you raise from the rich loam-land?

CHORUS. Dynasties out of earth, sons of the home-land!

ALISE. Grapes beneath our feet, rich from the vine, earth-smelling wine . . .

CHORUS. Blood of the vine, to strengthen our sons!

Into this serenity comes Aretini, representing Fascism. He symbolically takes the land from the people for the good of the state. Alise's calls for revolution are ignored, and the people commit to work for the state:

ALISE. (*Screaming.*) I alone then, stand against you!

ARETINI. You want the earth!

ALISE. The whole earth, new and young again!

ARETINI. Bah! Don't be absurd, you're a child.

ALISE. I was, you made me something else.

ARETINI. And you turn against me.

ALISE. (*To Chorus wildly.*) Help me: do you want your sons to be killed? Destroy him now!

CHORUS. Our feet are clay, rooted in the earth. . . . Dynasties out of the earth . . .

ARETINI. They shall make sons of steel, suckled on blood.

ALISE. I'll carry the flag then. (*From her breast she pulls out a red flag, ties it to the gun she carries.*) I too have a song!

ARETINI. You are alone.

ALISE. I sing a song, I carry a flag! (*Alise sings the "International" in Italian.*) (244–45)

With that, a Fascist soldier, at Aretini's command, stabs Alise through the palms with a bayonet and her dedication to the revolutionary cause is secure.

As the flashback ends, Fascist and Communist forces converge on stage. Led by Aretini and Rubeloff, two choruses stand on either side of the stage, exchange threats, and ignore the pleas for the people from Alise. In the end, Alise's cries for help are ignored, and the people's revolution fails. As the play closes, David, mortally wounded, plants a red flag. Comforted by Alise, he huddles next to an overturned taxi and dies. In the midst of this apocalypse, Tim steps out of the cab and asks drunkenly, "How do I get home? Christ, for love a' pity, where do I go home?" (276). Then a shot rings out, he falls dead, and the final curtain falls.

The International is an unremitting critique of the societal forces in both the East and the West that, in the opinion of many left-wing artists such as Lawson, were spinning dangerously out of control. Lawson's pessimistic view of the future and the innovative dramaturgy employed to convey it were similar to those used in Gaston Baty's production of Pierre MacOrlan's novel *La Cavaliere Elsa*, produced at the Studio des Champs-Elysées in Paris in 1927, and Piscator's *The Good Soldier Schweik,* produced at Piscator's Proletarian Theatre (the Volksbühnen) in 1928. To be sure, the production footnotes, written by Lawson and included in the published text, include descriptions of innovative (perhaps proto-epic) dramaturgical practices and procedures that are remarkably similar to those of other left-wing artists working in the West.

> *The International* is a musical throughout. It requires full musical score along modernistic lines with special emphasis on broken rhythms, machine noises and chanting blues. This necessitates singing voice for a number of the actors. The chanting is a weaving of jazz rhythms with orchestral backgrounds.
>
> The chorus, divided into two parts, eight women in each part, is a combination of jazz treatment with the dignified narrative strophe and antistrophe of Greek drama. Their dancing is also adapted from simple revue formations to suit the needs of swaying tragic movement inherent in the play.
>
> The method is new and requires new form of presentation. The drama is a formalized pattern or symphony. The music must have the same quality as the play itself.
>
> Woven with the original musical material use is made of "The International," "The Birth of the Blues" and other well-known tunes.

> Noise of battle and shooting indicated in Act III and IV is entirely formal and part of the musical structure.
>
> [. . .] All chorus movements, unless otherwise indicated are on the fore-stage and second level so that they function in an area generally separated from the movement of the other characters. [. . .] (7–8)

Clearly, as were Piscator in Germany and Baty in France, Lawson was deeply invested in the process of developing "new form[s] of presentation" that had at the core the rejection of naturalism and the embracing of symbol-rich visuals and sounds. However, unlike his international cohorts who overtly supported a doctrinal approach to leftist politics, in *The International* Lawson shows little partiality in his criticism, attacking forces on the political right, middle, and left. The aggressive American capitalists Spunk and Fitch, who speak of "spread[ing]" and "cultivat[ing]" the world, are neatly juxtaposed against the derisive Communist Rubeloff, who dreams of inciting world revolution, and the sadistic Fascist Aretini, who thrives on military conquest (19–20). Significantly, none are sympathetically drawn.

The people of the world in the play are mere pawns, caught in the middle of a deadly game played by these various governmental regimes willing to destroy anyone to insure victory. Even those working-class characters who arise and answer the revolutionary call—such as Gussie the prostitute, a character who may be taken as Lawson's symbol for the United States (that is, a blues-singing whore), and the chorus of stenographers, a group that idealistically connects their rebellion for sexual liberty with the triumph of the people's revolution—are situated as figures who lack the proper material and mental resources and are thus doomed to fail. This cynical outlook accords with the pessimistic view of the world's future that Lawson held at that time: the end of civilization is at hand and there is no hope.[55] This sense of doom is most obvious in his portrayal of two main characters, David and Alise.

While the character Tim clearly symbolizes the working class, a decidedly un-Marxist member of the proletariat who is destined to die at the hands of bourgeois-inspired imperialism and destruction, it is the middle-class David who offers the best indication of the playwright's thought at this time. Lawson later wrote, "I felt intuitively that a second world catastrophe was certain. The young middle-class intellectual who dies as bombs fall on New York is me. I saw no hope in revolution, only destruction and the death of millions."[56] This deep cynicism is forcefully epitomized in the scene between David and Karneski in act 1, when the young American's desperate appeals to the Soviet general to delay the firing of the cannon are ultimately for naught. As the cannon accidentally discharges, thus prompting the bloody revolution that will reverberate throughout the world, there is a prevailing tone of absurd and tragic inevitability. The coming revolution is presented not as a step toward a brighter tomorrow but as an accident that will have catastrophic consequences. Thus David's altruism and idealism, as expressed in his desire "to see the working-class, be it . . . or see the world," is doomed to fail despite his valiant and selfless efforts (30).

The character Alise also embodies this pessimism. While she seeks a cloudy eschatological socialist truth, in the end she is as powerless as Bill Weed in *Nirvana* who tragically decides his optimal option is to end his days in a space capsule, floating for all time above the earth. As is the artist-intellectual in that earlier text, the revolutionary Alise is doomed to be a lost wanderer in an unknown universe. Unlike Bill, however, the consequences for Alise are even more dire as there is not even the promise of a mystical cosmic order to guide her. There is, instead, only death and the faint and fleeting hope that the socialist cause she has dedicated her life to will someday be rectified and realized. Lawson seems to suggest, however, that if left to those such as Alise—a stagnant and one-dimensional figure akin to the soulless characters in *Loud Speaker*—the likelihood of the people's revolution occurring, let alone succeeding, is exceedingly remote. Alise's absolute devotion to the revolution, while impassioned, is also strangely detached from anything approximating human inspiration, creative imagination, and individual will. The actions she engages in have no rational purpose and her commitment to socialism is little more than a programmed response. Near the end of *The International*, as David is dying in her arms, Alise can only speak romanticized and abstract rhetoric: "I carry change like a serpent in my breast [. . .] We are alone here" (274). While these words have a mystical tone reminiscent of *Nirvana*, they also suggest a vast emptiness. Alise's slightly optimistic vision of the future, the only faint expression of hope in the whole script, is similarly intangible and expressive of romantic notions of the socialist cause:

> ALISE. We are pilgrims seeking a flag . . .
>
> DAVID. Plant a flag here . . . New York . . . a bee-hive . . . a pyramid of stone . . .
>
> ALISE. It will grow higher, we will be dead . . . (274–75)

Even this faint hope is cut short, however, by the proletariat Tim being shot dead in the street.

Thus, unlike *Roger Bloomer* and *Processional*, which emanate rays of hope in the wake of violence and greed, *The International* offers no hope. Instead, the destruction of New York City in the script is a literal fulfillment of what was only dreamed of in *Roger Bloomer*: "What doom will come to this place, what doom, oh, hungry city? Your thrones will fall and your buildings will crash together, Singer and Woolworth will go to dust. . . . Death will come in a whirlwind breaking your sky towers" (*Roger Bloomer*, 117).

As was becoming standard, the critical response to the New Playwrights' production of *The International* in January 1928 was anything but kind.[57] The critics writing for the mainstream press were, for the most part, merciless. Steven Rathburn, writing for the *Brooklyn Eagle*, claimed that "the dramatic bombshell of a world revolution was a dud."[58] In the *Evening World*, E. W. Osborn pondered the playwright's pessimistic view of the future: "Apparently Mr. Lawson finds the world on the brink of something or other, and means to set labor force as a means of stopping whatever is going on." He concluded by suggesting that the playwright "might have named this one 'Recessional.'"[59] In his review for the *New York Journal*, "Mr. Lawson Writes Another Ear-Splitting Upheaval," John Anderson described the play as a "crowded, inchoate, and exquisitely tiresome rookus" and charged Lawson with "confus[ing] the stage with the soapbox" and "intellectual vertigo."[60] Alexander Woollcott was the most acidic and blunt, referring to it in a short and curt review as "excruciatingly uninteresting."[61]

A few critics writing for the mainstream saw promise and progress amid the many problems. Surprisingly, Brooks Atkinson applauded Lawson's commitment to new forms of writing: "In both *Roger Bloomer* and *Processional* he essayed new forms, and in *The International* he bursts still another stage wall."[62] In a review published in the *American*, a critic identified only as C. H. praised the play as "Lawson's most ambitious attempt" and the New Playwrights' commitment to change: "Blessed with freedom, the New Playwrights' know no restraint, and that is a fault. But they are working with new forms, new ideas and are unafraid experimenters, and that is a virtue."[63] Gordon M. Leland, a long-time admirer of Lawson's work, referred to Lawson as "a writer of modern philosophy in expressionistic play form" and found "many noteworthy points in *The International*. [. . .] The author's satire and irony have sharpened among other things. Subtlety has improved the good taste of his work, tho he still rightly calls a spade a spade. The scene in the house of ill repute is a masterpiece of expression, and one of the best in the play. In other scenes, too, he turns occasionally from finding new mediums to using old mediums with increasing facility."[64] Thomas Van Dyke hypothesized that "Lawson, realizing that there may be but one end to his play, found the results bitter to swallow and was considerably muddled when forced to add a coda his mind could not accept," but he was nonetheless impressed with the playwright's attempt to rein in such an immense topic: "Just as *Processional* was a cross-section of this frenetic epoch in American civilization, *The International* used the same form but on a much larger canvas, giving a cross section of the entire world, with its focus ranging from Thibet to New York."[65]

Given the pessimistic view of the revolution and the unflattering portrayal of the Soviet Union, it is not surprising that most writing for the left-wing press found great fault in *The International.* Most notably, Sender Garlin of the *Daily Worker* commended Lawson for his "honest and courageous attempt to treat a subject which thus far has been strictly taboo in the American bourgeois theatre," but he denounced the playwright for his "intellectual confusion" and "romantic" notions of the revolution.[66] Dos Passos, who had provided the scene designs for the production, wrote a letter to Garlin, defending Lawson and the play: "[*The International* is a] very personal and subjective emotional outburst expressing one man's feelings under the impact of our world today. [It] is a broad cartoon of the dynamics of current history. It uses all the stock cartoon figures and ideas, warping them to its own purpose. Because it is the first time this has been done on the American stage everybody comes out flustered and starts cursing the play out for not being 'realistic' or a number of things that it never intended or wanted to be."[67] The next day, in a lengthy response, Garlin countered that while "the technique in *The International* [was] interesting and significant," he still found the play to be "based on misconceptions of the nature of the world revolution and of the key figures who dominate its operations."[68] A week later, Dos Passos fired back. He objected to Garlin's comments, not because they disputed the value of the play but because they seemed "to be written from the same angle as those in the capitalist press, the angle of contemporary Broadway 'realism.'"[69]

While the Garlin–Dos Passos debate raged, Joseph Freeman, editor of *New Masses*, visited Lawson. During a "long but friendly" visit, Freeman pointed out what he perceived to be the serious ideological errors in *The International* and Lawson's other plays. At the time, Lawson found it strange that Freeman, who was noted for his aesthetic sensibilities, made no reference to the artistic values in the plays. Lawson recalled the discussion: "We talked at cross purposes. I spoke of the need to break the mold of 'bourgeois' forms and sterile emotions, and Joe answered with an analysis of the world situation. I listened carefully, but even in *political* terms, I could not accept his formulations. I believed my vision of doom was nearer to reality than his faith in the triumph of 'the masses.'"[70] Ironically, in due course Freeman came to deny the lessons he sought to teach Lawson, and Lawson came to accept them and teach them to others.[71] For the time being, however, Lawson was unable to embrace the idea of a working-class revolution, and his commitment to artistic rebellion and zealous individualism remained his guiding concerns.

Even so, by the early summer of 1928 the singular and unwavering commitment to artistic rebellion that had governed Lawson in his metaphysical phase and his tenure with the New Playwrights was, on some level, being compromised. In May, as one of his final acts as a functioning member of the New Playwrights, Lawson wrote and edited the copy for a pledge pamphlet sent to all season ticket holders. The message on the pamphlet demonstrates the playwright's deepening internal conflict. At the top of the first page of that text, under the heading "The New Playwrights' Theatre," are two phrases presented as credos: "experiment in playwriting and play production" and "pledged to be a stronghold of liberal and radical opinion." Beneath these two phrases, Lawson inscribed by hand, "We must keep up this double work of innovation and ideas."[72] It seems, then, that when Lawson departed for Hollywood later that summer he took with him a twofold ideal, to be both an artist-rebel and a political revolutionary. While he did not yet have a clear understanding of how to reconcile these two goals, he was consumed by "a thirst to find my place in the world—the part of the world in which I intended, whether I consciously knew it or not at the time, to live my life."[73]

En Route for the Dialectic Decade

In his essay "Towards Dialectical Criticism," Marxist literary critic and cultural theorist Fredric Jameson offers a compelling summation of the development, application, and implications of what he terms "dialectical thought."[74] According to Jameson, "dialectical thought" differs in principle from the more naïve "nonreflexive thinking mind" because of the method and manner of perception each system applies when confronting problems or dilemmas. Whereas the individual engaged in a nonreflexive mode of thinking aims to resolve such problems or dilemmas through application of commonsensical, conservative, and habitual means that merely reinforce the presuppositions and cosmology of an essentialist reality, the individual engaged in a dialectical mode of thinking seeks to both engage and transcend the "operative procedures of the nonreflexive thinking mind." This individual does so by adopting the practice of "converting those problems into their own solutions at a higher level, and making the fact and existence of the problem itself the starting point for new research." In turn, the notion of the "real" in relation to philosophy, art, politics, and science is, through the application of dialectical thinking, exposed not as natural or innate but is instead the material consequence of habitual and deeply entrenched suppositions and belief systems. Such suppositions and belief systems—these "rules of some private hobby"—are made "real" through the force of normalizing repetition. Jameson argues,

> [T]he most sensitive moment in the dialectical process [occurs when] the entire complex of thought is hoisted through a kind of inner leverage one floor higher, in which the mind, in a kind of shifting of gears, now finds itself willing to take what had been a question for an answer, standing outside the previous exertions in such a way that it reckons itself into the problem, understanding the dilemma not as a resistance of the object alone, but also as the result of a subject-pole deployed and disposed against it in a strategic fashion—in short, as the function of a determinate subject-object relationship.

Significantly, such shifts away from the processes of "everyday mental atmosphere" do not come easily or without consequence. When the operative procedures of the "everyday mode of thought" give way to "overelaborate and oversubtle" dialectical thinking, the individual must be prepared to answer charges from some that this newly adopted mode of mental operations engages in "perversely hairsplitting" abstraction. Moreover, this "brutal rupture [. . .] this cutting of knots" brings with it a sense of "breathlessness" in one's metal operations. Jameson describes this mental state in evocative terms: "[There is] something of a sickening shudder we feel in an elevator's fall or in the sudden dip of an airliner. That recalls us to our bodies much as it recalls us to our mental positions as thinkers and observers. The shock indeed is basic, and constitutive of the dialectic as such: without this transformational moment, without this initial conscious transcendence of an older, more naïve position, there can be no question of any genuinely dialectical coming to consciousness."[75]

Applying Jameson's model of "dialectical coming to consciousness" as something of an archetypal pattern for that process, one may suggest that the changes in tone and intent in the texts examined in this chapter—both those composed by as well as many of those aimed at Lawson—include traces of a "brutal rupture," one that resonated on both personal and cultural levels. When examined as discursive objects, these various literary and cultural texts reveal the presence of a historically specific social energy that implicated and ultimately altered the ideals, practices, and products of liberal intellectuals and culture makers such as Lawson as well as the conterminous American left in the latter years of the 1920s. That is to say, the "shock" of the shift for those on the cultural left, from what Jameson terms "normal object-oriented activity of the mind" toward "dialectical self-consciousness," is encoded in the content and form of the aforementioned texts. As such, Lawson's incipient personal struggle (or his "problem" or "dilemma"), to reimagine his aesthetics and politics and reconceive their connection, was a moment of "breathlessness" wherein his "entire complex of thought [was] hoisted through a kind of inner leverage one floor higher." This moment of breathlessness may be viewed as both product and producer of a larger ideological conflict in the social and cultural spheres in this historical moment.

On the level of biography, this shift is apparent in contrasting the shape and scope of theatrical expression forwarded and practiced by Lawson in "Debunking the Art Theatre," "The New Showmanship," and *Loud Speaker* against the decidedly different view promoted and practiced in "What Is a Workers Theatre?," *The International*, and the pledge pamphlet from the summer of 1928. For Lawson, this "brutal rupture [. . .] this cutting of knots" with the procedures of nonreflexive thought, and subsequent embracing of dialectical thought, may be linked to his transformational moment or "midnight in Boston." Here, the playwright first transcended the "older, more naïve position" of "The New Showmanship" and instead began to seek and to come to terms with the more politically assertive requisites and revolutionary ideals of "a Workers Theatre." Moreover—and at the risk of being accused of "perversely hairsplitting" Lawson's position and condition in this historical moment—it seems plausible to propose that the abject experience of "midnight in Boston" had a twofold effect. In part, the experience in Boston prompted the move *away from* the declarative, sedentary, essentialist, and absolutist construct and tone that underpins the title and, indeed, whole of "The New Showmanship"—that is, "the theatre of the future [. . .] *is, here and now, an actuality.*" Simultaneously, however, it also prefigured the move *toward* the more inquisitive, dialectical, materialist, and forward-looking construct and tone at play in "*What* is a Workers Theatre?"—"we are out *to find and coordinate.*"[76]

Thus, in the wake of the executions of Sacco and Vanzetti, there began for the playwright a process of distancing from the commonsensical mode of thought as well as a concurrent advancing toward dialectical thought, as was manifest in Lawson's stated desires to "find my place in the world"[77] and more overtly connect his "art" to "social problems."[78] Likewise, Lawson's efforts to supplant the declarative tone and object-oriented activity of his earlier plays for an inquisitive tone and dialectical impulse—a shift referenced in the very titles of the aforementioned manifestos of 1927—seemed only to further complicate his already strained connection to the ideals and practices of the aesthetic-centered, and tacitly progressive democratic, art theatre of Cheney et al. The playwright's bid with "The New Showmanship"—to return to the "honorable principles [. . .] of telling a story" that is both "pictorial and dynamic"—was concomitantly revealed a "simplification [. . .] draw[ing] its forces from a host of buried [bourgeois] presuppositions."[79] The texts Lawson authored for and about the theatre in the year following his "midnight in Boston" may be read as both self-reflexive attempts on the part of the playwright to move beyond the conditions of "normal everyday mental atmosphere" as well as circulating discursive objects linked to the "political sea change" as charted by Denning, which sought to reconstitute the American left along the lines of revolutionary ideology and forge modes of artistic expression that would convey the deadening experience and exploitative nature of the capitalist system and bourgeois culture. Indeed, Lawson was just one among many on the left who were "attempt[ing] to reconstruct modernism, to tie [. . .] formal experimentation to a new social and historical vision, to invent a 'social modernism.'"[80]

Nonetheless, as is made clear in the debate between Dos Passos and Garlin following the production of *The International*, as well as the playwright's meeting with Freeman wherein the noted champion of American left pointed out the playwright's ideological errors (most notably, Lawson's pessimistic vision of the coming revolution), none of the dramatic or theoretical texts Lawson composed during his time with the New Playwrights, or for that matter before, were sufficiently in line with the precepts of those who had more fully and emphatically embraced the revolutionary, dialectical view of the world. The playwright's own call for a "Debunking [of] the Art Theatre," ironically an agenda that was more forcefully and convincingly argued in the essay "What Is a Workers' Theatre?," may be viewed as a continuance of the endeavor on the part of Lawson to distance himself from the noncommercial theatre community of the Theatre Guild variety. For its part, the once supportive community of liberal critics who had just a few years prior believed Lawson to be one of the most "promising" avant-garde playwrights in New York was now perplexed and in some cases irritated. This community of critics penned responses and evaluations of Lawson's latest dramatic texts and those texts in production that at best voiced their confusion and at worst, hostility and suspicion respecting the playwright's choices. The charges this community of liberal critics levied at Lawson, of mistaking the stage for a soapbox, as well as critiques from the left-wing press regarding the absence of anything approximating a hard-line Marxist stance in the playwright's texts, left the playwright in a precarious and untenable position.

By mid-1928, Lawson found himself between and thus vulnerable to and, in many respects, at the mercy of the critical conceits of two powerful groups within the larger noncommercial theatre community, each forging and championing oppositional systems of value founded on competing ideologies. Lawson was, in short, neither fish nor fowl, neither "artist-rebel" nor "revolutionary," or, to call upon Jameson's model once again, betwixt and between the two positions (or "floors") suitable for any playwright seeking to work in the larger noncommercial theatre community in the United States. No longer satisfied with results born from "the operative procedures of the non-reflexive thinking mind," which had led to a series of form-dominated responses to the particular problems in question (that is, capitalism and bourgeois culture), Lawson would spend the final years of the 1920s and the first years of the 1930s struggling along "the thorny path to commitment," grappling with these problems and honing the mental and artistic abilities needed to "[convert] those problems into their own solutions at a higher level."[81]

Lawson as a child, ca. 1904. Courtesy of Jeffrey Lawson.

Lawson, ca. 1925. Courtesy of Jeffrey Lawson.

Roger rescued by the Ragged Man in act 2 of the Marguerite Barker production of *Roger Bloomer*. Special Collections Research Center, Morris Library, Southern Illinois University Carbondale.

Louise rejecting Mr. Rumsey's marriage proposal in act 3 of the Marguerite Barker production of *Roger Bloomer*. Special Collections Research Center, Morris Library, Southern Illinois University Carbondale.

Roger going toward the lighted doorway in act 3 of *Roger Bloomer*. Illustration by Roland Young.

"Jazzin' up the big strike!" in act 1 of the Theatre Guild production of *Processional*. Setting by Mordecai Gorelik.
Photograph by Francis Bruguière.

Jim forcing Sadie into the mine in act 3, scene 2 of the Theatre Guild production of *Processional.* Setting by Mordecai Gorelik.

Photograph by Francis Bruguière.

Dynamite Jim hung on a fence in act 3, scene 3 of the Theatre Guild production of *Processional*. Setting by Mordecai Gorelik. Photograph by Francis Bruguière.

The chorus girls from the Richard Aldrich and Alfred de Liagre production of *The Pure in Heart*. Special Collections Research Center, Morris Library, Southern Illinois University Carbondale.

Annabel sitting in the tenement awaiting her fate in act 2, scene 3 of the Richard Aldrich and Alfred de Liagre production of *The Pure in Heart*. Special Collections Research Center, Morris Library, Southern Illinois University Carbondale.

A Stranger with a Beard casting his spell in act 3 of the New Playwrights' production of *Loud Speaker*. Setting by Mordecai Gorelik.

The interior of the abandoned factory from the Theatre Union production of *Marching Song*. Setting by Howard Bay.

4

The Thorny Path to Commitment

Bury the past, put it in the ground and throw dirt on it—
—John Howard Lawson, *Success Story*, 1932

In his book *Days of the Phoenix: The Nineteen Twenties I Remember* (1957), literary critic and defender of the lyrical left, as well as that movement's various progeny, Van Wyck Brooks recalled, "Over the gate of the thirties one seemed to see the words, 'Abandon hope, all ye who enter here.'"[1] Lawson would later remark that in many respects, Brooks's recollection of the deep-seeded cynicism troubling many former artist-rebels accurately encapsulated his "own mood" at the dawn of the 1930s. By situating Dante's frequently used description of the woeful warning suspended over the gates of hell as conterminous to the doubt and despair haunting the cultural left at the beginning of the new decade, the playwright believed Brooks had offered a keen and apt summation of the state of a once vibrant community. Lawson also believed, however, that missing from Brooks's recollection of the early 1930s was a recognition that this "anguish [. . .] impelled" many on the left in the years that followed toward "a new consciousness."[2] Despite their disagreement on the capacity of this mood to bring about change and prompt a renewed awareness of social conditions, Brooks and Lawson agreed that the youthful and exuberant energy, unbridled irreverence, and escalating optimism that had created and sustained the avant-garde community and the experimental mode in the United States, from its inception in the years immediately preceding World War I through the early and mid-twenties, was, by 1930, a fading memory. For many on the left, the virtues and sanguine ideals of the forward-looking, groundbreaking movement had slowly been superseded, replaced by bitterness, pessimism, and a cavalier attitude often predicated on the fatalistic question, "what does it matter, anyway?"

Lawson points to the "dissolution" of *The Little Review*, "one of the liveliest and most enduring publications of the avant-garde," in the spring of 1929 as a telling milestone in the history of the experimental arts community. For him, this event revealed the sickly state of the entire movement at that historical moment.[3] In her farewell editorial, coeditor Margaret Anderson wrote a stinging diatribe aimed at those "confused" artists:

> I began *The Little Review* because I wanted an intelligent life.
>
> By intelligent life I didn't—and don't—mean (1) the ability to follow an argument, (2) the capacity for documentation, (3) the gift of erudition, authority, strong physical vibrations, or any other primary signs by which people seem to get labeled intelligent at the moment when I am finding them particularly uninteresting.
>
> By interesting I meant = creative opinion. [. . .]
>
> The thing I wanted—would die without—was conversation. The only way to get it was to reach people with ideas. Only artists had ideas. . . . and of course only the very good ones. So, I made a magazine exclusively for very good artists of the time. Nothing more simple for me than to be the art arbiter of the world.
>
> I still feel the same way—with a rather important exception. As this number will show, even the artist doesn't know what he is talking about. And I can no longer go on publishing a magazine in which no one really knows what he is talking about. It doesn't interest me. [. . .]
>
> So, if anyone feels he should like to buy *The Little Review* and go on publishing all the first-rate creative expressions of these confusions, I am perfectly willing to sell it. And I will read it with interest—because of the confusions and because of the beauty of their expression.
>
> Only, don't let me hear any more about "it's the artist who transforms life." I know it. But I'm not particularly interested at the moment of transformation. I want a little illumination.
>
> Of course I won't start that other kind of review. I wouldn't really have the patience: everyone becomes too angry when expert opinion is brought to bear upon his pretences, his satisfaction in living the

human cliches. I would take years to get down to a little decent discussion of the world psyche.[4]

The tone of acidity and defeat in Anderson's prose may be linked to the answers she received to a questionnaire sent to those on the cultural left associated with the magazine. In the autumn of 1928, many in the United States avant-garde community were asked by the editors of *The Little Review* to respond to ten questions, including, "What do you look forward to?," "What do you fear most from the future?," "What is your world view?," "What is your attitude toward art today?," and "Why do you go on living?" Many of the answers printed in the final issue of *The Little Review* (prefaced with Anderson's editorial) reflect the dire psychological state of the American avant-garde movement at the end of the decade. Novelist Djuna Barnes wrote nothing more than "I am sorry, but the list of questions does not interest me to answer. Nor have I that respect for the public" (17). Prefacing her short, sharp, and sarcastic responses, Emma Goldman commented that the questions were "terribly uninteresting" (36). Responding to "What do you fear most from the future?," anarchist Alexander Berkman wrote, "That there ain't any" (19). To "What is your world view?," poet Richard Aldington simply replied, "Despair" (11).[5]

Lawson would later recall that the lack of hope in these responses "reflected the tensions of a disintegrating movement, which had reached a point at which the sanctity of the written and spoken word as a form of communication was called into question."[6] In light of this, it may be argued that the playful precepts of automatic writing, one of the favorite tools of the lyrical left that called for a heightened awareness of language via free association, had (d)evolved over the course of the twenties into the nihilistic notion that there is no meaning in language and, for that matter, life. The works from this period of two of Lawson's fellow artist-rebels, poets e. e. cummings and Hart Crane, are endowed with this nihilism and, thus, may be read as representative examples of the dramatically shifting discursive formations within the larger cultural field of the American left.

By the late 1920s, cummings had reconceived his mode of expression, replacing his unique wordplay imbued with sexuality, erotic desire, and subtle critique of puritanical morality with subtextual tones of violence, hopelessness, and death:[7]

          2 boston
Dolls;found
with

Holes in each other

’s lullaby and
other lulla wise by UnBroken
LULLAlullabyBY

the She-in-him with
the He-in-her(&

both all hopped
up)prettily
then which did
lie
Down, honestly

now who go(BANG(BANG[8]

Crane wrote in 1928: “The spiritual disintegration of our period becomes more painful to me every day, so that I now find myself balked by doubt at the validity of practically every metaphor I coin.”[9] Not long after writing this, Crane, wracked with self-doubt and despair, committed suicide.[10]

This overwhelming sense of hopelessness at the end of the twenties, which produced, shaped, and organized a social energy that irrevocably altered the verbal, aural, and visual practices of many American avant-garde artists such as cummings and Crane, was a deeply ironic development as it was created, in part, by the sudden failing of the very social and economic systems that had been a favorite target of many in the experimental arts community for more than a decade. For many years, countless members of the avant-garde, like an insurgent army, had haphazardly and, in many respects, playfully attacked the bourgeois and capitalist power structures and social order. Nonetheless, quite often the central intent of this community of self-proclaimed “radicals” was to challenge and overturn, via ironic playfulness, traditional ideals in art and literature rather than bourgeois sociopolitical structures as a whole. Throughout most of the 1920s, a considerable number in the larger community of experimental theatre artists and critics, continuing in the practice of the lyrical left, persisted in the view that art should be neither dogmatic nor didactic and that the modernist avant-garde vision and revolt was unconditionally, first and foremost, about aesthetics. Moreover, while many within this community held that capitalism and the bourgeois social and political system was evil and perverse to the core—as exemplified in the executions of Sacco and Vanzetti—they also viewed that hegemonic system as an all-powerful and unassailable entity that could only be destroyed by some extraordinary, incomprehensible, and highly unlikely disaster, not by aesthetics. When the plunging figures on the Wall Street stock exchange board exposed that the existing political, economic, and social system had an Achilles heel that no one had projected, these artist-rebels were thrown into a chaos they had metaphorically envisioned and championed but never considered would actually happen.[11] Hence, aesthetic visions of economic and social collapse—such as Roger Bloomer's vision of an economic apocalypse: "Singer and Woolworth will go to dust. . . . Death will come in a whirlwind breaking your sky towers" (117)—suddenly no longer seemed abstract poetizations or metaphors for the exploitative nature of the capitalist system but instead prophetic warnings that presaged the daily news headlines, circa October 1929.

Unfortunately, many experimental artists such as Lawson, who had for years lamented the social, political, and economic systems as "morally bankrupt" and even prophesied disaster, found themselves unable to provide any concrete responses to a very real crisis.[12] Prompted by the horrors of the first world war, these aesthetes within the larger so-called lost generation, who had for years created ideal illusions of a shimmering new world just beyond the "lighted doorway," found themselves unwilling and/or unable to respond when confronting a new and omnipresent reality engendered by the social and economic chaos of 1929. In the end, the requirements of dealing with the concrete hardships presented by the Depression broadened the already existing schism in the avant-garde community. There were some, such as cummings, Crane, and Brooks, who in their own ways chose to bemoan and deny the material world and the pressing crises in the social arena. There were others, however, who sought to understand reality as it had been shaped by the new social conditions, orient themselves to the specifics of left-wing revolutionary ideology, and commit to an agenda of rethinking and revising their aesthetic practices. Eventually, Lawson would choose to ally himself with the latter group.

Throughout the twenties, Lawson sought to secure a position of leadership in the rebellion against the main currents in American art. While he, like other artist-rebels of the period, held "that the rebellion in the arts [was] a harbinger of a revolution and release of the human spirit," his central concern was always the furtherance of nonrealistic, experimental forms of theatrical expression—to "break down the walls of the theatre."[13] Still, by the time he departed from the faltering New Playwrights' Theatre in the summer of 1928—and in the wake of a slipping reputation with one-time sympathetic critics who had supplanted the word "promising" with the word "confusion" in their evaluations of his work—Lawson held that his vision of artistic rebellion was in need of reevaluation. All the promise of aesthetic revolt in the theatre, which arguably reached its pinnacle in 1925 when the miners erupted from the stage into the audience in *Processional*, was, by the summer of 1928, a passing memory. The practices and procedures of aesthetic rebellion underpinning these texts from the 1920s seemed dolefully idyllic and ideologically deficient in light of the executions of Sacco and Vanzetti and the failing of the New Playwrights' Theatre. What is more, when the stock market plummeted the next year, the immense changes taking place in American society forced Lawson to reconsider his position and goals as an artist in the United States. He recalled:

> [I]n the United States [of the early 1930s], I was more a stranger than I had ever been. I had thought of [the United States] as a spiritual wasteland, but now the unknown land was filled with unknown people—shivering on breadlines, opposing farm foreclosures, sullen crowds in the cities, lost children on the roads.
>
> My conscience was touched. But I could not relate my own problems as a [middle-class intellectual] writer, my experience in the twenties, my griefs, hopes, and aims, to this new phenomenon.[14]

Thus, at the dawn of the 1930s, Lawson found himself "without the mental resources" to deal with the "common experience of most Americans."[15] While he still longed to identify with and, in turn, poeticize and theatricalize "the dilemma of modern man," he became less and less concerned with the abstract (that is, Freudian and metaphysical) struggles of universal and abstract "modern man" and more concerned with "the harsh reality of the American scene." As yet, however, the playwright had little idea of how to connect with such issues or, for that matter, parlay his burgeoning concern into a form he believed suitable for theatrical expression. Throughout the first years of the decade, Lawson's struggle to identify with and present this "harsh reality" would initiate a process that would eventually propel him from hopelessness to hope, from ambivalence to commitment, and from "artist-rebel" to "political revolutionary."

The struggle between these two positions was a fundamental force in the playwright's life during this period and shaped in profound ways the nature of his thinking as well as his mode of artistic expression. Manifest most obviously in his composition and Group Theatre production of the script *Success Story* (1932) and in the cultural text of

Lawson's tenure as president of the Screen Writers' Guild, circa 1933, this personal struggle was coupled to and deeply embedded within the shifting and dynamic social and cultural currents in the United States at the turn of the decade. As discursive objects to be read, then, these aesthetic and theoretical texts and recorded experiences (that is, cultural texts) are endowed with traces of the dynamic social energy of the shifting American left in the first years of the 1930s.

Success Story

In May 1928, Waldo Frank commented in his essay "Our Arts: The Re-Discovery of America" that Lawson's plays disturbed him because the "mirrored jungle is employed clumsily to voice a spiritual assertion which would be magnificent [. . .] if it were organic and conscious."[16] This charge so puzzled the playwright that he felt moved to lay aside his current projects—a rewriting of *The Jazz Tragedy* now entitled *The Pure in Heart* and an adaptation for the stage of Theodore Dreiser's novel *Sister Carrie*[17]—and review his earlier scripts in light of Frank's criticism. What Lawson discovered as he reread his scripts from the 1920s both alarmed and troubled him. In *Roger Bloomer*, *Processional*, *Loud Speaker*, and *The International*, he found that despite his commitment to the development of new forms of drama, he had consistently imposed "exaggerated dramatic patterns" and "jazz-cartoon characters" on a number of "modern situations." In *Nirvana*, his one attempt to make a more "conscious and organic" assertion, he had become "bogged down in subjectivity." The core of the problem, Lawson later remarked, was his own "half-lost identity":

> [M]y plays were deficient in psychological depth because they dealt with people as symbols—and I tended to think of myself in the same way. I had never succeeded in portraying a character in three, much less, in four, dimensions. [. . .] Sadie Cohen [. . .] began as a caricature and became a person when she joined the procession of Americans. This is what I had done—avoided full acknowledgment of my identity and endeavored to find my place in the American procession. This was still my purpose. I was still destined to "write the crazy epic of this day." But first of all, I had to know myself [. . .]

In an effort "to know" himself, Lawson began writing in pencil, "at breakneck speed," a play entitled *Death in an Office*.[18] By the end of June 1928, he had completed a rough draft of the script, which contained the essential structure of what eventually became *Success Story*.[19]

Lawson had hoped to secure a New York production for the new script during the 1928–1929 theatre season. However, these plans were waylaid when, in the weeks immediately following his completion of that first draft, the playwright was offered and accepted a three-month contract to write screenplays for MGM. An initial offer to work for the studio had come earlier that year, while Lawson was still heavily involved in the work of the New Playwrights' Theatre. At that point, because of his commitment to the company, he did not accept this offer. However, when MGM reissued their proposition in the summer of 1928, Lawson accepted. Arriving in Hollywood in the late summer of that year, Lawson began what would be a nearly four-year repose from the theatre.

His initial success in the film industry came quickly. In late 1928, on the strength of his second screenplay, *Dynamite*, cowritten with Jeanie Macpherson and directed by Cecil B. De Mille, Lawson was awarded a long-term contract with MGM.[20] Despite such achievements in the film industry, Lawson continued to write plays and pursue opportunities in the theatre. Moreover, after only two years, he had become increasingly frustrated with the operating procedures of the studio system. Most notably, and as was typical for contract writers, Lawson held that he was not receiving due credit for his writing. As a result, in the summer of 1930 he broke his contract with MGM and returned to New York, purchasing a rambling twenty-room colonial house at Mastic Beach, Long Island. Notwithstanding his hopes of a triumphant return to the theatre, Lawson was unable to secure opportunities for productions of his scripts on the New York stage. Therefore, and with his debts mounting, in late 1930 Lawson was forced to obtain another screenwriting contract, this time with RKO. Over the course of the next year, through late 1931, Lawson worked for RKO, traveling back and forth from New York to California on numerous occasions. However, this appointment too proved fleeting when, at the end of 1931, William Le Baron, the producer at RKO who had hired Lawson, was fired. Soon thereafter, and with little warning or just cause, Lawson was also terminated.

Through these experiences, Lawson came to hold a very negative view of the studio system. Nonetheless, when he first accepted a screenwriting contract, he was buoyed by the promise of a career in Hollywood. Indeed, later in life, Lawson commented that his initial choice to work in the film industry was motivated by his budding interest in cinematic techniques and how they could be applied to the stage, his growing disdain for the New York critics, the foreseeable failure of the New Playwrights, and his need to provide for his family, which now included two young children.[21] Writing in 1934, Harold Clurman offered another insight on Lawson's "flight" to Hollywood:

> He [Lawson] is unable to support himself by his earnings as a playwright either in the big theatres of Broadway or in the little theatres of Greenwich Village. He adapts himself to Hollywood and, one might say, he enjoys it! Here the legend of "prosperity" takes on every sign of reality; here the miracle of American abundance becomes a continuous show. Here, moreover, he meets people who are neither fussed about "art" or about "ideas." The motives are frankly an industry, executives are financial magnates, the writer is a man with a definite job with clearly marked problems, restrictions, ends. Here people come and go, many contacts are made, everybody and everything is passed in review. Work, money, personalities, excitement—the big world at last, a front row at the American pageant![22]

During this period, the course of Lawson's life was profoundly affected by a series of national events that foregrounded the plight of the underclass in the United States. Three incidents that had a particular effect on the playwright were the bloody conflict between management and union textile workers in Gastonia, North Carolina, in the spring of 1929; the 6 March 1930 march by a million jobless workers in a dozen American cities who called for relief and unemployment insurance; and the Scottsboro Boys case, which began in March 1931 when nine African American males were herded off a train in Paint Rock, Alabama, and charged with the rape of two white girls. As Lawson read newspaper accounts of these and other events, he found himself mesmerized by the working-class people at the center of the conflicts.[23] Still, he thought himself unable and unqualified to include their stories in his creative endeavors. This inability to act forced Lawson into a period of intense soul-searching that led to a disturbing recognition:

> Thinking of myself as a rebel, as I had throughout the [twenties], I was forced to examine my relationship to our society and to the class of people who did its toughest work. It was clear enough that I had no connection with them at all. I had no way of breaking my isolation and was not even sure I wanted to find a way.
>
> I could not brush aside the questions that plagued my mind. I followed the *New Masses* more carefully, because it reported the lives and conditions of workers, and gave me a feeling that I belonged to the same world, or the same continent. [. . .]
>
> [Still,] I was not tempted to seek any personal participation in these activities. Participation was not a serious question for me. [. . .] I distrusted politics and [. . .] was adverse to the time consuming role of an activist.[24]

"The questions that plagued [Lawson's] mind" began to appear as a motif in his writing. Indeed, the script *Success Story* may be read as a documentation of the playwright's attempt to offer answers to some of these troubling questions.

However, it is within the treatments of an unfinished script entitled *Red Square*, written in the summer of 1931, that the essence of this discord is perhaps most clear. Like many liberal and leftward-leaning intellectuals in the United States in the early 1930s, Lawson shared an increasing interest in the Russian Revolution and the rise of the Soviet Union. Unlike some of his more ardent revolutionary peers, however, Lawson was troubled by much of what he saw and was very guarded about the possibilities of the Soviet system. Out of this concern came the idea for *Red Square*. Lawson recalled:

> I was shocked by the news of Mayakovsky's death, and I intended to make his suicide the climax of a play which would cover the history of the Soviet Union, seen largely from the viewpoint of an American intellectual who spends several years there and falls in love with a Russian woman. I could never attain any clear perspective on the play, or even crystallize a scene. But during 1931, in intervals when I was able to spare time from my film tasks, I scribbled random notes. I knew very little about Lenin, but wondered whether he could have met James Joyce when they were both in Zurich during the First World War. They had apparently visited the same cafes, the Odeon and zur Linde. I decided to begin my play with an imaginary meeting between the author of *Imperialism* and the author of *Ulysses*. I regarded both as great intellectual leaders, representing opposing forces—the power of politics and the power of art.

The proposed end of the script illustrates Lawson's view at this time. The American intellectual finds as much frustration under Communism as he did under capitalism and returns to the United States, "convinced that the creative individuality is the enemy of all social systems."[25] It seems, then, that for Lawson in the first years of the 1930s, any system that demanded his unwavering commitment in both political life and artistic expression was an anathema. Paul Buhle, historian of the political and cultural left, notes that the view Lawson held at this time was widespread in the community of liberal and leftward-leaning intellectuals living in the United States:

> The defeat of the American left [in the years immediately following World War I] had suspended the intellectuals in an all-too-familiar political vacuum where popular radicalism seemed the lucky fate of

> people in another time or place. The task of reconceptualizing social prospects under the changed conditions of mass society found them tragically ill-prepared. Marxist texts and formal training therefore helped them very little in understanding their own milieu. [. . .] Marxist parties offered them a variety of practical experiences but *at a heavier price than most would finally be willing to pay.*
>
> Their common source of wisdom was "Progressive" social science and its methods [. . .] The Progressive currents in philosophy and economics [. . .] inclined young radicals towards analogous over-simplifications. With abundant energy and clarity, the radicalized intellectuals thus excoriated the inequities, exploitation, and self-made mythologies of their time. Rarely did their probes satisfy their own intuitive sense of more complex relations between ideas and reality.[26]

While Lawson had a developing interest in the "common experience of Americans," he, like so many other radicalized intellectuals, was unable and/or unwilling to find a suitable compromise for synthesizing that interest with his artistic vision, and, moreover, he viewed "politics" and "art" as "opposing forces."

Lawson took a decisive step toward scrutinizing his belief that art and politics were oppositional when, in January 1932, he sought out the advice of Edmund Wilson, champion of the socially conscious novel, who was then serving as associate editor for the *New Republic.* One year prior, in an essay entitled "An Appeal to Progressives," Wilson threw down a proverbial gauntlet when he called on American "radicals and progressives who repudiate[d] the Marxian dogma and the strategy of the Communist party," and who hoped "to accomplish anything valuable," to "take Communism away from the Communists, and take it without ambiguities or reservations, asserting emphatically that their ultimate goal is the ownership of the means of production by the government."[27]

Wilson's revolutionary zeal was born, in the first place, from his distrust of the bureaucratic, Lovestone-era Communist party (that is, the WP), which forwarded "American exceptionalism," the right-wing theory that allowed for the coexistence of capitalism and Communism; and, in the second place, from a guarded optimism he held for the newly reconstituted party (the CP-USA) under the stewardship of Earl Browder.[28] Upon Lovestone's expulsion from the party in mid-1929 and the subsequent advent of Browder (who, for all practical purposes, was the leader of the CP-USA beginning in mid-1930), the party moved decisively to the left, forsaking categorically the moderation implied in Lenin's NEP and, in so doing, became securely aligned with Stalin's ultraliberal Third Period policies. From this point forward, the right-wing views of the Lovestoneites—and, indeed, all factions and factionalism—were intolerable. While this alliance with Moscow would in due course result in a "byzantine organization [. . . that] demanded a loyalty that confused discipline and indoctrination," in the first years of the 1930s many radicalized middle-class intellectuals, who had been distrustful of Communist politics proper, found the CP-USA's newfound revolutionary ethos and focus promising.[29] Wilson's essay of early 1931 may well be viewed as a circumspect vote of confidence in the new, leftward-leaning and Soviet-friendly CP-USA. To that end, he writes:

> [I]t seems to me impossible at the present time for people of [Herbert] Croly's general aims and convictions [previously addressed by Wilson as progressive liberals in the tradition of Hamiltonian centralization] to continue to believe in the salvation of our society by the gradual and natural approximation to socialism [once] called progressivism, but which has generally come to be known as liberalism. That benevolent and intelligent capitalism on which liberals have always counted has not merely not materialized to the extent of metamorphosing itself into socialism—it has not even been able to prevent a national disaster of proportions which neither capitalists nor liberals foresaw and which they both profess themselves unable to explain. [. . .]
>
> [T]he truth is that we liberals and progressive have been betting on capitalism [. . .] And now the abyss of bankruptcy and starvation into which the country has fallen with no sign of any political leadership which will be able to pull us out, liberalism seems to have little to offer [. . .]
>
> What we need in this country is *a genuine opposition*, and it is a long time since the liberals have been one. A genuine opposition must, it seems to me, openly confess that the Declaration of Independence and the Constitution are due to be supplanted by some new manifesto and some new bill of rights. It must dissociate its economics completely from what is by this time a purely rhetorical ideal of American democracy, though it has since the first days of the republic been bound up in our minds with the capitalist system. [. . . A]n American opposition must not be afraid to dynamite the old shibboleths and conceptions and to substitute new ones as shocking as possible.[30]

In the final chapter of his study of modernist literary trends, *Axel's Castle*, also from 1931, Wilson echoed this mass appeal for "a genuine opposition." With this text, however, his plea for revolutionary change was aimed at those within the literary and intelligentsia communities:

> I believe therefore that the time is at hand when these writers [that is, Yeats, Proust, Eliot, Stein, Valéry, Joyce], who have largely dominated the literary world in the decade 1920–1930, though we shall continue to admire them as masters, will no longer serve us as guides. [. . .]
>
> The writers with whom I have here been concerned have not only, then, given us works of literature which, for intensity, brilliance and boldness as well as for architectural genius, and intellectual mastery of their materials, rare among their Romantic predecessors, are probably comparable to the work of any time. Though it is true that they have overemphasized the importance of the individual, that they have been preoccupied with introspection sometimes almost to the point of insanity, that they have endeavored to discourage their readers, not only with politics, but with action of any kind—they have succeeded in effecting in literature a revolution analogous to that which has taken place in science and philosophy: they have broken out of the old mechanistic routine, they have disintegrated the old materialism, and they have revealed to the imagination a new flexibility and freedom. And though we are aware in them of things that are dying—the whole belle-lettristic tradition of literature perhaps, compelled to specialize more and more, more and more driven in on itself, as industrialism and democratic education have come to press it closer and closer—they none the less *break down the walls of the present* and wake us to the hope and exhalation of the untried, unsuspected possibilities of human thought and art.

Although Lawson was at this moment unwilling to accept Wilson's challenges unconditionally, he was nonetheless fascinated by the call for a "genuine opposition" as well as the charge for artists to "break down the walls of the present." In light of these appeals, Lawson initiated a program of study whereby he reconsidered his own claim made years before, to "break down the walls of the theatre."[31] To that end, and in an effort to find his way through his paradoxical view regarding the relationship of art and politics, in the spring of 1932 Lawson had a series of informal meetings with Wilson, and under the latter's tutelage, the playwright read Marx. By way of these discussions with Wilson, the idea of Communism entered Lawson's consciousness "not [yet] as something I accepted or liked, but as an American force, which had moral and intellectual implications that could not be ignored." After his work with Wilson, by the summer of that year the cornerstone of Lawson's commitment to revolutionary politics was in place. While Lawson therefore officially continued to hold a non-party position for the next two years, in his mind was "planted [. . .] the idea of an American reality that was radical" and the desire to put that reality on stage.[32]

In the late summer and early autumn of 1932 and upon the heels of his meetings with Wilson, Lawson, who had not been able to secure a screenwriting contract since being dismissed from RKO at the end of 1931, at last sold two scripts for the theatre. *The Pure in Heart* was purchased by the Theatre Guild, and the newly formed Group Theatre secured the rights to *Success Story. The Pure in Heart*, slated for previews in Baltimore, Pittsburgh, Hartford, and Boston before commencing its New York run, opened in Baltimore on 3 October to scathing reviews. On 10 October, it moved to Pittsburgh where George Seibel of the *Pittsburgh Sun-Telegraph* wrote, "Instead of *The Pure in Heart* it should be called *The Feeble in Mind*."[33] Needless to say, the Guild closed it four days later and canceled its New York engagement. *Success Story*, faring considerably better, opened on 26 September 1932 and ran for a respectable 120 performances.

Set in New York City, *Success Story* tells of the magnificent rise and fall of Solomon Ginsberg, a Russian-American Jew. The scene of the play is confined to the "richly furnished" private office of Raymond Merritt, head of the Raymond Merritt Advertising and Sales agency.[34] The first act takes place on a summer afternoon in 1928. In a discussion with Rufus Sonnenberg, a Wall Street banker, Merritt reveals that he has decided to move his privately held business into the public sphere by selling stocks. He and Sonnenberg, who is financing this development, talk of the seemingly indomitable stature of American big business and exchange ideas on how to get ahead in that arena. Into this scene—which echoes in a fascinating manner the opening dialogue between the characters Fitch and Spunk in *The International*—enters Sol, a "tough, uncouth, sombre" young man who is an office boy in the statistics department of the agency (16). Through exposition, it is revealed that Sol obtained the job because his lover and childhood friend, Sarah Glassman, is Merritt's private secretary. He and Sarah are self-professed radicals who have spent their whole lives in the poverty-stricken East Side tenements of New York City. Unlike Sarah, who is willing to wait for the revolution, Sol's impoverished upbringing has left him impatient, angry, and desperately ambitious. Merritt and Sonnenberg barely acknowledge Sol's existence, and when they leave the office, the young man explodes:

SOL. There's no future without money, I must get it . . . I been waiting for a break ever since I was born!

SARAH. We had one good break, each other.

SOL. What good is that? When you're in bad with life, two is no better than one. [. . .]

SARAH. You have changed some, Sol.

SOL. Sure I'm changin'. I had enough watchin' other people rake in the money, people like that fool, Merritt—Sometime I'll get my mitts on that bozo an' when he comes up for air he'll be all bloody, an' then I'll bust up the whole place 'cause it smells of money . . . break up these little partitions that shut off one fool from another fool . . . to Hell with 'em, yours for the revolution, signed, Solomon Ginsberg!

SARAH. That would be a big help for the revolution, wouldn't it?

(*Pleading.*)

YOU and me have learned a lot together, we've studied and read and gone to meetings. . . .

SOL. Sure, we're chock full of Marx and Lenin, but when you come up against a cheap capitalist grafter like Merritt, you fall for him. [. . .] I'm sick to death of radical meetings an' sour-faced people an' cheap gab. . . . (38–40)

When Merritt returns, Sol insults him. Merritt threatens to fire him and then, amused by the young man's passion and bluntness, offers him an opportunity to write advertising copy for an important client.

As Sol sits alone in the office at the desk, Agnes Carter, Merritt's "delicious blonde" mistress, enters (54). The act closes with Sol fluctuating between his attraction and repulsion for Agnes and all that she represents:

SOL. Suppose I tell you what I think a' you?

AGNES. You have, you told me I was Venus.

SOL. Sure. D'you know what I think a' Venus? Beauty? Bah, what's beauty? Don't I know you're a rotter? Sure I do . . . You're a piece a' pink fluff for the luxury trade—what's more . . . you're a parasite, a slave, a white slave an' blood sister to a street walker.

AGNES. You're out of luck from now on, Ginsberg—

SOL. You're sore, 'cause I tell you what's what.

AGNES. No . . . I kind of want you . . .

SOL. For a lover, you mean . . . is that what you mean, huh?

AGNES. No, just to crack the whip over you, any man that's so mad must be easy to get. . . .

SOL. If I had a million dollars I'd buy you, 'cause your skin's all gold—

AGNES. You wouldn't get me, so that's that.

SOL. Wanna bet?

AGNES. Get the million first, then I'll bet.

SOL. I will . . .

AGNES. Wild, aren't you . . . crazy? You'd take me now and smash me . . . wouldn't you, with one hand? You'll be sorry you ever called me names . . . I'll crack the whip . . . (97–99)

Act 2 takes place two years later, in 1930. Sol's ambitions have paid off. He has become a significant figure in the firm and has betrayed his revolutionary notions:

SARAH. [. . .] you've changed [. . .] Sol, I'm afraid for you, afraid you are riding for a fall.

SOL. What are you criticizing me for? Anybody would think it was a crime for a guy to make good—

SARAH. No, it's fine if that's what you want.

SOL. What do you think I want?

SARAH. I wish I knew and I wish I could give it to you.

SOL. I'll get what I want without you—

SARAH. So it seems—

SOL. Watch my dust—say, it gives me a kick to look back at the radical type we used to fall for—that stuff's a religion for misfits—Huh! I'm no misfit, I know where I belong—

SARAH. That sounds like a Rotary club speech—

SOL. That's bunk too—most everything's bunk when you know your way round—the trick is, to use the bunk without being taken in—

SARAH. Why are you so bitter about it?

SOL. Me bitter! I'm laughing—looking back at a raw kid that got drunk on the words he found in books—God! It seems like a million miles away—I haven't been near the East Side in a year . [. . .]

SARAH. Sol . . . now and then, the way you smile or something, I see you like you used to be! Where's the boy I used to know, named Sol Ginsberg—

SOL. That kid is dead. . . . Bury the past, put it in the ground and throw dirt on it— (109–12)

As the act progresses, Sol threatens to reveal to Sonnenberg that Merritt has used company money to cover his private loses in the stock market. When he demands a promotion, a raise, and the power to determine the financial direction of the firm, Merritt, under the threat of blackmail, is eventually forced to surrender control of the firm. Agnes, enthralled by Sol's "romantic and impossible" notions, agrees to marry him, while Sarah is disdainfully thrown aside (170).

Act 3 takes place two years later, in 1932. Merritt has been forced to hand over all his financial interest in the firm to Sol, who has invested wisely and has assumed ownership of the office and company. As Sol works at his desk, Sarah, who still works for the firm, reminisces. She speaks of their old lives and associations that "haunt [. . .] like a memory" and claims, much to the amusement of Sol, that the world "still needs changing" (196). When Agnes drops by to visit, it is instantly clear that their marriage is falling apart. She threatens to leave Sol, he responds, "I'd like to kill you just to see you squirm," and leaves in a rage to wander about the city (221). When Sol returns to his office at dawn, he finds Sarah waiting for him. As he takes a gun from his pocket and lays it on the desk, he turns to Sarah:

> SOL. Been walking through the streets for hours—zowie, it was cold . . . too cold to think—too cold to breathe—Can you help me?
>
> SARAH. If I could, Sol—
>
> SOL. How about it Sarah? Why don't you shoot me yourself? You'd save me a lot of trouble.
>
> SARAH. One of your jokes—
>
> SOL. Never more serious in my life! [. . .] Help me, Sarah—there's so much between us! (227–28)

Sarah agrees to help him, and he responds by trying to seduce her. Suddenly comprehending, Sarah sees that Sol is attempting to use her as he used everyone and everything in his life. As he clutches Sarah to his chest, she cries, reaches for the gun on the desk, raises it to Sol's side, and fires. Sol is adamant that the gun must be found in his own hand so that it will have the appearance of a suicide. Agnes and Merritt enter after a night on the town. Sol, who is dying, speaks only to Sarah:

> SOL. One time there was a Jew named Christ dressed up like a rainbow, he told the world plenty, maybe there'll be some more like him. . . . Me, I don't care! I'm only thinking of myself. Put me in a solid silver coffin with gold cupids—don't matter what it costs. . . .
>
> *(Starts to laugh, stiffens in Sarah's arms.)* (243)

The play ends with Sarah and Merritt standing silently in shock as Agnes takes control and creates an alibi:

> AGNES. . . . He was locked in here and he killed himself. We came down—we three together, and found the door locked. Get that straight, somebody's got to use their head—take that telephone and call somebody—take that telephone, Raymond—
>
> *(Merritt helplessly picks up the telephone.)*
>
> Get the police; tell 'em exactly what I say: take hold of that phone and call them—Tell the police it's a suicide, tell 'em he had a nervous breakdown . . . too much work . . . too ambitious. . . . (244–45)

Her voice continues as the curtain falls.

Lawson worked on *Success Story*, on and off, for four years. During that time, he incorporated suggestions from Dos Passos, Basshe, and Frank. The playwright would later comment that with the writing and rewriting of *Success Story* "came the death of my former self."[35] By grappling with the inner conflict dividing Sol's desire for recognition, money, and success from his idealism and interest in social struggle, Lawson began to "purge and strengthen" his own life.[36] The playwright's newfound focus is immediately apparent. Gone are the abstract methods and the one-dimensional characters that had dominated his first five scripts. In their place are realistic methods and three-dimensional characters capable of psychological development.

In addition to the shifts in dramatic structure and character, the thematic focus is altered to include a more pointed attack on American bourgeois society and capitalism. Nonetheless, in these first years of the 1930s, Lawson was still unwilling to accept without condition the precepts of the Communist revolution. The specifics of Lawson's advancement toward this more overt though not-yet-revolutionary political position are clarified in his correspondence with Harold Clurman preceding the Group Theatre production.

In the early summer of 1932, when the Group Theatre accepted *Success Story* for production, Lawson began a correspondence with Clurman. Over the next few months, Clurman made a number of suggestions for revision that were incorporated by Lawson. However, at the beginning of August, Clurman began to question the nature of Sarah's political commitment. The letters from Lawson concerning this issue provide a clear indication of the direction and state of his thinking at this time.

The debate was instigated by a letter from Clurman dated 8 August wherein he suggested that Lawson should make a number of revisions to the script, particularly regarding the character of Sarah:

> [At the end of act 3,] Sarah's responses to Sol's pleas for help are weak and vague. After all, she is the clearest person in the play and a *communist* (which means a person with a definite point of view) and it is important in the last scene of the play, before the climax, she *tell* Sol very clearly and passionately what is really the matter with him and what is the tragedy and significance of his whole story. This is of the *utmost* importance. Without it the play will not be ideologically clear and many people will misunderstand Sol and the importance of his story. Although Sarah must not mention her communism in this speech it might be helpful to you in writing it to see it from that angle so that you can make Sarah *precise* as well as passionate.[37]

Two more letters from Clurman, sent on 9 and 10 August, pursued this and other related issues.

Lawson vehemently opposed these changes and said so in a bombastic letter dated 11 August. When he arrived at Dover Furnace the next week to work with the group, he brought with him a lengthy written statement entitled "Communism in relation to *Success Story*." In this missive, which was distributed to the entire company, Lawson declared that Sarah could not be regarded as a "serious communist" because "her emotional clarity springs from an inner feeling, not a political belief." He continued:

> I take full responsibility for having been vague about this in our previous conversations—my reason being that my ideas have changed so much since my first creation of "Success Story" that I wasn't sure how the radical thought in the play would work out until I subjected it to thorough study during the present revision. I am now convinced that the communism mentioned in the play is simply a cultural background for Sol and Sarah, to which she clings and on which he turns his back, but which has no deep significance for either of them.

Lawson went on to describe his own personal development in relation to the play:

> I am increasingly convinced of the revolutionary function of literature, and am continually trying to orient myself toward such an approach. I trust that my future work will gradually develop a clear revolutionary point of view. But clarity is the first essential of such a point of view. To pretend that "Success Story" has a fundamentally revolutionary approach would be to confess my own bankruptcy as an author. I do not regret that "Success Story" is not a radical play (in the political or ideological sense); I think it needs no apologies; it is (in my estimation) a completely *honest* play as it stands. The references to

Communism have exactly the right tone—Sarah's connection with old comrades, Sol's mystic expression of union with the people in cellars. This is characteristic of these people—but let us have no delusions on this score: it is *not* Communism!

While I am not a Communist, I have given much thought to the theory of it. I don't qualify as an expert, but I want to guard myself against being guilty of anything so palpably unsound as to hint that Sarah represents a Communist (or any sort of revolutionary) point of view. The girl has some of the failings of the worst type of philosophical anarchist, and this is to her discredit. If a woman is a Communist, she does not spend her best years as a secretary and executive in an advertising office; she does not destroy her whole life because of a purely Victorian idea of love and faith; she does not find the solution of a personal problem in the neurotic gesture of killing the thing she loves. Sarah is a great woman, great because of the depth and validity of her emotion, but if her Communism were anything more than lip service, she would have done none of these things. If any ideologist at Dover Furnace thinks he can reconcile this sort of thing with revolutionary thought, please shoot him in the head: it won't hurt him!

Lawson concluded the statement with the following: "Insofar as 'Success Story' succeeds at being a clear study of certain processes of character in relation to environment in our day and age, it has revolutionary significance—but in no other sense."[38]

Thus, while Lawson's desire to "orient [himself] toward" the "revolutionary function of literature" and his explication that *Success Story* was a "study of certain processes of character in relation to environment in our day and age" indicates further progression away from his singular aesthetic focus of the twenties, he was clearly not yet ready to raise the red flag of political revolution. Clurman's recollection of Lawson's visit to Dover Furnace further supports this contention: "From time to time [Lawson] vented opinions that had led us to believe that though he was definitely of progressive, even radical opinion, he was violently opposed to official communist doctrine."[39] Lawson's unfinished play from that same summer, *Red Square*, clearly espouses the idea that party membership meant subservience to the party line.

Still, despite Lawson's apparent renouncing of any official association with the Communist Party, the characters and structure of *Success Story* indicate that he had abandoned the nonrealistic methods that dominated his scripts from the 1920s and adopted, either consciously or unconsciously, the stringent restrictions of socialist realism. Furthermore, the play's biting and overt attack on the dangers of capitalism and the myth of the American dream seem to echo, in a general sense, the Communist Party line and, therefore, its presence indicates a change in Lawson's thinking. This transformation of thought may be further clarified in a comparison of the characters Sol Ginsberg and Roger Bloomer.

Lawson himself suggested that, in many ways, Sol could be viewed as Roger grown up.[40] At the beginning of *Success Story*, Sol, like Roger, is alienated from society. However, unlike Roger, who never clearly defines the internal, abstract, Freudian desires that prompt his alienation, Sol clearly and angrily articulates that it is the result of external forces, specifically his economic background and ethnic heritage, that have created and sustained his alienation. This awareness and ability to critically assess the materiality of his existence clearly separates Sol from Roger and promotes in the former a drive to belong to—and in some respects shape—the society that has shunned him. The movement away from the young man battling shadows in a surreal nightmare, toward the business man in a realistic office fighting for social recognition and economic gain, clearly marks a change in Lawson's thought. Unlike the abstract and often clouded social commentary in *Roger Bloomer*, *Success Story* voices a clear and articulate indictment against bourgeois society, specifically capitalism. Indeed, the thematic center of the script is the condemnation of the society that stimulates and glorifies power and social status in light of monetary wealth. This overt indictment against capitalism is augmented by the double tragedy in the script.

In addition to the most perceptible tragedy in the play, Sol's ill-fated drive to achieve "success at any price," there is another tragedy.[41] That is to say, the "death in [the] office" that closes the play is the culmination of two tragedies, Sol's and Sarah's, each making a comment on the dire state of bourgeois society and the payment that society exacts from its subjects. Nonetheless, as Lawson mentioned in his statement to the group, the death of Sol is not a rationally conceived punishment levied by one clearly committed Communist (that is, Sarah) on a fallen comrade (that is, Sol) for betraying an ideological creed. Rather, Sarah, driven beyond reason by socially determined forces and "Victorian ideas of love and faith," destroys the one thing she has always believed in and loved. Lawson spoke very passionately and directly about the romanticized worldview that was implied in Sarah's final actions in "Communism in relation to *Success Story*":

> The final scene is on a heroic scale (at least, it ought to be): the killing is an act of justice; but we mustn't forget that this act of justice is committed by a woman in a neurotic state as her only way of escape,

> and that she regrets it immediately afterward. Her next thought is equally neurotic: to suffer and atone! This sense of sin and atonement is part of [her] social heritage. Sarah might eventually *grow up* to a point which she could see this series of acts in their proper balance, but any such development on her part is another play.
>
> Sarah reaches a point of poetic intensity at which she is able to see a complete picture of Sol's downfall. But this is not because she has a set belief: it's because she believes in nothing but him. Her whole course of action is predicated on this. There is no time in the play when her alleged communism means less to her than in these moments.[42]

Both Sol and Sarah have been victimized—and in the case of Sol, destroyed—by the society in which they are forced to exist. Seen from this angle, *Success Story* documents what might happen when good people who have been alienated by an evil society are given passage into that society. Throughout the script, as Sol and Sarah establish themselves in the bourgeois world, the revolutionary spirit that fostered them is slowly traded away.

This ill-fated view of the revolutionary spirit created a minor stir in the left-wing press. While many in that arena ignored the September 1932 Group Theatre production, those who did respond viewed it as an apologia for bourgeois society.[43] Representative of this view is the anonymous review that appeared in the *Daily Worker*, which dismissed the play as just another episode of "the Eugene O'Neill bourgeois reactionary variety, in which the audience is asked to weep over the sexual problems of a finance-capitalist swindler."[44]

The notices in both the liberal and mainstream press were somewhat better. Gilbert Gabriel was moved by the play and found that it reached "that motion of inevitability which is beyond mere commotion, and which is the highest desire of the theatre, anywhere, anywhen."[45] Similarly, Joseph Wood Krutch thought it "a sober, intense, and vehement drama. [. . .] Mr. Lawson has treated a familiar story from an original angle. [. . .] He neither glorifies 'success' nor indulges in that now conventional satire on big business and advertising, instead he is concerned with the dark and terrible abysses in the soul of an ambitious man, and leaves us shuddering at the spectacle of one who can torture himself as well as others because of a lust for power which brings neither joy nor satisfaction to anyone."[46] In the end, however, the words of Brooks Atkinson offer both the best evaluation of *Success Story* and a suggestion of how the play fits within the larger mosaic of Lawson's career.

In the first of his two reviews for the *New York Times*, Atkinson commented that while the play was "not particularly original," it was "a stinging indictment," full of "moral fervor" and "savage passion."[47] The next week, when he considered the play again, Atkinson was less enthusiastic. While he still thought it was "the most stimulating of the new plays" and praised the group for selecting "a manuscript that is crumpled and blotted by a restless idea," he saw in it indications of a playwright who was not sure of his goal:

> Mr. Lawson lacks style, and *Success Story* as a play writhes as neurotically as its hero. It is underwritten in minor parts; it makes bewildering conclusions; it is impulsive, and it mixes pungent and poetic writing with plain rodomontade. [. . .]
>
> [A]lthough Mr. Lawson's characters are raw with feeling, they never think. [. . .] Something of that sort must be true of Mr. Lawson himself. His feelings are nervous and shrill; his emotions are as hot and groping as a tongue of flame. But he has little of the cold deliberation that shapes plays into fully articulate pieces of work.[48]

Atkinson's view was apparently widely held. Writing two years later, Clurman made a similar point: "*Success Story* is an important step forward: it brings Lawson to the point of sensing that the human principle involved in capitalism must finally prove itself destructive. A social philosophy—somewhat vaguely stated—begins to emerge from the passionate complaints of this play."[49] Despite Clurman's faith in the future, Lawson would continue to struggle for almost three more years with how to present "the harsh reality of the American scene." Nonetheless, Lawson's "vaguely stated . . . social philosophy" was in the first years of the 1930s slowly beginning to find a specific form.

The Writer in Hollywood

Late in 1932, following the Group Theatre's production of *Success Story*, the lack of theatre work in New York brought about by the deepening Depression forced Lawson to return to Hollywood and MGM.[50] Though the move seemed at the time to be a compromise—in that he had grown to view the studio system in Hollywood as "ruthless and irresponsible"—it nonetheless led to one of the most significant events in the playwright's life.[51]

In early February 1933, Lawson was one of a small number of screenwriters brought together by the shared conviction that an organization needed to be formed to advance and defend their economic and artistic interests.[52] In addition to Lawson, the most active participants in these early meetings were Lester Cole, Louis Weitzenkorn, Oliver Garrett, and Ralph Bloch. By the end of February, this core group had expanded to include some twelve to fourteen active participants. The majority of those involved were not highly politicized. Still, from the start most members in the organizing group positioned themselves in one of two broadly defined ideological camps.

The left side was led by Sameul Ornitz, Lester Cole, and John Bright. Though none other than Ornitz were Communists at this time, the leftist group was decidedly militant, sworn to creating in Hollywood a powerful trade union that would regard screenwriters as workers and could, through the threat of strike, advocate for improvements in the profession. On the right side were "many of the most successful screenwriters in Hollywood." Howard Green, Rupert Hughes, Edwin Justus Mayer, and Louis Weitzenkorn led this more conservative faction. Believing the group should function more as a professional lobby, the rightists were somewhat more libertarian in their agenda. As such, the primary goals for those in this group on the right were for individual screenwriters to receive artistic credit and maintain legal control of their work. Events in the arena of national affairs in the spring of 1933 would impel the two disparate factions to join forces.[53]

On Monday, 6 March 1933, in an effort to calm the nation's spiraling inflation, newly elected president Franklin Roosevelt ordered the closure of all banks. Two days later, the president of MGM, Louis B. Mayer, believing that the closure of the banks was indicative of greater economic problems to come, panicked and cut the salaries of all non-union studio employees by 50 percent. Within a few days, the executive heads of the other major studios in Hollywood followed Mayer's lead and made similar pay cuts aimed at all non-union employees. Among the many non-unionized artisans affected by this policy were hundreds of contract screenwriters, including Lawson. Lawson recalled his feelings when Mayer announced the pay cut at MGM and how the producers' actions brought the disparate writers with different aims and ideologies together. "I was sitting close to Mayer. He spoke with unrestrained emotion, and tears trickled down his cheeks as he explained that he too would cut his salary by half. Mayer's tears moved me—but not to sympathy. I was not crying but thinking. [. . . His] tears gave me an emotional insight into the system of power. I knew most of the men and women in that room; Mayer was taking blatant advantage of us and misusing whatever creative power we possessed. That misuse bound us together and set us to action."[54] Thus, by imposing a pay cut, the producers galvanized the widely divergent screenwriters, creating in their ranks a mood of militancy and community.

On Friday, 10 March, two days after the pay cut was announced, the organizing group of screenwriters, now "bound [. . .] together," reconvened and began to plan a course of action. Member Oliver Garrett brought to the meeting his lawyer and friend Lawrence Beilenson, who delineated the legal steps required for the establishment of a trade union. The organizing group continued to meet with Beilenson every night for the next few weeks and thus began the process of formalizing its identity and setting its agenda.

As a first step, it was agreed the group would assume the name of an almost defunct social organization called the Screen Writers' Guild that had a tenuous tie to the Authors' League of America.[55] With their name in place, the group moved forward by defining its method of organization. In order to bind the disparate membership together and to meet the peculiar circumstances of unionization in a field where there had been no trade-union consciousness, Beilenson advised that the group adopt a contract method of organization.[56] Each member of the Guild would be required to sign the contract. In so doing, he or she pledged to abide by the Code of Rules, which would later be established by three-fourths vote of the membership, and was required to pay $100, which went into a strike fund. The contract would not become effective unless one hundred and fifty screenwriters signed it by 21 April 1933.

On 6 April, after a month of organizational meetings, some two hundred screenwriters gathered at the Hollywood Knickerbocker Hotel to pledge their support to the newly reconstituted Screen Writers' Guild. The meeting opened with Lawson reading to those gathered a contract that called for fewer hours, higher wages, regularized hiring practices, and union-directed salary arbitration. Underlying the rather weighty legal language was a simple but radical idea clearly expressed in one of the first lines of the preamble: "writers are the creators of motion pictures."[57] These words, seemingly clear and straightforward, spelled revolution in the film industry as every contract for writers' material or services clearly stated that the studio, and not the writer, was author of the material.[58] The screenwriters' reaction to these words was later recalled by Lawson: "There was no stormy applause. There was tension and fear. I said I would be the first to sign the contract, and asked who in the hall would join me. Slowly, one by one, hands were raised. When about half those present had raised their hands, people rose to their feet, and everyone's hands were in the air."[59] By the end of the night, 173 had signed the contract.[60] The meeting closed with the election of officers and executive board. Lawson was unanimously elected president; Frances Marion, vice president; Joseph Mankiewicz, secretary, and Ralph Bloch, treasurer.[61] Regarding this moment and his appointment, Lawson recalled:

> The emotion I felt was new and potent. I had always had a feeling about collective action. The need of working with others was strong in me. This was the faith of the New Playwrights; I had believed in it with passion as a collective, and the gap between my concept of a democratic association and the actual operation of the Playwrights—partly due to my own faults and the immaturity of all of us—had wounded me. [. . .]
>
> Now, my life and the lives of other writers seemed bound together. Their trust in me gave me a sense of responsibility and purpose that was related to my dignity as a person and my aims as an artist. I had never thought of myself as a lonely truth-seeker. Now I saw a hope that I could really make a serious artistic contribution to films, and that in doing so, I would serve others as well as myself.[62]

Lawson echoes this sentiment in the Davis and Goldberg interview published in *Cineaste*:

> [T]he case of the Hollywood Ten goes back to the formation of the Screen Writers Guild in 1933, and I am very proud of the fact that I was a leading figure in organizing the Guild. It was a dedication I felt deeply toward the writer, toward the freedom of the writer within the limits imposed by the industry, toward enlarging those limits so that the writer could do a more effective creative job. I felt this very strongly, although my ideas about how and to what extent it could have been done have varied through the years and would be quite different today. But I regard that meeting at the Knickerbocker Hotel in 1933 as the beginning of a cycle of my life, a determination, a commitment to give my life and my professional activity to this cause. It was a logical beginning of the events that came to a crisis in 1947 [the HUAC hearings] and that sent me to jail in 1950 and 1951.[63]

Lawson's election to the office of president was of little surprise. His previous association with the Dramatists Guild, the only part of the Authors' League that functioned in any way as a trade union, gave him a degree of union experience that most of the other members of the organizing committee lacked.[64] Moreover, Lawson was one of the few in the organizing group who was willing to "throw caution to the wind, urging that the organization was a must, action was imperative, [and the producers'] abuses unforgivable."[65] His passionate commitment to the cause fostered an unusually high level of trust from most of the other members. Lawson's experience and commitment aside, his selection was primarily a result of his centrist position.[66] During the previous month's organizational meetings, he had surfaced as leader by his ability to bring together the right and left factions. Quite simply, Lawson knew success would come only if those involved would put aside their differences and unite under the central idea expressed in the preamble of the contract: writers are the creators of motion pictures.[67]

Lawson's commitment to the center was short lived. At the end of May, he was suddenly released from his contract with MGM.[68] Though he did not fight the issue, as he was willing to work full time on behalf of the Guild, the clear breach of contract and the incapacity to respond pushed Lawson to adopt a more radical stance. This new position first became apparent during the early summer of 1933 when he officially reconstituted the Guild's relationship with the parental Authors' League in "hope[s] that [. . .] writers in all fields [would] back each other in strike action," and advised on the forming of the Screen Actors' Guild.[69] Lawson's commitment to the militant faction became even more pronounced in the autumn of 1933, at the National Industrial Recovery Act (NIRA) hearings in Washington, D.C.

Throughout the summer and autumn of 1933, the federal government held hearings in Washington under the provisions of NIRA, which stipulated that a Code of Fair Practice be established by each major industry in the country.[70] Lawson and Beilenson wrote numerous letters to the Authors' League seeking sponsorship to the meetings where they could voice the Screen Writers' Guild's demand for the inclusion of bargaining rights in the film industry code. Marc Connelly, president of the League, finally agreed that significant improvements for screenwriters were possible if the Guild was included under NIRA and thus sanctioned the trip.[71]

On 22 August, Lawson left for two days of preparatory meetings in New York with the executive board of the Authors' League. In New York, League official Louise Silcox was assigned to accompany Lawson to the meetings in Washington. Though her official office was secretary and treasurer of the League, Silcox's duties were much more extensive. She was the principal spokesperson for the League and in charge of all the activities of the League's guilds. Silcox provided an interesting contrast to the liberal Lawson. She was a Republican, deeply suspicious of Roosevelt's New Deal, and, according to Lawson, "spiritually at home in the nineteenth century." Still, she had a profound influence on Lawson. "Louise and I had totally different visions of the writer's function, but we were both fiercely dedicated to the writer's welfare. We never doubted each other's probity. I don't know whether she would have been pleased or shocked to know that she played such a unique part in my education. There was no one, with the possible exception of Edmund Wilson, who had such an influence on my becoming a Communist."[72]

Lawson and Silcox arrived in Washington on 25 August. After just three days of preliminary meetings with federal officials, it was perfectly obvious to them both that the Guild had no weight in Washington, that the code was being prepared to satisfy the producers' wishes, and that any hope for inclusion of collective bargaining into the code was lost. In a bitter letter to the Guild dated 28 August, Lawson reported that "certain deadly sections" of the code were being "designed to destroy competition and perpetuate the producers' arbitrary and undemocratic control over the creative workers in the Motion Picture industry."[73] With little hope for major advances, Silcox and Lawson began to lobby for the inclusion of clauses in the code that would limit the studios' unchallenged privileges of freezing salaries and eliminating competition for the services of creative personnel. Their efforts reaped few results. In a last-ditch effort, Silcox and Lawson tried to ally the Guild with the powerful American Federation of Labor. Though AFL president William Green lauded the proposal and promised full support and cooperation, Federation officials immediately rejected the proposal on the grounds that writers were not workers.[74] By the time of the NIRA hearings for the film industry, held on September 12, 13, and 14, Silcox and Lawson had been virtually shut out of the process and were not even allowed to make a statement. Surprisingly, when Lawson returned to Hollywood, he made his report to a "packed, cheering meeting of the Guild." While very little had been accomplished in real results concerning the code, the membership saw Lawson's trip to Washington as a "wake-up call" to the producers. In the words of Lawson, "[I]t alleviated fears; it gave us dignity."[75]

As expected, the completed Motion Picture Industry Code that was sent to the president for approval in October 1933 openly favored industry management. To add insult to injury, several of its key clauses "effectively functioned as salary-limiting devices that amounted to permanent government-sanctioned pay cuts."[76] Obviously missing were revisions recognizing the newly founded Guild or improving the status of writers in the film industry. Thus, it was no great surprise that the code, signed by Roosevelt on 27 November, read as if it had been written by the producers. What was a surprise was the president's executive order that accompanied the code, which stated that because film artists were "engaged in purely creative work" certain provisions would be indefinitely suspended.[77]

As written, the code made it illegal for one producer to "entice" an employee from another studio with an offer of better pay. The fact that countless, detailed procedures had to be followed before an offer could be made to employee at another studio all but disallowed an open market in the motion picture industry and, thus, took the right of choice away from actors, directors, and screenwriters. With the executive order, Roosevelt suspended the provisions that supported these procedures and, thereby, disabled the producers' plan to use the code as a legally sanctioned "weapon" against the artistic personnel whose skills and talents made them valuable.[78]

Roosevelt's stunning move sent shock waves through the industry. Unaware of all the positive repercussions inherent in the executive order, and without consulting Lawson, the executive board of the Guild sent a highly contemptuous telegram to the White House denouncing the code for "its failure to establish collective bargaining rights," to safeguard writers against blacklisting, or to recognize the existence of the Screen Writers' Guild.[79] Authors' League officials were livid with the board's renegade actions. They viewed the telegram as a serious breach of League protocol and threatened to terminate sponsorship of the Guild. Lawson, who was in New York at the time, pleaded with the League to delay any such action and wrote a detailed letter to the executive board explaining that the telegram they sent was not only prohibited under the governing policies of League, but also unwarranted in light of the provisions of the executive order. Lawson argued that the executive order constituted a significant step in the right direction in that it gave screenwriters new prestige and could eventually have a positive effect on their position in Hollywood. Upon receiving Lawson's letter, the board held an all-night meeting, reversed its decision, and apologized to the League and the White House.[80]

While the board's quick change of heart was prompted in part by Lawson's letter, the more compelling motive inducing their acquiescence was their observation of the immediate consequences Roosevelt's executive order had on the film industry. Caught completely off guard, the producers were furious and had lashed out in a flurry: first with private threats against individual Guild members and later with public statements attacking Roosevelt's executive order and, what is more significant, the Guild. This denunciation of the Guild was the producers' first public acknowledgment that such a group existed. A few days after the order was made public, the head of NIRA, General Hugh S. Johnson, feeling the pressure of the producers' lobby, issued a "clarification" that contradicted what the president had stated in his executive order.[81] A telegram from the Guild's executive board to Lawson shows how quickly and fully they had adopted the viewpoint of Lawson and the League officials: "Johnson's clarification ruins all we had accomplished under the Code . . . We are feeling tremendous pressure from the producers . . . This should make abundantly clear that straight arguments and reasonable representations mean nothing. Influence is all that counts. Fact that producers made such an issue of writer exemption shows importance of work done by you and the League."[82]

Under a directive from the Authors' League, Lawson immediately went to work on having Roosevelt's executive order "reaffirmed." In an emergency meeting with Sol Rosenblatt, the NIRA coordinator for the film industry, Lawson threatened to go to the press with "the power of four thousand authors" if the executive order was not immediately reaffirmed.[83] On 2 January 1934, General Johnson wrote a second letter in which he rejected all charges of intentionally opposing the aims of Roosevelt and vaguely reaffirmed the executive order. Despite the letter's cryptic nature, it was clearly a victory for the Guild.[84]

On 4 January 1934, Lawson wrote to the executive board that the main effect of his encounter with General Johnson was "to make [the General] look extremely foolish."[85] In truth, the effect of this encounter and, for that matter, the entire proceedings in Washington during the latter half of 1933 was more far-reaching. On an organizational level, the Guild under Lawson had proved that it was an increasingly powerful force that could not be ignored. Despite the exclusion of collective bargaining from the film industry code, there arose within the Screen Writers' Guild a feeling of power brought about by their collective activity. Under Lawson, the Guild established that first year a direction and confidence that would never be lost.

On a more personal level, the experience, especially the time in Washington, provided Lawson with a great education in politics and their relation to art. Although he had certainly evidenced strong thoughts on the controlling and corrupting hand of big business since the early 1920s, Lawson was stunned at the influence exercised by corporations on the United States government. In 1973 he recalled,

> Being in Washington [in 1933], totally frustrated in the effort to get recognition for the Screen Writers Guild, I learned a great deal about the establishment and about Washington politics. The process of radicalization—which began for me at dawn on the battlefield in France when I was driving ambulances near Hill 301—that process of education in the meaning of the social structures of capitalism in the United States was continued and given a decisive turn by my function as the head of the Screen Writers' Guild. I learned there was no compromise you could make with the Establishment.[86]

The difficulty in getting anything done in Washington forced Lawson to adopt a strident socialist stance, which would prove an important stepping-stone in his journey toward his eventual undying commitment to Communism. Lawson would later remark that through his tenure as president of the Guild he had "learned to respect working class people" and came to "the threshold of commitment."[87] The significance of his Guild activity was perceived by others as well: when called before HUAC in October 1947, Lawson was asked about membership in only two organizations—the Communist Party and the Screen Writers' Guild. Although he refused to admit membership in either group on the grounds that the congressional hearings were unconstitutional, there was little question that the empowering, potent, and life-altering experiences with the Screen Writers' Guild, in particular his experience in Washington in the summer and autumn of 1933, had led Lawson to his unwavering commitment to radical causes and revolutionary politics. In his memoirs, Lawson himself offers a candid but zealous assessment of the effect his term as president of the struggling Screen Writers' Guild had on him. "I [. . .] learned lessons I would never forget. My view on politics was shaped [. . .]. It was a milestone on the thorny path to commitment."[88]

Prefiguring Commitment

In the first years of the 1930s, Lawson, troubled by the recognition that he was "without the mental resources" to deal with the "common experience of most Americans," endeavored to shift away from a nonreflexive mode of thinking. To his mind and the minds of his critics, this normal mode of thought had led to the abstract, mystical, and, in some cases, "clumsily" applied aesthetic central to his dramas in the 1920s. In its place, Lawson began to gravitate toward embracing a dialectical mode of thought. This served as a guiding force in his efforts to forge a new aesthetic suitable for expressing his vision of "the harsh reality of the American scene."[89] As charted throughout the course of this chapter, Lawson's ever-evolving mode of thought and, by extension, the shape and scope of his method of artistic expression were in dynamic interplay with the extraordinarily vibrant sociopolitical and cultural currents in the United States at the turn of the decade. Of particular importance were those social energies flowing within the various communities that constituted the cultural left.

As is illustrated in the composition and production of *Success Story* as well as in Lawson's tenure as president of the Screen Writers' Guild, the playwright's orientation toward revolutionary politics found new force and specificity in the first years of the 1930s. His shifting from artist-rebel to revolutionary—a shift that was not yet completed in the first years of the 1930s—was inextricably bound up in the questions with which Lawson grappled during this time. Nonetheless, while the playwright came to believe that the (his) aesthetic rebellion of the twenties had failed, he also continued to hold, in manner typical of many of the heirs of the lyrical left, a deeply seeded distrust of organized politics born from that community's commitment to ardent individualism as well as the lingering pledge its members held to an agenda of rebellion, not revolution. Correspondingly, Lawson found he was unable to distance himself entirely from the pessimism and fatalism that ensnared other members of the avant-garde such as Van Wyck Brooks, Margaret Anderson, e. e. cummings, and Hart Crane. The never-completed *Red Square*, which forwarded the view that individual creativity would be compromised by any commitment to a political belief system, as well as *Success Story*, which poeticized the revolutionary spirit as a naïve position that was destined to fail, participated as a social currency in this economy of pessimism. It would take the harsh critical and disastrous commercial failure of his next two scripts in production—*The Pure in Heart* and *Gentlewoman*—in the spring of 1934 to bring to a head this evolving and increasingly unbearable personal dilemma. Therein, the nihilism and fatalism of the decaying lyrical left would at last give way to the optimism and hope that Lawson would find in his commitment to the people's revolution.

As part of his intellectual process, in the first years of the 1930s Lawson, like many others in the wildly variant community of leftward-leaning intellectuals, struggled with and, in turn, helped determine and shape the emerging and always vacillating requirements of what would eventually be termed and codified as "literary Marxism" at the first American Writers' Congress, held in April 1935.[90] In these years immediately following the stock market crash, the direction of this developing conception, labeled by some of its proponents as "the Marxist objection," was forged and refined in large part in the heated struggle between competing representational discourses.

On the one side were those who self-identified as New Humanists. Included in this group were intellectuals and literati such as Irving Babbitt, Paul Elmer More, and Seward Collins (who would become one of the leading apologists for Hitler and Mussolini in the United States). Broadly speaking, this group declared naturalism and other "modernist" modes of artistic expression (that is, naturalism, realism, and the host of nonrealistic -isms that had emerged in the first decades of the twentieth century) and thought (that is, Einstein-inspired relativity, Freudianism, and Nietzschian atheism) decadent, vulgar, and failed attempts. They sought instead to defend and uphold what they perceived as traditional literary values, classical norms, and restrained ideals and advocated a forceful doctrine of moderation and restraint. On the other side were those who were haphazardly grouped together and labeled inappropriately by the New Humanists as "antihumanist." Those in this group were widely dissimilar in their political views and included liberal (that is, social democrats) and left-wing (that is, Marxist) critics and authors, ranging from the ranks of the ultrarevolutionary, such as Michael Gold and V. F. Calverton, to the slightly more moderate, such as Malcolm Cowley, Katherine Anne Porter, and Edmund Wilson. Together this community of radicals and revolutionaries championed "realism" and, in the case of the group's more revolutionary participants, labeled New Humanism "literary fascism."[91] The terms of artistic expression and evaluation in the United States during this period were dictated by the social energy born from this unresolved struggle pitting New Humanism against antihumanism.

For Lawson, as it was for most who held progressive democratic or revolutionary views, the New Humanist stance was, for all practical purposes, seens as a reactionary (if not fascist) movement that opposed progress in the arts and, by extension, upheld the bourgeois world order.[92] In the pages of the revolutionary *New Masses* and the liberal *New Republic*, as well as in a 1930 volume of eclectic essays, *The Critique of Humanism: A Symposium*, edited by Hartley Grattan, New Humanism was situated as a patently conservative political and social force that sought to assault the emancipated modern spirit in general and naturalism and realism in particular. Edmund Wilson's essay of March 1930, "Notes on Babbitt and More"—which significantly predates his aforementioned revolutionary essay "An Appeal to Progressives"—may be viewed as a representative antihumanist polemic.

Written in response to the Babbitt and More–edited volume *Humanism in America: A Symposium*, Wilson works to methodically expose the system of boldly conservative ideas underpinning New Humanism as, ironically, inhuman, antidemocratic, authoritarian and oppositional to culture. Moreover, he seeks to discredit Babbitt's and More's self-proclaimed position as defenders of genuine human values as a politically motivated guise, masking their fervent desire to forward bourgeois high culture as legitimate and valued culture. Central to Wilson's critique is a measured, critical unpacking of Babbitt's appropriation of Plato. Wilson writes:

> Babbitt surely did not learn from Plato, whom he invokes [. . .], that we should feel so sure of our own opinions that we need not moderate with other people who happen to have different ones. The hero of Plato's novel of ideas is, of course, Socrates, but Plato's dialogues are a novel, none the less, and the impression, I think, that most people get from them, though they may not be persuaded by Socrates' opinions, is that the world has a good many aspects and that there is a good deal to be said on all sides. The people in Plato who follow Babbitt's precept that we "should not be moderate in dealing with error" are the judges of Socrates. I doubt whether even Aristotle was so sure that he was right as Babbitt. If Mr. Babbitt wants to find a tradition for his policy of dealing with error, he must look not to the Academy and the Lyceum, but to the councils of the inquisition, the revolutionary tribunal of the Terror and—to come closer to Professor Babbitt's home—Dedham Courthouse and Boston State House.[93]

Though clearly pointed, Wilson's critique seems moderate when compared to that of Michael Gold, a fellow traveler in the antihumanist struggle. In his barbed essay from the autumn of 1930, "[Thornton] Wilder: Prophet of the Genteel Christ," Gold sarcastically described the writing style of critical darling Wilder as "diluted Henry James." The staunch defender and champion of Marxist literary practice accused Wilder of writing pieces that belonged in "a museum, not a world," and of "peopling a devitalized world, an historic junkshop, with moldy characters" who spent their lives "brooding over their little lavender tragedies" with "tender irony." Gold noted his utter distaste for the "falseness" of Wilder's thought and his "tailor-made rhetoric, [the] language of death." Likewise, he found the widely celebrated author's books and plays to benefit in both content and form the needs of the decaying "parvenu class" that was searching for "a short cut to the aristocratic emotions." Quite simply, then, Gold believed "Wilder's goal [was] to comfort the status quo." He was the poet laureate of "a small sophisticated class that has recently arisen in American—our genteel bourgeoisie," an author of sentimental stories, written in a moldering tone and serving a degenerating class. As such, Gold believed Wilder's cultural work was born from, and instrumental in the continual production of, the New Humanist (masking a fascist) representational discourse.[94]

Clearly, though Gold's tone is decidedly more strident than that of Wilson, these two cultural critics shared an agenda in these first years of the 1930s: exposing the New Humanists as defenders not of genuine human values but of the bourgeois hegemonic order. Even so, while facing this common enemy, these antihumanists differed in how each sought to deal with the worldview forwarded by the likes of Babbitt and More. For Gold, the response envisioned was simple and harsh: the complete toppling and utter destruction of the systems of ideas and power underpinning the New Humanist mode, to be followed by the establishment of the new world order (that is, Communism). For Wilson, who had in 1930 not yet committed to this revolutionary Marxist agenda, the response to New Humanism was still one of individual opposition and rebellion: an assaulting and altering (as opposed to destruction) of the traditional structures and authorities. These competing views of Gold and Wilson regarding the method of response to New Humanism may be read as indicative of the chasm still separating progressive democrats from revolutionaries in the first years of the 1930s.[95]

There were some, such as Joseph Freeman, who had successfully shifted from the mode of rebel as defined by the lyrical left and assumed the role of revolutionary—"Individual rebellion has passed out of me and I would like nothing more than to be a disciplined worker in the movement," Freeman said.[96] However, there were many more, Lawson among them, who were as yet unwilling to subvert and constrain individual desire for the good of the people's revolutionary cause. There was nonetheless during these first years of the Depression a growing belief on the part of many progressive democrats that Marxism in general, and the CP-USA in particular, held possibilities of organization for social action on a mass scale. Thus, for Wilson, the threat posed by New Humanism initiated a profound alteration in his system of ideas wherein he came to believe that writers and artists could play an integral part in "break[ing] down the walls of the present" that separated his metaphorical "Axel's Castle" from "the City of Man."[97] As did Wilson, Lawson slowly began to awaken to the view that Communism was "an American force, which had moral and intellectual implications that could not be ignored."[98] It would be under the strain of his experiences in the middle years of decade, that this view, begrudgingly held by Lawson, would at last blossom into a deeply held revolutionary perspective.

Lost like Hamlet in His Inner Conflict

All the time I was running in circles in the dark, I wasn't even born yet.

—John Howard Lawson, *The Pure in Heart*, 1934

Near the beginning of her study *Contingencies of Value: Alternative Perspectives for Critical Theory*, Barbara Herrnstein Smith theorizes the dynamic interplay between the artist's art and the critical audience:

> Every literary work—and, more generally, artwork—is thus a product of a complex evaluative feedback loop that embraces not only the ever-shifting economy of the artist's own interests and resources as they evolve during and in reaction to the process of composition, but also the shifting economies of her assumed and imagined audiences, including those who do not yet exist but whose emergent interests, variable conditions of encounter, and rival sources of gratification she will attempt to predict—or will intuitively surmise—and to which, among other things, her own sense of the fittingness of each decision will be responsive.

Smith goes on to explicate the powerful, albeit always mutable, nature of creation, evaluation, and judgment, focusing on the elaborate relation between systems of aesthetic value and "the multiple social, political, circumstantial, and other constraints and conditions to which [those systems of aesthetic value] are responsive."[1] Smith's notion of contingent value that both determines and is determined by a myriad of overt and covert forces, institutional and individual desires, and verbal and nonverbal discourses, proves especially helpful when considering the developments in the theatre of the mid-1930s, and, by extension, that theatre's connection to the cultural dynamics in the United States of that historical moment.

As argued in the preceding chapters, over the course of the 1920s and early 1930s, the so-called left in the United States was in truth comprised of many communities. Each group within the "left" had specific aims and agendas, and they spanned a remarkably wide spectrum. Included within this widely construed "left" were communists of every sort—the Browder-led CP-USA and the two principle splinter groups, the right opposition led by Jay Lovestone and the left opposition (that is, Trotskyites) led by James Canon—as well as socialists and a large assortment of more moderate social democrats. In the middle years of the 1930s, however, and in the face of a growing Fascist threat (both at home, in the guise of New Humanism, and abroad, in the guise of Nazism), many of the chasms separating these various groups were slowly spanned. While it would be impossible and imprudent to pinpoint one particular event that initiated this closing of gaps, one salient occurrence was undoubtedly Michael Gold's call in the April 1933 issue of *New Masses* for "a united front of all working class parties and liberal groups. [. . .] Every anti-fascist is needed in this united front. There must be no base for factional quarrels."[2]

Gold's call for collaboration among the various factions comprising the numerous ideologically disparate liberal and left communities—between revolutionaries and social democrats, between working-class laborers and middle-class intellectuals, between rebellious aesthete moderns and champions of proletariat literature and art—was driven by his resolute conviction that fascism in all its forms, and a force even more evil than bourgeois capitalism, posed a considerable threat to all humanistic values. This threat, believed Gold, could only be defused and defeated by an unprecedented union of all who identified as "liberal" and "left wing" in the United States.

The dramatic and ominous rise of Nazism in Germany, culminating with Hitler's installation as chancellor, was cause enough for Gold—who had over the course of the preceding five years as editor of *New Masses* assumed a role that might be described as "literary commissar" of the CP-USA—to endorse a suspending of the dogmatism and factionalism (forwarded, in part, by Gold's own sectarian writings of the late 1920s and early 1930s) that had disassociated, one from another, the various leftist and liberal communities for almost two decades. In *The Rise and Fall of The American Left*, Diggins offers a cogent explanation of this sudden shift on the part of Gold and, in succession, the CP-USA away from the view of other progressive and liberal groups they had held in the late 1920s and early 1930s:

> [This view] rested largely on the theory of "social fascism," a notion first developed in the early 1920s by European Communists in an effort to undermine the social democrats in Germany and elsewhere. In accordance with this thesis communists were instructed to turn "class against class" so that in the end only two classes (the proletariat and bourgeoisie) would confront one another in mortal combat. In order to discredit liberals and socialists, the CP took the position that all those who were not communists were class enemies and that liberal-social democracy and fascism were expressions of the same repressive bourgeois state, the only difference being the former was "masked" and the latter "naked." In Germany, communists thus scorned socialist attempts to oppose Hitler's rise to power, and in the United States communists attacked [1932 presidential nominee from the Socialist Party] Norman Thomas and President Roosevelt as "social fascists." The communist strategy presumed that fascism reflected capitalism's "final crisis"; hence whatever tactic would expedite Hitler's advent to power was a victory for communism ("After Hitler, Our Turn!"). But when Hitler consolidated power and made it clear that fascism was anything but a transitory phenomenon, and when Roosevelt seemed to salvage American capitalism, the theory of social fascism had to be abandoned. Instead of predicting fascism's imminent collapse, communists now described it as an imminent threat. The USSR responded by joining the League of Nations and signing a mutual defense pact with France, and the Comintern [which dictated policy for the CP-USA] announced the new policy of the Popular Front.
>
> The Popular Front [. . .] represented a complete volte-face. Whereas the CP had previously insisted on class struggle, it now called for collaboration with the bourgeoisie. It had formerly exalted the Soviet system of government; now it extolled the virtues of American democracy. It had once preached internationalism; now it praised nationalism. American communists embraced the new course without so much as a blush of embarrassment, hailing socialists as fellow comrades and praising Roosevelt as an enlightened statesman.[3]

In light of this "complete volte-face," there occurred a discernable transformation in the shape and scope of the discursive and intertextual determinations, as well as the verbal and nonverbal discourses, within the various left communities in the United States. Specifically, in the wake of Gold's call for unity and culminating with the authorizing of the Popular Front in 1935, the emergent view that Fascism was a looming and portentous threat altered in significant ways the social energy that organized and established the practices of creating and responding to cultural outpourings, including texts generated for and about the theatre.[4] As these diverse leftist and liberal communities began to unify and mobilize under the ideology of a Popular Front or "united front" as envisioned by Gold, there was subsequently a shift in the particular way these texts for and about the theatre were produced, consumed, and valued. Simultaneously, liberal and leftist theatre artists and critics, regardless of party affiliation or ideological creed, began to reorganize their methods and modes in light of this paradigmatic shift. There was, consequently, in the middle years of the 1930s, a series of events taking placing within the leftist community writ large, and by extension within the community of theatre artists and critics, that seem the very embodiment of Smith's theoretical model. The texts written by and about the theatre in this historical moment were concurrently producers and material products within a "complex evaluative feedback loop," one that "embrace[d] not only the ever-shifting economy of the artist's own interests and resources as they evolve[d] during and in reaction to the process of composition, but also the shifting economies of [the] assumed and imagined audiences," who were, in turn, producing and responding to the "emergent interests" of a united left as engendered by the ideology of the Popular Front.[5]

Specific responses in the theatre to this readjusted social energy were as numerous and varied as the liberal and left-wing communities that created them. Moreover, factionalism continued to persist. For a brief time, however, beginning in the middle years of the 1930s and continuing through the end of the decade, playwrights, producing organizations, and critics, sharing a common belief in the transformative power of the theatre, invested their work with a heightened and overt social consciousness. This very often resulted in a supplanting of the ardent individualism so central to progressivism and, by extension, the lyrical left with an increased stress on the power of collective action. Perhaps above all else, however, this social energy of the mid-1930s prompted in artists a renewed commitment to offer specific and detailed solutions to social ills and fascist impulses without abstraction and ambiguity. Thus, *materialist aesthetics*, defined by Ira Levine as "a symbiotic interplay between social conditions and theatrical activity," at last seemed to have gained a more widespread acceptance.[6]

In terms of theatrical production, this social energy produced a variety of fascinating results.[7] There was the formation of the Theatre Union, which opened its first production, *Peace on Earth* by Albert Maltz and George Sklar, on 29 November 1933. In early 1934, this group also produced, to considerable acclaim, *Stevedore* by Sklar and Paul Peters. Both plays presented sympathetic and affirming portraits of working-class life, political activism, and militant unionism. Likewise, the Shock Troupe of the Workers' Laboratory Theatre, a group with ties to the CP-USA, had begun staging works in the late 1920s and publishing the magazine *Workers' Theatre* (a precursor to the Popular Front publication *New Theatre*) beginning in 1931. In November 1933, they dramatized and staged to considerable acclaim V. J. Jerome's poem *Newsboy*, creating a twelve-minute agitprop that pitted the capitalist press against the left-wing press. During this same period, the German-language Proletbuehne was producing plays on the streets and in union halls, as was Artef, the Yiddish-language Workers Theatrical Alliance. Further, the League of Workers' Theatres (a consortium that included the Workers' Laboratory Theatre and the Theatre Collective, and served as the predecessor to the New Theatre League) had grown from an fledgling union of twelve affiliated groups at its founding in 1931 into a formidable producing organization with close to three hundred members, all in a matter of three years.

The new social spirit in the theatre in the United States was not restricted to the small, noncommercial, or workers' theatres. In early 1933, George S. Kaufman and Morrie Ryskind, who had a huge success in 1931 with the musical satire *Of Thee I Sing*, returned with a sequel, *Let 'Em Eat Cake*. In November 1933, John Wexley's strike play, *Steel*, made a brief Broadway run of twelve performances. Early the following year, his *They Shall Not Die*, one of two plays produced in the first months of 1934 that dealt with the Scottsboro Boys case, was produced to much acclaim by the Theatre Guild. Additionally, the commercial stage in New York of 1933 saw the arrival of Brecht and Weill's *Threepenny Opera*, Jack Kirkland's dramatization of Erskine Caldwell's novel *Tobacco Road*, and the continued presence of the socially inclined Group Theatre.

Buoyed by the possibilities of this new atmosphere in the theatre, in the first months of 1934 Lawson refused nomination for a second term as president of the Screen Writers' Guild and returned to New York with an eye toward reviving his theatrical career. In the three years following, three of Lawson's scripts, *The Pure in Heart* (1934),

Gentlewoman (1934), and *Marching Song* (1937), were produced in New York. Additionally, he wrote and published numerous theoretical writings, principally his book-length study *Theory and Technique of Playwriting* (1936). In all of these texts, there remain discursive traces of the escalating internal struggle pitting the playwright's conception of aesthetic rebellion against his maturing political ideology that was increasingly revolutionary. As material phenomena, these dramatic and theoretical texts, as well as the critical texts created in response to his work, were inextricably linked to a larger representational discourse unique to the emergent and, eventually, codified Popular Front. As such, these texts may be read as discursive objects that include both overt and tacit traces of the historically specific social energy born from the social and cultural currents of the "united" left in the United States at this historical moment.

The Pure in Heart and *Gentlewoman*

The Pure in Heart may be traced to the rough outline for *The Jazz Tragedy*, circa 1924. At that time, the artist-rebel Lawson considered it a sequel to *Processional*, wherein he could apply the methods of that script to a story about life in New York City. In the outline for this early version, the protagonist, Annabel Sparks, is described as "the Sadie Cohen of Broadway."[8] Following a rough draft of the script written in June 1926 under the title *The Social Whirl*, Lawson completed *The Pure in Heart* in the summer of 1928, immediately before his first foray into the film industry. At that point, and following the encouragement of Joseph Freeman, the playwright submitted the script to the Theatre Guild. The Guild's 1932 production, directed by Theresa Helburn, closed to disastrous reviews during its pre-Broadway, out-of-town run. The script subsequently underwent extensive revision during the summer and autumn of 1933. This round of revisions was completed in January of the next year. Notwithstanding the modifications made at various times during the early 1930s, on the whole the structure, tone, and theme of the script clearly belong to the Lawson of the twenties with the continued, though more limited, use of various nonrealistic and presentational techniques, the abstract rejection of the bourgeois moral code and the impassioned championing of individualism as the thematic core. There are nevertheless a small number of startling adjustments made to the presentation of that thematic center, alterations clearly linking *The Pure in Heart* to Lawson's mode of thought and pessimistic worldview of the early 1930s.

The Pure in Heart tells the story of Annabel Sparks, a young woman who runs away from her small-town home to the bright lights of New

York City. The exterior of the Sparks' family home, "a small-town shack" in upstate New York, provides the setting for the first scene of act 1.[9] As the curtain rises, Annabel enters. She is "an attractive, eager girl of nineteen [. . . who] might be almost any girl in any American town, just out of high school, half way out of adolescent affairs, not knowing where to turn, bubbling over with energy and sentimentality" (3–4). Through Annabel's discussions with Ma and Pa Sparks, the family's appalling financial problems are brought to light. Pa Sparks "ain't got a penny" and Ma Sparks cannot find "a quarter for the iceman" (5). Annabel talks of how she is tired of the family's financial woes and the limitations of her small town. She is tortured by the promises of "next Christmas," feels "[l]ike breaking everything to pieces, shooting things, smashing things," and dreams of running away to New York and the theatre, where "[w]ith a little practice [she] could dance as good as Joan Crawford" (8–10). When a letter arrives from a friend who has gone to New York, Annabel's desire to leave her small-town life only intensifies:

> ANNABEL. 'Way inside there's a little fire burning, a fire no bigger'n a minute, but sometimes I feel like it would burn me to a black cinder. (*She stops, overcome by her own feelings*) Let me go! Let me do it, 'cause it's what I got to do—help me, Mommer—all I want is some money. [. . .] I could catch the six-fifteen—there's just time. (*Decisively*) I want to be on that train! If you won't give me the money, I'll go anyway. You can't stop me. [. . .] I know what I want and I'm going to get it. (11–12)

The scene ends with Annabel stealing money from her parents and running for the train. As she goes, she calls to her parents and the world, "There's music playing in New York! I want to shuffle off and find that music. I want to go out where it's spilling like a fountain!" (14).

With no break in the action, and as jazz music swells, the first scene dissolves into the second scene of act 1: the stage of a theatre in New York. The setting on the stage, though half-finished, is that of a Broadway musical comedy that "has a rich, mysterious, romantic quality, suggesting the glittering, and fictitious beauty which Annabel is seeking" (15). While stagehands move about, removing what was the Sparks' home and adjusting lights, a variety of people come and go. There is Junius Mellon, a kindly millionaire who hopes to back the production; Matt Swann, a "hard-boiled" director and producer; Dr. Martin Goshen, a cynical, hard-drinking playboy who is Swann's partner; and Edwina Raleigh, Goshen's lover and an aging "Goddess of the silver screen" who is trying to breathe life into her dying career (16). In addition to the company members, there is Dr. Goshen's younger brother, Larry Goshen, a "good-natured tough kid" who just got out of jail and wants to "get away some place, it doesn't matter where" (37). Annabel enters and begs Swann to put her in the chorus. Although Swann chases her away, she promises to "drop in again" (31). When she returns, she is surprised to find the stage empty except for Larry. He flirts with her, but she flatly rejects him and talks of her dreams of success on the stage. As Larry leaves, Swann enters. The first act ends with Annabel agreeing to sleep with Swann in exchange for a part in the chorus.

The first scene in act 2 takes place one week later in the apartment of Dr. Goshen. Annabel and Goshen have just made love and she is "a little tight, bright-eyed, [and] hysterical" (57). Goshen glibly warns her against "bedroom hysterics" and his nihilism becomes apparent. A knock at the door interrupts their conversation. Annabel exits to the bedroom and Larry enters. He tells his brother that he has failed to get an honest job, has "gotten into another jam," and needs a thousand dollars. As he talks with Martin, it becomes clear that Larry's life has been a series of bad breaks and that his tough facade hides a lost soul:

> LARRY. [. . .] you can't help being what you are. You're safe, you always been safe 'cause you had cash. Money's what counts, money's the whole works.
>
> GOSHEN. You're wrong—
>
> LARRY. Sure, I'm wrong, 'cause I'm on the outside looking in: go out and sit on park benches, go down to the waterfront and talk to the working stiffs. You learn things when you're down and out. I'm not sore at you, Martin, you're flabby and you take it easy and you're full of words right up to your neck. You're an ornament to society, that's you; you can see a lot of bright lights from your window, but you can't see the working stiffs walking down there in the dark—
>
> GOSHEN. Why all this talk about workers? You're not a worker!
>
> LARRY. No, I'm nothing. That's the trouble. I don't belong any place, I don't care—society's a mangy con game, from top to bottom—to hell with it . . . (66)

Larry and Martin's talk is interrupted by another knock at the door. Edwina enters and discovers Annabel. In a rage over Goshen's infidelity, she immediately calls Swann at the theatre and has Annabel fired. With that, Edwina exits, followed by Goshen. The scene closes with Annabel and Larry, two loners with uncertain futures, left alone in the apartment.

As the second scene of act 2 opens, Goshen's apartment is dismantled by stagehands and the stage of Swann's theatre is again revealed. It is the final dress rehearsal and the chorus girls are singing and dancing. The song-and-dance routine is abruptly interrupted when Edwina misses a cue. Swann storms on stage, yells at the entire company, and abruptly sends everyone home. All have exited the stage except a few stagehands and Mellon, who has been watching from the wings, when Annabel enters. She begs Mellon to "make [Swann] change his mind" and let her back in the show (88). Although he refuses to interfere with the production, Mellon, like everyone else, is intrigued with Annabel's fiery spirit and offers to help her develop her talent by paying for training with no strings attached. At the height of happiness, Annabel turns to leave and finds herself face to face with Larry. He is being trailed by the police and has come to find his brother. When a detective enters, there is "a brief tense struggle, and muffled shot, and the detective falls dead" (96). Unexplainably drawn to Larry, Annabel chooses to follow him, thus forsaking the offer just made by Mellon, all the while claiming, "I don't care, I want to go with him, I don't want anything else" (97).

The third scene in act 2 takes place the next evening in a room in a tenement. As the youngsters wait for a man to smuggle them into Canada, Larry paces the floor nervously and Annabel tries to calm him by talking about their future. With police sirens wailing in the distance, Larry begs her to leave and she refuses, confessing, "I'd rather die, I'd be dead if I went on living." As the sounds of sirens grow louder, Larry muses:

> LARRY. [. . .] Maybe some place is different—I don't know: where they'd keep busy working, digging, plowing, building cities too, laying one brick on another brick . . . (*As if he were seeing the simplicity of it*). There's nothing bad with all that stuff. People could be happy, people could build things, work without stealing, love without going crazy— (106–8)

The scene ends with them walking out of the door and into a dark hall:

> LARRY. It's dark.
>
> ANNABEL. (*As they disappear*). Don't mind the dark. (110)

After the stage goes to black, several shots ring out.

The final scene takes place in the theatre that same evening. Behind a gauzy curtain the chorus dances, "shadowy figures swaying with dream-like precision" (111). As Edwina stands at the center of the curtain ready to make her entrance, Goshen enters followed by Swann:

> GOSHEN. . . . My brother and the girl have been killed . . . shot to death in the hall of a tenement.

EDWINA. (*Turns to him harshly*). Why tell me now, do you want to spoil my entrance?

SWANN. What's going on here? There's your cue, Edwina . . . Hurry up.

Edwina parts the curtain and enters, light floods the stage, wild music plays, Goshen and Swann are "silhouetted against the blaze of light," and the front curtain falls (111).

Harold Clurman referred to *The Pure in Heart* as "Lawson's swan-song to the jazz-and-racket age."[10] In many ways, Clurman's brief description is fitting. Structurally, the script does represent Lawson's last foray into the style from the twenties. The realistic mode Lawson employed with aplomb in *Success Story*, while not completely abandoned, is, nonetheless, amended with the familiar mixture of jazz music and techniques borrowed from nonrealistic dramatic forms. Moreover, many of the characters are one-dimensional and cartoon-like. Martin Goshen, for example, is a character type, not unlike the Man in the Silk Hat in *Processional*, who speaks for the decaying and unfulfilled bourgeoisie:[11] "Look at me! In a sense I'm a man of the world. But look at me more closely: I'm supposed to be a doctor; I haven't had a patient since I left medical school; I inherited money, I fell in love, I played the market, I lost a fortune . . . So what? I don't know the answer" (61). Of all the characters, only Larry and Annabel break from the boundaries of stereotype to become fully realized characters. In this way, they are similar to Dynamite Jim in *Processional*, who exists as the only individualized character in a dramatic world that is otherwise populated by one-dimensional, grotesque figures. Still, while Annabel and Larry gain individual status and are used by Lawson to perform a dramatic function borrowed from his technique in the twenties, the ideas they express, the choices they make, and the destinies they are forced to accept, provide a clear indication that they are linked to Lawson's mode of thought in the early thirties. This synthesis of a dramaturgical method quintessentially related to the 1920s and mode of thought unique to the early 1930s may be further explored through an explication of the similarities and differences in Lawson's drawing of Roger Bloomer and his drawing of Annabel Sparks and Larry Goshen.[12]

While Annabel's individualistic desire to escape from her small town and go to New York City is not unlike the individualistic desire of the young disillusioned protagonist in *Roger Bloomer*, there are a number of key differences. Whereas Annabel initially leaves her home propelled by the superficial want of celebrity and material success, Roger flees Iowa driven by the weighty aim, albeit naïve, to find metaphysical truth. Despite their differing objectives, for both protagonists the journey to New York City is an affirmation of their ardent and emerging individualism, born from the burning desire to define who they are in the world. While both Roger and Annabel eventually rise above the forces opposing them in their quests for agency—which involves for Roger an intensifying resolve to live the life he wants and for Annabel a radical and wholesale reconfiguring of what she values and desires—with Annabel, Lawson provides an account of the bleak future following that victory. Annabel's story involves not only her triumph over her puerile desire to achieve celebrity and material success, as well as her ability to adopt a life goal that is nobler, but also the tragic consequences of that choice. For her, then, individualism is first realized in her callow want of celebrity and material success, then reconfigured in her accepting of the very different life offered by Larry, and, in the end, brutally punished.

Less complex is *Roger Bloomer.* As argued in chapter 2, the whole of that earlier script deals with little more than the young man's spiritual sojourn and a strengthening of his resolve to "go it alone." Significantly, it is only in the final moments, when Roger triumphs over the shadows in his dreams and moves toward "a bright ray of light" illuminating an "open door," that there is any suggestion whatsoever that he has achieved his goal (225). Unlike Annabel's violent and tragic future that is fully realized on stage—and that may be read as a poetization of the playwright's view that tragic and inevitable consequences accompany ardent individualism—there is never a concrete manifestation of Roger's future. In the final moments of the script, though, Lawson strongly suggests that the young man's future is bright and full of hope. For Roger, then, individualism is first realized, forged, and strengthened in his struggles against oppression, and, in the end, rewarded. It is this optimistic ending, wherein the individualized hero secures agency and triumphs, that marks *Roger Bloomer* as a script written in the early twenties and separates it from the pessimistic view of individualism underpinning *The Pure in Heart.*

Larry too performs a dramatic function suggestive of Lawson's earlier scripts, but he also expresses ideas that mark him as a product of the early thirties.[13] As with the playwright's dramas from the twenties, the social critique implied in *The Pure in Heart* is overwhelmed by the focus on dramatic techniques. Amid the formal devices of metatheatricality, one-dimensional characterization, and jazz music are a handful of overt and thoroughly romantic denunciations of bourgeois society, all of which come from Larry, an instinctively good soul—an "everyman" who is kin to Roger Bloomer—who has been thrown unprepared into a deadening and evil environment and corrupted. In the second half of the play, Larry provides an almost constant albeit poeticized commentary on the decadence of bourgeois society. Near the end he proclaims, "We were wrong all along, but we didn't want to be like that, we didn't decide what we were going to be" (107). While few of his lines are as overtly politically inflected as this one, his constant references to an unattainable ideal world provide a much more concrete and pessimistic image of the future than the abstract and optimistic view conveyed via the image of "far off, listen, the tread of marching people singing a new song" (*Roger Bloomer,* 225). Thus, while *The Pure in Heart* relies on dramatic techniques borrowed from the twenties, the ideas expressed and actions taken by the two main characters represent Lawson's confused and pessimistic thinking in the early thirties.

The Pure in Heart—independently produced by Richard Aldrich and Alfred de Liagre Jr.—opened at the Longacre Theatre on 20 March 1934 and closed after seven performances.[14] In an essay published in the *New York Times* two days before the play's disastrous run, Lawson tried to express his idea of revolutionary theatre such as it was in the spring of 1934. In reading the essay through a materialist lens, it becomes clear that Lawson was still straddling two worlds and two definitions of revolutionary theatre. At the beginning of the essay, the guidelines he suggests for creating such a theatre could be mistakenly thought as pulled from "The New Showmanship," his first, aesthetic-centered manifesto for the New Playwrights' Theatre: "The use of stairways and platforms in stage design is only one aspect, although the one that most frequently comes to mind. Abstraction or stylization in make-up and general movement is another. Expression of radical or revolutionary sentiment is another. And projections of poetic and fantastic states of being another." Near the end of the essay, however, his definition for the revolutionary theatre takes on a decidedly different tone, one akin to his ideas expressed in "What Is a Workers Theatre?": "This then is the theatrical experimentation I believe in: experiment with insurgent and intransigent ideas, experiment with plans for re-making a clearly tottering world, experiment with the essential desires and torments of characters acutely aware of life around them and its most immediate and urgent problems."[15] It seems, then, that while Lawson continued to desperately hold onto the ideal that formal experimentation was the main concern of the revolutionary theatre, he still could not dismiss the idea that the theatre should also address "immediate and urgent problems" of people living in a "tottering world."

Lawson's attempt to straddle two worlds is further demonstrated in his program note for the March 1934 production: "*The Pure in Heart* is an attempt to achieve a mood quite foreign to the realistic theatre [. . .] It is rather an effort to bring a certain sort of poetry into the theatre. This is not the poetry of blank verse and measured sentences. It is the poetry of the New York streets, the turbulent, crude rhythm of the dynamic world in which we live."[16] Lawson's noble intention to bring together "poetry" and "the crude rhythm of the dynamic world" was apparently perceived as confusion or lack of commitment by left-wing critics. Many in this camp had evidently had enough of Lawson's indecision, and ignored the play altogether. Of the critics writing for the mainstream press, only Brooks Atkinson, who found "Mr. Lawson's cosmopolitan rhapsody [. . .] stirring," wrote a somewhat favorable review. Nonetheless, Atkinson's note that the most striking aspect of the play for him was the concurrence of "an old impression that [. . .] Lawson is an interesting playwright" suggests that the critic saw little progress beyond the bounds of what had brought the playwright some measure of success the previous decade.[17] "Ever since 'Processional' he has resisted easy filing. There is something of that old carousel-like drama in this current piece. [. . .] It is the dance of the phantoms of New York, tabloid in its material and mystic in its philosophy. [. . .] But still confusion dogs the characters and the play and leaves the theatregoer perplexed by the ending. To put it baldly, 'The Pure in Heart' is not resolved, and that is a pity." The other doctrinal reviewers were less forgiving and railed against the production and Lawson. Percy Hammond sarcastically thanked Lawson for giving him an evening in the theatre appropriate for "feverish napping [. . . only] disturbed now and then by the author's drowsy memories of plays by other melodramatists,"[18] and John Anderson dismissed it as "a hodge-podge of banal scenes."[19] With *The Pure in Heart*, Lawson satisfied neither the majority of the critics nor the public.

Gentlewoman, which opened two days after *The Pure in Heart*, fared little better. In the words of Lawson, "[It] too demonstrated the war within myself."[20] Act 1 of *Gentlewoman* takes place in the library of Jack and Gwyn Ballantine's house, which "radiates wealth and good taste."[21] Jack has been called out of town on business, and Gwyn, a "queenly" woman who "has poise and brains" and "is disarmingly direct," is hosting a dinner party (124). As the action commences, dinner has just ended and all have retired to the library where they talk about collective farming in Russia, Freud, the possibility of another world war, and the unemployed. In addition to Gwyn, there is Elliott Snowden, a "genteel, good-tempered, negatively likable" man in his thirties who is a Harvard graduate, a famous novelist, and in awe of Gwyn (118); Connie Blane, Elliott's girlfriend, fresh out of finishing school; Dr. Morris Golden, a "dry and scientific" psychoanalyst (124); Mrs. Kate Stoneleigh, a "vigorous, metallic, hard-boiled" woman of sixty and Gwyn's aunt (123); Colonel Fowler, a retired military man who has just returned from a trip to Russia where he consulted on engineering projects; and Havens, the "correct and non-committal butler" (120). Into this refined scene enters Elliott's friend Rudy Flannigan. Rudy is a hard-drinking, wildly irresponsible writer who "has a penetrating mind, has read and thought a good deal, but has never coordinated his ideas clearly" (131). Eventually all exit except Gwyn and Rudy. Gwyn flirts with him, all the while laughing at his crude attempts to sweep her off her feet. Rudy, in turn, constantly ridicules her lavish lifestyle. While the conversation is light, it is apparent that they have engaged in a multifaceted battle, pitting working class against upper middle class and male against female. Their playful sparring becomes more heated and dissolves into a moment of full disclosure:

GWYN. . . . I'm afraid to look ahead.

RUDY. No, you're not.

GWYN. I am, I'm frightened. (*She laughs softly*) I've told you so many lies this evening—I've pretended to be calm, but my head is crowded with strange thoughts . . . (*She stands before him, as calm as a statue, but a strange vibration in her voice*) I can even imagine myself dropping this gown from my shoulders and standing before you!

RUDY. (*Moved, quite a new tone in his voice*). I don't want you to.

GWYN. I know: That's why I dare suggest it—

RUDY. Perhaps, if I wait . . .? (*She shakes her head. He adds quite simply*). You see I've fallen in love with you!

GWYN. You don't understand your own feelings—one minute you gobble me up as if I were a bit of hors d'œuvre and the next minute you think you are in love. . . . Perhaps some day people will learn to understand themselves. (155–56)

This awkward moment is interrupted and the acts ends abruptly when Vaughn, Jack Ballantine's business associate, enters and announces that Jack has committed suicide on the train to Washington.

The second act takes place six weeks later and is set in Gwyn's sitting room. Dressed in black and sitting in front of the fireplace, Gwyn is visited by "a cross-section of [her] friends," each providing exposition that fills in the last six weeks and each offering a different way for Gwyn to get on with her life (184). First comes Colonel Fowler, who reveals that Jack's business dealings were less than up front: insurmountable debts led him to suicide, and all Gwyn's holdings, including the house, must be liquidated to pay off the creditors. As he prepares to leave he awkwardly offers to marry Gwyn, and she politely declines. Next, Dr. Golden enters and reveals that Jack's death was brought about by not only financial troubles, but also "psychic impotence [. . .] the sense that he was no longer adequate" (167). As he exits, he too offers to aid Gwyn, suggesting that his counseling services might be helpful. Rudy enters next, tells her to "stop flirting with corpses," and tries to coax her to take a chance with him. Much to his dismay, the future he paints terrifies Gwyn, his bravado offends her, and she asks him to leave. Rudy responds with anger:

> RUDY. I was a fool to get into this, dizzy, dazzled by a jewel in a jewel box. There's a bread line just around the corner, hundreds of 'em with the wind whistling through their pants—and you sit in here smeared with perfume and emotion! To hell with it.
>
> *(Gwyn takes all this without emotion. She stops him as he turns to the door.)*
>
> GWYN. Wait. What you say is true—I admit I'm a coward—I want to hold you in my arms and I can't—I can't have an affair with you, it wouldn't work. When a woman is in love, she wants understanding and dignity and beauty . . . love is important, like having babies and being born— (172–73)

Sensing a moment of vulnerability, Rudy tries to kiss Gwyn only to be interrupted by the entrance of Mrs. Stoneleigh. Rudy storms from the room, and Mrs. Stoneleigh offers to take Gwyn on vacation to the Riviera. When Gwyn declines the offer, Mrs. Stoneleigh exits. Elliott then enters, and he too offers Gwyn the chance to get away. His proposal is interrupted by Rudy who returns and again attempts to sweep Gwyn off her feet. This time Gwyn confesses that she is intrigued with the idea of them "together, in a little room up six flights of stairs," but again refuses (185). With that, Rudy humbly confesses that he too is trying to find his way in life. Gwyn, deeply touched by his new-shown vulnerability, immediately changes her mind. The act ends with her and Rudy leaving the room, and Gwyn declaring, "It's good to burn bridges" (186).

The first scene of act 3 occurs six months later. Gwyn has moved out of the Ballantine mansion and into an apartment with Rudy, using funds provided by Mrs. Stoneleigh. As the curtain rises, Rudy is sitting at his typewriter struggling to finish an article and Connie is lying on the couch smoking a cigarette. They have just made love, and Connie tries to make conversation. As they talk, it becomes clear that neither of them has deep feelings for the other and that they only came together out of their resentment of Gwyn. Connie is angry because of Elliott's unwavering dedication to Gwyn and Rudy is angry because of Gwyn's attempt to tame him. Gwyn enters, and it appears that she is delighted with her new life. In light conversation with Connie, Gwyn admits that when money runs short she turns to Mrs. Stoneleigh. Connie exits and Rudy confesses the indiscretion with Connie, admits that it was an act of anger, and claims that Gwyn's inability to accept their lot in life drove him to infidelity. In the course of conversation, it becomes clear that Gwyn will not adopt Rudy's vision of life. While she is anxious "to find a way to live—a way that means something, that touches reality," she cannot change her nature (203). Likewise, Rudy admits that he is unwilling to change: "I've got no illusions about myself, Gwyn—I'm lazy and soft—but I went to a school of muscle and sweat and I know what it means" (204). Now that it is clear that they will never reconcile, Gwyn sends Rudy away. As Rudy leaves, Elliott enters. The scene ends with Gwyn revealing that she is pregnant and that she "planned it deliberately, to make [Rudy] settle down—I didn't want a child—I deserve to be put on the rack and tortured" (206).

The last scene takes place the following morning in the library of the Ballantine mansion. The furniture is covered with sheets and all the personal effects have been removed in preparation for the new owners. Colonel Fowler, Mrs. Stoneleigh, and Elliott enter one after the other. All have heard that Gwyn has returned to the house and have come to offer their help and advice. Gwyn refuses their offers and dismisses them. Rudy enters and they talk one last time:

GWYN. What you told me yesterday—the starving people—

RUDY. Been worrying about that?

GWYN. If that's where reality lies, I don't want to escape.

RUDY. (*Seriously*). If you want to go after that sort of reality, you have to do it alone.

GWYN. And you?

RUDY. Me too! Maybe you want it, but we'd never find anything like that together.

GWYN. Why not?

RUDY. Too tied up in each other . . .

GWYN. Could we find it alone?

RUDY. (*Rises, deeply troubled*). I'm not much good . . . might get somewhere in ten years if I had the nerve—

GWYN. (*In a frightened whisper, searching his face for the answer*). Why not with me?

RUDY. No, I'd go on doing this sort of thing, get in an emotional mess and get drunk to settle it. As long as I'm with you, I have no courage . . . I feel responsible, worry about you whether you want me or not . . . worry about money and write books. Books are all right if you can make 'em spit fire and lead . . . I don't want to write, don't know enough. I don't want to sail over the battle on a pink cloud pounding a typewriter. (217)

With that Rudy leaves, determined to make a difference in the world. Elliott enters and he and Gwyn talk about the future:

ELLIOTT. (*Deeply troubled, pleadingly*). Sooner or later, you'll stop rebelling, you'll grow old, fighting all the bright new confusion just the way Aunt Kate has fought you, always losing and smiling, because bitterness wins in the end . . .

GWYN. You're looking in the wrong crystal ball, there's nothing but the past in yours.

ELLIOTT. There's nothing but the past in the future.

GWYN. Even the child in me knows better than that.

ELLIOTT. Why should anything be different? He'll go through the mill, tapped for bones, at Yale, the Stock Exchange and an assortment of women.

GWYN. Our children won't play at life in boudoirs and offices: they'll face something different whether they like it or not. If you and I look in the crystal ball we'd turn to stone; we're not fit for the future, we're little people, we comfort ourselves with little passions, we waste ourselves with little fears, we walk in a funeral procession—towards a red horizon; we can't see the cities burning and the marching armies—there's blood in the sky. (220)

As the play closes, and upon the ashes of her personal sacrifice, Gwyn too commits herself to change. She is determined to raise a child who will not repeat her mistakes: "perhaps I can make a child who won't be afraid, he'll take sides and die—but there's always a chance, he might live and make a new world" (221).

Lawson commented that the idea for *Gentlewoman* was born out of his desire to "meet the requirements of Broadway" and, at the same time, "deal with a meaningful contemporary theme." "I was not unmindful of the box office, and I was desperately anxious for the success that had always eluded me. This was in some sense a challenge to my craftsmanship; I needed to prove that I could master conventional techniques in order to adventure more boldly in uncharted territory."[22] In some ways, Lawson achieved his goal. The ill-fated romantic relationship between Gwyn, the intelligent upper-middle-class woman, and Rudy, the unstable and romanticized revolutionary, has many of the structural and thematic markings of the conventional drawing-room play. This core story, complete with a callow social theme, is indeed kin to commercially successful scripts written by U.S. playwright S. N. Behrman for the Broadway stage in the 1930s. Nonetheless, Behrman's enviable facility with the well-made play form, coupled with his overriding desire to write dramas that were first and foremost commercially viable, separates his endeavors from Lawson's attempt to grapple with weighty contemporary issues within a conventional dramatic structure. While a formalist analysis of *Gentlewoman* would most certainly reveal the script to be a hodgepodge of melodramatic clichés and stereotypes of the most obvious sort, what is of concern here is the underdeveloped idea resting at the thematic center of that text.

Gwyn, a member of the educated upper middle class, in due course comes to realize that the old world order on which her life was based is materially and spiritually exhausted. Romantic love and solitary reflection are shown to be inadequate tools for dealing with the new chaotic times. Eventually she decides to "enter the fight" by committing to do all she can to raise her child in a world that is better or send him to a war to make it better. Similarly, Rudy, a member of the working class, comes to realize that all his talk of revolution does little more than mask his indecisiveness. In the end, he too makes a commitment to join with the forces that will create a new and better tomorrow. Thus, out of the failed relationship between Gwyn and Rudy comes a commitment for both.

Despite the implied nobility of each character's final decision, most of the script is given over to documenting their ambivalent waffling. Scene after scene conveys their tortured musings and inability to act or commit. Furthermore, when Gwyn and Rudy do at last accept the responsibility of commitment, their choices are presented as not only difficult, but as contrition. Harold Clurman commented on Lawson and his portrayal of commitment:

> Lawson himself at the time was a little like both of his protagonists, deeply in sympathy with the gentlewoman of the past, brutally impatient with the softness that made him cling to her, aware that he could not long dwell within this dual consciousness, eager for the

> conflagration ahead that would ultimately burn and temper all to a new wholeness and strength.
>
> Every aspect of the play betrayed an ambiguity that derived from Lawson's intense groping. The social problem that was the center of the play's meaning could not be identified with any particular situation, for what was clearly visible struck the audience as merely the depiction of a rather stupid love affair.[23]

Thus the thematic center in *Gentlewoman* may be viewed as something of an autobiographical testament to the confused and tortured state of the playwright's thinking in early 1934.

As with *The Pure in Heart*, *Gentlewoman* was an enormous commercial and critical failure. Opening on 22 March (two days following the doomed production of *The Pure in Heart*), the Group Theatre production of *Gentlewoman* closed after only twelve performances.[24] Of the reviewers writing for the mainstream press, again only Brooks Atkinson offered a critique that was at all positive. In his review for the *New York Times*, Atkinson postulated that *Gentlewoman*, though at times unfocused and not as engaging as either *Roger Bloomer* or *Processional*, was an adequate revoicing of Lawson's recurring theme: "moderns adrift on the sea of life." Overall, however, he was unmoved: "The mystic forms suit [Lawson] better. For when he arranges modern bewilderment into the realistic pattern of three acts his characters look unreal, his ideas look sophomoric and the playgoer suspects that Mr. Lawson is out of his soundings. [. . .] When he writes in a realistic style he lets himself down and the theatregoers out."[25] Other critics writing for the mainstream press were far less forgiving. While John Anderson saw it as nothing more than a "yammering match between two extraordinarily dull people,"[26] Percy Hammond dismissed Lawson as "a grave and juvenile thinker about solemn subjects."[27]

Though the critiques from those writing for the mainstream presses were in keeping with how Lawson's scripts had traditionally been reviewed in those publications, the reaction from the critics writing for the liberal press was increasingly negative and hostile. Representative of this view is the harsh critique of Joseph Wood Krutch. Writing for *The Nation*, Krutch, a political conservative who nonetheless had in the 1920s been among those who had championed Lawson as the bright hope for the American theatre, voiced the frustration of many:

> Mr. Lawson continues to merely bubble and stew. He has become the author of one other interesting play, "Success Story," and the perpetrator of several which deserve to stand near the bottom of any list it

> would be possible to draw up. Some of us were disposed to be unduly kind to them on the theory that they were all promising, but a promise broken too often ceases to have much value and I, for one, have come to the end of my patience. I am weary of being expected to be very much exited about situations which are never very clearly defined. If Mr. Lawson does not tell us pretty soon what all his shooting is about, it will be time to take away his gun.[28]

Krutch's desire for clarity and definition was echoed by reviewers writing for the left-wing press. While most in this camp once again ignored the production altogether, the few who did respond voiced a common complaint: while Lawson is a playwright proficient in the forms suitable for the bourgeois theatre, his scripts in no way express the ethos of the coming revolution. In her post-production review for *New Theatre*, Jennie Held wrote, "John Howard Lawson is [. . .] still tied up in knots. [. . .] After *Success Story* I thought Lawson had cleared away all his torments. [. . .] Not at all. His people still cry for gold at the end of the rainbow, still see that it is nothing but tin, the system still twists and chokes them, and in the end the solution is death. [. . .] Somewhere in these plays there is a buzzing about workers—when will John Howard Lawson make that voice real?"[29] In like manner, Melvin Levy, writing for the *Daily Worker*, criticized Lawson for his romanticized and ignoble characterization of the proletariat, and labeled the character Rudy "a communist Casanova."[30] Clearly, then, for most of the critics writing for both the liberal and left-wing presses, Lawson's inability and/or unwillingness to offer specific and detailed solutions to social ills, and correspondingly his continued reliance on methods that favored abstraction and ambiguity, was intolerable in an era facing a very real Fascist threat.

Lawson responded to the reviews for *Gentlewoman* and *The Pure in Heart* by firing off a lengthy and heated letter to the editor sent to most of the major metropolitan New York newspapers. In the missive, which was later revised and included as "A Reckless Preface" to the published scripts, Lawson claimed that American theatre was "in a sickly condition"; described it as "an expression of the middle class mind"; and charged the New York critics with "incompetence," describing them as "a small group of men who, with no recognizable qualifications" delivered "shallow and partial judgments with an Olympian finality" that "seriously hamper[ed] the normal activity of the theatre."[31] Lawson asserted that he and others[32] who dealt "uncompromisingly with revolutionary themes" had been attacked mercilessly by these critics "attempting to preserve the outworn sophistication and fake aestheticism of Broadway," and he urgently called for "a detailed study of the class bias of the critics" (vii):

> I have no desire to charge the reviewers, collectively or individually, with conscious dishonesty or intentional unfairness. I do not suspect them of conspiratorial plotting against the well-being of authors and actors. Probably no one has been more consistently harassed by the critics than myself, yet I am sure they come to a Lawson opening with a kindly desire to like what they see. They don't like it because it puzzles them. For this very reason, I believe a play of mine offers a particularly good test of a critic's capacity. If he understands his job and takes his responsibility seriously, he must be particularly careful of his approach to the experimental or difficult. He must be careful to avoid narrow-minded finality; he must attempt to strike a balance between his own limitations and the limitations of the performance. (x)

The most serious problem in the theatre, according to Lawson, was the power the critics held over production. "It seems to me that this control amounts to rigid dictatorship," he wrote. "It is true that the barrier erected between the play and the public is a temporary one. With money and time the barrier can be broken down. But money and time are not frequently available" (x). Regarding his two most recent plays, neither money nor time was available. As a result, both "were closed by an irresponsible dictatorship" (xi). While he agreed that both *The Pure in Heart* and *Gentlewoman* were "faulty in many respects," as an artist he was "anxious to correct them." The critics, however, were uncooperative in this respect. They met the works with "wholesale condemnation" and thus destroyed any positive value that the plays might have held (xiii–xv). Lawson then made an impassioned call for change:

> To my way of thinking, there is only one satisfactory answer to the problem: the writer, actor or director who wishes to do genuinely creative work cannot function in the Broadway system. The stupid control exercised by the critics is an integral part of that system. The only answer is to turn resolutely to the building of the revolutionary theatre. The enthusiastic crowds at "Peace on Earth" and "Stevedore" are convincing proof that a new audience exists; an audience which is in complete contrast to the jaded respectability of Broadway; an audience which disregards the trivial judgments of the reviewers, which is ready to roar its approval of plays which deal straightforwardly with real issues. (xvii)

The essay ended with Lawson again confronting the "dictatorship" of the critics. "[T]hese dictators," Lawson wrote, "are neither greatly respected nor generally trusted; the public accepts them thoughtlessly; the professional theatre laughs at them, deriding their ignorance and narrow-mindedness—and bowing helplessly to their irresponsible control. Why?" (xvii–xviii).

Upon the heels of this letter, and only one week after the failures of *The Pure in Heart* and *Gentlewoman*, Lawson's friend and fellow former New Playwright Michael Gold, who had not written a review while the shows were in production, offered Lawson some harsh advice. In his *New Masses* article "A Bourgeois Hamlet in Our Time," Gold followed up on the line of questioning introduced by Held in her *New Theatre* review. He began by describing his first impression of Lawson ten years before, when the Theatre Guild "produced a most unusual play, *Processional*":

> It was one of the first attempts on the American stage to portray industrial America. Talent of a high order was obvious in its writing, yet the stark reality of its subject matter was sicklied over with vapors from another world. [. . .] Lawson had tackled a strike theme, it is true, but the strike, in his limited vision, was comprehended as it might have been by a cub reporter for a tabloid newspaper. [. . . Still, t]he play was greeted with much sympathy in the left-wing press. It was clear that this was the first essay of a gifted fellow-traveler, and that young writer ought not to be condemned for not having read Marx.

Gold then compared Lawson to Hamlet, "lost [. . .] in his inner conflict," and asked, "What have you learned in these ten years?" The answer the critic provided for Lawson was shockingly blunt: "In Lawson's case the answer tragically seems to be 'Nothing. I am still a bewildered wanderer lost between two worlds, indulging myself in the same adolescent self-pity as my first plays. Hence my lack of maturity and esthetic or moral fusion.'" Gold contended that time and again in his plays, Lawson had "botched [. . .] the revolutionary theme" and the proletarian aesthetic, and "projected his own confused mind on the screen of history." While Lawson's "synthetic concoctions" began with "some fundamental truth," they always "dissolve[d] back into the solipsist's world of unreality." Gold concluded, "When a man has achieved a set of principles, when he knows firmly he believes in them, he can, like the Soviet diplomats, make compromises, box office or otherwise. Until then, a man or an author is forever betraying the fundamentals. This is what Lawson and the liberals always do; he has no real base of emotion or philosophy; he has not purified his mind or heart."[33]

One week later, Lawson responded to Gold's criticisms in a letter to the *New Masses* entitled "Inner Conflict and Proletarian Art." Lawson began the letter by "unhesitatingly" admitting that "70 percent of Mike's attack" was true:

> I would not be worth my salt as an author if I were not acutely familiar with the problems facing me in breaking away from bourgeois romanticism and being of some genuine literary use to the revolution. [. . .]
>
> Mike Gold deliberately ignores the historical background which is ultimately connected with my development as a dramatist. He ignores my repeated statements (with which I assume he is familiar) that my work to date is utterly unsatisfactory in its political orientation, that the left tendency in my plays has been clouded and insufficiently realized, and that the only justification for my existence as a dramatist will lie in my ability to achieve revolutionary clarity.

Lawson went on to define himself as a "fellow-traveler," praise Marxist criticism as "the only criticism with which [he was] in the least concerned," ponder and accept the criticism that he has "betrayed [. . .] the revolutionary working-class either in [his] writing or [his] personal activity," and ask for contact with the working class in order to find the ideological and aesthetic clarity that was demanded by the Marxist critics. Lawson concluded by musing, "'Where do I belong in the warring world of two classes?' I'm sorry the question bores Mike, but I intend to make my answer clear with due consideration, and with as much clarity and vigor as I possess."[34]

Offering more advice on 24 April, Gold asserted that Lawson had actually hurt the revolutionary movement by portraying the proletariat revolutionary, first as "some sort of neurotic girl who flirts from place to place in a meaningless nightmare" (Alise in *The International*); then as "a frenzied money-maker for whom the revolution is only a brief emotional outlet of his personal frustration" (Sol in *Success Story*); and lastly as "a Bohemian, '90 percent faker and ten percent revolutionist'" (Rudy in *Gentlewoman*). In so doing, the well-meaning playwright had given the bourgeois spectators who frequented uptown theatre productions the kind of picture they wanted to see. Gold closed with this claim: "Lawson is lost between two camps. This muddles his every concept, and makes him incapable of presenting even a strong and authentic picture of decay. [. . .] Lawson is no novice. I will confess, I have always been puzzled by someone who could sit on a fence as long as he has. If my review was too harsh, perhaps, it may make him angry enough to climb down from that fence."[35]

When the commercial and critical failures of *Gentlewoman* and *The Pure in Heart*, Lawson's response to the critics, and the attack from Gold all converged in the spring of 1934, the dilemma that had been evolving and torturing Lawson since the far-off days with the New Playwrights was at last brought to a head. Unable to satisfy the mainstream, liberal, or left-wing critics, the public that populated the commercial theatres of New York, or himself, Lawson had no choice but to get to the root of his conflict. With ringing charges of romantic introspection, abstraction, confusion, and lack of commitment coming from virtually every quarter, Lawson at last would heed Gold's advice and "climb down from that fence."

Marching Song

In the days immediately following Gold's challenge, Lawson met with Earl Browder at his New York office. Lawson told Browder of his interest in "practical activity" and writing about the working class. Soon thereafter, Lawson was on a train to Birmingham, Alabama, to meet with the Scottsboro Boys. Following his visit with the accused, Lawson was heckled and threatened by members of the White Legion Knights, arrested, held for a few hours, and put on a northbound train. Upon his return to New York, Lawson published his observations of the trip in a series of articles printed in May in the *Daily Worker* and *New Masses*. Realizing the explosive nature of the story, the mainstream but leftward-leaning *New York Post* then commissioned Lawson to write a series of exposés on the White Legion in Alabama, which were published in a series of front-page stories.

In July of that same year, Lawson returned to Georgia and Alabama as part of a delegation sponsored by the National Committee for the Defense of Political Prisoners, the American Civil Liberties Union, the International Labor Defense, and the Herndon Defense Committee. Upon their arrival in Atlanta, the group was detained for a few hours for being "Anarchists," "Communists," and "part of the red set-up."[36] The next day, in Birmingham, as the delegation was leaving the county courthouse, Lawson was arrested on the charge of criminal libel,[37] held for a few hours, and, once again, told to get out of town.

Following this second visit to Alabama, Lawson was offered a contract with Columbia Pictures. His position with this studio proved more short-lived than his tenure with MGM one year before. The president of Columbia, Harry Cohn, strongly encouraged all studio employees to financially support Republican candidate Frank Merrian in the California gubernatorial race. Although Lawson did not agree with Democratic candidate Upton Sinclair,[38] he resented the practice of requiring a contribution. When Cohn demanded a donation of one dollar from his new employee, Lawson flatly refused and was fired.

Lawson's "practical activit[ies]" did not go unnoticed. In the June issue of *New Theatre*, left-wing critic Lester Cohen wrote in his prefatory remarks to Lawson's essay "Towards a Revolutionary Theatre: The Theatre—The Artist Must Take Sides": "Just yesterday Lawson was a respected citizen. [. . .] And today, John Howard Lawson is a seeming disturber of the peace, an exile from the fair state of Alabama—a public enemy. Why? Because Lawson has crossed the class line, because the range of his interests extended beyond ordinary responsibilities." Cohen concluded his remarks by claiming that Lawson had joined the rank of revolutionary writers who "are experiencing the mass-life and the mass-problems of our time, the writers who will give us living literature and the living theatre of the modern world."[39] Lawson's essay that follows Cohen's vote of confidence further demonstrates the playwright's newfound ideological clarity.

In the first part of "Towards a Revolutionary Theatre," Lawson asserted that the new era of class consciousness in the United States necessitated revolutionary changes in the theatre. While noting that the recent critically and commercially successful New York productions of *Stevedore*, *Peace on Earth*, and *They Shall Not Die* were indeed "tremendously significant" in the "development of a genuine American theatre" that sought to "dramatiz[e] the class struggle directly and uncompromisingly," Lawson cautioned that these productions needed to be viewed as only a "beginning" for the revolutionary theatre. Sounding very much like Gold, Lawson went on to assert that a careful Marxist analysis of these texts and the productions would reveal "certain serious [ideological] faults" that could not be addressed as long as revolutionary theatre artists sought to work within the "traditional pale-pink, art-for-art's sake" environment of a "sick and debilitated" Broadway system, which was "a [capitalist] business organism, whose methods and operations are as clearly defined as those of Wall Street." Lawson continued:

> The revolutionary theatre is on the threshold of its vital growth. [. . . A]t the same time, it is inevitable that a split between the theatre of the workers and the theatre of the reactionary bourgeoisie will become gradually more pronounced. As the class struggle grows more intense and more openly apparent, it is reflected more clearly in the various arts: The compromisers, the escapists, artists who chatter about "pure

> art" find that they are no longer able to hide behind their aesthetic liberalism. The artist is *forced* to recognize the elementary facts of the economic struggle; he is *forced* to take sides.

Theatre workers, he charged, who "profess a confused and half-hearted liberalism" by employing a "veneer of aesthetic liberalism" needed to do as he had done and "take sides," "orient themselves toward the left," and find "political clarity." In so doing, they would be able to participate in "the living force of proletarian art, offering fresh themes, fertile experimentation, and real integrity." Lawson concluded this impassioned plea for "revolutionary" change with a fervent and critical evaluation of his own work, focusing on the plays produced while he was a member of the New Playwrights' Theatre, and an earnest call to arms:

> [The New Playwrights' Theatre] played an important part in initiating the first steps toward a class-conscious theatre. These steps were tentative and lacking in political clarity, but the New Playwrights did an important job, both in the quality of the plays produced, and in the confused but courageous insistence with which they raised the slogan: "The theatre for social protest [. . .] a theatre pledged to the production of plays revolutionary in method and theme."
>
> But we are living in an era of revolutionary change. Confused and half-hearted liberalism is no longer possible. [. . .] Class-conscious workers in theatre should propagandize for an extension of the movement, appeal to other workers, attack reactionary press and reactionary management, stress the need of developing new audiences, expose the shoddy standards of Broadway. There is only one direction in which the drama can move forward: it must join the march of the advancing working class, it must keep pace with the quickening momentum of the revolution.[40]

Clearly, unlike the New Playwrights' manifestos Lawson penned in the late 1920s, which called first for aesthetic rebellion in the American theatre, "Towards a Revolutionary Theatre" was an unabashed and unapologetic call for political revolution.

In the autumn of 1934, Lawson's passionate appeal became even more pronounced. In his essay "Straight from the Shoulder," published in the November 1934 issue of *New Theatre*, Lawson wrote that because it was "the first obligation of the revolutionary writer" to be "*specific* in regard to party and political questions," then "the playwright must organize his technique from this point of view." He went on to criticize many so-called revolutionary playwrights, claiming that they tended to fall prey to "literary romanticism" and, as a result, produced works "muddled by symbolism," "humanitarian vagueness," and "Freudian escape." Revolutionary theatre artists needed to reject these tendencies and, instead, write with "dynamic clarity. [. . .] I say emphatically that it is not the business of the Proletarian theatre to *aid* this escape. In fact, that is the business of bourgeois art; the function of revolutionary drama is to circumvent this escape; it is successful in proportion to its ability to *force* partisanship upon the audience." If revolutionary playwrights are successful in their endeavors to "*force* partisanship," then they will have written plays that are "greater [. . .] in the truly Aristotelian sense." The essay closed with Lawson encouraging all revolutionary theatre artists to "bring detailed understanding to the problems which mean life and death to the working class," and he announced that it was his "aim to present the Communist position, and to do so in a most specific manner." Lawson followed up on this resolute pledge by joining the Communist Party in early 1935.[41]

As playwright of no little status, the CP-USA immediately sought to incorporate Lawson into official activities. His first major function as a spokesperson for the party came in April 1935 when he addressed the First American Writers' Congress. Lawson, who would later refer to the event as "a declaration of revolution in the arts,"[42] opened his address, entitled "Technique and the Drama," with a call for "detailed technical [that is, Marxist] analysis" of the theatre and, specifically, the playwright's craft. He offered a "crude, admittedly over-simplified" four-step approach for play construction and analysis founded upon the classic tradition of Aristotelian conflict: "(a) Conflict and action involve the exercise of the conscious will toward a goal; (b) this involves social judgments and social purpose; (c) it may be assumed that the dramatist's conception of social meaning and purpose will determine the exact form of the conflict; (d) then construction is not merely a pitcher into which the social content is poured, but is the core of social content itself." With this model in place, Lawson offered a brief analysis of the work of Ibsen, the last great writer of "the end of the middle-class era."

> [Ibsen] dissects the bourgeois family with surgical vigor, showing its inertia, its bitterness, its confused moral values. But the *structure* of Ibsen's plays conforms very directly to the social content: instead of developing the action gradually, his plays begin at a crisis. Clayton Hamilton says, "Ibsen caught his story very late in its career, and revealed the antecedent incident in little gleams of backward dialogue." What is the reason for this form? The explanation lies in the fact that

> Ibsen has invented a technique which exactly fits *his* social material: the final psychological crisis of the middle-class family.

Lawson claimed that while Ibsen's technique had been fitting for his era, that method, which embraced idleness, passivity, and Freudian musings, had outlasted it usefulness and was now influencing the theatre in negative ways. Using the works of Eugene O'Neill and George S. Kaufman to exemplify his point, Lawson declared that the contemporary American theatre had been "infected" by Ibsen's passive method that had at its core "the denial of growth and dynamic development." He cited specifically the practice of beginning the play at crisis and illuminating the past in the course of the action as a technique that led to "the denial of the conscious will."

> The crisis is diluted and the backward-looking moments are emphasized, so that the play (in many cases) is all exposition and no crisis. Drama depends on action and logic. But mystic [that is, Freudian] philosophy negates action and denies logic. Thus the playwright, whose point of view is tinged with mysticism, expresses a dread of action, a lost desire for emotional stability. He achieves this by delaying or avoiding conflict. This may satisfy the playwright, but it does not satisfy dramatic construction. When the dramatist runs away from life, he runs away from his own play.

Lawson closed his address by warning that as long as the contemporary American playwright denied "the conscious will," the "growth and dynamic development" of the American theatre would be obstructed.[43] At this point, Lawson's explanation of "the conscious will" was incomplete and his thoughts on how to revolutionize the American theatre were immature. Nevertheless, a skeletal framework of his methodology for a new revolutionary theatre was put in place.

In early 1936, the impassioned call made in "Towards a Revolutionary Theatre" and the practical methodology outlined in "Technique and the Drama" were merged and expanded in Lawson's book *Theory and Technique of Playwriting*. Lawson divides the study into two parts. The first half involves a sweeping account of the development of western drama and its connection to and dependence on philosophy. Describing his investigation as "clinical," Lawson's chief concern is tracing the rise and fall of humanist ideology, manifested in the notion of "individual will," as an impulse in the drama.[44] In mapping "the close connection of philosophy and dramatic thought," Lawson offers detailed considerations of several philosophers whose ideas influenced drama. Hegel, whose notion of the dialectic, as evident in the conflict between the free individual and the conditions imposed by the environment, is dramatized in Goethe's *Faust*; Schopenhauer, whose argument that will is divorce from consciousness, impulse rules over logic, and happiness is achieved through inertia and passive contemplation, is dramatized in the last plays of Ibsen; and James, whose "principle of pure experience," which positions the individual as a fragmented and irrational entity, is dramatized in the later plays of O'Neill (that is, after *The Hairy Ape*) (88). Having defined a pattern of philosophy and its application to the structure of drama, Lawson at last arrives at the following thesis: the "influential trends in modern thought that deny mankind's ability to exert any rational control over his existence" have led to the overuse of an outdated dramatic structure where "moods and fears replace courage and consistent struggle to achieve rational goals" (85). The first half of the study closes with a call for the "serious artist [. . .] to break from the mold of outworn ideas, to *think creatively*." While this struggle will no doubt cause "serious inner conflict," the creation of new and revolutionary dramatic forms, ones that portray humankind's conscious struggle to realize aims and desires, will emerge (158, emphasis in original).

In the second half of the book, Lawson introduces his method of revolutionary playwriting. Working from the premise that because "the drama deals with social relationships, the dramatic conflict must be a social conflict," Lawson posits the following "basis" for his method: "The essential character of drama is social conflict in which the conscious will is exerted: persons are pitted against other persons, or individuals against groups, or groups against other groups, or individuals or groups against social or natural forces—in which the conscious will, exerted for the accomplishment of specific and understandable aims, is sufficiently strong to bring the conflict to a point of crisis" (168). From this point, Lawson discusses in detail conflict, action, and unity, following closely the method outlined at the beginning of his address "Technique and the Drama." The study concludes with a brief comparison wherein Lawson likens his method to "the method of socialist realism," which could rise above subjective romanticism and the mechanical constraints of naturalism and thus eliminate confusion in the drama, and a rationale of why his new method is necessary (208).[45]

> In the early nineteen-twenties, the more rebellious spirits in the theatre talked of breaking down the walls of the playhouse; the moldy conventions of the drawing room play must be destroyed; the drama must be created anew in the image of the living world. These declarations were vitally important; but those who attempted to carry out

the task had only an emotional and confused conception of the living world of which they spoke. They succeeded in making a crack in the playhouse walls, through which one caught a glimpse of the brightness and wonder which lay beyond.

This was the beginning: the serious artist who caught a fleeting glimpse of the free world knew [. . .] that he must leave the mist of dreams and see reality "free and awake." This could not be done by selecting bits of reality piecemeal or by building a dramatic patchwork of fragmentary impressions. Since the drama is based on unity and logic, the artist must understand the unity and logic of events. This is an enormously difficult task. But it is also an enormously rewarding task: because the real world which the artist seeks is also the audience of which he dreams. The artist who follows Emerson's advice to look for "beauty and holiness in new and necessary facts, in the field and roadside, in the shop and mill," finds that the men and women who are the stuff of drama are the men and women who demand a creative theatre in which they may play an active part.

The living theatre is a theatre of the people. (302)

Upon completing *Theory and Technique of Playwriting*, Lawson began to work on his next script, *Marching Song*. While he had initially conceived the idea for this dramatic text in the summer of 1932 while in residence with the Group Theatre at Dover Furnace, the idea remained unexplored until the summer of 1936. Lawson's recollection of the writing experience during that summer indicates that the goal he sought in his dramatic writing was a product of his own endeavor "to break from the mold of outworn ideas, to *think creatively*": "I was engaged in the summer of 1936, in the most difficult dramatic task I had ever undertaken. In *Marching Song* I hoped to create a lyrical poetic form which would express the suffering and hope of people who had not been shown on the American stage—the workers who were beginning to organize the great mass-production industries. It seemed to me a great epic of our time; it was the essence, the soul of all I had ever attempted to do in the theatre."[46] In this passage, Lawson's lofty objective is quite clear: to create a new dramatic form wherein he could merge the story of "suffering and hope of [. . .] the workers," an indication of his newfound commitment to documenting the struggles and triumphs of the working class, with a "lyrical poetic form," a career-long ambition dating back to his work in the twenties. By bringing together the heightened and, at times, poetic language with the hot topic of labor strife, Lawson sought to make manifest his dream of a "theatre of the people."

Marching Song is set inside the abandoned factory of the now-defunct Winkle Wheel Company on the outskirts of Brimmerton, an industrial city in the Great Lakes region that is home to the Brimmer Motor Company. As the first act opens, Jenny Russell is discovered sitting alone in the factory, rocking her baby and singing softly. Through various conversations with the homeless, unemployed men who live in the shadows of the abandoned factory, it is revealed that Jenny's husband Pete has been fired and blacklisted from the Brimmer Company for trying to organize a union local. Now, under order of the Brimmer Company, the local bank has foreclosed on the Russells' home, leaving Jenny, her sister Rose, the baby, and Pete without a home.

Pete and his friend Hank enter carrying belongings from the house. As they talk about Pete's situation, Hank, who is a member of the strong electrician's local, asks why Pete's union has not become involved. Pete answers bitterly: "The union? Nothin' left of it but the name. I was down there yesterday, office full o' men and women askin' for help. The union's got no money an' no plans. They make a lousy settlement an' we're left holding the bag."[47] As Pete continues to speak, "a procession of men and women" slowly enter, carrying the Russells' belongings (66). With the floor of the factory full of people, Bill Anderson, the new leader of the union local, enters. Anderson has spread the word of the Russells' eviction and has called for a union meeting in the abandoned factory. After Anderson brings the meeting to order, he calls for a sit-down strike in order to get Pete and the other fired men back to work. Emotions grow and someone yells, "I tell you [Anderson's] a red!" Anderson replies:

> BILL. I'll tell you who I am. Most of you don't know me: I never got around much. I worked on the brake-drum assembly for eleven years, put a nut in a grease cap an' tighten six bolts. Most of you was in some place else in the same plant. Pete's case is tied up with all of us, inside or out, with everybody in this town an' other towns. Don't think we're alone here. We're doing our stuff right now on a belt that goes seven times 'round the world! (*A pause.*) I got three things to propose: first we go to the bank to get Pete Russell put back in his house. . . . If they turn us down, we go to the relief, demand they give 'em a place to live an' move 'em into it free. . . . If we don't get any satisfaction there, there's one thing left to do: we take this furniture an' put it back in the house where it belongs. Them that want to do it raise their hands—them that's ready to join us, raise up your hands! (70–71)

Slowly, one by one, everyone in the factory, except for Jenny and Pete who are standing apart from the crowd, raise their hands. As the crowd turns slowly toward Pete and Jenny, a "jagged flash of lightening cuts across the scene," a "terrific roll of thunder" sounds, and Jenny and Pete raise their hands (71–72).

Act 2 takes place in the afternoon of the next day. As Pete, Jenny, and Bill talk, it is revealed that the attempt to put the Russells back in their house was met with an attack from the police and thugs hired by the company. While Pete and Jenny are pessimistic about the future, Bill is energized. As he tells Pete of the leaflets he has been distributing all over town, Lucky Johnson, an African American who was brought in by the company as a scab worker, arrives with the news that he has persuaded the other scabs to join the union. While Bill congratulates "Brother Johnson" and thanks him for his work, Pete calls him racially charged names, refuses to believe Lucky's claim that he and the other scabs knew nothing about the union or the strike, and declines Lucky's offer to shake hands. When news arrives that the workers at the plant have sat down on the job, the factory floor floods with people, and Bill addresses them in a passionate speech wherein he outlines the demands the workers have made. When he finishes, Hank starts to sing, the crowd joins in and they march out of the factory into the street, leaving Bill, Jenny, Pete, and a few of the unemployed men alone on stage. Bill turns to Pete and Jenny:

> BILL. Come on, Pete.
>
> JENNY. (*Clinging to Pete.*) Don't do it, Pete. Don't go with them.
>
> BILL. You're a living part of the union, Pete. Can't cut yourself off no more'n you'd cut off your own hand.
>
> JENNY. I knew it would be like this. It begins with a small thing and it grows like a storm, it's nothing to you now, there's no job to save. They come to you making promises, but it's you that must give your pain and hunger. Haven't you given enough?
>
> BILL. What's the matter with you, don't you see what this means? It's like you got a spotlight on you, whether you want it or not. The way people see you, you're bigger than yourself like a man makes a big shadow. (84–85)

This tense scene is interrupted by the entrance of Jenny's sister, Rose, who offers to go to work for the union. As Rose and Bill make plans, Jenny begs her to reconsider. Rose leaves the factory and Pete explodes:

> PETE. (*Turns on Bill violently.*) You think you're a big shot, set yourself up for a little tin Jesus. Go ahead and see what you get. Maybe you won't feel so big when the shooting starts. That's what you're heading for only you're too dumb to know it. You gab about the workers but every worker in this town is gonna be worse off the way this is gonna

turn out. O.K. Go ahead, shoot the works, I don't care if they blast you to hell. (86)

Pete exits with Jenny, and Bill appeals to the homeless men to join in the march and then exits. As the homeless men talk, Mr. Winkle, who owns the abandoned factory, enters. Pete returns and he and Winkle talk of the days when the factory was thriving. In a gesture of kindness, Winkle offers Pete a job and promises to set things straight with the bank. They exit and Binks, a New York thug hired by the Brimmer Company, enters and searches for Bill. When the unemployed men offer him no help, Binks exits. Soon after Binks leaves, Bill enters, wounded from an explosion at the union office. He is being chased by Inspector Feiler, a cruel police officer who has been bought off by the company. As Bill prepares to hide in the furnace of the factory, Pete enters smoking a cigar that Winkle gave him. Ambivalent to the cause, he stands idly by and watches as Bill scrambles into the furnace. Winkle enters with Jenny and they all talk about the Russells' new life. The discussion is interrupted by the arrival of Feiler, who has followed Bill to the factory. As Feiler questions all in the factory, it becomes apparent that Pete knows the whereabouts of Bill. Winkle turns to Pete:

> WINKLE. . . . Speak up, Russell. I'm depending on you. Whatever your personal opinion may be, you must co-operate with the law. . .
>
> JENNY. Pete . . . It's your life, Pete. A chance to live . . . you know how I worried about the baby . . . Seems like the baby's life you're holding in your hands . . .
>
> (PETE *is in agony.*)
>
> PETE. Jenny . . . help me, Jenny . . .
>
> JENNY. (*Hesitantly, watching his face, trying to understand what he is going through.*) You got to do what you know is right, Pete.
>
> PETE. (*Turns firmly to* WINKLE *and* FEILER.) I got nothing to say about Bill Anderson. (109–10)

With that, Winkle takes back his offer to help the Russells and he and Feiler exit. Pete turns to Jenny:

> PETE. (*Slowly, searching his mind, trying to make it clear.*) I had to do it. I kept thinking of the men sitting there in the plant, in the motor assembly, sitting there where I worked. I'm there with 'em, can't cut myself off no more'n I'd cut my arm.
>
> JENNY. Why did you ask me to help you?
>
> PETE. (*Simply.*) I needed to.
>
> JENNY. (*In a strange voice.*) You needed me?

PETE. I know how you feel, I know the bitterness of you.

JENNY. Do you?

PETE. All you cared about was the house.

JENNY. (*Bursts out in a voice of tortured passion, showing a violence which she has never before suggested.*) You think I want a house to die in? You think I want to sit there dying till you come in with liquor and perfume on you. I got a heart in me and the house was my heart 'cause it's you, the house was you and no other thing. You talked to me about love at one time. When was that? Is the memory in you?

PETE. It's my job to take care of you an' I can't do it, I'm too weak for it.

JENNY. (*More gently.*) Then what's happened to us, Pete? Why have we been like strangers?

PETE. All I want is to keep you warm, you an' the baby, keep you warm with my arms around you. I got no strength for it.

JENNY. It's all right, Pete. (*He takes her in his arms, crushing her against him.*)

PETE. Your heart's beating like it would break.

JENNY. That's what it's been doing for a long time . . . you don't know. (111–12)

The first scene in the last act takes place later that afternoon. Rose enters followed by her boyfriend, Joe. Rose reveals to Joe that Bill is still hiding in the furnace and that she is working for the union. Joe, who is ambivalent about the strike, is troubled by Rose's sudden commitment and begs her to run away with him. Rose, angered by this proposal, leaves. Left alone, Joe finds a cigarette and when he hears someone approaching, retires to a dark corner. Binks enters with his henchmen and Pete, who is questioned and then beaten when he refuses to answer. Pete is sent away. As Binks and his men talk, they discover Joe in the shadows. Under threat of torture, Joe reveals the whereabouts of Bill. When the men check the furnace, Bill is gone. Binks turns once again to Joe, who reveals there is a massive picket line being planned for the evening. The thugs leave and Joe stands alone until Hank arrives with Lucky. Soon thereafter, Bill enters and reveals that he heard Joe betray him and escaped through a pipe. Bill and Hank exit, leaving Lucky to organize the crowd, which has gathered while the men have been talking. Jenny enters carrying her dead baby. She speaks to the crowd:

JENNY. I was sick with fear to make my baby safe. . . . It's lonely to be afraid. (*She looks around wonderingly at the crowd.*) You're the same as me, wanting your children to live. [. . .] (*As if she is beginning to *understand.*) That's why you're here, so you can be together, to make each other strong to hold the lives of your children. (*With increasing passion.*) I want to give life to this in my arms, but I can't. My flesh won't keep her warm, my breath won't give her breath. I'll go with you. Give me strength to carry her, so I can make her warm again with hunger and hope. (*Carrying the baby held rigidly in front of her, she turns toward the door.*)

The scene ends with the entire crowd moving slowly "toward the lighted doorway," and Pete and Lucky coming face to face:

LUCKY. You walk with me?

PETE. I'll walk with you, brother. (148)

The final scene takes place later that night. As the curtain rises, Binks and his men, drunk and laughing, are standing in a circle around a smoldering ashcan with hot pokers in hand. Joe stands apart from the crowd, terrified. The men separate, showing Bill, "lying face downward on the ground. He is bare to the waist and his feet are bare," and he has just been branded (150). The sounds of an approaching crowd filter into the factory, and Binks signals his men to "Shut him up!" As the group of thugs close in around him, Bill speaks "as if he were repeating a lesson": "Lay down your tools . . . Strike for the right to live free . . . General strike . . . " (154). Binks and his men exit to face the oncoming crowd, leaving Bill's lifeless body on the floor. People flood into the factory, fleeing the police and thugs who have used machine guns and tear gas. Suddenly, the stage goes to dark except for moonlight cutting across the stage. The men in the power plant have turned off the electricity that feeds the entire city. With only the moonlight illuminating him, Lucky climbs up a ladder to a window to look out over the darkened city. He speaks, in part to himself and in part to the people below him on the floor of the factory.

LUCKY: No light but the moon shining from here to nowheres. But there's people, more'n you could count if you never quit counting. Streets full of quiet people. . . . We stopped the power 'cause it's us that made it! Electric power comes from the sky, but it's us that hold it in our hands with the sparks flowing from our hands. We put a saddle on the lightning like you saddle a mule! We strung them wires . . . We built them motors! You hear me, you multitude, power is people!

While Lucky speaks, the people who fill the stage slowly rise to their feet "from their broken and despairing positions," until all are standing as the curtain falls (158).

The fundamental thought of *Marching Song* is established in the first moments.[48] Jenny, quietly singing to her baby in a dismantled factory, talks with Fergus, one of the homeless men who lives in the factory:

FERGUS. How do you happen to be sitting there?

JENNY. I just want to rest a little.

FERGUS. Is that a place to rest, on a cold stone, with the day just breaking?

JENNY. I get the sun here. It's a real comfort to feel the sun.

FERGUS. Has your house no windows to let the sun in?

JENNY. It's all right here, safe from the cold wind blowing from the river.

FERGUS. Aren't there four walls to your house to shut out the wind?

JENNY. (*Rises and screams suddenly as if her voice were torn from her body.*) No. (15)

This despondent cry of "No" is echoed throughout the rest of the play and can be taken as evidence of Lawson's attempt to rise above the subjectivity of bourgeois romanticism to which he had fallen victim with *Gentlewoman* and, in turn, so thoroughly condemned in *Theory and Technique of Playwriting*. This rejection of romanticism is carried throughout the play and may be seen in the playwright's approach to theme and technique.

Thematically, there are two impulses at work in *Marching Song*. While the first and most obvious idea, the conflict between capital and labor, certainly has overtones of the easily romanticized notion of absolute good versus absolute evil, another issue that lies with that theme at the core of the play is treated in a stark and uncompromising manner: the dilemma of commitment. While a study of the first issue would further demonstrate Lawson's commitment to revolutionary politics, a study of the latter issue is far more valuable here, in that it provides remarkable access into the mind of Lawson at this time.

At the end of the first act, when Pete and Jenny, who are standing apart from the crowd, raise their hands to join the crowd in putting back the furniture, there is not only fear and excitement but reluctance in the commitment they are making. The multilayered dynamic that surrounds their commitment was not a new idea for Lawson or unique to *Marching Song*. Indeed, *Gentlewoman* also shows conversion to the revolutionary cause not as a relief to the confused soul looking for solace but as an "invitation to suffering" that would torment the spirit but, at the same time, "purify and humanize" the alienated soul.[49] Still, while *Gentlewoman* and *Marching Song* share the theme of commitment, their presentations of that theme are markedly different.

As I have argued, in *Gentlewoman* the dilemma of commitment is presented as a highly romantic venture. As Rudy and Gwyn wallow in their ambivalence, the ramifications and rewards of commitment, though constantly alluded to, are never demonstrated. Instead, their struggle never progresses beyond the highly romantic notion that commitment is good because it is noble. Conversely, *Marching Song* focuses on not only the agonizing choice of commitment but also the ramifications of that choice. Out of Jenny and Pete's reluctant commitment comes even more intense struggles: the sit-down strike in the factory, which they refuse to join, the questioning of Pete by Winkle and Feiler, and the death of their child. Therefore, unlike the taxi drivers in *Waiting for Lefty* who are easily won over to the cause by the murder of their organizer, Pete and Jenny are continually forced to question and think critically about their decision.[50]

While not as overt as the thematic design, the technique of *Marching Song*, as seen in stylistic and structural methods, shows further evidence of Lawson's explicit attempt to reject bourgeois romanticism and satisfy his desire "to create a lyrical poetic form which would express the suffering and hope of [working] people."[51] Stylistically, the language in *Marching Song* may be characterized as a poetic intensification of ordinary speech. Similarly, the printed text includes many detailed suggestions from Lawson regarding gesture and movement that could only be described as stylistically exaggerated. Structurally, *Marching Song* seeks to satisfy Lawson's call for script "construction [to be] not merely a pitcher into which the social content is poured, but [. . .] the core of social content itself."[52] To be sure, the dilemma of commitment in *Marching Song* is conveyed not just in its thematic design but also through a plot structure that is poignant, direct, and relentless. As the play involves very few moments of exposition, the focus is instead upon Jenny and Pete's constant struggle to achieve rational goals. They are never given a chance to elude the social conflict they face and, consequently, the dramatic conflict is never delayed or compromised. The multiplication of difficulties faced by Jenny and Pete, the unbearable responsibility of each choice they face, is the key to the suspense in the play. For example, in the scene between Jenny and Pete at the end of act 2, Pete, faced with the questions of Winkle and Feiler, cries out, "Help me, Jenny." A moment later Jenny asks, "Why did you ask me to help you?," to which Pete responds "I needed you. . . . All I want is to keep you warm, you an' the baby, keep you warm with my arms around you. I got no strength for it" (111–12). Pete's "confession of weakness," brought about by the psychological effects of the dilemma of commitment, creates a new bond between him and Jenny. Furthermore, it is this confession of weakness, and not heroics, that prompts the climactic action in the last act.[53] While subtle, Lawson's technique, involving both stylistic and structural choices, is another clear sign of the playwright's attempt to create a "theatre of the people" wherein the constraints of bourgeois romanticism are eliminated.

Despite Lawson's advances with content and form, the February 1937 Theatre Union production of *Marching Song* did not, in the playwright's estimation, succeed. Director Anthony Brown—who had recently had enormous success with *Tobacco Road*—and producer Lem Ward allowed the piece to "wallow in the shadow of naturalism [. . .] that was heavy over the American theatre at this time." Therefore, the poetic interpretation of the raw tensions in society that Lawson had envisioned was "obscured" by fellow artists who relied on "lyric probing" that "turned aspiration to rhetoric."[54] To that end, it is impossible to assess unconditionally the merit of *Marching Song*. Certainly, its faults are manifold. Even so, these faults are inextricably interwoven with virtues. In his own evaluation of the piece, Lawson writes, "It attempts too much; it is on a relentlessly ambitious [and] impossible scale; it dreams of a 'people's theatre' which does not correspond to the consciousness of any conditions in the American theatre or the relationship of the theatre to the life of its time. I have no regret for the rebellious spirit, the dream of impossibilities that made *Marching Song* a unique effort to create a new kind of theatre, a new consciousness."[55]

Ironically, *Marching Song* was the only play Lawson ever wrote that was favorably reviewed by a majority of the critics of the mainstream press. This was due, in part, to the impact of the play and partly to the aforementioned growth and influence and popularity of the left-wing theatre in light of the Popular Front in the mid- and late thirties. Some in the mainstream raved. John Mason Brown of the *New York Post* spoke of "the skill and suspense of the scenes" and claimed it was the "most stirring [Lawson] has written since the far off days of *Processional*."[56] Richard Watts Jr., who also found it to be "Lawson's best drama since the now classic *Processional*," commented that while a "good editorial blue pencil would unquestionably have been a great help [. . .] *Marching Song* is a powerful and exciting drama."[57] Arthur Pollack made no stipulations in his short review: "*Marching Song* burns with indignation skillfully expressed."[58] Gilbert Seldes of *Scribner's* offered a more extensive analysis: "[Lawson] has taken the staple elements of melodrama and transformed them into a propaganda play which is remarkably successful as a play. [. . .] The vitality and conviction of *Marching Song* make the polite politics of the season look sick, and make us wonder whether the polite plays were not always invalid."[59]

While no one in the mainstream damned the play outright, there were those who had reservations. Wilella Waldorf commented:

> Mr. Lawson is bent on giving us a comprehensive picture of the grinding poverty, political pandering, official stupidity, mob violence and hired gun play that so often makes newspaper headlines in times like these. [. . .] Mr. Lawson is so busy painting his picture and so fascinated with its details that he has not bothered to get good and mad and slash out in the vigorous manner of some earlier, and probably less intelligent, Theatre Union plays. His play is full of melodramatic happenings, but it fails to pack a good melodramatic wallop, the sort of thing the gallery loves to applaud and roar over.[60]

Likewise, Brooks Atkinson wrote: "Mr. Lawson is a writer of brilliant scenes which he etches with savage humor. He also has considerable trouble making a coherent play out of them. Although most of *Marching Song* is alive and most of the dialogue is crisply worded, it makes a tortured progress down the labor union street."[61] Similarly, Burns Mantle thought that while the play made "a clear, frank statement or picture of believable conditions," the playwright and the Theatre Union had "missed an opportunity":

> It is, in the minds of Mr. Lawson and his producers, another statement for the cause of labor. But to me it is merely another statement.
>
> Just why the propagandists who are so eager to benefit the workers through drama will continue to merely repeat the injustices and brutalities practiced against them in strike times, and not make some intelligent effort to prove their cause and their campaigns justified, it is difficult to understand.
>
> What they should be told, and shown as well, is what the workers are fighting for and why they are willing to sacrifice everything for their compromise victories.[62]

As was typical, the doctrinal conservative John Anderson was the most critical. While he begrudgingly admitted that "Mr. Lawson can write lines of searing heat; he can sting his drama to mordant and ferocious laughter," he found *Marching Song* "slow in its development, trite in its statement and unresolved in its conclusion, a play that grows luke-warm at best and reaches no emotional pitch anywhere."[63]

Significantly, and as might be expected, the notices from the left-wing press were highly favorable. Charles E. Dexter wrote a glowing review in the *Daily Worker*:

> The play you have been waiting for is here at last. It is John Howard Lawson's *Marching Song* and you may as well line up at the box office and get your tickets now. For it is the Theatre Union's greatest production. [. . .] *Marching Song* is a great show as well as an impressive social drama. There is not a dull moment in it and many an episode that will stir you to anger, melt you to sympathetic tears, tickle you to laughter and, finally, urge you to action. For this is not a great American play but today's American reality, as fresh as the headlines on your newspaper.[64]

In his review, Nathaniel Buchwald made a similar claim: "*Marching Song* is a captivating and poignant drama. It is the best labor play, the most eloquent and poetic dramatization of the class struggle of our time. [. . .] It is the most profound drama, despite the familiar formula of the labor play, 'we suffered, we fought, we won.' The magic of the author's creative imagination plus his clear thinking has turned this formula into a living, palpitating dramatic composition."[65]

In addition to the positive reaction from the left-wing press, the New York State committee of the CP threw its full support behind the play. The committee sent out a letter, signed by the State Organization-Education Committee, that read in part: "It can definitely be pointed out that this play accurately depicts the times from a class conscious point of view. It is not only a good play from the standpoint of theatre technique but is a really powerful piece of propaganda, the sort of thing which, in the cultural field, can educate and arouse interest in the labor movement." The letter ended by encouraging all members and organizations of the party "to do everything possible in the direction of encouraging attendance [. . . and] in guaranteeing that this fine play will get over the critical two or three week period [. . .] to play before hundreds of thousands of additional New York workers."[66]

In the end, *Marching Song* won critical applause and a fervent response from a limited audience and ran for sixty-one performances. Despite the largely positive critical and commercial response, Lawson saw the play as evidence of his inability to find a dramatic method that corresponded with his political ideology:

> [*Marching Song* is] a consummation of negations or barriers that is so painful that it seems to me that words must burn the paper. It was the end of a process that began in the twenties; it was the failure of what was projected by the New Playwrights'. [. . .] The problem of converting what I felt, what I had to express, into an aesthetic form that I knew—to make the whole experience, including the blood and

> anger [of the working class] my own, was beyond my powers. [. . .] It was at last clear to me, the theatre could not provide the substantial involvement [my] political commitment now required. [. . . I]t marked the wholly unexpected end of my public career in the theatre.[67]

With *Marching Song*, Lawson attempted to incorporate a revolutionary theory of playwriting and take his place alongside other artists who saw artistic expression as a tool for political revolution and were committed to portraying through an artistic medium the evils of capitalist society. While the script stands today as a fine example of the proletarian movement in the theatre, it marked, for Lawson, a moment of transition. On the one hand, it indicates the end of the playwright's decade-long struggle to understand and put on stage the "harsh reality of the American scene."[68] On the other, it connotes the beginning of his life as a revolutionary activist whose primary quest was the advancement of the people's revolution. Unable to find a method wherein he could bring together his art and political commitment and unwilling to continue to write plays that privileged form over function, Lawson would in the months that followed leave the theatre behind and pursue political activism (supported through his screenwriting) on a full-time basis. Joseph Wood Krutch's review of *Marching Song* offers an intriguing and concise summation of Lawson's choice: "For a very long time the trouble seemed to be that Mr. Lawson did not know what he thought, but when he at last found out he seemed to know almost too well. Before he embraced Communism he was too confused to write a really effective play; since his conversion he has been almost too clear. Knowing all the answers is, for a playwright, almost as bad as not knowing any."[69]

Crisis and Commitment

The numerous overt and covert social, political, and economic forces; institutional and individual desires; and verbal and nonverbal discourses that created, empowered, and sustained the social energy of the Popular Front in the United States in the 1930s forged and underpinned a unified albeit diverse American left. By turns, the theatrical landscape within this cultural front was at once vibrant and in many respects precarious. This was particularly so for those such as Lawson, who in the early part of the decade continued to hold a view of art and politics grounded in a belief system rooted in the ethos of progressivism, the same belief system that had provided the foundation for the lyrical left and that movement's various progeny throughout the 1920s. In the early and middle years of the 1930s, many Popular Front theatre artists, producers, and critics, though ideologically incongruent at their base, were drawn together in the cause of anti-Fascism. In support of this cause, they invested their works for and about the theatre with a heightened sense of social consciousness and, by extension, a commitment to offer specific and detailed solutions to social ills. Broadly speaking, there was within this larger community of progressives and revolutionaries a foregoing of the endorsement of individualism and a move toward embracing the view that hope and power was founded in collective action and the quest for social justice.

Upon his return to the theatre in the first months of 1934, Lawson entered a three-year period wherein his ideas regarding art, politics, and the intersection of those forces would be challenged and shaped anew by this emergent and fervent social energy. It was during the earliest part of this final period of his career in the New York theatre that Lawson's penchant for writing scripts that relied on formalist experimentation, abstraction and/or ambiguity—and, moreover, forwarded a worldview that although perhaps radical, was pessimistic, romanticized, and, thus, tethered to progressive-era individualism—was ignored by audiences and, perhaps more significantly, brutalized by critics of nearly every type. The playwright's art and politics in turn were altered in fundamental ways.

This profound change in the middle years of the 1930s, though seemingly abrupt, was in truth a consequence of a developmental process dating back to the 1920s. During his career in the theatre, through a series of events that might well be labeled "crises," Lawson gradually came to believe that the existing theory of progressive democracy was archaic and flawed. He increasingly adopted the view that this idealistic body of thought, which had determined his worldview, no longer held the power to solve political, social, and economic problems. Hence, his emergent faith in the Marxist view of the world called into question the fundamental generalizations of the bourgeois and capitalist world order.

For Lawson, the belief that there had been a complete failure of existing rules of this order came about in the middle months of 1934. This was due, specifically, to the commercial and critical failures of *The Pure in Heart* and *Gentlewoman*. More broadly speaking, however, this elemental shift was a consequence of the observed discrepancies between his desire to hold fast to the practices and procedures of artistic rebellion while simultaneously endeavoring to secure his position within the community of revolutionaries who were out to change the world. When it became clear that he could no longer balance these two objectives and that they were, in fact, mutually exclusive, Lawson "climb[ed] down from that fence" and embraced Communism with unwavering commitment. Correspondingly, the new vocabulary and concepts offered by Communism were put to immediate use in the form of numerous theoretical works, most principally *The Theory and Technique of Playwrighting* and his script *Marching Song*.

For the few short years following his commitment, Lawson was an ardent and vocal supporter of Popular Front politics. His unwavering, albeit newly found, commitment to the more revolutionary branch (that is, the Communists) of that larger liberal and leftist community impelled the playwright to accept and espouse a view regarding the relationship of art and politics that would prove exceedingly unpopular and, in some cases, criminal in decades to follow. By the end of the 1930s, the "united front," as Gold and others had envisioned and created, faltered and collapsed. This was due in large part to the divisions engendered by the Hitler-Stalin nonaggression pact of August 1939. The ideological divides, which previously separated those who were revolutionary and thus vehemently anti-war from those who were progressive and thus supportive of the U.S. government's defense preparations and aid to the Western democracies, were again installed. While there would be a brief return to a conciliatory relationship between these two ideologically opposed groups following the German attack on Russia in June 1941, which led to the Browder-sanctioned "class peace" and "win the war" policies, the union of progressives and revolutionaries ended as the 1930s came to a close.

It may be convincingly argued that the desire to lay bare the exploitative nature of capitalism and the bourgeois world order would never again garner the widespread and impassioned support it had in the 1930s, hence the oft-used description "The Red Decade" in reference to that ten-year period. Still, for the most committed of comrades in the United States, which included Lawson, this point was moot. The prospect of returning to the precepts of progressivism and the bourgeois world order, even in its most radical of forms, was viewed as a traitorous move and a step backwards toward lonely isolationism born from an antiquated brand of bourgeois-inspired individualism. Thus, upon rectifying his own crisis of commitment in the middle years of the 1930s, Lawson would spend a large portion of the remainder of his life seeking to ferment and invoke a similar crisis in the larger cultural field, leading to the widespread commitment of all peoples.

Though it is beyond the aims of this study to explicate in detail all the ways in which Lawson sought to promote the people's revolution in the decades that followed, it is essential to consider in closing a short essay that demonstrates the depth and profundity of Lawson's revolutionary perspective. In "A Crisis in the Theatre," written immediately prior to the Theatre Union's production of *Marching Song*, Lawson's vision of the world he hoped to help create and his place in it is set forth with vigor and clarity. Furthermore, the views expressed in this essay serve as a fascinating bellwether, gauging the impact of that commitment on his conception of art and his practice as an artist.

Near the end of "A Crisis in the Theatre," published in *New Masses* in December 1936, Lawson writes:

> Today the people of the United States are awakening to new political needs and pressures which affect every phase of the country's life. The theatre reflects this crisis. The progressive movement [of the early 1920s] has reached a new stage; a richer and more complex dramatic culture is needed. The theatre does not respond to this need in an *accidental* manner; it is not simply that some dramatist takes a notion that it would be pleasant or profitable to write a particular type of play. The dramatist responds to definite trends which affect his professional activity and methods of work, and which are part of the general social trend.[70]

In terms of specific proposals and observations regarding the shape and scope of proletariat drama and theatre, there is little in this essay that does not appear in other pieces written by Lawson in the first months and years following his commitment to Communism. The arguments central to the essay—his call for the equating of dramatic conflict with social conflict, his contention that playwrights must write with clarity and specificity regarding social action, and his contrasting of the dying bourgeois theatre against that emergent and dynamic form that empowers the working class—are discussed more fully and forcefully in other texts, some of which are explicated above. Nonetheless, in my reading of his body of work from this period, I have found few instances analogous to this paragraph from this short essay where Lawson's complete acceptance and embracing of dialectical thinking is so succinctly illustrated.

Here, Lawson clearly implies his newfound certitude in the material power of cultural circulation of social energy (that is, for Lawson, the ability of "the general social trend . . . to affect") within an economy of negotiation and exchange. The revolutionary artist, whose art is (indeed must be) a social act, both determines and is determined by the larger culture. This artist is simultaneously a subject, whose every move is conditioned by the power of that culture, and acting agent, capable of autonomous, albeit limited and provisional, action and self-direction. Such action and self-direction is instrumental in the emergence of a new social consciousness that will lead humankind away from the "dead past" of individualized, "middle-class thought" and into a future of collective "social action."[71]

Notably, then, for Lawson, this "crisis in the theatre" was correlative to and necessarily ingrained within a larger crisis in the culture of the United States (and beyond). Significantly, his primary focus following his commitment became inspiring this crisis in the larger cultural field. Deeply embedded within his desire to forward a vision of theatre that was "richer and more complex" was a more fundamental and resolute belief in the certainty, promise, and hope of the people's revolution. On a metaphysical level, this intensely held belief would allow Lawson at last to reconstitute fundamentally his ontological and epistemological bearings and thus ease his divided conscience. On the level of the material, the impact of this belief upon his view of art and the practice of the artist was equally profound. Quite simply, within a dialectical cosmology, art was no longer regarded as an isolated field of inquiry distinct from politics. Any discussion of "spanning" or "bridging" those fields of inquiry merely reinforced the faulty and dying system of belief that positioned them as discrete and oppositional. Art and politics were instead constituted as two of the many coterminous fields of inquiry embedded within the larger cultural field. In light of this view disallowing the separation of artistic practice from other social practices, then, comes the psychological orientation to not draw a distinction between one's art and one's politics. One's art is one's politics. Thus, no longer bound to his "artist-rebel" identity—an identity that positioned art and politics as isolated and self-serving activities—Lawson was instead able to construe his art as necessarily rooted within and bound to his revolutionary perspective. *Marching Song* was a material manifestation of this newfound perspective.

Significantly, however, with recognition of and commitment to the belief in the interconnectivity of "theatre" and "world" came a level of hopefulness that Lawson had not heretofore known or, for that matter, believed could exist.[72] The fact that he chose, following the production of *Marching Song*, to forgo the theatre as an arena from where he would advance the revolutionary cause (favoring instead political activism supported through his employment in the film industry), may therefore be read not as a defeat or a failing. It was instead an expression of his hope in the people's revolution, a belief that he could better support social action toward that goal through other endeavors, as well as a vital step in his journey to "find his place in the world." If the theatre would not enable him to advance that revolutionary action, to express that revolutionary view, and to help others find that place, then he would need to look elsewhere.

Many scholars and critics suspicious and/or hostile to this sort of categorical choice have cast Lawson's commitment to the revolutionary cause, a commitment that came to outweigh by far his allegiance to the theatre, as an indicator of the manipulative nature of the Communist worldview. Lawson never saw it as such. Rather, as the 1930s came to a close, the onetime artist-rebel came to the conclusion that the theatre was no longer a suitable arena for him to advance the revolutionary perspective and express his undying hope in the prospect of a brighter tomorrow awaiting all the peoples of the world. It is this newfound and undying hope, I contend, that is key to understanding Lawson's exit from the theatre.

His hope was no longer that of the lyrical left or of progressive democracy, a hope placed in individual introspection. His hope was also no longer that of the "art theatre," a hope in aesthetic liberalism that was contingent upon one's ability to create art that was valued in terms of its formalist experimentation and vague social critique. Nor was his hope that of the New Playwrights, a naïve and fleeting hope masking his divided conscience that eventually gave way to fear, pessimism, and lonely isolationism. Neither was his hope that of the Popular Front, a hope that relied on a diluted and concealed conception of the social realities that in effect buttressed antiquated views of the world. Rather, his was a hope born from the resolute and secure view that one's actions, art or otherwise, make the world, that all humans are connected to and therefore responsible for one another, and that power resides not in the individual, divorced from the social whole, but in the union of all peoples. It was, in the end, this hope that at last led Lawson to the threshold of a "lighted doorway," bravely facing a new tomorrow. However, unlike the hope of Roger Bloomer, who was encouraged "to go it alone," this was hope in the power of community (225). This was a hope keenly expressed in the final line of *Marching Song*: "You hear me, you multitude, power is people!" (148).

Epilogue: The Rebel Now Revolutionary

In yourself you must find the secret. [. . .] Go it alone, Roger [. . .]

—John Howard Lawson, *Roger Bloomer*, 1923

You hear me, you multitude, power is people!

—John Howard Lawson, *Marching Song*, 1937

In the autumn of 1937, Lawson participated in what would prove to be his final New York production: a Federal Theatre Project remounting of a revised *Processional.* Lawson, who had been hired to serve as an advisor on the production, was unsatisfied with the revisions and left for California before it opened on 13 October. Concerning the alterations he and directors Lem Ward and John Bonn made to the script, the playwright later commented, "I endeavored to present the [stereotypical] characters more realistically and sympathetically, and the result was far from satisfactory; it destroyed the intensity and style of the play."[1] A reading of the retailored text confirms Lawson's critique. The modernist "discordant jumble"[2] of avant-garde dramaturgical modes and popular entertainment forms, anachronistic characters, and half-finished plot lines central to the much-celebrated 1925 version are all unified, refined, and, in large part, made inert in the 1937 version. Moreover, the Marxist critique merely hinted at in the earlier version is pushed toward the fore in the later version, which results in a script that verges on propaganda. Despite Lawson's reservations, the Federal Theatre Project's *Processional* ran for eighty-one performances. When it closed, the playwright's New York theatre career came to an unceremonious end.

This end was not, of course, immediately apparent. In 1938, Marxist critic Eleanor Flexner wrote that *Marching Song* was a "new beginning" for Lawson who now "took his place among the leading playwrights in the new school of militant and explicit social statements. [. . .] Lawson's interest in the experimental form dates from his earliest play; in addition, he is alone among his contemporaries in traveling the path from confused dissatisfaction with the theatre and with society at large to where, his point of view at last solidly integrated, we can expect from him his best work."[3] Lawson, however, never followed up on this "new beginning" envisioned by Flexner. Instead, in the latter months of 1937 he returned to Hollywood, this time for good.

Initially, Lawson viewed his return to Hollywood as a temporary circumstance, born from his desperate financial situation. Hired to work on the film *The River Is Blue*, a screenplay written by Clifford Odets and Lewis Milestone, Lawson ventured West with members of the Group Theatre who had been hired to work on that film. When Odets's script proved problematic, independent producer Walter Wagner offered Lawson the opportunity to rewrite it.[4] The result was *Blockade*, a film that attempted to deal with the Loyalist struggle against Fascism in Spain. The ultimate commercial and critical success of *Blockade* led to a series of long-term contracts for Lawson, first with Warner Brothers, until 1940, and then Columbia Pictures, until 1945.[5]

Later in life, Lawson would describe the years 1937 through 1947 as "ten years of uneventful [artistic] life."[6] Though he worked on and off on a theatrical script entitled *Parlor Magic*, his screenwriting work became his primary vocation in a professional sense. More broadly speaking, however, it was during this period that political activism became his life's work. Beginning in the late 1930s and continuing through the end of the 1940s, Lawson emerged as a leader of numerous radical and revolutionary organizations. He served on the board of the Hollywood Anti-Nazi League in the late 1930s; he was an organizer and leading participant in the Second Writers Congress of 1937, the Third Writers Congress of 1939, and the Fourth Writers Congress of 1941; he functioned as secretary for the American Society for Technical Aid to Spanish Democracy (a group with official ties to the CP-USA); he was a cofounder of the American Peace Mobilization and later the American People's Mobilization; he was a major player in the Hollywood Independent Citizens Committee of Arts, Sciences, and Professions, which brought together radicals like Dalton Trumbo and moderates like Ronald Reagan for the reelection campaigns of California governor Culbert Olson in 1942 and President Roosevelt in 1944; he played a leading role in organizing the Writers Congress at the University of California at Los Angeles in 1943; he served on the editorial board for *Hollywood Quarterly* (a predecessor of the *Quarterly of Film, Radio and Television* and, subsequently, *Film Quarterly*), which was published by the radical Hollywood Writers Mobilization; he was on the organizing committee for the Conference Against Thought Control held at the University of California at Los Angeles in 1947; and he was appointed to the editorial board of the Popular Front publication *Mainstream* and became a contributing editor to *Masses and Mainstream*.

In addition to these activities, Lawson became the leader of the Hollywood branch of the CP-USA. When he returned to California in 1937, Lawson found in Hollywood a struggling Communist community composed of people who wanted and needed, as he did, a well-organized and functioning party.[7] Lawson's reputation as a person of action and his ability to organize—in large part based on his work with the Screen Writers' Guild earlier in the decade—led to his election as leader of the Hollywood cell of the party in 1938. He served in that capacity until 1945 when Stalin rejected Browder's "class peace" and "win the war" policies, which called for the long-term coexistence of capitalism and communism in the United States.[8] Lawson, who had been tied to Browder since his indoctrination into the party ten years before, was blamed for failing the membership and his leadership role was reduced somewhat. Even then, however, he continued to be one of the leading apologists for Soviet activity and a staunch defender of Marxism (if not necessarily the Communist Party line).

Lawson's political activism did not go unnoticed by the government. In 1940 and 1943, he was one of the principal subjects of an investigation conducted by the Joint Fact-Finding Committee on Un-American Activities of the California State Legislature. Chaired by the reactionary Jack Tenney, this committee sought to expose Communists in the film industry. In 1941, his screenplay *Four Sons* was one of twenty-five films subjected to scrutiny of the Martin Dies–chaired U.S. Senate subcommittee investigating war propaganda.[9] Though these investigations uncovered little in the way of incriminating evidence, they did prompt his dismissal from Columbia Pictures in 1945 and, moreover, led directly to his being included as one of the infamous

Hollywood Ten who were called before the House Committee on Un-American Activities in 1947.[10]

Summoned before HUAC in October 1947, Lawson was the first of the so-called unfriendly witnesses that made up the Hollywood Ten to testify. His testimony, which consisted of his attempt to read a prepared statement, was cut short when he refused to answer questions regarding his memberships in the CP-USA and the Screen Writers' Guild.[11] When charged with contempt and convicted, Lawson, as did the other members of the Hollywood Ten, appealed first to the U.S. Court of Appeals, claiming that their right of free speech had been violated. When the U.S. Court of Appeals upheld the convictions in 1949, they attempted to appeal the convictions to the U.S. Supreme Court. In April 1950, that body ruled they would not review the cases. Shortly thereafter, the Hollywood Ten were sent to jail.

Lawson, along with Dalton Trumbo, served his sentence in the Federal Correctional Institution in Ashland, Kentucky, from June 1950 through April 1951. While imprisoned, he remained remarkably active, corresponding with various radical organizations and writing. In late 1950, he published *The Hidden Heritage*, his cogent Marxist historical analysis of the cultural and political structures underpinning class struggle in the United States.[12] During his time in prison, he also completed a poetic satire, *In Praise of Learning*, and an outline of his book *Film in the Battle of Ideas*, which was subsequently published in 1953.[13] Upon his release, Lawson returned to California. Throughout the remainder of the 1950s, he devoted most of his time toward lecturing, but he did also complete a script entitled *Thunder Morning*, a sequel to *Marching Song*.[14] While he worked occasionally as a screenwriter during this period, his efforts were always uncredited due to the blacklist.

In the spring of 1961, Lawson left for Moscow to attend the Moscow Film Festival. During his visit, he fell ill and was forced to undergo two major operations. While convalescing in Russia, Lawson completed another book, *Film, the Creative Process*, which reflected his growing interest in existentialism, and a new version of *Parlor Magic*, performed in East Germany and the Soviet Union in 1963.[15] Upon his recovery, he was offered a temporary appointment to the Film Association of the Soviet Union. He returned to the United States from the USSR in May 1963. From 1963 until his death in San Francisco on 11 August 1977, Lawson engaged in a focused study of Sartre and Camus. During these final years, he also worked on his autobiography and sought out opportunities to lecture.

Throughout his life, Lawson was concerned with how to be both a good artist and a responsible member of society. Finding the intersection of his art and his politics was never a simple matter and often resulted in a complex and contentious internal struggle. By Lawson's own admission, the apex of that struggle paralleled the years of his theatrical career.[16] Thus, his scripts and theoretical writings on the theatre from the twenties and thirties may be viewed as material manifestations chronicling one man's journey to define who he was and where he belonged in the world, as he ventured from "artist-rebel" to "political revolutionary." As I have sought to demonstrate in the preceding chapters, by considering the elaborate system of interchanges, negotiations, and shifting economies that informed and was informed by Lawson's composition of those various texts—that is, his symbiotic relation to the material world that surrounded him in this historical moment—we are offered a more balanced and nuanced view of not only the playwright's life but also the broad cultural connections linking those texts to the larger milieu. In arguing that Lawson was both a product and producer of the social energy specific to this era, I have endeavored to chart some of the ways in which the playwright's writings for and about the theatre were powerful instruments of aesthetic and/or social change, inextricably imbued with a dynamism that did not merely reflect but instead energetically and, in some cases, radically reshaped culture. By reading these various texts authored by Lawson as material phenomena that absorbed, carried, and actualized the social energy of their time, I have suggested a modified and arguably more inclusive view of this moment in the history of the theatre in the United States.

In closing, I would like to recount one event of a more personal nature, an event that in many respects underscores the spirit that has been an instrumental force in the composition of this study. It is an event that began innocently enough a number of years ago, when I was first beginning to publicly present my research on Lawson. Following a presentation at an academic conference, one member of the audience asked me to justify my time spent on "the life of a failed playwright." I was, at the time, in no small way offended by the remark, and yet I did not know quite how to respond. As is typical when placed into an awkward circumstance, I stumbled through some incoherent remarks, noting the troubling and subjective nature of a term such as "failed" and suggesting that an accurate history of the theatre during the interwar years in the United States was yet to be written. As I concluded, I turned the question back toward the audience member and asked, "Why do you claim he failed?" The individual's response to my convoluted answer and subsequent follow-up question was short and precise: "He failed because he wasn't able to achieve what he set out to do in the theatre and then he quit."

From a certain advantage, it could be argued convincingly that the audience member's summation of Lawson's career was apropos. In the 1920s, Lawson did struggle to create a dramatic form suitable for expressing his vision of a dynamic country. And then in the 1930s, his attempts to write scripts that bridged his interests in dramatic form and his emerging revolutionary political stance were often marred by indecision and thus proved not entirely effective. Having noted this, however, I am resolute in my belief that the summation of Lawson's career offered by that audience member is fundamentally wrong. It is wrong not because I hold some romantic view of Lawson's place in the history of the American theatre but because it equates departure with failure.

When Lawson chose to leave the theatre in the late 1930s, it was because he felt it was not an appropriate forum for him to express his revolutionary perspective. His career in the theatre in the 1920s and 1930s was a stage in the development of that perspective, and his departure therefore a moment of transition moving beyond that stage. Simply put, then, to summarize his career as "failed" is not only too simple, it is also shortsighted in that it neglects to consider the ways in which Lawson's career in theatre in the interwar years made him who he was in the years and decades that followed. More broadly speaking, and as I hope my study has established, common categorical labels for Lawson such as "failed," "propagandistic," and even "left-wing" not only reduce and isolate his remarkable and varied career but also undergird and advance totalizing narratives regarding the theatre and, moreover, the political and cultural left in the United States of the twenties and thirties.

In reading Lawson's aesthetic and theoretical texts as cultural texts—ones that produce and are produced by a myriad of institutional and discursive determinations—I have sought to continue the work of those who have gone before me in the endeavor to grant agency to those figures from the past such as John Howard Lawson who are marginalized and, in some cases, erased by the exacting force of totalizing narratives. I will leave it to others to continue to analyze cultural texts so as to further challenge and revise these historiographic practices and, moreover, to seek, as I have sought, to not only write but to right the historical record.

Appendix
Notes
Bibliography
Index

Appendix: Plays Written by John Howard Lawson and Their Production History, 1923–1937

Roger Bloomer, 1923. Produced by the Equity Players, opening on 1 March 1923. Directed by Shelley Hull. Produced independently by Marguerite Barker and Lawson on 15 March 1923.

Processional, 1925. Produced by the Theatre Guild, opening on 12 January 1925. Directed by Phillip Moeller.

Nirvana, 1926. Produced by Noble, Ryan, and Livy, opening on 3 March 1926. Directed by Robert Peel Noble.

Loud Speaker, 1927. Produced by the New Playwrights' Theatre, opening on 2 March 1927. Directed by Harry Wagstaff Gribble.

The International, 1928. Produced by the New Playwrights' Theatre, opening on 12 January 1928. Directed by Lawson.

Success Story, 1932. Produced by the Group Theatre, opening on 26 September 1932. Directed by Lee Strasberg.

The Pure in Heart, 1934. Produced by Aldrich and De Liagre Jr., opening on 20 March 1934. Directed by Edward Massey.

Gentlewoman, 1934. Produced by the Group Theatre, opening on 22 March 1934. Directed by Lee Strasberg.

Marching Song, 1937. Produced by the Theatre Union, opening on 17 February 1937. Directed by Anthony Brown.

Notes

Introduction: Writing and Righting a Revolutionary's Life

1. Gilbert Gabriel, "Rhapsody in Red," *New York Telegram-Mail*, 13 January 1925, in the John Howard *Lawson Papers*, box 4, folder 4, Special Collections, Morris Library, Southern Illinois University at Carbondale, collection 16. Hereafter, I use the following method to document materials drawn from this archive: *Lawson Papers*, followed by "b." indicating *box* or "pkg." indicating *package*, followed by "f." indicating *folder* (when applicable), followed by "p." indicating *page* (when applicable). This review is reprinted in Montrose Moses and John Mason Brown, eds., *The American Theatre as Seen by Its Critics* (New York: Cooper Square Publishers, 1967), 313–15.

2. Sheldon Cheney, *The Art Theatre*, revised ed. (New York: Alfred A. Knopf, 1925), 4.

3. Gordon M. Leland, "Review of *The International*," *The Billboard*, 28 January 1928, pp. 11, 89.

4. Harold Clurman, *The Fervent Years: The Group Theatre and the Thirties* (1948; reprint, New York: Da Capo Press, 1983), 93.

5. Murray Kempton, *Part of Our Time* (New York: Simon and Schuster, 1955), 184.

6. Louis Broussard, *American Drama: Contemporary Allegory from Eugene O'Neill to Tennessee Williams* (Norman: University of Oklahoma Press, 1962), 50–55.

7. Walter Benjamin, *Understanding Brecht*, translated by Anna Bostock (London: New Left Books, 1973), 87.

8. Alan Wald, "Culture and Commitment: US Communist Writers Reconsidered," in *Writing from the Left: New Essays on Radical Culture and Politics* (London: Verso, 1994), 68.

9. Catherine Gallagher and Stephen Greenblatt, *Practicing New Historicism* (Chicago: University of Chicago Press, 2000), 9.

10. Heyman Zimel, "Messiah of the New Technique," *American Hebrew*, 25 March 1927, 693. Here, I use the term *modern* in the historical sense as defined by Raymond Williams in his essay "When Was Modernism?" included in *The Politics of Modernism*, edited by Tony Pinkley (London: Verso, 1989), 31–36. Nonetheless, I do not mean to endorse (nor does Williams) the view that there is a simple or easy categorization of modernism, one based entirely on periodization or an absolutely defined and shared set of concerns. Indeed, as the following study will indirectly demonstrate, I hope to problematize those essentializing notions of the "modern" and suggest, instead, a more fluid rendering of that term, one comprised of numerous, diverse, and contesting practices and theories. In turn, I will endeavor to show the ways in which Lawson was part of a community of "modern" theatre artists who were constantly reshaping the discursive formations of "modernism."

11. Barrett H. Clark and George Freedley, eds., *A History of Modern Drama* (New York: Appleton Century, 1947), 706. Clark authors the entry on the United States that includes his consideration of Lawson.

12. Felicia Hardison Londré and Daniel J. Watermeier, *A History of North American Theatre: The United States, Canada, and Mexico: From Pre-Columbian Times to the Present* (New York: Continuum Publishing, 1998).

13. Bernard Hewitt, *Theatre U.S.A., 1668 to 1957: A History by Eyewitnesses* (New York: McGraw-Hill, 1959), 355–57; and Garff B. Wilson, *Three Hundred Years of American Drama and Theatre* (Englewood Cliffs, NJ: Prentice-Hall, 1982), 276.

14. Ethan Mordden, *The American Theatre* (New York: Oxford University Press, 1981), 130.

15. Morgan Himmelstein, *Drama Was a Weapon: The Left-Wing Theatre in New York, 1929–1941* (New Brunswick, NJ: Rutgers University Press, 1963); Clay Reynolds, *Stage Left: The Development of the American Social Drama in the Thirties* (Troy, NY: Whitston, 1986); Malcolm Goldstein, *The Political Stage: American Drama and Theater of the Great Depression* (New York: Oxford University Press, 1974); Jordan Miller and Winifred Frazer, *American Drama between the Wars: A Critical History* (Boston: Twayne, 1991); and Sam Smiley, *The Drama of Attack: Didactic Plays of the American Depression* (Columbia: University of Missouri Press, 1972). Lawson apparently thought very little of most of the studies on American theatre of the 1920s and 1930s published during his lifetime. He expresses his strong opinion respecting such studies in notes written in the 1960s regarding his association with the Group Theatre. A typical remark is the one aimed at Himmelstein's study. Lawson describes it as "an absurd description of the left-wing theatre [of the 1930s]" (Autobiography, *Lawson Papers*, b. 96, f. 2).

16. Useful period-specific studies by Ronald H. Wainscott, *The Emergence of the Modern American Theatre, 1914–1929* (New Haven: Yale University Press, 1997), and C. W. E. Bigsby, *A Critical Introduction to Twentieth Century American Drama*, vol. 1, *1900–1940* (Cambridge: Cambridge University Press, 1982), do offer more balanced treatments of Lawson's career. Nonetheless, the expansive scope of these studies disallows a thorough analysis of his career.

17. See Thomas Allan Greenfield, *Work and the Work Ethic in American Drama, 1920–1970* (Columbia: University of Missouri Press, 1982); Collete A. Hyman, *Staging Strikes: Workers' Theatre and the American Labor Movement* (Philadelphia: Temple University Press, 1997); and Roberta Lynne Lasky, "The New Playwrights Theatre, 1927–1929," PhD dissertation, University of California, Davis, 1989.

18. See Ira A. Levine, *Left-Wing Dramatic Theory in the American Theatre* (Ann Arbor: UMI Research Press, 1985); Anne Fletcher, "The Theory and Practice of Mordecai Gorelik (1925–1935): Emblem for the Changing American Theatre," PhD dissertation, Tufts University, 1992; and Mark Fearnow, *The American Stage and the Great Depression: A Cultural History of the Grotesque* (Cambridge: Cambridge University Press, 1997). Other thematic or area studies of note are Mardi Valgemae and Harry T. Moore, *Accelerated Grimace: Expressionism in the American Drama of the 1920s* (Carbondale: Southern Illinois University Press, 1972); and Kathleen Malia Trainer, "The Dissident Character in American Drama of the 1930s," PhD dissertation, University of Notre Dame, 1983.

19. Liliane Claire Randrianarivony-Koziol, "Techniques of Commitment in the Thirties: A Study of the Selected Plays of John Howard Lawson," PhD dissertation, Indiana University, 1982; and Beverle Rochelle Bloch, "John Howard Lawson's *Processional*: Modernism in American Theatre in the Twenties," PhD dissertation, University of Denver, 1988. See as well Richard Peter Benoit, "A Hegemonic Analysis of John Howard Lawson and the New Playwrights Theatre," PhD dissertation, Kent State University, 2000.

20. I am referencing here Thomas Carlyle's "great man" theory so popular with nineteenth-century biographers. Such humanist modes of biography position the human subject at the fore and romanticize the subject's acts. In this study, I have sought instead to demonstrate how the expressive acts of the subject (i.e., Lawson) as well as his critics are embedded deeply in the historical moment in which they existed. Works informing my understanding of biography include *Interpretive Biography*, by Norman K. Denzin (Newbury Park, CA: Sage Publications, 1989); *The Art of Literary Biography*, edited by John Batchelor (New York: Oxford University Press, 1995); and *Biography as History*, by Stephen B. Oates (Waco, TX: Markham Press, 1991).

21. Richard Peyron Brown, "John Howard Lawson as an Activist Playwright: 1923–1937," PhD dissertation, Tulane University, 1964, iv.

22. Harrison William McCreath takes a similar approach in "A Rhetorical Analysis of the Plays of John Howard Lawson," PhD dissertation, Stanford University, 1965. McCreath endeavors "to investigate the ideas and the techniques of an American dramatist [. . .] through a comprehensive rhetorical analysis" (1). His is a rigorous study that scrutinizes Lawson's written scripts and the rhetorical effect these texts have on the reading audience (5).

23. Robert Merritt Gardner, "International Rag: The Theatrical Career of John Howard Lawson," PhD dissertation, University of California, Berkeley, 1977, v.

24. "Social energy" was coined by Stephen Greenblatt in *Shakespearean Negotiations: The Circulation of Social Energy in Renaissance England* (Berkeley: University of California Press, 1988), 6.

25. In *History and Criticism* (Ithaca, NY: Cornell University Press, 1985), Dominick LaCapra argues that historical documents, such as Lawson's aesthetic and theoretical texts, should be viewed as "texts that supplement or rework 'reality' and not mere sources that divulge facts about 'reality'" (11).

26. Christopher Caudwell, *Illusion and Reality: A Study of the Sources of Poetry* (1937; reprint, New York: International, 1963), 11, 100.

27. In *Marxism and Literary Criticism* (Berkeley: University of California Press, 1976), Terry Eagleton argues against the work of Caudwell and other "vulgar" Marxist critics. Eagleton contends that Caudwell, as well as other English-language Marxist critics from the 1930s, "lacks a sufficiently dialectical understanding" of the relationship of content and form, and thereby posits a literary theory that is haunted by the idealism of English Romanticism and, therefore, "more akin Shelley than to Stalin" (23, 54). To be fair, the dogmatism and Romanticism in the work of Caudwell and other Marxist contemporaries of the 1930s may in part be justified by the fact that he was writing at a time of worldwide economic depression, which undoubtedly buttressed his belief that capitalism was undergoing its final crisis and that bourgeois culture was in its death throes.

28. Jeffrey L. Sammons, *Literary Sociology and Practical Criticism: An Inquiry* (Bloomington: Indiana University Press, 1977), 7–8.

29. Tony Bennett, "Texts in History," in *Post-Structuralism and the Question of History*, ed. Derek Attridge, Geoff Bennington, and Robert Young (New York: Cambridge University Press, 1987), 63–67.

30. Bennett, "Texts in History," 69–70.

31. Bennett, "Texts in History," 70–71.

32. Greenblatt, *Shakespearean Negotiations*, 14.

33. Bennett, "Texts in History," 72.

34. Bennett, "Texts in History," 75; and Greenblatt, *Shakespearean Negotiations*, 12–13. I believe it is important to add a caveat regarding my attempt to "suspend . . . my own reading practices." In situating this as a principle aim of my study, I do not wish to imply a belief in the possibility of objective history. I trust that my readings will not be perceived as authoritarian truth claims; I freely admit that I bring to my analysis of text and context interpretations and readings that are informed by my own experiences and passions as a white, middle-class, heterosexual, male academic who, although living in the capitalist-democratic West, is inclined toward a socialist view of the world. Thus I hold that Lawson's texts are knowable only insofar as one is able to piece together the mutable historical reading patterns and discursive formations that determined their meanings. His texts, like all texts, are material phenomena whose meanings were, and continue to be, discursively reordered by specific social and material conditions. In the words of Bennett, it is "a question of studying texts in light of their readings, readings in lights of their texts" ("Texts in History," 74).

Sources informing my view of the practice of historical investigation include Behan C. McCullaugh, *The Truth of History* (New York: Routledge, 1998); Richard J. Evans, *In Defense of History* (New York: Norton, 2002); Georg G. Iggers, *Historiography in the Twentieth Century: From Scientific Objectivity to the Postmodern Challenge* (Middletown, CT: Wesleyan University Press, 1997); Norman Wilson, *History in*

Crisis? Recent Directions in Historiography (Englewood Cliffs, NJ: Prentice-Hall, 1998); and John Lewis Gaddis, *The Landscape of History: How Historians Map the Past* (Oxford: Oxford University Press, 2002).

35. H. Aram Vessar, *The New Historicism* (New York: Routledge, 1989), xi.

36. Gallagher and Greenblatt, *Practicing New Historicism*, 12.

37. In Lawson's unpublished autobiography, circa the early and mid 1960s, the playwright repeatedly uses the term *artist-rebel* to describe himself in the late twenties and early thirties and *political revolutionary* to describe himself following his commitment to communism in the mid-thirties. Various drafts of this work are contained in the *Lawson Papers*, boxes 91–100, under the titles of *A Way of Life, The History of a Writer's Mind, A Calendar of Commitment,* and *Another View of the Twenties and Thirties.*

38. See Rita Barnard, *The Great Depression and the Culture of Abundance* (New York: Cambridge University Press, 1995); Mark Fearnow, *The American Stage and the Great Depression: A Cultural History of the Grotesque* (Cambridge: Cambridge University Press, 1997); Rena Fraden, *Blueprints of a Black Federal Theatre, 1935–1939* (New York: Cambridge University Press, 1994); and Michael Denning, *The Mercury Theatre: Orson Welles and the Popular Front* (London: Verso, 1992).

39. Barnard, *The Great Depression*, 12.

1. The Awakening

"The Awakening" is one of the suggested working titles for the first part of Lawson's autobiography.

1. Autobiography, *Lawson Papers*, b. 92, f. 2. Lawson's more detailed account of his response to his mother's death reads:

> It was not primarily a feeling of lost love, but rather of injustice, fury and despair. My anger had been building up for years, because my mother had been sick since the time of my birth, I had never had a chance to know her love; I was seldom allowed to enter the sick room, and was reprimanded whenever I made noise in the house. [. . . T]he insecurity I felt at her death was communicated by my father. A man of forty-eight left with three children of whom the oldest is thirteen, is tragically bereaved and may be actually expected to build a new life. But there could be no new life for my father: his love for my mother was so idealized that it amounted to worship. [. . . S]he was his soul. (*Lawson Papers*, b. 92, f. 2., pp. 9–10)

2. Autobiography, *Lawson Papers*, b. 92, f. 1, p. 17.

3. Autobiography, *Lawson Papers*, b. 92, f. 2.

4. Autobiography, *Lawson Papers*, b. 92, f. 1, p. 25.

5. Autobiography, *Lawson Papers*, b. 92, f. 2.

6. Autobiography, *Lawson Papers*, b. 92, f. 1, p. 25.

7. Period accounts of these events are included in Lawson's childhood scrapbook, *Lawson Papers*, b. 1, f. 5.

8. The script for *Savitri* is in the *Lawson Papers*, box 62, f. 4.

9. Autobiography, *Lawson Papers*, b. 95, f. 2, p. 26.

10. *Louise* challenged conventional ideas of operatic grandeur. The character Louise, played by Mary Gardner, is a Parisian working girl. The settings, to Lawson's recollection, were "realistic" and "uncouth" (Autobiography, *Lawson Papers*, b. 99, f. 13). The Ash Can exhibition showed paintings by a group of American painters known as "The Eight" who explored hyperrealism. They first displayed their work at the MacBeth Gallery in New York in the spring of 1908.

11. Robert H. Hethmon, interview with John Howard Lawson, 25 April 1964, *Lawson Papers*, b. 39, f. 1 (hereafter cited as "Hethmon interview"). Also see *Lawson Papers*, b. 3., f. 2, for various papers from Lawson's time at Williams.

12. John Howard Lawson, "Art for Cube's Sake," *Literary Monthly* (May 1913), *Lawson Papers*, b. 3, f. 2.

13. The script for *A Hindoo Love Drama* is in the *Lawson Papers*, b. 62, f. 5 and 6, and b. 63, f. 1.

14. Hethmon interview.

15. Kirkpatrick was to remain Lawson's literary agent for many years.

16. In 1915, the "little theatre" movement was thriving in the United States. Lawson saw a number of plays at the Bandbox Theatre featuring the Washington Square Players (who later became the Theatre Guild). He was interested in their ideas and even tried his hand at episodic structure with a script entitled *Souls: A Psychic Fantasy*, but he was told by Kirkpatrick that his best opportunities lay with the commercial theatre (Autobiography, *Lawson Papers*, b. 99, f. 13). *Souls* was neither sold nor produced. The script for *Souls* is in the *Lawson Papers*, b. 63, f. 2 and 3.

Some elements of another embryonic piece, entitled *The Silver Cord*, would resurface in the form of *The Mad Moon*, circa 1919, and *A New England Fantasy*, circa 1924, both of which served as early manifestations of *Nirvana*. Notes on *The Silver Cord* are in the *Lawson Papers*, b. 63, f. 4.

17. *Standards* tells the story of two young men in desperate need of money who go searching for financial help in New York. Following an exposition-laden first act, in the second act they visit a night club, a millionaire's home, a "den of crime," and the house of a preacher. Via this episodic structure, Lawson endeavors to compare and contrast the various standards or moral attitudes of these different segments of society. The script for *Standards* is in the *Lawson Papers*, b. 64, f. 1.

18. *The Spice of Life* (aka *The Butterfly Lady*) tells the story of an upper-class young woman who refuses to go through with her planned marriage. The play uses different genre qualities in each act (e.g., act 1 is a drawing room comedy; act 2, melodrama; act 3, farce; and act 4, musical comedy). The script for *The Spice of Life* is in the *Lawson Papers*, b. 64, f. 2 and 3. The construction of *Servant-Master-Lover* (aka *The Laughing Lip*) is similar to that of *Standards*: a central idea that is explored through a series of second-act episodes. The story concerns a young man who, in an attempt to win the love of a woman, demonstrates that he can play three roles: her loyal servant, her domineering master, and her romantic lover. The script for *Servant-Master-Lover* is in the *Lawson Papers*, b. 63, f. 5 and 6.

19. Newspaper reviews for the productions of both *Servant-Master-Lover* and *Standards* are in the *Lawson Papers*, b. 3, f. 4.

20. Hethmon interview.

21. There is some confusion as to this date and subsequent timeline for the years 1917–1919. In some drafts of Lawson's autobiography, he places his departure date as February 1917. See note 25 in this chapter and note 1 in chapter 2.

22. Autobiography, *Lawson Papers*, b. 94, f. 10, pp. 26–41.

23. John Howard Lawson, "No Man's Land," ed. Mandy Lawson, *The Lost Generation Journal* 5 (1977–78): 12–13.

24. Autobiography, *Lawson Papers*, b. 92, f. 1, p. 61.

25. As with his date of departure from the United States, there is some confusion as to when this epiphany on the haystack occurred. In some drafts of Lawson's autobiography, he places it in the first weeks of April 1917. In other drafts, he places it in the first days of September of that same year. The September date seems more likely given the historical record. Specifically, in a number of drafts of his autobiography, Lawson notes that he began writing *Roger Bloomer* in the days following the French infantry's capture of Hill 304 on the western front, which took place on 24 August 1917. Thus, if Lawson was serving when Hill 304 was captured, the September date would prove accurate. What is more, I can find no record of a French advance on Hill 304 at any point in April 1917.

Nonetheless, there is some anecdotal evidence supporting the April date (and, by extension, the February departure date from the United States referred to in note 21). Principally, in various drafts of the autobiography, Lawson contends he left the Norton-Harjes in the days immediately following the entry of the United States into the war, circa 6 April 1917, and spent the summer months of 1917 in Paris. If this is true, he could not have been involved with the French advance on Hill 304 circa late August 1917. In an interview conducted by Dave Davis and Neal Goldberg, entitled "Organizing the Screen Writers' Guild: An Interview with John Howard Lawson," and published in *Cineaste* 8, no. 2 (1977), Lawson remarks he began writing *Roger Bloomer* following an advance on Hill 301. I can find no evidence of an advance on Hill 301 in April or August 1917.

Lawson's recollection of the battle (be it the taking of Hill 304, Hill 301, or another) that, in part, inspired the writing of *Roger Bloomer* is chilling:

> [W]e had followed blindly as the infantry moved forward. There were two of us operating each vehicle. In the noise and confusion, mud and corpses, I lost my way. With my ambulance separated from the others, we didn't know whether we were ahead of the advance or behind it. The smell of death changed to the bitter-sweet smell of mustard gas. Adjusting our gas masks, we pushed on. Finally we found a dressing station, and wounded men were loaded into slots for stretchers. We rode bumping through shell holes, as dawn exposed the wasteland that had been the forest of Avocourt. Most of the men in our charge were dead on arrival. We made the same journey a hundred times. The worst moment was always the end—worse than the guns and gas—when we opened the ambulance and counted those who had died on the road. ("No Man's Land" 12)

26. Autobiography, *Lawson Papers*, b. 91, f. 1, p. 14a.

27. "The Metaphysical Phase" is the term Lawson uses to describe the years 1923–1926. It serves as the title for a chapter in one draft of his autobiography. Dos

Passos was, at this time, working on what would become his novel *One Man's Initiation, 1917.*

28. Emma Goldman, *The Social Significance of the Modern Drama* (1914; reprint, New York: Applause, 1987), 1.

29. Sheldon Cheney, *The Art Theatre: Its Character as Differentiated from the Commercial Theatre, Its Ideals and Organization, and a Record of Certain European and American Examples* (1917; revised, New York: Alfred A. Knopf, 1925), 3. Irwin Granich (aka Michael Gold), "Towards Proletarian Art," *Liberator*, February 1921, 21.

30. Cheney, *The Art Theatre*, 15–16.

31. Cheney, *The Art Theatre*, 263–64.

32. Cheney, *The Art Theatre*, 3, 264, and 105.

33. Walter Long, "A Sociological Criticism of the American Drama," published in serial in *Modern Quarterly*, nos. 2 and 3, 1925; Floyd Dell, "Literature and the Machine Age," *Liberator*, November 1923; and V. F. Calverton, *The Newer Spirit: A Sociological Criticism of Literature* (New York: Boni and Liveright, 1925).

34. Gold's association with the theatre began with the Provincetown Players who produced his one-acts *Ivan's Homecoming* and *Down the Airshaft* in 1917. In 1920 the group produced his one-act *Money*. For excellent accounts of Gold's career, see John Pyros, *Mike Gold: Dean of American Proletarian Writers* (New York: Dramatika Press, 1979); and Michael Folsom, ed., *Mike Gold: A Literary Anthology* (New York: International Publishers, 1972).

35. Folsom, *Mike Gold: A Literary Anthology*, 7, 10, and 62.

36. Granich (aka Gold), "Towards Proletarian Art," *Liberator*, February 1921, 20–21.

37. Michael Gold, "Editorial," *Daily Worker*, 17 February 1925, 1. Quoted in Levine, *Left-Wing Dramatic Theory in the American Theatre*, 66.

38. Michael Gold, "Go Left, Young Writers," *New Masses*, January 1929, 3–4.

39. See Colette A. Hyman, *Staging Strikes: Workers' Theatre and the American Labor Movement* (Philadelphia: Temple University Press, 1997).

40. In his introduction to *The Cambridge Companion to Modernism* (Cambridge: Cambridge University Press, 1999), editor Michael Levenson offers the following interpretation of the impulse to limit or "weed out" within modernism:

> Because its leading voices eagerly assumed not only the burdens of making new artifacts, but also the responsibility of offering new justifications, the misunderstanding of Modernism began at the start, began with ambition of writers and artists to set the terms by which they would be understood, where this often meant setting the terms by which others would not qualify for understanding. This circle of initiates was closed not only against the unwashed public, *but also against rival artists who were excluded from the emerging narrative of Modernism triumphant.* In the last twenty years this once dominant narrative has lost its power to control responses to the period, and we now have a dramatically enlarged perception of the range and reach of achievement. What once seemed the exclusive affair of "modern masters," the "men of 1914" (as Wyndham Lewis called them), now stands as a complex of inventive gestures, daring performances, enacted also by many who were

> left out of accounts of early histories of the epoch, histories offered first by the actors themselves and later produced within an academic discourse, willingly guided by the precedents of the eminent artists. (2–3; emphasis added)

In light of Levenson's reading, the emerging split I am suggesting within the noncommercial theatre community might be viewed as microcosmic within a macrocosmic event. That is, the "closing" of the "modernist" theatre, such as it was defined and narrated by Cheney et al., to those such as Gold who sought to promote new theories and practices, was linked to a larger impulse imperative in the modernist impulse.

41. Levine, *Left-Wing Dramatic Theory*, 1–2.

42. Thomas S. Kuhn, *The Structure of Scientific Revolutions*, 2nd ed. (Chicago: University of Chicago Press, 1970). Kuhn defines *paradigm* as an "implicit body of intertwined theoretical and methodological belief that permits selection, evaluation, and criticism" (16–17); *anomaly* as "the recognition that nature has somehow violated the paradigm-induced expectations that govern normal science" (52–53); *crisis* as "the result of anomaly," which is defined as the "[f]ailure of existing rules" (68) and realization that the existing paradigm is "ridden by dogma" (75); and *emergence* as "the transition from a paradigm in crisis to a new one from which a new tradition of normal science can emerge," which is "a reconstruction of the field from new fundamentals" (84–85).

43. Thomas F. Connolly, *George Jean Nathan and the Making of Modern American Drama Criticism* (Madison, NJ: Fairleigh Dickinson University Press, 2000), 13.

44. George Jean Nathan, "Drama as an Art" in *The Critic and the Drama* (New York: Alfred A. Knopf, 1922), 33–34.

45. Connolly, *George Jean Nathan*, 47.

46. Along with Nathan, I include as part of this community of progressive critics the aforementioned Sayler, Cheney, and Goldman, as well as Waldo Frank, Hiram Moderwell, Clayton Hamilton, Archibald Henderson, and Van Wyck Brooks.

47. John Patrick Diggins, *The Rise and Fall of the American Left* (1972; reprint, New York: W. W. Norton, 1992), 94. The term "lyrical left" is credited to Floyd Dell. My reflections on the lyrical left are, in part, informed by Diggins's account of this historical moment. I also draw upon Sidney Lens, *Radicalism in America* (New York: Thomas Y. Crowell, 1969); Malcolm Cowley, *Exile's Return: A Literary Odyssey of the 1920s* (New York: Viking Press, 1951); Paul Buhle, *Marxism in the United States* (London: Verso, 1987); Theodore Draper, *The Roots of American Communism* (1957; reprint, Chicago: Ivan R. Dee, 1989); and Christopher Lasch, *The New Radicalism in America, 1889–1963: The Intellectual as Social Type* (New York: Alfred A. Knopf, 1965).

48. "Radical" as distinct from "revolutionary." For the purposes of my study, the former is defined as one who seeks to make *extreme changes* to existing sociopolitical or cultural views, habits, conditions, and/or institutions. The latter is one who seeks the *complete* overthrow of the existing sociopolitical or cultural views, habits, conditions, and/or institutions.

49. Joseph Freeman, *An American Testament* (New York: Farrar and Rinehart, 1936), 50.

50. Diggins, *The Rise and Fall of the American Left*, 95.

51. See Bourne's "The War of Intellectuals," published in *Seven Arts* in June 1918.

52. Louis Fraina, *Revolutionary Socialism: A Study of Socialist Reconstruction* (New York: Communist Press, 1918), 63; Diggins, *The Rise and Fall of the American Left*, 101–6.

53. Diggins, *The Rise and Fall of the American Left*, 109–13.

2. Break Down the Walls of the Theatre

The title of this chapter is a phrase Lawson used in reference to his work in the 1920s. He uses the phrase in his autobiography and in his interview with Robert Hethmon.

1. Once again, there is some confusion regarding these dates. In some drafts of Lawson's autobiography, he contends that after the United States entered the war on 6 April 1917 he, Dos Passos, and a half-dozen other Norton-Harjes volunteers were offered but declined transfers to U.S. military ambulance units, citing moral objections, and instead went to Paris to await new orders. This timeline supports the view, referred to in note 21 of chapter 1, that Lawson departed from the United States in February 1917, not June. It also disallows his presence at the taking of Hill 304 in August of that same year.

In addition to Dos Passos, Lawson also spent considerable time with Robert Hillyer, who later became a well-known poet. Hillyer, who was a former classmate of Dos Passos at Harvard and also a volunteer with the Norton-Harjes, was one of the young men who stayed in Paris illegally.

2. Autobiography, *Lawson Papers*, b. 97, f. 6, p. 49.

3. During his brief return to the United States in 1919, Lawson completed two scripts, *The Mad Moon* and *Humanlike*. These two scripts were neither sold nor produced. Nonetheless, Lawson imported many of the names of the characters as well as the central idea of a moral conflict between a young poet and stodgy puritanism from *The Mad Moon*—which can be traced to the outline of *The Silver Cord*, circa 1915—into *A New England Fantasy*, completed in 1924. This script, in turn, served as the basis for *Nirvana*. The script for *The Mad Moon* is in the *Lawson Papers*, b. 64, f. 4., and b. 66, f. 2. I can find no evidence of *Humanlike* other than Lawson's reference to it in his autobiography.

4. On 2 January 1920, federal police under the direction of Attorney General A. Mitchell Palmer and his aide J. Edgar Hoover seized thousands of people in thirty-three cities on charges of un-American activity. This was one of the first events in Hoover's ascent to power. Hoover had been appointed chief of the Anti-Radical Division of the Department of Justice on 1 August 1919. A series of small raids were conducted in November of that same year. The second and main series of raids took place on 2 January 1920.

5. Lawson's time in Paris predated the exile of many of the more commonly celebrated American expatriates. Further, he questioned much of the subsequent romanticizing of the era on the grounds that it softened and simplified the rebellion of those involved.

6. Autobiography, *Lawson Papers*, b. 99, f. 6, p. 886.

7. Lawson's exposure to expressionism began while at Williams, when he was introduced to the work of Frank Wedekind. Prior to seeing the aformentioned plays in production, Lawson also had read the work of Ernst Toller and Walter Hasenclever.

8. Autobiography, *Lawson Papers*, b. 95, f. 3, pp. 95–105.

9. Lawson finished only act 1 of *Processional* at this time. Lawson writes of the time, "The plays begun in Paris [in 1920] were not produced until many years later, and underwent vital changes, but what I wrote from April to September is the record of a transformation in my ideas of art and the theatre's forms and potentialities. Many members of my generation came in contact with these ideas at an earlier or later date. But for me, the shock of recognition was concentrated in those five months of 1920" (Autobiography, *Lawson Papers*, b. 99, f. 13, p. 114).

10. Autobiography, *Lawson Papers*, b. 99, f. 13, p. 115.

11. Autobiography, *Lawson Papers*, b. 95, f. 3, pp. 95–106a. Also, by early 1921, Lawson had run out of money. To support his family, he took a job with the Red Cross in Paris.

12. John Howard Lawson, *Roger Bloomer* (New York: Thomas Seltzer, 1923), 5–7. Subsequent references to the script appear parenthetically in the text.

13. The following studies explicate just a few of the many literary works that poeticize the force of urban space and urbanization on the structuring of the human, adolescent psyche: Peter Preston and Paul Simpson-Housley, *Writing the City: Literature and the Urban Experience* (New York: Routledge, 1994); Graham Clarke, ed., *The American City: Literary and Cultural Perspectives* (New York: St. Martin's Press, 1988); John Twyning, *London Dispossessed: Literature and Social Space in the Early Modern City* (New York: St. Martin's Press, 1998); and Graeme Gilloch, *Myth and Metropolis: Walter Benjamin and the City* (Cambridge, MA: Blackwell, 1996).

It is important to note as well that Lawson was aware when he was writing *Roger Bloomer* that the "youngster going to the city" was a very common theme. He viewed his adoption and subsequent alteration of this familiar narrative line as something of a guerilla tactic: attacking the bourgeois society of which he was a part and yet so detested from the inside. He later wrote regarding his use of this approach, "In declaring myself an artist-rebel, I asserted—for the first time—my birthright as an American. This was my being, my personality, and I had to declare it" (Autobiography, *Lawson Papers*, b. 92, p. 68).

14. In suggesting this parallel between Lawson and the fictional Roger, I do not mean to make an authoritarian truth claim. Rather, I contend that reading Lawson's life, like reading his play, is one valuable method for illuminating the materiality of both. To that end, it is perhaps important to note that late in his life Lawson did remark that "Roger is me" (Autobiography, *Lawson Papers*, b. 95, f. 3, p. 16). Regarding this conflation of dramatic personae and playwright, in his study *Modern German Drama* (New York: Grove, 1959), H. F. Garten notes that the expressionistic hero is "identical with the author's self" (107).

15. Diggins, *The Rise and Fall of the American Left*, 140.

16. Lawson notes the parallel of Roger to Ibsen's Reverend Brand in an early draft of his autobiography (Autobiography, *Lawson Papers*, b. 93, f. 2).

17. Broussard, *American Drama*, 53. In the chapter "Elmer Rice and John Howard Lawson," in *American Drama: Contemporary Allegory from Eugene O'Neill to Tennessee Williams*, Broussard offers a number of useful observations regarding *Roger Bloomer* and the ways in which it does and does not serve the expressionistic mode in a purely formal and thematic sense. Where Broussard's analysis falls short, however, is in his positioning of Lawson as a lesser talent than Rice based solely on the relative success of both playwrights in the application of expressionist techniques. Broussard situates expressionism as an immutable and unassailable artistic mode and, thereby, evaluates the success of those working with that mode based solely on the constancy in their application of the techniques associated with it.

18. I draw from the detailed history of German expressionism provided in Garten's *Modern German Drama*.

19. The reordering that occurred within the expressionistic mode in both Germany and the United States (i.e., the various changes made to tone and technique when the shift was made from mysticism to activism) may perhaps be read as another manifestation of a larger, macrocosmic shift, one that reordered the rules and orders of discourse for those artists in the West who were leftward leaning. I am thinking specifically of a larger repositioning of artists on the left who responded to World War I (either affirming or condemning it) by engaging in concrete praxis as opposed to ethereal and individualized introspection. For theatre artists writing in the expressionistic mode, this shift is perhaps specifically manifested in the restructuring of the expressionistic hero and that figure's overarching act, altering the heroic act from one that is largely subjective and internalized (i.e., the spiritual sojourn) to one that is social and externalized (i.e., the social insurgent).

20. In a letter to Richard Peyron Brown, Lawson wrote, "*Roger Bloomer* is sometimes compared to *The Adding Machine*, but there is an essential difference: Rice's play is pessimistic, whereas *Roger Bloomer* ends with affirmation of the human spirit; out of the nightmare, Roger emerges to 'face the music.'" Quoted in Brown, "John Howard Lawson as an Activist Playwright: 1923–1937," 34–35.

21. Autobiography, *Lawson Papers*, b. 99, f. 13, p. 114–15.

22. Autobiography, *Lawson Papers*, b. 99, f. 13, p. 117 (emphasis in original).

23. *Roger Bloomer*, 1920, *Lawson Papers*, b. 65, f. 1, p. 133. Box 65, folder 1 contains the working drafts of *Roger Bloomer* circa 1920.

24. Lawson himself noted the connection between Roger's dream and his budding interest in Dada. He writes, "I identified with the dadaist [. . .] the grotesque and the absurd could create an extraordinary tension between the audience and the performers, and I endeavored to achieve this quality in Roger's nightmare" (Autobiography, *Lawson Papers*, b. 95, f. 3).

25. Lawson notes in his writings that later in life, he came to view Roger's passivity as expressed in the early drafts of the script as "a deficiency which is endemic in expressionism [. . . a deficiency that] has been handed on to the theatre of the absurd" (Autobiography, *Lawson Papers*, b. 99, f. 13, p. 115).

26. Ernst Toller, *Transfiguration*, in *Seven Plays* (London: John Lane the Bodley Head, 1935), 105.

27. *Roger Bloomer*, 1920, *Lawson Papers*, b. 65, f. 1, pp. 30–31.

28. Hethmon interview.

29. In my research, I have failed to find any source (e.g., production prompt book) that would illuminate the changes imposed by Hull. The only prompt book included in the Lawson archive is from the Barker remounting of the play (see *Lawson Papers*, b. 66, f. 3). However, according to Lawson the changes imposed by Hull were extensive to the point that he felt, in many respects, that the Equity Players' production in no way reflected his intent.

30. Expressionistic drama was wildly popular in the art theatres in New York during the first years of the 1920s. The Theatre Guild alone produced Rice's *The Adding Machine*, which opened a little over two weeks after *Roger Bloomer* on 18 March 1923; Capek's *R. U. R.*, which opened on 9 October 1922; Kaiser's *From Morn to Midnight*, which opened on 21 May 1922; and Toller's *Man and Masses*, which opened on 14 April 1924.

31. Kenneth Macgowan, review of *Roger Bloomer*, Equity Players, 48th Street Theater, New York, *Wheeling (WV) News*, 11 March 1923, *Lawson Papers*, b. 4, f. 1. In *The Art Theatre*, Cheney offers a fascinating period account of the founding and objectives of the Equity Players, which specifies many of the problems facing that company on an organizational level and, thus, illuminates why the company struggled with Lawson's script. Cheney's critique focuses on the decision of the board members to go head to head with Broadway, to quickly forsake the staging of contemporary experimental pieces for the likes of Shaw and Ibsen, as well as their "half-hearted attempt" to support the work through a subscription audience (79). There is a sense that while Cheney wants to throw his full support behind this company, he is nonetheless troubled by their direction (Cheney, *The Art Theatre*, 76–80).

32. Letter from Shelley Hull to Lawson, 18 March 1923, *Lawson Papers*, b. 4, f. 1.

33. Hethmon interview.

34. Autobiography, *Lawson Papers*, b. 93, f. 2, p. 175a.

35. Kenneth Macgowan, review of *Roger Bloomer*, Greenwich Village Theatre, New York, *Evening Globe*, 13 April 1923, *Lawson Papers*, b. 4, f. 1. The cast for the Equity Players' production included Henry Hull (husband of the director Shelley Hull) as Roger and Mary Fowler as Louise. In the remounted production, Roger was played by Alan Bruce, who had played some of the supernumerary roles in the Equity Players' production.

36. I believe it necessary to offer a clarification regarding my use of the terms *conservative* and/or *mainstream*, *liberal*, and *left-wing* in relation to the media critics responding to Lawson's work. Broadly speaking, I have labeled "conservative" and/or "mainstream" those critics who were not only writing for doctrinal presses but were exceedingly suspicious—not to mention brutal in their summations—of theatre artists who were seeking to advance the mode and scope of theatre beyond the institutionalized European playwriting and stagecraft practices of the late nineteenth century (e.g., the well-made play form). I have labeled "liberal" those critics who championed new methods and forms. While a number of these so-called liberal critics wrote for mainstream publications (e.g., Stark Young's tenure as critic with the *New York Times* in the middle years of the 1920s), others wrote for liberal publications that overtly cited as part of their editorial policy the advancement of progressive democracy (e.g., *New Republic* and *The Nation*). Finally, I have labeled "left-wing" those critics who measured cultural outpourings in terms of how they did or did not

aid the advancement of socialist or communist agendas. More often than not, these so-called left-wing critics wrote for publications where the editorial policy was firmly grounded in the conventions of revolutionary politics (e.g., *New Masses*).

37. Alan Dale, review of *Roger Bloomer*, Equity Players, 48th Street Theater, New York, *Hartford Times*, 10 March 1923, *Lawson Papers*, b. 4, f. 1.

38. John Corbin, review of *Roger Bloomer*, Equity Players, 48th Street Theater, New York, *New York Times*, 2 March 1923, 18:3.

39. John Corbin, review of *Roger Bloomer*, Equity Players, 48th Street Theater, New York, *New York Times*, 11 March 1923, 1:3.

40. Dana Burnett, letter to the editor, *New York Times*, 18 March 1923, *Lawson Papers*, b. 4, f. 1.

41. David Gray, letter to the editor, *New York Herald*, 8 April 1923, *Lawson Papers*, b. 4, f. 1.

42. Caroline Wise, letter to the editor, *New York Call*, 23 March 1923, *Lawson Papers*, b. 4, f. 1.

43. Copy of letter sent to Lawson in *Lawson Papers*, b. 4, f. 1.

44. Ludwig Lewisohn, "Native Plays," review of *Roger Bloomer*, Marguerite Barker, Greenwich Village Theatre, New York, *The Nation*, 21 March 1923, 346.

45. Stark Young, "Forward Equity," review of *Roger Bloomer*, Marguerite Barker, Greenwich Village Theatre, New York, *New Republic*, 21 March 1923, 100–101.

46. Anita Block, review of *Roger Bloomer*, Marguerite Barker, Greenwich Village Theatre, New York, *New York Call*, 30 March 1923, *Lawson Papers*, b. 4, f. 1.

47. Autobiography, *Lawson Papers*, b. 93, f. 2, 4.

48. John Dos Passos, foreword to *Roger Bloomer*, viii.

49. John Howard Lawson, letter to the editor, *New York Times*, 18 March 1923, *Lawson Papers*, b. 4, f. 1.

50. Autobiography, *Lawson Papers*, b. 99, f. 13, pp. 117–19.

51. *Processional*, 1920, *Lawson Papers*, b. 65, f. 2, p. 1. Referenced is the draft of act 1 completed in the summer of 1920. Various working drafts of *Processional* are included in box 65, folders 2–6. Box 66, folder 1 includes Lawson's research on the strikes in Mingo County, West Virginia, and southern Illinois.

52. I am using the term "materialist aesthetics" as defined by Levine in *Left-Wing Dramatic Theory in the American Theatre*: "a symbiotic interplay between social conditions and theatrical activity" (1).

53. Autobiography, *Lawson Papers*, b. 99, f. 13, p. 119. Later in life, Lawson noted the ways in which the early draft of the script was connected to the larger cultural field: "There was absolutely no originality in any of these ideas. They were drawn from the literature and art of the period. But the combination of them in a play dealing with American labor conflict was new, and was beyond my power. I could not evolve a satisfactory form—I could only assemble incongruous bits and pieces of action" (Autobiography, *Lawson Papers*, b. 99, f. 13, p. 120).

54. Autobiography, *Lawson Papers*, b. 95, f. 3, p. 106a.

55. Autobiography, *Lawson Papers*, b. 99, f. 13, p. 121.

56. Autobiography, *Lawson Papers*, b. 95, f. 3, p. 106a.

57. A working outline for *Processional* from the summer of 1923 offers some insight into the script's development at this point:

Plot Outline:

I. Labor in agony of strike. People go on laughing, smiling as if nothing had happened—A man escapes—he knows nothing about the strike, caught by gigantic forces, feeling way in clouds of coal work. He escapes in confusion.
II. Everything turns in ruins around the man—He learns the truth—Vague revolt stirs in him—He goes out carelessly to die—Irony of events saves him again but a woman traps him.
III. The same irony of the individual's case turns the whole industrial dispute into an absurd farce—After me cometh a builder.
—America is the only modern country where caste or loss of it are of extreme importance.
—What about Jim singing "The International"
—No attempt should be made to convey subtle or allegorical meaning—events happen for their own sake.
—Major themes: revolution, mothers and men, religion and politics.
—All sex is absolutely primitive.

(included in *Lawson Papers*, b. 65, f. 3)

58. My attempts to find more information regarding these two events have revealed very little. The various drafts of Lawson's autobiography do little more than make passing reference to what were surely two monumental occurrences in the playwright's personal life. Concerning his brother's suicide, there is certain evidence in some drafts of Lawson's autobiography that the playwright believed his brother's death was, at least in part, a result of the force of puritanical restrictions. In regards to his separation and eventual divorce from Kate in 1925, there is some evidence that they continued to have a amicable relationship.

59. See "Paris Dada" in Annabelle Melzer, *Dada and Surrealist Performance* (1976; reprint, Baltimore: Johns Hopkins University Press, 1994), 137–60. Lawson was at this time also invested in a deep study of T. S. Eliot's "The Waste Land."

60. Autobiography, *Lawson Papers*, b. 94, f. 4, p. 205.

61. Autobiography, *Lawson Papers*, b. 94, f. 5, p. 227.

62. John Howard Lawson, *Processional* (New York: Thomas Seltzer, 1925), 4. Subsequent references to the script appear parenthetically in the text.

63. The Theatre Guild insisted that the stage direction "through the audience" be changed to "through the orchestra pit." Later in life, Lawson commented that this action was linked to the company's commitment to two nineteenth-century notions, psychological realism and psychic symbolism, and its refusal to go beyond these modes of theatrical presentation. Lawson recalled, "The Guild was committed to illusion and it accepted a variety of illusions, from 'slice of life' to the symbols and dreams of expression. But none of these styles broke with the 'mystery' of the stage event, which was perceived as separation between the stage and the spectators. *Processional* broke the proscenium and spilled into the audience" (Autobiography, *Lawson Papers*, b. 94, f. 6, p. 264).

64. Introduction to *Processional* in *Contemporary Drama: European, English and Irish, American Play*, ed. E. Bradlee Watson and Benfield Pressey (New York: Scribner's, 1961), 849.

65. See Julia Walker, *Expressionism and Modernism in the American Theatre: Bodies, Voices, Words* (Cambridge: Cambridge University Press, 2005), for an outstanding consideration of *Processional* as it relates to expressionism.

66. "Dada Manifesto, 1918," reprinted in *Modernism: An Anthology of Sources and Documents*, ed. Vassiliki Kolocotroni, Jane Goodman, and Olga Taxidou (Chicago: University of Chicago Press, 1998), 279.

67. See Autobiography, *Lawson Papers*, b. 94, f. 6, p. 251a, for the playwright's discussion of the influence of Picasso's setting for *Parade* on *Processional*. Also see note 73 for more information regarding the execution of this scene by designer Mordecai Gorelik.

68. Given the venomous tone in *Processional*, it seems appropriate to categorize Lawson as kin to those Dadaists such as George Grosz, whose focus was more squarely on the political force of his montages, as opposed to someone like Kurt Schwitters, whose vision of Dada was more formalist. Indeed, I would argue that the evidence clearly suggests that Lawson was in the mid 1920s diametrically opposed to the view espoused by Schwitters: that one should take art for what it evokes, not what it references.

69. Later in life Lawson described Jim as "a primitive whose instinctive violence is a central factor of American life and the source of rebellion that can lead to a better future" (Autobiography, *Lawson Papers*, b. 95, f. 3, p. 106a).

70. There is, I believe, another parallel between Jim and Yank in O'Neill's *The Hairy Ape*. Dynamite Jim in *Processional*, as is Yank (aka Robert Smith) in O'Neill's script, is presented as a person whose surname is no longer needed. However, whereas Jim successfully moves toward a place where he reclaims his surname and, by extension, his individuality, Yank, despite all his efforts, is removed further and further from anything approximating this type of agency.

71. Autobiography, *Lawson Papers*, b. 94, f. 6, p. 237.

72. *Processional*, 1920, *Lawson Papers*, b. 65, f. 2.

73. *Processional* was Gorelik's first Broadway design. Other notables in the cast and crew included June Walker as Sadie, Blanche Friderici as Mrs. Flimmins, and George Abbott as Dynamite Jim. Also of note, Alvah Bessie, Sanford Meisner, and Lee Strasberg were cast in supernumerary roles.

About Gorelik's design, Lawson later wrote, "[I]t seemed to me that an unbelievable meeting of minds occurred. [. . . Gorelik's] scenic investiture of *Processional* was the most decisive factor in sustaining and supplementing the values of the script. [. . .] Gorelik's design for the vaudeville curtain in the first scene, the street of a coal town with Fourth of July decorations and painted flags, was like any other vaudeville curtain, and yet wholly different, an imaginative angry comment on the town, the insincerity of our patriotism, the desecration of the spirit" (Autobiography, *Lawson Papers*, b. 94, f. 5, p. 224 and f. 6, p. 251a).

74. Percy Hammond, review of *Processional*, Theatre Guild, Garrick Theatre, New York, *New York Herald-Tribune*, 13 January 1925, 12.

75. Alan Dale, review of *Processional*, Theatre Guild, Garrick Theatre, New York, *Hartford Times*, 13 January 1925, *Lawson Papers*, b. 4, f. 4.

76. Burns Mantle, "The New Guild Play Wild, Weird and Woozy," review of *Processional*, Theatre Guild, Garrick Theater, New York, *Daily News*, 13 January 1925, 24.

77. Alexander Woollcott, review of *Processional*, Theatre Guild, Garrick Theater, New York, *New York Sun*, 13 January 1925, *Lawson Papers*, b. 4, f. 4.

78. George Jean Nathan, review of *Processional*, Theatre Guild, Garrick Theater, New York, *American Mercury*, March 1925, 372–73.

79. I have found no evidence of reviews of the Theatre Guild's production of *Processional* written by left-wing critics.

80. Stark Young, review of *Processional*, Theatre Guild, Garrick Theater, New York, *New York Times*, 18 January 1925, 7: 1.

81. Stark Young, review of *Processional*, Theatre Guild, Garrick Theater, New York, *New York Times*, 13 January 1925, 17: 1.

82. Heywood Broun, review of *Processional*, Theatre Guild, Garrick Theater, New York, *The World*, 18 January 1923, 9: 4.

83. Gilbert Gabriel, "Rhapsody in Red," review of *Processional*, Theatre Guild, Garrick Theater, New York, *New York Telegram-Mail*, 13 January 1925, *Lawson Papers*, b. 4, f. 4. This review is also reprinted in *The American Theatre as Seen by Its Critics*, ed. Montrose Moses and John Mason Brown (New York: Cooper Square Publishers, 1967), 311–13.

84. Copy of letter sent to Lawson in *Lawson Papers*, b. 4, f. 1. Others who signed include Gladys Brown and Arthur Davison Ficke.

85. Thornton Wilder, "The Turn of the Year," *Theatre Arts Monthly*, March 1925, 152–53.

86. Alexander Woollcott, "Life Behind the Scenes—Elmer Rice on *Processional*," *New York Sun*, 19 January 1925, *Lawson Papers*, b. 4, f. 4.

87. Autobiography, *Lawson Papers*, b. 99, f. 6, p. 879.

88. Autobiography, *Lawson Papers*, b. 100, f. 3, p. 474.

89. Autobiography, *Lawson Papers*, b. 92, f. 7, p. 250.

90. Autobiography, *Lawson Papers*, b. 94, f. 4, p. 205.

91. A handwritten script of *New England Fantasy*, circa 1924, is in the *Lawson Papers*, b. 66.

92. Lawson wrote of the script, "Written from May 25 to April 20 1924, the *Fantasy* contains the whole basis for *Nirvana*. It is a turning point in my personal history and tells so much about my mental and emotional life that I find it almost unbearable to read" (Autobiography, *Lawson Papers*, b. 94, f. 5, p. 206).

93. John Howard Lawson, *Nirvana*, typescript, 1926, act 1, p. 47, in *Lawson Papers*, b. 67, f. 2 and 3. *Nirvana* was never published. Subsequent references to the script appear parenthetically in the text.

94. *Nirvana* program, March 1926, *Lawson Papers*, b. 5, f. 1.

95. Autobiography, *Lawson Papers*, b. 94, f. 6, p. 264.

96. Concerning Breton, I have drawn from both Bettina Knapp's *French Theatre 1918–1939* (London: Macmillan, 1985) and Melzer's *Dada and Surrealist Performance*.

97. André Breton, "Manifesto of Surrealism" (1924), in *Manifestos of Surrealism*, translated by Richard Seaver and Helen R. Lane (Ann Arbor: University of Michigan Press, 1974), 37–38; also Knapp, *French Theatre*, 17–18. Lawson would later note that he was at this point growing increasingly suspicious of Freudian psychoanalysis. He points to one particular meeting in the spring of 1926 with Dr. Smith Ely Jeliffe, a leading psychiatrist in the first decades of the twentieth century. In a

meeting with Jeliffe, the discussion turned to *Nirvana*. According to Lawson, Jeliffe "talked for hours about Bill's homosexuality," which Lawson had never considered. Lawson contends that this meeting was a "big event which caused me to question psychoanalysis" (Autobiography, *Lawson Papers*, b. 94, f. 8). In another section of his autobiography, Lawson remarks:

> It is misleading to describe [my] change in the mid 20s as from Freud to Einstein. Freud maintained ascendancy—and so did sex—but the afflicted psyche, denied earthly satisfaction, unable to communicate on a human level, sought contact with the stars. Science guided the arts toward mysticism and distrust of reason: keystones of modern thought—from the plural vision of cubism to the vague of expressionism. [. . . Thus] I turned from Freud to Jung because Jung's theory of archetypal myths embedded in the unconscious mind seemed to me more fruitful than Freud's single-minded dedication to the Oedipus Complex. (Autobiography, *Lawson Papers*, b. 99, f. 13)

98. Lawson makes passing reference regarding his indebtedness to surrealism in Autobiography, *Lawson Papers*, b. 94, f. 6, p. 264.

99. In his review of Lawson's work, focusing specifically on *Nirvana*, Kelsey Allen offers a similar reading. Allen's review was published in *Women's West*, 4 March 1926, and is included in *Lawson Papers*, b. 5, f. 1.

100. Autobiography, *Lawson Papers*, b. 94, f. 9.

101. Autobiography, *Lawson Papers*, b. 94, f. 6, p. 245, and Hethmon interview.

102. Brooks Atkinson, review of *Nirvana*, Noble, Ryan, and Livy, Greenwich Village Theater, New York, *New York Times*, 4 March 1926, 19: 1.

103. Burns Mantle, review of *Nirvana*, Noble, Ryan, and Livy, Greenwich Village Theater, New York, *Daily News*, 6 March 1926, *Lawson Papers*, b. 5, f. 1.

104. Alexander Woollcott, review of *Nirvana*, Noble, Ryan, and Livy, Greenwich Village Theater, New York, *The World*, 4 March 1926, *Lawson Papers*, b. 5, f. 1.

105. Percy Hammond, review of *Nirvana*, Noble, Ryan, and Livy, Greenwich Village Theater, New York, *New York Herald-Tribune*, 14 March 1926: 5: 1.

106. Arthur Pollack, review of *Nirvana*, Noble, Ryan, and Livy, Greenwich Village Theater, New York, *Brooklyn Eagle*, 4 March 1926, 12A.

107. Gilbert Gabriel, review of *Nirvana*, Noble, Ryan, and Livy, Greenwich Village Theater, New York, *New York Sun*, 20 March 1926, 4.

108. Joseph Wood Krutch, "Hard Facts," review of *Nirvana*, Noble, Ryan, and Livy, Greenwich Village Theater, New York, *The Nation*, 17 March 1926, 295.

109. It should be noted that Lawson purports, in his autobiography, that Michael Gold and Joseph Freeman both wrote scathing reviews of *Nirvana*. I can find no further evidence of these reviews. It should also be noted that Lawson withheld *Nirvana* from publication.

110. Copy of letter from Lawson to Gilbert Gabriel, March 1926, in *Lawson Papers*, b. 5, f. 2. Lawson was not alone in his praising of the script. He received letters of ardent support from some members of the liberal literati. Perhaps the most passionate came from Marc Connelly in a letter dated 4 March 1926. In part, Connelly wrote, "*Nirvana* is miles ahead of *Processional* [. . .] the conception and your fidelity

to it are magnificent. [. . .] I don't know when I've felt the theatre being used as a real church more reverently or effectively" (*Lawson Papers*, b. 5, f. 1).

111. Autobiography, *Lawson Papers*, b. 100, f. 1.

112. Autobiography, *Lawson Papers*, b. 94, f. 5, p. 237.

113. Autobiography, *Lawson Papers*, b. 100, f. 1.

114. Stephen Greenblatt, "Towards a Poetics of Culture," in *The New Historicism*, ed. H. Aram Vessar (New York: Routledge, 1989), 12.

115. Gilbert Gabriel, "Rhapsody in Red," 312.

116. Autobiography, *Lawson Papers*, B. 94, f. 9.

3. To Beat the Drums of Rebellion

The title of this chapter is drawn from critic John Mason Brown's column "Intermission," published in the April 1928 edition of *Theatre Arts Monthly*. Brown used the phrase to describe Lawson's scripts.

1. Diggins, *The Rise and Fall of the American Left*, 143.

2. Significantly, neither Sacco nor Vanzetti came from peasant families. Both were sons of modestly prosperous farmers, Sacco from the south of Italy, Vanzetti from the north. Both had immigrated in 1908, seeking a democratic republic. Their optimism and hope for such a state in the United States quickly eroded, and both struggled to find work and, subsequently, became very active in radical politics. The two men, in fact, first met when each was participating in a strike rally. So profound was their disillusionment that at the outbreak of World War I, both moved to Mexico along with some sixty of their anarchist compatriots. Sacco returned to the United States at the end of 1917. Vanzetti returned in 1918.

3. Lens, *Radicalism in America*, 280.

4. Lens, *Radicalism in America*, 280.

5. Diggins, *The Rise and Fall of the American Left*, 143.

6. Autobiography, *Lawson Papers*, b. 94, f. 10, p. 323. Lawson was arrested during the march for obstructing the sidewalk.

7. *Crisis* as, once again, defined by Kuhn: "the result of anomaly" brought about by the "[f]ailure of existing rules" (68) and realization that the existing paradigm is "ridden by dogma" (75).

8. In chapter 1 of his study *The Communist Party of the United States: From the Depression to World War II* (New Brunswick: Rutgers University Press, 1991), Fraser M. Ottanelli explicates the various factions in the Communist movement in the United States in the 1920s and how this factionalism led to shrinking membership. He also describes how the stage was set during this decade for unification and expansion under the leadership of Earl Browder in the 1930s.

9. Autobiography, *Lawson Papers*, b. 99, f. 6, p. 886.

10. Copy of letter from Lawson to Gilbert Gabriel, March 1926 in *Lawson Papers*, b. 5, f. 2.

11. Autobiography, *Lawson Papers*, b. 94, f. 10, pp. 318–9b. "Midnight in Boston" is the working title for a chapter in Lawson's autobiography.

12. Lawson's desire to be associated with those who were active in left-wing politics in the United States might also be seen in his appointment to the board of the newly created *New Masses* in the spring of 1926.

13. John Howard Lawson, "Debunking the Art Theatre," *New Masses*, June 1926, 22–30; emphasis in original.

14. Cheney, *The Art Theatre*, 15, 16, 3, and 264.

15. Notice, *New Masses*, June 1926, 29.

16. An invitation was also extended to Eugene O'Neill, who declined to join. Faragoh's first foray into playwriting was *Pinwheel*, produced by Irene and Alice Lewisohn at the Neighborhood Playhouse in 1927. He followed Lawson to Hollywood after the dissolution of the New Playwrights' Theatre. His only other script of note, *Sunup to Sundown*, was produced on Broadway in 1938. His screenplays include *Her Private Affair* (1929), *Frankenstein* (1931), *Little Caesar* (1931), and *Becky Sharp* (1935). He died in 1966. In the early 1920s, Basshe was connected with the Provincetown Players, working primarily as a stagehand and stage manager. His script *Adam Solitaire* was produced by that group in 1925. Following the dissolution of the New Playwrights, Basshe continued to work in theatre, primarily as a stage manager. He had a few short pieces produced by some smaller workers' theatre groups in New York in the 1930s, including *John One Hundred* (1936), *Snickering Horses* (1938), and *The Turbulent Waters* (1938). His full-length play *Doomsday Circus*, though never produced in New York, was staged in Germany and Los Angeles. He died in 1939 at the age of forty.

Lawson would later write, "Basshe and Faragoh were the most gifted playwrights I have ever known. All three of us found it difficult, after 1928, to find a place in the theatre. Faragoh followed me to Hollywood, but never abandoned writing plays. Basshe continued to write brilliant, erratic, inspired theatre pieces—he could not discover or create a theatre that would meet the challenge of his imagination" (Autobiography, *Lawson Papers*, b. 100, f. 2, p. 383).

17. In her study *People's Theatre in Amerika* (New York: Drama Book Specialists, 1972), Karen Malpede Taylor offers the following amusing account of the first meeting between Kahn and the would-be New Playwrights:

> The luncheon to plan their New Playwrights Theatre took place at the Bankers Club, the central gathering place for Wall Street's moguls. It was probably an intentionally ironic gesture on Kahn's part because he knew about the playwrights' radical sympathies. Gold meant to counter by attending the luncheon without socks, but Faragoh, who stole enough Banker Club stationary to placate his creditors throughout the Depression, insisted on lending a pair of his own. Gold used to sign his letters to Kahn "your class enemy"; yet the relationship between the playwrights and their benefactor was always cordial. Kahn and the four [Dos Passos was in Europe and not present for any of the early organizational meetings] were unlikely conspirators, but where else could a non-commercial theatre turn for funds? (7)

18. Hethmon interview.

19. Miller and Frazer, *American Drama between the Wars*, 101.

20. Autobiography, *Lawson Papers*, b. 94, f. 10, p. 331a. Lawson offered another intriguing evaluation of the New Playwrights in a speech delivered at the American Studies Association's Theatre Symposium, held at San Fernando State College in 1961:

> [The New Playwrights' Theatre was] an expression of our desire to enliven the stage. [. . . This] was a worthy aim however much we may have been mistaken and confused in our approach. [. . . Our] intentions were publicized in statements made in defense of our productions—bold pronouncements, largely written by me, calling for drama that would have the slang and vitality, the casual meaning and nuances of American life. It was one thing to issue manifestos about plays and another to write them and get them on the stage. Had our plays been as promising as our manifestos, it is still doubtful that we could have found an audience to look at them. (Manuscript of speech is included in *Lawson Papers*, b. 36, f. 1)

21. Gold, for example, was the only member who was actively involved in the Communist Party.

22. Hethmon interview. For the first season, the company leased an abandoned music hall on 52nd Street. The opening of the theatre was heralded by Basshe's manifesto "The Revolt on 52nd Street," published in the *New York Times*, 27 February 1927, 7:4.

23. Autobiography, *Lawson Papers*, b. 94, f. 10, pp. 333–34. Gold's *Fiesta* was also rehearsed but did not make it to production during the first season.

24. For the second and third seasons, the New Playwrights leased a small theatre at 40 Commerce Street which had been renamed the Cherry Lane. The opening of this season was heralded by Dos Passos's manifesto "Towards a Revolutionary Theatre," published in *New Masses*, December 1927, 20. Edward Massey directed both *The Belt* and *Hoboken Blues*.

25. Gold began to serve as senior editor in the spring of 1928. His association with that publication, however, dated back to its founding in the spring of 1926. At that point, Gold, along with Hugo Gaellert and Joseph Freeman (to name a few), created *New Masses* in large part because they were troubled by the turning of the *Liberator* into a wholly political magazine with few literary and aesthetic concerns. Despite the state-of-the-art design and contributions by many well-known writers, *New Masses* faltered along for two years, often kowtowing to the "middle-of-the-road" contextual demands of the Garland Fund, the liberal though democratic foundation that funded the magazine. In 1928, however, when the Garland Fund stipend was exhausted, Gold became senior editor. Gold immediately set out to reorganize the faltering magazine, opting for a plainer (i.e., less expensive) format, a more revolutionary political stance, and a pledge to privilege the publication of "workers' art and literature."

26. The third season included productions of nonmember Upton Sinclair's *Singing Jailbirds* and Dos Passos' *Airways, Inc.* Lawson, Dos Passos, and Gold all remained on the executive board. At some point near the end of 1928 or early 1929, Faragoh too left New York for Hollywood. There are numerous letters addressed to Lawson and Faragoh in California from Basshe and Dos Passos that chart the dissolution of the company. Dos Passos was the first to resign, in March 1929, following the production of *Airways, Inc.*

27. *New York Times*, 26 April 1929, 29.

28. Autobiography, *Lawson Papers*, b. 91, f. 1., p. 365.

29. Lasky, "The New Playwrights Theatre," 206–7.

30. Autobiography, *Lawson Papers*, b. 100, f. 2, p. 383; emphasis in original.

31. John Howard Lawson, "The New Showmanship," *Pinwheel* program, February 1927, 1, 4. In *Lawson Papers*, b. 5, f. 2.

32. John Howard Lawson, "What Is a Workers Theatre?" *New York Sun*, 12 November 1927, 40. Also in *Lawson Papers*, pkg. 1.

33. Ottanelli, *The Communist Party of the United States*, 9–16.

34. Autobiography, *Lawson Papers*, b. 94, f. 10, p. 320.

35. Michael Denning, *The Cultural Front* (London: Verso, 1997), 59–60.

36. *A Jazz Tragedy* would evolve into *X Plus Y*—leading to *The Invisible Mob*, and eventually, *Loud Speaker*—as well as *The Social Whirl*—leading to *The Pure in Heart*. *Lawson Papers*, box 68 includes the handwritten notes for *A Jazz Tragedy*, dated August 1924 (f. 2); a typewritten script for *X Plus Y*, dated December 1924, and typewritten outline for revisions, dated 16 December 1924 (f. 3); a handwritten script for *The Invisible Mob*, dated June 1925 (f. 1); and a handwritten script for *The Social Whirl*, dated May/June 1926 (f. 2). Box 69 includes a typewritten script for *The Invisible Mob*, dated July 1925 (f. 1), as well as the final draft of *Loud Speaker*, dated 2 March 1927 (f. 2).

37. *X Plus Y*, 1924, *Lawson Papers*, b. 68, f. 3.

38. *The Invisible Mob*, 1925, *Lawson Papers*, b. 68, f. 1.

39. The work of Meyerhold had been featured at the 1926 International Theatre Exhibition. Regarding the New Playwrights' fondness for constructivism, Taylor writes, "The New Playwrights' seized upon constructivist staging as a way to make the interior revolt of expressionism functional. (Meyerhold was equally drawn to Amerikan [*sic*] jazz and vaudeville, whose use in the plays [New Playwrights' Theatre] members pioneered. In 1928 William Gropper reported from the Soviet Union in the *Daily Worker* that Meyerhold was planning productions of *Processional* and *The Belt*, which opened the [New Playwrights' Theatre's] second season. The productions never materialized)" (*People's Theatre in Amerika*, 8–9).

40. John Howard Lawson, *Loud Speaker* (New York: Macaulay, 1927), 17–18. Subsequent references to the script appear parenthetically in the text.

41. Autobiography, *Lawson Papers*, b. 100, f. 2, p. 331a.

42. Autobiography, *Lawson Papers*, b. 100, f. 2, p. 331a.

43. *Loud Speaker* was directed by Harry Wagstaff Gribble and designed by Mordecai Gorelik. Seth Kendall played Collins.

44. Bernard Smith, "Machines and Mobs," *New Masses*, March 1928, 23.

45. Percy Hammond, review of *Loud Speaker*, New Playwrights' Theatre, 52nd Street Theatre, New York, *New York Herald-Tribune*, 3 March 1927, 14.

46. Burton Davis, review of *Loud Speaker*, New Playwrights' Theatre, 52nd Street Theatre, New York, *New York Telegraph*, 3 March 1927, *Lawson Papers*, pkg. 1.

47. George Winchell, review of *Loud Speaker*, New Playwrights' Theatre, 52nd Street Theatre, New York, *New York Evening Graphic*, 3 March 1927, *Lawson Papers*, pkg. 1.

48. Brooks Atkinson, "The Play: Steeplechase Drama," review of *Loud Speaker*, New Playwrights' Theatre, 52nd Street Theatre, New York, *New York Times*, 3 March 1927, 27.

49. George Jean Nathan, review of *Loud Speaker*, New Playwrights' Theatre, 52nd Street Theatre, New York, *American Mercury*, May 1927, *Lawson Papers*, pkg. 1.

50. Autobiography, *Lawson Papers*, b. 100, f. 2, pp. 331a and 332.

51. The movement of the KMT into Nanjing was part of Chiang's Northern Expedition. Beginning in July 1926, the Northern Expedition was formed to rid China of regional warlords and reunite the country under one central government. It was launched from the KMT base in Guangzhou. This military action was an outgrowth of the nationalist ideology proposed by KMT leader Sun Yat-sen in the first years of the 1920s. Sun's basic ideology, "The Three Principles of Nationalism, Democracy, and Socialism," was charged with the spirit of anti-imperialism and national unification. In 1923, in an endeavor to forward his agenda and buttress the feeble KMT military forces, Sun forged an alliance with the Soviet Union, and its proxy, the Chinese Communist Party. In turn, Chinese Communists received orders from the Comintern to join the KMT. The next year the KMT began to be reorganized along Leninist lines. When Sun died in 1925, Chiang began to move the KMT to the right.

My understanding of Chinese politics in the 1920s has been shaped by Jonathan D. Spence, *The Gate of Heavenly Peace: The Chinese and Their Revolution, 1895–1980* (New York: Penguin, 1982), and Arif Dirlik, *The Origins of Chinese Communism* (New York: Oxford University Press, 1989).

52. After being expelled from the KMT, the CCP split into two factions and went underground. One faction attempted to organize urban uprisings. The other, headed by Mao, retreated to the countryside of central China, where it mobilized peasant support, formed a peasant army, and set up several soviet governments. The first faction would eventually join Mao in central China.

53. The archive does not include any working drafts of *The International.*

54. John Howard Lawson, *The International* (New York: Macaulay, 1927), 9. Subsequent references to the script appear parenthetically in the text.

55. Autobiography, *Lawson Papers*, b. 100, f. 2, p. 367.

56. Autobiography, *Lawson Papers*, b. 94, f. 10, p. 327a.

57. Production personnel for *The International* included settings by Dos Passos, music by Edward A. Ziman, and choreography by Don Oscar Becque. Lawson instructed Ziman to compose a score in the tradition of *Rite of Spring.*

58. Steven Rathburn, review of *The International*, New Playwrights' Theatre, Cherry Lane Theatre, New York, *Brooklyn Eagle*, 16 January 1928, *Lawson Papers*, pkg. 1.

59. E. W. Osborn, review of *The International*, New Playwrights' Theatre, Cherry Lane Theatre, New York, *Evening World*, 16 January 1928, 12.

60. John Anderson, "Mr. Lawson Writes Another Ear-Splitting Upheaval," review of *The International*, New Playwrights' Theatre, Cherry Lane Theatre, New York, *New York Journal*, 16 January 1928, B2.

61. Alexander Woollcott, review of *The International*, New Playwrights' Theatre, Cherry Lane Theatre, New York, *The World*, 16 January 1928, 11.

62. Brooks Atkinson, review of *The International*, New Playwrights' Theatre, Cherry Lane Theatre, New York, *New York Times*, 16 January 1928, 24: 4.

63. C. H., review of *The International*, New Playwrights' Theatre, Cherry Lane Theatre, New York, *New York American*, 16 January 1928, 24.

64. Gordon M. Leland, review of *The International*, New Playwrights' Theatre, Cherry Lane Theatre, New York, *The Billboard*, 28 January 1928, 11, 89.

65. Thomas Van Dyke, review of *The International*, New Playwrights' Theatre, Cherry Lane Theatre, New York, *New York Telegraph*, 16 January 1928, 2.

66. Sender Garlin, "Lawson Play an Ingenuous Drama of the Revolution," review of *The International*, New Playwrights' Theatre, Cherry Lane Theater, New York, *Daily Worker*, 16 January 1928, 4.

67. John Dos Passos, letter to editor, *Daily Worker*, 20 January 1928, 4.

68. Sender Garlin, "Response to John Dos Passos," *Daily Worker*, 21 January 1928, 6.

69. John Dos Passos, letter to editor, *Daily Worker*, 28 January 1928, 6.

70. Autobiography, *Lawson Papers*, b. 100, f. 2, p. 368a; emphasis in original.

71. Autobiography, *Lawson Papers*, b. 94, f. 10, p. 331.

72. John Howard Lawson, leaflet for pledges, New Playwrights' Theatre, April 1928, *Lawson Papers*, pkg. 1.

73. Autobiography, *Lawson Papers*, b. 100, f. 2, p. 387.

74. "The Dialectic Decade" is the suggested working title for a chapter in Lawson's autobiography.

75. Fredric Jameson, "Towards Dialectical Criticism," in *Marxism and Form: Twentieth Century Dialectical Theories of Literature* (Princeton, NJ: Princeton University Press, 1971), 307–8.

76. Emphases in titles and quotes from "The New Showmanship" (*Pinwheel* program, February 1927, 1, 4. *Lawson Papers*, b. 5, f. 2) and "What Is a Workers Theatre?" (*New York Sun*, 12 November 1927, *Lawson Papers*, pkg. 1) are added.

77. Autobiography, *Lawson Papers*, b. 100, f. 2, p. 387.

78. Lawson, "What Is a Workers Theatre?," *Lawson Papers*, pkg. 1.

79. Lawson, "The New Showmanship," *Lawson Papers*, b. 5, f. 2; and Jameson, "Towards Dialectical Criticism," 308.

80. Jameson, "Towards Dialectical Criticism," 308; and Denning, *The Cultural Front*, 59–60.

81. Autobiography, *Lawson Papers*, b. 96, f. 2, p. 356; and Jameson, "Towards Dialectical Criticism," 307.

4. The Thorny Path to Commitment

1. Van Wyck Brooks, *Days of the Phoenix: The Nineteen Twenties I Remember* (New York: Dutton, 1957), 184.

2. Autobiography, *Lawson Papers*, b. 100, f. 3, pp. 478–79.

3. Autobiography, *Lawson Papers*, b. 100, f. 3, pp. 475–76.

4. Margaret Anderson, editorial, *The Little Review*, May 1929, 3–4. Subsequent references to this issue of *The Little Review* appear parenthetically in the text.

5. Autobiography, *Lawson Papers*, b. 100, f. 3, p. 475–76.

6. Autobiography, *Lawson Papers*, b. 100, f. 3, p. 477.

7. Autobiography, *Lawson Papers*, b. 100, f. 3, p. 477; and Frederick J. Hoffman, *The Twenties: American Writing in the Postwar Decade* (New York: Free Press, 1962). 83–87.

8. e. e. cummings, "[IX] y is a WELL KNOWN ATHLETE'S BRIDE" (1931) in *Poems 1923–1954* (New York: Harcourt, Brace and Company, 1954), 228–29.

9. Crane in Hoffman, *The Twenties*, 263.

10. In his autobiography, Lawson briefly mentions Crane and cummings as examples of those artists who were not "impelled" toward "renewed social awareness" by "anguish." Instead, they, as did many others, chose to disavow the force of the social and "languish in a state of hopelessness" through a process of "aesthetic escapism" (Autobiography, *Lawson Papers*, b. 100, f. 3, pp. 473–79).

11. Autobiography, *Lawson Papers*, b. 100, f. 3, p. 475.

12. Autobiography, *Lawson Papers*, b. 100, f. 3, p. 477.

13. Autobiography, *Lawson Papers*, b. 100, f. 3, p. 482.

14. Autobiography, *Lawson Papers*, b. 100, f. 3, pp. 480–81.

15. Autobiography, *Lawson Papers*, b. 100, f. 3, pp. 473–74.

16. Waldo Frank, "Our Arts: The Re-Discovery of America," *New Republic*, 9 May 1928, 344. See also Autobiography, *Lawson Papers*, b. 100, f. 2, pp. 390–91.

17. Drafts for the incomplete scripting of *Sister Carrie* are included in *Lawson Papers*, b. 70, f. 1 and f. 2.

18. Autobiography, *Lawson Papers*, b. 100, f. 2, pp. 391–93. Notes and a rough draft of *Death in an Office* are included in *Lawson Papers*, b. 70, f. 3.

19. Upon completing *Death in an Office*, Lawson began to write a play entitled *Saga Center*. I have not been able to find a complete copy of this script. *Lawson Papers*, b. 71, f. 1 includes notes and a detailed outline. Lawson's description and critique of it is interesting:

> The action takes place in the dusty central square of a village on the prairie. I had to go back to my feelings about America when I settled in Paris in 1920, and I made the leading character [a] French woman, Felicite Green. Felicite is married to [. . .] Ben Green. [. . .] Ben is a small farmer, whose radical activities cause him to be murdered by the Ku Klux Klan. After his death, Felicite has a love affair with the politician who, as head of the Klan, ordered the murder. The bitter scenes between them bear a curious resemblance to the scenes between the rich racist and the prostitute in Sartre's *The Respectful Prostitute*. In the end, the politician defies the Klan and reveals the truth about the murder; he and Felicite escape from his enraged followers.
>
> The attempt to deal with American fascism as a psychological phenomenon was important. But the characters were so far beyond my understanding that they seem to be loaded with inexplicable emotion. This is especially true of Felicite: she is involved in the action, yet she is never really a part of it. There is no sense of her passion for the wealthy politician, and her French background has no precise meaning in terms of her American experience. (Autobiography, *Lawson Papers*, b. 100, f. 2., pp. 393–94)

20. Writing for the *Internet Movie Database*, film reviewer Ron Kerrigan offers the following plot summary for *Dynamite*.

> Wealthy Cynthia is in love with not-so-wealthy Roger, who is married to Marcia. The threesome is terribly modern about the situation, and Marcia

will gladly divorce Roger if Cynthia agrees to a financial settlement. But Cynthia's wealth is in jeopardy because her trust fund will expire if she is not married by a certain date. To satisfy that condition, Cynthia arranges to marry Hagon Derk, who is condemned to die for a crime he didn't commit. She pays him so he can provide for his little sister. But at the last minute, Derk is freed when the true criminal is discovered. Expecting to be a rich widow, Cynthia finds herself married to a man she doesn't know.

Lawson's other screenplays from this period include *Dream of Love*, *The Ship from Shanghai*, *Our Blushing Brides*, *The Sea Bat*, *Bachelor Apartment*, *Goodbye Love*, and *Success at Any Price*. For a more thorough discussion of Lawson's screenwriting career, see Gary Carr's "The Left Side of Paradise: The Screenwriting of John Howard Lawson," PhD dissertation, University of Texas, Austin, 1975.

21. Autobiography, *Lawson Papers*, b. 95, f. 1. Sue and John Howard Lawson's son Jeffrey was born in the summer of 1926. Their daughter Amanda was born three years later.

22. Harold Clurman, foreword to John Howard Lawson, *With a Reckless Preface: Two Plays "The Pure of Heart" and "Gentlewoman"* (New York: Farrar and Rinehart, 1934), xxi–xxii.

23. Autobiography, *Lawson Papers*, b. 100, f. 3, pp. 488–90.

24. Autobiography, *Lawson Papers*, b. 100, f. 3, pp. 495–500.

25. Autobiography, *Lawson Papers*, b. 100, f. 3, pp. 485–86.

26. Paul Buhle, *Marxism in the United States: Remapping the History of the American Left* (London: Verso, 1987), 156; emphasis added.

27. Edmund Wilson, "An Appeal to Progressives," *New Republic*, 14 January 1931, 234–38. See also Autobiography, *Lawson Papers*, pp. 499–500.

28. See chapter 3 for a more thorough account of "American exceptionalism" and the shifting of power within the Communist movement in the United States.

29. Diggins, *The Rise and Fall of the American Left*, 151.

30. Wilson, "An Appeal to Progressives," 234–38; emphasis added. See *Lawson Papers*, b. 100, f. 3, pp. 499–504, for the playwright's discussion of his relationship with Wilson and the force of his influence.

31. Edmund Wilson, *Axel's Castle: A Study in the Imaginative Literature of 1870–1930* (1931; reprint, New York: Charles Scribner's Sons, 1959), 292–98; emphasis added.

32. Autobiography, *Lawson Papers*, b. 100, f. 3, pp. 487–501.

33. George Seibel, review of *The Pure in Heart*, Theatre Guild, Nixon Theatre, Pittsburgh, *Pittsburgh Sun-Telegraph*, 11 October 1932, *Lawson Papers*, pkg. 1.

34. John Howard Lawson, *Success Story* (New York: Farrar and Rinehart, 1932), 3. Subsequent references to the script appear parenthetically in the text.

35. Autobiography, *Lawson Papers*, b. 100, f. 3, p. 527.

36. Autobiography, *Lawson Papers*, b. 100, f. 2, p. 393.

37. Harold Clurman, letter to John Howard Lawson, 8 August 1932, *Lawson Papers*, b. 5, f. 5; emphasis in original.

38. John Howard Lawson, "Communism in relation to *Success Story*," August 1932, *Lawson Papers*, b. 5, f. 5; emphasis in original.

39. Clurman, *The Fervent Years*, 93.

40. Autobiography, *Lawson Papers*, b. 100, f. 3, p. 521.

41. *Success at Any Price* was the title of the film adaptation of the script, written by Lawson.

42. Lawson, "Communism in relation to *Success Story*," *Lawson Papers*, b. 5, f. 5; emphasis in original.

43. The Group Theatre production of *Success Story* was directed by Lee Strasberg. The cast included Luther Adler as Sol and Stella Adler as Sarah. Lawson wrote of the production:

> Stella Adler and her brother, Luther, who played Sarah and Sol, were more affected by their early training with their father, Jacob Adler, than by the Stanislavsky method, and they played with a fire which identified them with the Jewish feeling of the play—a feeling of moral betrayal of a tradition rather than an abandonment of youthful radicalism.
>
> It seemed to me that Strasberg, who had come from the ghetto in Galacia to the United States when he was nine years old, and whose formative years were spent on the East Side, was moved to make the Jewish theme dominant, and to orchestrate the performance around it, although it is hard to tell how far Strasberg's direction was affected by the special intensity that Stella and Luther brought to their performances. (Autobiography, *Lawson Papers*, b. 100, f. 3, p. 526)

44. Review of *Success Story*, Group Theatre, Maxine Elliott Theatre, New York, *Daily Worker*, 3 October 1932, 1.

45. Gilbert Gabriel, review of *Success Story*, Group Theatre, Maxine Elliott Theatre, New York, *The American*, 27 September 1932, *Lawson Papers*, b. 5, f. 7.

46. Joseph Wood Krutch, "Mr. Lawson Comes Back," review of *Success Story*, Group Theatre, Maxine Elliott Theatre, New York, *The Nation*, 12 October 1932, 336–37.

47. Brook Atkinson, review of *Success Story*, Group Theatre, Maxine Elliott Theatre, New York, *New York Times*, 27 September 1932, 24:4.

48. Brooks Atkinson, "Pushing Ahead," review of *Success Story*, Group Theatre, Maxine Elliott Theatre, New York, *New York Times*, 2 October 1932, 9:1.

49. Clurman, foreword to *With a Reckless Preface*, xxiii–xxiv.

50. "The Writer in Hollywood" is the working title for a chapter in Lawson's autobiography.

51. Ceplair and Englund, *The Inquisition in Hollywood*, 61. Also see Dave Davis and Neal Goldberg, "Organizing the Screen Writers' Guild: An Interview with John Howard Lawson," *Cineaste*, 8, no. 2 (1977), 4–11, 58.

52. See *Lawson Papers* b. 96, f. 2, and b. 100, f. 3 and f. 6 for the playwright's thoughts on the development of the Screen Writers' Guild as recorded in drafts of his autobiography.

53. Ceplair and Englund, *The Inquisition in Hollywood*, 25–26.

54. Autobiography, *Lawson Papers*, b. 100, f. 3, p. 566.

55. Autobiography, *Lawson Papers*, b. 96, f. 2, p. 341.

56. For example, Actor's Equity had recently failed in its attempt to unionize film actors. Lawson later recalled that there were a number of participants in these early meetings who would not have participated had it not been for the legalized contract approach to organization: "[Bielenson and I] believed that writers could not be held together without some sort of legal tie which would correspond to their understanding of contractual obligation. Union-organization in itself was not enough, and many of the people whose participation we needed would shy away at even the mention of a union" (Autobiography, *Lawson Papers*, b. 96, f. 2, p. 342).

57. Autobiography, *Lawson Papers*, b. 96, f. 2, p. 342. Screen Writers' Guild constitutions, statements, and contracts are in the *Lawson Papers* b. 6, f. 4.

58. Autobiography, *Lawson Papers*, b. 96, f. 2, p. 343.

59. Autobiography, *Lawson Papers*, b. 96, f. 2, p. 343a.

60. Concerning the methods used to secure the signatures, Lawson writes the following:

> About seventy-five writers at the meeting signed the contract. Many others scurried away, shame-faced in their escape. The [newly elected officers and Executive] Board met after the meeting, and we selected the names of prominent writers whose support would be decisive for us in the coming weeks. We decided that a group of us would visit them that very night and secure their signatures. We spent the next six hours, until dawn, going from house to house[,] from the Hollywood Hills to the sea. Most of those we visited argued with us, some with a touch of desperation. There is no doubt that we exerted a good deal of pressure, and the arguments were not always gentle. I remember one writer opened his front door—it must have been four o'clock in the morning; he was wearing a bathrobe and surveyed us sleepily. "Must I sign?," he asked. I said, "Yes, you must!" The others nodded and the signature was given. (Autobiography, *Lawson Papers*, b. 96, f. 2, p. 344)

61. The executive board included Oliver Garrett, Howard Green, Grover Jones, Dudley Nichols, and Louis Weitzenkorn.

62. Autobiography, *Lawson Papers*, b. 96, f. 2, pp. 343–43a.

63. Davis and Goldberg, "Organizing the Screen Writers' Guild," 8.

64. Autobiography, *Lawson Papers*, b. 96, f. 2, p. 341.

65. Autobiography, *Lawson Papers*, b. 100, f. 3, p. 565.

66. Autobiography, *Lawson Papers*, b. 96, f. 2, p. 344a, and Ceplair and Englund, *The Inquisition in Hollywood*, 27–28.

67. Autobiography, *Lawson Papers*, b. 100, f. 3, p. 567.

68. Lawson offers the following summation of his treatment in the weeks preceding his dismissal from MGM: "There was no change at the studio the day after [the meeting at the Knickerbocker Hotel. Nonetheless] I soon realized I was being watched; the papers in my desk were examined during my absence; an attractive young woman who was a bit-player in films made an affront to attract me which was so naïve that I felt obligated to tell her that she too was a worker and should not lend herself to the dark schemes of the producers" (Autobiography, *Lawson Papers*, b. 96, f. 2, p. 345).

69. Autobiography, *Lawson Papers*, b. 96, f. 2, p. 346. In joining ranks with the Authors' League, the Guild also allied itself with the Dramatist Guild, the Newspaper Guild, and the Radio Writers Guild. See Ceplair and Englund, *The Inquisition in Hollywood*, 36.

70. Autobiography, *Lawson Papers*, b. 100, f. 3, p. 569.

71. Autobiography, *Lawson Papers*, b. 96, f. 2, p. 346.

72. Autobiography, *Lawson Papers*, b. 100, f. 3, p. 583.

73. John Howard Lawson, letter from Lawson to the Guild, 28 August 1933, *Lawson Papers*, b. 6, f. 3. This letter was later published in *Screen Writer News*. See as well Autobiography, *Lawson Papers*, b. 100, f. 3, p. 585.

74. Autobiography, *Lawson Papers*, 100, f. 3, pp. 586–87.

75. Autobiography, *Lawson Papers*, b. 96, f. 2, p. 349. Also, in late September 1933, RKO, which had, following his dismissal from MGM, hired Lawson to adapt *Success Story* for the screen, informed the playwright that the characters Sol and Sarah would no longer be Jewish. Lawson was furious. However, due to the nature of his contract, he was unable to do anything. Lawson's inability to control his creative work merely added fuel to an already smoldering fire. In *Success at Any Price*, Douglas Fairbanks Jr. played Sol, and Colleen Moore played Sarah.

76. Ceplair and Englund, *The Inquisition in Hollywood*, 29.

77. Autobiography, *Lawson Papers*, b. 96, f. 2, p. 351a.

78. Autobiography, *Lawson Papers*, b. 100, f. 3, pp. 590–91.

79. Autobiography, *Lawson Papers*, b. 96, f. 2, p. 352.

80. Autobiography, *Lawson Papers*, b. 100, f. 3, pp. 592–93.

81. Autobiography, *Lawson Papers*, b. 100, f. 3, p. 594.

82. Ralph Bloch, letter from Guild Board (Ralph Bloch) to Lawson, 6 December 1933, *Lawson Papers*, b. 6, f. 3. Autobiography, *Lawson Papers*, b. 100, f. 3, p. 585.

83. Autobiography, *Lawson Papers*, b. 96, f. 2, p. 354.

84. Autobiography, *Lawson Papers*, b. 96, f. 2, p. 356.

85. John Howard Lawson, letter to Guild, 4 January 1934, *Lawson Papers*, b. 6, f. 3.

86. Davis and Goldberg, "Organizing the Screen Writers' Guild," 8.

87. Autobiography, *Lawson Papers*, b. 100, f. 3.

88. Autobiography, *Lawson Papers*, b. 96, f. 2, pp. 352a-356.

89. Autobiography, *Lawson Papers*, b. 100, f. 3, pp. 473–74.

90. The First American Writers' Congress was held at the Mecca Temple in New York City on 26, 27, and 28 April 1935. Over 200 delegates from twenty-six states attended, as well as 150 writers, who attended as guests, and 4,000 spectators.

91. V. F. Calverton, "Literary Fascism," *New Masses*, April 1930.

92. See Autobiography, *Lawson Papers*, b. 100, f. 3, pp. 491–98, for Lawson's thoughts on the New Humanist/antihumanist debate.

93. Edmund Wilson, "Notes on Babbitt and More," *New Republic*, 19 March 1930. Reprinted in Edmund Wilson, *A Literary Chronicle, 1920–1950* (New York: Doubleday Anchor Books, 1956), 146–60. The reference to Dedham Courthouse and Boston State House is, of course, intended to invoke the memory of Sacco and Vanzetti and, in turn, equate Babbitt with those who, in the opinion of Wilson, were responsible for their deaths.

94. Michael Gold, "Wilder: Prophet of the Genteel Christ," *New Republic*, 22 October 1930, 267. Gold's essay "Proletarian Realism," published one month prior, may be viewed as a companion piece to his critique of Wilder. In this essay, Gold proudly proclaimed himself "the first American writer to herald the advent of a world proletarian literature and a concomitant to the rise of the world proletariat," and he cited nine objectives the working-class artist should try to embrace (*New Masses*, September 1930, 4–5).

95. Lawson recalls these competing views when he writes that he was "moved" by Wilson's "careful, literate studies of the philosophy and ethics of [New] Humanism," and yet found Gold's consideration of those same issues "inappropriate [. . .] the tone of his [Gold's] critical writing made me uneasy." Autobiography, *Lawson Papers*, b. 100, f. 3, p. 494–96.

96. Joseph Freeman, *An American Testament* (New York: Farrar and Rinehart, 1936), 663.

97. Edmund Wilson, *Axel's Castle*, 298.

98. Autobiography, *Lawson Papers*, b. 100, f. 3, p. 487.

5. Lost like Hamlet in His Inner Conflict

The title of this chapter is drawn from Michael Gold's critique of Lawson, "A Bourgeois Hamlet in Our Time," published in *New Masses* on 10 April 1934.

1. Barbara Herrnstein Smith, *Contingencies of Value: Alternative Perspectives for Critical Theory* (Cambridge, MA: Harvard University Press, 1988), 45 and 28.

2. Gold's letter is part of "Against the Fascist Terror in Germany," *New Masses*, April 1933, 11. In this issue of *New Masses*, the editors published letters from fourteen writers who had responded to a call in the March 1933 issue, requesting comments on Hitler's recent advent to the seat of chancellor in Germany on 30 January 1933. In addition to Gold, the issue included letters by Roger N. Baldwin, Heywood Broun, Waldo Frank, Granville Hicks, Sidney Hook, Scott Nearing, James Rorty, and Isidor Schneider. The issue also included Joseph Freeman's essay "The Background of German Fascism." See Ottanelli, *The Communist Party of the United States*, 58.

3. Diggins, *The Rise and Fall of the American Left*, 173–74.

4. At the Seventh World Congress in 1935, the Comintern officially altered its ultraleftist and isolationist stance by calling for a "Popular Front" of all peoples and parties who opposed Fascism. The CP-USA immediately deserted its heated and vocal opposition to Roosevelt's New Deal and, moreover, sought to reintegrate party leaders into liberal, social democratic organizations and mainstream trade unions. Regarding the latter, the CP-USA played a central role in organizing emerging unions for the Congress of Industrial Organizations (CIO) and, for the first time since the years immediately preceding World War I, gained significant representation and, thus, considerable power in a number of unions. However, with the signing of the Hitler-Stalin nonaggression pact in August 1939, and the onset of World War II that immediately followed, the Comintern abruptly altered its policy, ending its criticism of Nazi Germany and denouncing the war as an "imperialist" venture enacted by Great Britain and France. In the United States, the CP-USA, following the Comintern's directive, vigorously opposed all defense preparations and aid to

the Western democracies, labeling all such efforts "war-mongering." Many of the now-Communist-dominated unions went on strike in support of this opposition. When Germany attacked Russia in June 1941, the Comintern's position on the war again changed overnight. Supplanting the term "imperialist" for "democratic" in its discussions of the war, the CP-USA, under the leadership of Earl Browder who sanctioned "class peace" and "win the war" policies, gave its full support to pro-war causes. In turn, strikes were opposed as a hindrance to the "democratic" war effort. See Ottanelli, *The Communist Party of the United States*, 58.

5. Smith, *Contingencies of Value*, 45. I must note that while I argue that there was a considerable "closing of gaps" during this historical moment, there continued to be numerous critiques written by both liberal and left-wing critics that bore the stamp of those respective worldviews. As my analysis of Lawson's scripts composed during this period will demonstrate, various dogmatisms still haunted critical discourse, sometimes profoundly so.

6. Levine, *Left-Wing Dramatic Theory*, 1.

7. For Lawson's recollection of the New York theatre scene circa 1934, see Autobiography, *Lawson Papers*, b. 100, f. 2, p. 601–5.

8. A handwritten outline for *The Jazz Tragedy* (circa 1924) and partial script for *The Social Whirl* (circa May–June 1926) is included in *Lawson Papers*, b. 68, f. 2.

9. John Howard Lawson, *The Pure in Heart*, in *With a Reckless Preface: Two Plays "The Pure of Heart" and "Gentlewoman"* (New York: Farrar and Rinehart, 1934), 3. Subsequent references to the script appear parenthetically in the text.

10. Clurman, foreword to *With a Reckless Preface*, xxii.

11. McCreath, "A Rhetorical Analysis of the Plays of John Howard Lawson," 155.

12. In his study "A Rhetorical Analysis of the Plays of John Howard Lawson," McCreath suggests a connection between *Roger Bloomer* and *The Pure in Heart*, but does not develop this line of thought. See pp. 151–52.

13. McCreath, "A Rhetorical Analysis of the Plays of John Howard Lawson," 157–59.

14. *The Pure in Heart* was directed by Edward Massey. Scenic design was by Jo Mielziner. The cast included Dorothy Hall as Annabel Sparks and James Bell as Larry Goshen. Gorelik had originally been commissioned to design the sets. However, Lawson found his designs "so striking" that he feared "they would distract attention from the actors." Late in life, Lawson admitted that dismissing Gorelik was a crucial mistake. Unable to control any other aspect of the production, he became "unreasonably critical of Gorelik's settings" (Autobiography, *Lawson Papers*, b. 100, f. 2, pp. 610–11).

15. John Howard Lawson, "Essays in the Theatre," *New York Times*, 18 March 1934, *Lawson Papers*, pkg. 1.

16. Program for *The Pure in Heart*, Aldrich and De Liagre Jr., Longacre Theater, New York, *Lawson Papers*, b. 5, f. 7.

17. Brooks Atkinson, "Dance of the Cosmopolis in 'The Pure of Heart' by John Howard Lawson," Review of *The Pure in Heart*, Aldrich and De Liagre Jr., Longacre Theater, New York, *New York Times*, 21 March 1934, 24:3.

18. Percy Hammond, "The Dreamy Mr. Lawson Talks Hysterically in His Sleep," Review of *The Pure in Heart*, Aldrich and De Liagre Jr., Longacre Theater, New York, *New York Herald-Tribune*, 21 March 1934, 14.

19. John Anderson, Review of *The Pure in Heart*, Aldrich and De Liagre Jr., Longacre Theater, New York, *New York Journal*, 21 March 1934, *Lawson Papers*, pkg. 1.

20. Autobiography, *Lawson Papers*, b. 100, f. 3, p. 606.

21. John Howard Lawson, *Gentlewoman*, in *With a Reckless Preface: Two Plays "The Pure of Heart" and "Gentlewoman"* (New York: Farrar and Rinehart, 1934), 117. Subsequent references to the script appear parenthetically in the text.

22. Autobiography, *Lawson Papers*, b. 100, f. 3, pp. 504, 606.

23. Clurman, *The Fervent Years*, 132–33.

24. *Gentlewoman* was directed by Lee Strasberg, with scenic designs by Mordecai Gorelik. The cast included Stella Adler as Gwyn Ballentine, Morris Carnovsky as Dr. Golden, and Lloyd Nolan as Rudy Flannigan. About his association with the Group Theatre, Lawson later wrote:

> I was drawn to the Group and yet I could not identify with them. I had doubts about their motives—largely because their motives were as mixed as mine. Yet they represented the only force in the American theatre which could bring my plays to the stage with skill and a measure of understanding. From the Group's point of view, or at least from the point of view of its three directors, I was the best hope for accomplishing their purpose—to bring fervor and imagination to the theatre, without a head-on collision with Broadway or the Broadway audience.
>
> The affinity between us was in part due to the fact that they suffered, as I did, from a divided conscience. [. . .]
>
> [With the staging of *Gentlewoman*, t]he Group's motives were as impure as mine: rehearsing the play in four weeks and bringing in Lloyd Nolan, an actor who had no previous experience with them, to play the male lead, the Group was guilty of the same sins of pride and ambition which afflicted me. (Autobiography, *Lawson Papers*, b. 100, f. 2, pp. 604–5 and 612)

25. Brooks Atkinson, Review of *Gentlewoman*, Group Theatre, Cort Theatre, New York, *New York Times*, 23 March 1934, 28:4.

26. John Anderson, Review of *Gentlewoman*, Group Theatre, Cort Theatre, New York, *New York Journal*, 23 March 1934, *Lawson Papers*, pkg. 1.

27. Percy Hammond, Review of *Gentlewoman*, Group Theatre, Cort Theatre, New York, *New York Herald-Tribune*, 23 March 1934, *Lawson Papers*, pkg. 1.

28. Joseph Wood Krutch, "Sound and Fury," Review of *Gentlewoman*, Group Theatre, Cort Theatre, New York, *The Nation*, 11 April 1934, 24–26.

29. Jennie Held, Review of *The Pure in Heart* and *Gentlewoman*, *New Theatre*, 9 April 1934, 19.

30. Melvin Levy, "The World of Theatre," Review of *Gentlewoman*, Group Theatre, Cort Theatre, New York, *Daily Worker*, 28 March 1934, 7.

31. Lawson, *With a Reckless Preface*, vii–x. Subsequent references to this essay appear parenthetically in the text.

32. Lawson specifically noted *They Shall Not Die* by John Wexley, *Peace on Earth* by George Sklar and Albert Maltz, and *Stevedore* by Sklar and Paul Peters.

33. Michael Gold, "A Bourgeois Hamlet in Our Time," *New Masses*, 10 April 1934, 28–29.

34. John Howard Lawson, "Inner Conflict and Proletarian Art," *New Masses*, 17 April 1934, 29–30.

35. Michael Gold, "Reply to Lawson," *New Masses*, 24 April 1934, 28–29.

36. Lawson as quoted in Brown, "John Howard Lawson as an Activist Playwright," 140.

37. This charge was a response to Lawson's description published in *New Masses* of the Birmingham court. He referred to it as a "kangaroo court."

38. Although Sinclair was running on the platform "End Poverty in California" (EPIC) through the development of people's cooperative, he did not garner the support of the CP-USA. Specifically, the CP-USA viewed Sinclair's platform as too dangerous and revolutionary in an era when the party was, instead, seeking to align itself with the doctrine of the Popular Front.

39. Lester Cohen, "Lawson Crosses the Class Line," *New Theatre*, June 1934, 5.

40. John Howard Lawson, "Towards a Revolutionary Theatre: The Theatre—The Artist Must Take Sides," *New Theatre*, June 1934, 6–7; all emphases in original.

41. John Howard Lawson, "Straight from the Shoulder," *New Theatre*, November 1934, 11–12; all emphases in original.

42. Autobiography, *Lawson Papers*, b. 99, f. 1.

43. John Howard Lawson, "Technique and the Drama," in *American Writers Congress*, ed. Henry Hart (New York: International, 1935), 123–28; all emphases in original.

44. John Howard Lawson, *Theory and Technique of Playwriting* (1936; reprint, New York: Hill and Wang, 1960), 157. Subsequent references to this book appear parenthetically in the text.

45. Later in life, Lawson would further refine his approach and term it "psychological naturalism." Regarding this term, he wrote:

> [I use "psychological naturalism" instead of "socialist realism"] not because I want to defend its mechanistic and defeatist use in the Soviet Union, but because ["socialist realism"] places the work of art in a restricted political framework and suggests that the aesthetic views of the Soviet Union, or even the policies of Josef Stalin, were the main factor in the course of cultural thought in the United States. I do not want to underestimate the Soviet influence, but it is not the main factor in the evolution of psychological naturalism, which is heavily influenced by Freudian and Existentialist concepts. (Autobiography, *Lawson Papers*, b. 99, f. 6, pp. 879–80)

46. Autobiography, *Lawson Papers*, b. 99, f. 5, p. 765.

47. John Howard Lawson, *Marching Song* (New York: Dramatist Play Service, 1937), 32. Subsequent references to the script appear parenthetically in the text.

48. Autobiography, *Lawson Papers*, b. 99, f. 5, p. 834.

49. Autobiography, *Lawson Papers*, b. 99, f. 5, p. 835.

50. Autobiography, *Lawson Papers*, b. 99, f. 5, p. 836.

51. Autobiography, *Lawson Papers*, b. 99, f. 5, p. 765.

52. Lawson, "Technique and the Drama," 124.

53. Autobiography, *Lawson Papers*, b. 99, f. 5, pp. 836–37.

54. Autobiography, *Lawson Papers*, b. 99, f. 5, p. 841. Lawson also notes that he originally submitted the script to the Group Theatre. When they turned it down, Lawson was "shattered."

55. Autobiography, *Lawson Papers*, b. 99, f. 5, p. 835.

56. John Mason Brown, Review of *Marching Song*, Theatre Union, Bayes Theater, New York, *New York Post*, 15 March 1937, 10.

57. Richard Watts Jr., Review of *Marching Song*, Theatre Union, Bayes Theater, New York, *New York Tribune*, 18 February 1937, 14.

58. Arthur Pollack, Review of *Marching Song*, Theatre Union, Bayes Theater, New York, *Brooklyn Eagle*, 18 February 1937, *Lawson Papers*, pkg. 1.

59. Gilbert Seldes, Review of *Marching Song*, Theatre Union, Bayes Theater, New York, *Scribner's*, April 1937, *Lawson Papers*, pkg. 1.

60. Wilella Waldorf, Review of *Marching Song*, Theatre Union, Bayes Theater, New York, *New York Post*, 18 February 1937, *Lawson Papers*, pkg. 1.

61. Brooks Atkinson, "John Howard Lawson's *Marching Song* Brings the Theatre Union to Broadway," Review of *Marching Song*, Theatre Union, Bayes Theater, New York, *New York Times*, 18 February 1937, 18:2.

62. Burns Mantle, Review of *Marching Song*, Theatre Union, Bayes Theater, New York, *Daily News*, 18 February 1937, *Lawson Papers*, pkg. 1.

63. John Anderson, "Embattled Strikers in New Play Mirrored Recent Headlines," Review of *Marching Song*, Theatre Union, Bayes Theater, New York, *New York Journal*, 18 February 1937, *Lawson Papers*, pkg. 1.

64. Charles E. Dexter, "*Marching Song* Vital As Today's Newspaper," Review of *Marching Song*, Theatre Union, Bayes Theater, New York, *Daily Masses*, 19 February 1937, quoted in Brown, "John Howard Lawson as an Activist Playwright," 151–52.

65. Nathaniel Buchwald, Review of *Marching Song*, Theatre Union, Bayes Theater, New York, *Daily Worker*, 21 February 1937, *Lawson Papers*, pkg. 1.

66. New York State Communist Party, State Organization-Education Committee, *Lawson Papers*, pkg. 1.

67. Autobiography, *Lawson Papers*, b. 99, f. 2, p. 441 and f. 5, p. 834.

68. Autobiography, *Lawson Papers*, b. 100, f. 3, p. 474.

69. Joseph Wood Krutch, "Strike Play," Review of *Marching Song*, Theatre Union, Bayes Theater, New York, *The Nation*, 27 February 1937, 249.

70. John Howard Lawson, "The Crisis in the Theatre," *New Masses*, 15 December 1936, 36; emphasis is in the original.

71. Lawson, "The Crisis in the Theatre," 36.

72. Greenblatt, *Shakespearean Negotiations*, 14.

Epilogue: The Rebel Now Revolutionary

1. Letter to Dr. Eberhard Burning, 8 May 1966, *Lawson Papers*, b. 38, f. 2. Three years later, Lawson echoed and developed this critique in a letter to Jack Salzman dated 29 January 1969:

I am not happy about the changes made in *Processional* for the 1937 Federal Theatre production: the attempt to "humanize" the cartoon figures of the black man [Rastus] and the Jewish characters [Sadie and Cohen] undercut the theatrical quality of the style. [. . .]

Processional is not really a social drama of the thirties; on the contrary, it is (in my own modest opinion) a remarkable experiment in a Brechtian theatricalist style which had an appreciable effect on the American theatre in 1925, and it may be regarded as the first serious attempt to create an American kind of theatricalism. [. . .] It points to the living newspaper and agitprop [of] the 1930s. (Copy of letter in *Lawson Papers*, b. 58).

2. Burns Mantle, "The New Guild Play Wild, Weird and Woozy," review of *Processional*, 24: 1–2.

3. Eleanor Flexner, *American Playwright: 1918–1938* (New York: Simon and Schuster, 1938), 285.

4. See Davis and Goldberg, "Organizing the Screen Writers' Guild," for Lawson's account of the return to California and the writing of *Blockade*.

5. Lawson's screenplays from this period include *Algiers* (1938), *They Shall Have Music* (1939), *Four Sons* (1940), *Action in the North Atlantic* (1943), *Sahara* (1943), *Counter-Attack* (1945), and *Smash-Up* (1946).

6. Autobiography, *Lawson Papers*, b. 99, f. 5, p. 850. Lawson also remarked, "I never abandoned the creative challenge of the theatre and never stopped writing for the stage. Hardly a day passed without my scribbling notes for one of my dramatic projects" (*Lawson Papers*, b. 99, f. 5, p. 853).

7. Autobiography, *Lawson Papers*, b. 99, f. 5, p. 853.

8. In May 1945, an article was published in the *Daily Worker* by Jacques Duclos of the French Communist Party. Duclos, who was most likely following a directive from Stalin, condemned Browder's "class peace" and "win the war" policies. At a meeting of the National Committee of the CP-USA in June, Browder was removed as general secretary. In February of the next year, he was expelled from the party.

9. The House Committee on Un-American Activities (HUAC) was established in 1938. From 1938 until 1944 it was officially a "temporary" committee, chaired by Martin Dies, a Democrat from Texas. It was under the watch of Dies that the Federal Theatre Project was investigated and closed. Through the maneuvering of John Rankin, a Democrat from Mississippi, HUAC became a "permanent" committee in January 1945. From 1945 through 1952, the committee was chaired by John S. Wood, a Democrat from Georgia. On various occasions, however, Wood relinquished the chair to J. Parnell Thomas, a Republican from New Jersey.

10. In addition to Lawson, the Hollywood Ten included Dalton Trumbo, Alvah Bessie, Albert Maltz, Samuel Ornitz, Herbert Bieberman, Ring Lardner, Lester Cole, Edward Dmytryk, and Adrian Scott. An eleventh, Bertolt Brecht, answered the committee's questions and then immediately left for Europe.

11. The complete transcript of Lawson's testimony, including the statement he was not allowed to read, is recorded in *Thirty Years of Treason: Excerpts before the House Committee on Un-American Activities, 1938–1968*, edited by Eric Bentley (New York: Viking, 1971), 153–65.

12. John Howard Lawson, *The Hidden Heritage: A Rediscovery of the Ideas and Forces That Link the Thought of Our Time with the Culture of the Past* (New York: Citadel Press, 1950). In his introduction, Lawson notes that he began the study in 1936.

13. Notes on and drafts of *In Praise of Learning* are included in the *Lawson Papers*, b. 72, f. 7 and b. 73, f. 1–2. John Howard Lawson, *Film in the Battle of Ideas* (New York: Masses and Mainstream, 1953).

14. Various drafts of *Thunder Morning* are include in the *Lawson Papers*, b. 73, f. 3–5.

15. John Howard Lawson, *Film, the Creative Process: The Search for an Audio-Visual Language and Structure* (New York: Hill and Wang, 1964).

16. Autobiography, *Lawson Papers*, b. 92, f. 1, p. 3.

Bibliography

I use the following method for documenting materials drawn from the Lawson Papers archive: "*Lawson Papers*," followed by "b." for *box* or "pkg." for *package*, followed by "f." for *folder* (when applicable) and followed by "p." for *page* (when applicable). The Lawson Papers Collection (collection 16) is housed in Special Collections in Morris Library at Southern Illinois University Carbondale.

Allen, Kelcey. Review of *Nirvana*, Noble, Ryan, and Livy, Greenwich Village Theatre, New York. *Women's Wear*, 4 March 1926.

Anderson, John. "Embattled Strikers in New Play Mirrored Recent Headlines," Review of *Marching Song*, Theatre Union, Bayes Theater, New York. *New York Journal*, 18 February 1937.

———. "Mr. Lawson Writes Another Ear-Splitting Upheaval," Review of *The International*, New Playwrights' Theatre, Cherry Lane Theatre, New York. *New York Journal*, 16 January 1928.

———. Review of *Gentlewoman*, Group Theatre, Cort Theatre, New York. *New York Journal*, 23 March 1934.

———. Review of *The Pure in Heart*, Aldrich and De Liagre, Jr., Longacre Theater, New York. *New York Journal*, 21 March 1934.

Anderson, Margaret. Editorial. *The Little Review*, May 1929.

Atkinson, Brooks. "Dance of the Cosmopolis in 'The Pure of Heart' by John Howard Lawson," Review of *The Pure in Heart*, Aldrich and De Liagre Jr., Longacre Theater, New York. *New York Times*, 21 March 1934.

———. "John Howard Lawson's *Marching Song* Brings the Theatre Union to Broadway," Review of *Marching Song*, Theatre Union, Bayes Theater, New York. *New York Times*, 18 February 1937.

———. "The Plays: Steeplechase Drama," Review of *Loud Speaker*, New Playwrights' Theatre, 52nd Street Theatre, New York. *New York Times*, 3 March 1927.

———. Review of *Success Story*, Group Theatre, Maxine Elliott Theatre, New York. *New York Times*, 27 September 1932.

———. Review of *Gentlewoman*, Group Theatre, Cort Theatre, New York. *New York Times*, 23 March 1934.

———. Review of *Nirvana*, Noble, Ryan, and Livy, Greenwich Village Theater, New York. *New York Times*, 4 March 1926.

———. "Pushing Ahead," Review of *Success Story*, Group Theatre, Maxine Elliott Theatre, New York. *New York Times*, 2 October 1932.

———. Review of *The International*, New Playwrights' Theatre, Cherry Lane Theatre, New York. *New York Times*, 16 January 1928.

Barnard, Rita. *The Great Depression and the Culture of Abundance*. New York, Cambridge University Press, 1995.

Batchelor, John, ed. *The Art of Literary Biography*. New York: Oxford University Press, 1995.

Benjamin, Walter. *Understanding Brecht*. Translated by Anna Bostock. London: New Left Books, 1973.

Bennett, Tony. "Texts in History." In *Post-Structuralism and the Question of History*. Ed. Derek Attridge, Geoff Bennington, and Robert Young. New York: Cambridge University Press, 1987.

Benoit, Richard Peter. "A Hegemonic Analysis of John Howard Lawson and the New Playwrights Theatre," PhD dissertation, Kent State University, 2000.

Bentley, Eric, ed. *Thirty Years of Treason: Excerpts before the House Committee on Un-American Activities, 1938–1968*. New York: Viking, 1971.

Bigsby, C. W. E. *A Critical Introduction to Twentieth Century American Drama*. Vol. 1, *1900–1940*. Cambridge: Cambridge University Press, 1982.

Bloch, Beverle Rochelle. "John Howard Lawson's *Processional*: Modernism in American Theatre in the Twenties," PhD dissertation, University of Denver, 1988.

Block, Anita. Review of *Roger Bloomer*, Marguerite Barker, Greenwich Village Theatre, New York. *New York Call*, 30 March 1923.

Bourne, Randolph. "The War of Intellectuals." *Seven Arts*, June 1918.

Breton, André. "Manifesto of Surrealism" (1924). In *Manifestos of Surrealism*. Translated by Richard Seaver and Helen R. Lane. Ann Arbor: University of Michigan Press, 1974.

Brooks, Van Wyck. *Days of the Phoenix: The Nineteen Twenties I Remember*. New York: Dutton, 1957.

Broun, Heywood. Review of *Processional*, Theatre Guild, Garrick Theater, New York. *The World*, 13 January 1925.

Broussard, Louis. *American Drama: Contemporary Allegory From Eugene O'Neill to Tennessee Williams*. Norman: University of Oklahoma Press, 1962.

Brown, John Mason. Review of *Marching Song*, Theatre Union, Bayes Theater, New York. *New York Post*, 15 March 1937.

Brown, Richard Peyron. "John Howard Lawson as an Activist Playwright: 1923–1937," PhD dissertation, Tulane University, 1964.

Buchwald, Nathaniel. Review of *Marching Song*, Theatre Union, Bayes Theater, New York. *Daily Worker*, 21 February 1937.

Buhle, Paul. *Marxism in the United States: Remapping the History of the American Left*. London: Verso, 1987.

Burnett, Dana. Letter to the editor. *New York Times*, 18 March 1923.

Calverton, V. F. "Literary Fascism." *New Masses*, April 1930.

———. *The Newer Spirit: A Sociological Criticism of Literature*. New York: Boni & Liveright, 1925.

Carr, Gary. "The Left Side of Paradise: The Screenwriting of John Howard Lawson," PhD dissertation, University of Texas, Austin, 1975.

Caudwell, Christopher. *Illusion and Reality: A Study of the Sources of Poetry*, 1937. Reprint, New York: International, 1963.

Ceplair, Larry, and Steven Englund. *The Inquisition in Hollywood: Politics and the Film Community, 1930–1960*. Berkeley: University of California Press, 1983.

Cheney, Sheldon. *The Art Theatre: Its Character as Differentiated from the Commercial Theatre; Its Ideals and Organization; and a Record of Certain European and American Examples*. New York: Alfred A. Knopf, 1917, 1925.

Clark, Barrett H., and George Freedley, eds. *A History of Modern Drama*. New York: Appleton Century, 1947.

Clarke, Graham, ed. *The American City: Literary and Cultural Perspectives*. New York: St. Martin's Press, 1988.

Clurman, Harold. *The Fervent Years: The Group Theatre and the Thirties*, 1948. Reprint, New York: Da Capo Press, 1983.

———. Foreword to John Howard Lawson, *With a Reckless Preface: Two Plays "The Pure of Heart" and "Gentlewoman."* New York: Farrar and Rinehart, 1934.

———. Letter to John Howard Lawson, 8 August 1932. *Lawson Papers*, b. 5, f. 5.

Cohen, Lester. "Lawson Crosses the Class Line." *New Theatre*, June 1934.

Connolly, Thomas F. *George Jean Nathan and the Making of Modern American Drama Criticism*. Madison, NJ: Fairleigh Dickinson University Press, 2000.

Corbin, John. Review of *Roger Bloomer*, Equity Players, 48th Street Theater, New York. *New York Times*, 2 March 1923.

———. Review of *Roger Bloomer*, Equity Players, 48th Street Theater, New York. *New York Times*, 11 March 1923.

Cowley, Malcolm. *Exile's Return: A Literary Odyssey of the 1920s*. New York: The Viking Press, 1951.

cummings, e. e. "[IX] y is a WELL KNOWN ATHLETE'S BRIDE" (1931). In *Poems 1923–1954*. New York: Harcourt, Brace and Company, 1954.

Dale, Alan. Review of *Processional*, Theatre Guild, Garrick Theatre, New York. *Hartford Times*, 13 January 1925.

———. Review of *Roger Bloomer*, Equity Players, 48th Street Theater, New York. *Hartford Times* 10 March 1923.

Davis, Burton. Review of *Loud Speaker*, New Playwrights' Theatre, 52nd Street Theatre, New York. *New York Telegraph*, 3 March 1927.

Davis, Dave, and Neal Goldberg. "Organizing the Screen Writers' Guild: An Interview with John Howard Lawson." *Cineaste*, 8:2 (1977).

Dell, Floyd. "Literature and the Machine Age." *Liberator*, November 1923.

Denning, Michael. *The Cultural Front*. London: Verso, 1997.

———. *The Mercury Theatre: Orson Welles and the Popular Front*. London: Verso, 1992.

Denzin, Norman K. *Interpretive Biography*. Newbury Park, CA: Sage Publications, 1989.

Dexter, Charles E. "*Marching Song* Vital As Today's Newspaper," Review of *Marching Song*, Theatre Union, Bayes Theater, New York. *Daily Masses*, 19 February 1937.

Diggins, John Patrick. *The Rise and Fall of the American Left*, 1972. Reprint, New York: W. W. Norton, 1992.

Dirlik, Arif. *The Origins of Chinese Communism*. New York: Oxford University Press, 1989.

Dos Passos, John. Foreword to John Howard Lawson, *Roger Bloomer*. New York: Thomas Seltzer, 1923.

———. Letter to the editor. *Daily Worker*, 20 January 1928.

———. Letter to the editor. *Daily Worker*, 28 January 1928.

Draper, Theodore. *The Roots of American Communism*, 1957. Reprint, Chicago: Ivan R. Dee, 1989.

Eagleton, Terry. *Marxism and Literary Criticism*. Berkeley: University of California Press, 1976.

Evans, Richard J. *In Defense of History*. New York: Norton, 2002.

Fearnow, Mark. *The American Stage and the Great Depression: A Cultural History of the Grotesque*. Cambridge: Cambridge University Press, 1997.

Fletcher, Anne. "The Theory and Practice of Mordecai Gorelik (1925–1935): Emblem for the Changing American Theatre," PhD dissertation, Tufts University, 1992.

Flexner, Eleanor. *American Playwright: 1918–1938*. New York: Simon and Schuster, 1938.

Folsom, Michael, ed. *Mike Gold: A Literary Anthology*. New York: International Publishers, 1972.

Fraden, Rena. *Blueprints of a Black Federal Theatre, 1935–1939*. New York: Cambridge University Press, 1994.

Fraina, Louis. *Revolutionary Socialism: A Study of Socialist Reconstruction*. New York: Communist Press, 1918.

Frank, Waldo. "Our Arts: The Re-Discovery of America." *New Republic*, 9 May 1928.

Freeman, Joseph. *An American Testament*. New York: Farrar and Rinehart, 1936.

Gabriel, Gilbert. Review of *Nirvana*, Noble, Ryan, and Livy, Greenwich Village Theater, New York. *New York Sun*, 20 March 1926.

———. Review of *Success Story*, Group Theatre, Maxine Elliott Theatre, New York. *The American*, 27 September 1932.

———. "Rhapsody in Red." *New York Telegram-Mail*, 13 January 1925. Reprinted in *The American Theatre As Seen By Its Critics* edited by Montrose Moses and John Mason Brown. New York: Cooper Square Publishers, 1967.

Gaddis, John Lewis. *The Landscape of History: How Historians Map the Past*. Oxford: Oxford University Press, 2002.

Gallagher, Catherine, and Stephen Greenblatt. *Practicing New Historicism*. Chicago: University of Chicago Press, 2000.

Gardner, Robert Merritt. "International Rag: The Theatrical Career of John Howard Lawson," PhD dissertation, University of California, Berkeley, 1977.

Garlin, Sender. "Lawson Play an Ingenuous Drama of the Revolution," Review of *The International*, New Playwrights' Theatre, Cherry Lane Theater, New York. *Daily Worker*, 16 January 1928.

———. "Response to John Dos Passos." *Daily Worker*, 21 January 1928.

Garten, H. F. *Modern German Drama*. New York: Grove, 1959.

Gilloch, Graeme. *Myth and Metropolis: Walter Benjamin and the City*. Cambridge, MA: Blackwell, 1996.

Gold, Michael. "A Bourgeois Hamlet in Our Time." *New Masses*, 10 April 1934.

———. Editorial. *Daily Worker*, 17 February 1925.

———. "Go Left, Young Writers." *New Masses*, January 1929.

———. Letter as part of "Against the Fascist Terror in Germany." *New Masses*, April 1933.

———. "Proletarian Realism." *New Masses*, September 1930.

———. "Reply to Lawson." *New Masses*, 24 April 1934.

———. (as Irwin Granich). "Towards Proletarian Art." *Liberator*, February 1921.

———. "Wilder: Prophet of the Genteel Christ." *New Republic*, 22 October 1930.

Goldman, Emma. *The Social Significance of the Modern Drama*. 1914. Reprint, New York: Applause, 1987.

Goldstein, Malcolm. *The Political Stage: American Drama and Theater of the Great Depression*. New York: Oxford University Press, 1974.

Gray, David. Letter to the editor. *New York Herald*, 8 April 1923.

Greenblatt, Stephen. *Shakespearean Negotiations: The Circulation of Social Energy in Renaissance England*. Berkeley: University of California Press, 1988.

———. "Towards a Poetics of Culture." In *The New Historicism* edited by H. Aram Vessar. New York: Routledge, 1989.

Greenfield, Thomas Allan. *Work and the Work Ethic in American Drama, 1920–1970*. Columbia: University of Missouri Press, 1982.

H., C. Review of *The International*, New Playwrights' Theatre, Cherry Lane Theatre, New York. *New York American*, 16 January 1928.

Hammond, Percy. "The Dreamy Mr. Lawson Talks Hysterically in His Sleep," Review of *The Pure in Heart*, Aldrich and De Liagre, Jr., Longacre Theater, New York. *New York Herald-Tribune*, 21 March 1934.

———. Review of *Gentlewoman*, Group Theatre, Cort Theatre, New York. *New York Herald-Tribune*, 23 March 1934.

———. Review of *Loud Speaker*, New Playwrights' Theatre, 52nd Street Theatre, New York. *New York Herald-Tribune*, 3 March 1927.

———. Review of *Nirvana*, Noble, Ryan, and Livy, Greenwich Village Theater, New York. *New York Herald-Tribune*, 14 March 1926.

———. Review of *Processional*, Theatre Guild, Garrick Theatre, New York. *New York Herald-Tribune*, 13 January 1925.

Held, Jennie. Review of *The Pure in Heart* and *Gentlewoman*. *New Theatre*, 9 April 1934.

Hethmon, Robert H. Interview with John Howard Lawson, 25 April 1964. *Lawson Papers*, b. 39, f. 1.

Hewitt, Bernard. *Theatre U.S.A., 1668 to 1957: A History by Eyewitnesses*. New York: McGraw-Hill, 1959.

Himmelstein, Morgan. *Drama Was a Weapon: The Left-Wing Theatre in New York, 1929–1941*. New Brunswick, NJ: Rutgers University Press, 1963.

Hoffman, Frederick J. *The Twenties: American Writing in the Postwar Decade*. New York: Free Press, 1962.

Hull, Shelley. Letter to Lawson, 18 March 1923. *Lawson Papers*, b. 4, f. 1.

Hyman, Collete A. *Staging Strikes: Workers' Theatre and the American Labor Movement*. Philadelphia: Temple University Press, 1997.

Iggers, George G. *Historiography in the Twentieth Century: From Scientific Objectivity to the Postmodern Challenge*. Middletown, CT: Wesleyan University Press, 1997.

Jameson, Fredric. "Towards Dialectical Criticism." In *Marxism and Form: Twentieth-Century Dialectical Theories of Literature*. Princeton, NJ: Princeton University Press, 1971.

Kempton, Murray. *Part of Our Time*. New York: Simon and Schuster, 1955.

Kerrigan, Ron. Summary of *Dynamite*. *Internet Movie Database*. http://www.imdb.com.

Knapp, Bettina. *French Theatre 1918–1939*. London: Macmillan, 1985.

Krutch, Joseph Wood. "Hard Facts," Review of *Nirvana*, Noble, Ryan, and Livy, Greenwich Village Theater, New York. *The Nation*, 17 March 1926.

———. "Mr. Lawson Comes Back," Review of *Success Story*, Group Theatre, Maxine Elliott Theatre, New York. *The Nation*, 12 October 1932.

———. "Sound and Fury," Review of *Gentlewoman*, Group Theatre, Cort Theatre, New York. *The Nation*, 11 April 1934.

———. "Strike Play," Review of *Marching Song*, Theatre Union, Bayes Theater, New York. *The Nation*, 27 February 1937.

Kuhn, Thomas S. *The Structure of Scientific Revolutions*. 2nd ed. Chicago: University of Chicago Press, 1970.

LaCapra, Dominick. *History and Criticism*. Ithaca, NY: Cornell University Press, 1985.

Lasch, Christopher. *The New Radicalism in America, 1889–1963: The Intellectual as Social Type*. New York: Alfred A. Knopf, 1965.

Lasky, Roberta Lynne. "The New Playwrights Theatre, 1927–1929," PhD dissertation, University of California, Davis, 1989.

Lawson, John Howard. "Art for Cube's Sake." *The Literary Monthly*, May 1913. *Lawson Papers*, b. 3, f. 2.

———. Autobiography. Various working titles including *A Way of Life*, *The History of a Writer's Mind*, *A Calendar of Commitment*, and *Another View of the Twenties and Thirties*. In *Lawson Papers*, b. 91–100.

———. "Communism in relation to *Success Story*," August 1932. *Lawson Papers*, b. 5, f. 5.

———. "The Crisis in the Theatre." *New Masses*, 15 December 1936.
———. "Debunking the Art Theatre." *New Masses*, June 1926.
———. "Essays in the Theatre." *New York Times*, 18 March 1934.
———. *Film in the Battle of Ideas*. New York: Masses and Mainstream, 1953.
———. *Film, the Creative Process: The Search for an Audio-Visual Language and Structure*. New York: Hill and Wang, 1964.
———. *The Hidden Heritage: A Rediscovery of the Ideas and Forces that Link the Thought of Our Time with the Culture of the Past*. New York: Citadel Press, 1950.
———. *A Hindoo Love Drama* (1913). *Lawson Papers*, b. 62, f. 5 and 6, and b. 63, f. 1.
———. "Inner Conflict and Proletarian Art." *New Masses*, 17 April 1934.
———. *The International*. New York: Macaulay, 1927.
———. *The Invisible Mob* (1925). Lawson *Papers*, b. 68, f. 1.
———. Leaflet to pledges of the New Playwrights' Theatre, April 1928. *Lawson Papers*, pkg. 1.
———. Letter to Gilbert Gabriel, March 1926. *Lawson Papers*, b. 5, f. 2.
———. Letter to Screen Writers' Guild Board, 4 January 1934. *Lawson Papers*, b. 6, f. 3.
———. Letter to the editor. *New York Times*, 18 March 1923.
———. Letter to the Screen Writers' Guild, 28 August 1933. *Lawson Papers*, b. 6, f. 3.
———. *Loud Speaker*. New York: Macaulay, 1927.
———. *The Mad Moon* (1919). *Lawson Papers*, b. 64, f. 4., and b. 66, f. 2.
———. *Marching Song*. New York: Dramatist Play Service, 1937.
———. *New England Fantasy* (1924). *Lawson Papers*, b. 66.
———. "The New Showmanship." In *Pinwheel* Program, February 1927.
———. *Nirvana* (1926). *Lawson Papers*, b. 67, f. 2 and 3.
———. "No Man's Land." Edited by Mandy Lawson. *The Lost Generation Journal* 5 (1977–78).
———. *Processional*. New York: Thomas Seltzer, 1925.
———. Program note for *Nirvana*, March 1926. *Lawson Papers*, b. 5, f. 1.
———. Program note for *The Pure in Heart*, March 1934. *Lawson Papers*, b. 5, f. 7.
———. *Roger Bloomer*. New York: Thomas Seltzer, 1923.
———. *Savitri* (1908). *Lawson Papers*, b. 62, f. 4.
———. *Servant-Master-Lover (Or, The Laughing Lip) (1916). Lawson Papers*, b. 63, f. 5 and 6.
———. *Souls: A Psychic Fantasy* (1915). *Lawson Papers*, b. 63, f. 2 and 3.
———. *The Spice of Life* (Or, *The Butterfly Lady*) (1916). *Lawson Papers*, b. 64, f. 2 and 3.
———. *Standards* (1915). *Lawson Papers*, b. 64, f. 1.
———. "Straight from the Shoulder." *New Theatre*, November 1934.
———. *Success Story*. New York: Farrar and Rinehart, 1932.
———. "Technique and the Drama." In *American Writers Congress*, edited by Henry Hart. New York: International, 1935.
———. *Theory and Technique of Playwriting*, 1936. Reprint, New York: Hill and Wang, 1960.
———. *Thunder Morning* (1955). *Lawson Papers*, b. 73, f. 3–5.
———. "Towards a Revolutionary Theatre: The Theatre—The Artist Must Take Sides." *New Theatre*, June 1934.

———. "What Is a Workers Theatre?" *New York Sun*, 12 November 1927.

———. *With a Reckless Preface: Two Plays "The Pure of Heart" and "Gentlewoman."* New York: Farrar and Rinehart, 1934.

———. *X Plus Y* (1924). *Lawson Papers*, b. 68, f. 3.

Leland, Gordon M. Review of *The International*, New Playwrights' Theatre, Cherry Lane Theatre, New York. *The Billboard*, 28 January 1928.

Lens, Sidney. *Radicalism in America*. New York: Thomas Y. Crowell, 1969.

Letter from Guild Board (Ralph Bloch) to John Howard Lawson, 6 December 1933. *Lawson Papers*, b. 6, f. 3.

Levenson, Michael, ed. *The Cambridge Companion to Modernism*. Cambridge: Cambridge University Press, 1999.

Levine, Ira A. *Left-Wing Dramatic Theory in the American Theatre*. Ann Arbor: UMI Research Press, 1985.

Levy, Melvin. "The World of Theatre," Review of *Gentlewoman*, Group Theatre, Cort Theatre, New York. *Daily Worker*, 28 March 1934.

Lewisohn, Ludwig. "Native Plays," Review of *Roger Bloomer*, Marguerite Barker, Greenwich Village Theatre, New York. *The Nation*, 21 March 1923.

Londré, Felicia Hardison, and Daniel J. Watermeier. *A History of North American Theatre: The United States, Canada, and Mexico: From Pre-Columbian Times to the Present*. New York: Continuum Publishing, 1998.

Long, Walter. "A Sociological Criticism of the American Drama." *Modern Quarterly*, Numbers 2 and 3 (1925).

Macgowan, Kenneth. Review of *Roger Bloomer*, Equity Players, 48th Street Theater, New York. *Wheeling (WV) News*, 11 March 1923.

———. Review of *Roger Bloomer*, Greenwich Village Theatre, New York. *Evening Globe*, 13 April 1923.

Mantle, Burns. "The New Guild Play Wild, Weird and Woozy," Review of *Processional*, Theatre Guild, Garrick Theater, New York. *Daily News*, 13 January 1925.

———. Review of *Marching Song*, Theatre Union, Bayes Theater, New York. *Daily News*, 18 February 1937.

———. Review of *Nirvana*, Noble, Ryan, and Livy, Greenwich Village Theater, New York. *Daily News*, 6 March 1926.

McCreath, Harrison William. "A Rhetorical Analysis of the Plays of John Howard Lawson," PhD dissertation, Stanford University, 1965.

McCullaugh, Behan C. *The Truth of History*. New York: Routledge, 1998.

Melzer, Annabelle. *Dada and Surrealist Performance*, 1976. Reprint, Baltimore: Johns Hopkins University Press, 1994.

Millay, Edna St. Vincent. Letter to the editor. Copy of letter sent to Lawson in *Lawson Papers*, b. 4, f. 1.

Millay, Edna St. Vincent, et al. Letter to John Howard Lawson, 21 January 1925. *Lawson Papers*, b. 4, f. 1.

Miller, Jordan, and Winifred Frazer. *American Drama between the Wars: A Critical History*. Boston: Twayne, 1991.

Mordden, Ethan. *The American Theatre*. New York: Oxford University Press, 1981.

Nathan, George Jean. "Drama as an Art." In *The Critic and the Drama*. New York: Alfred A. Knopf, 1922.

———. Review of *Loud Speaker*, New Playwrights' Theatre, 52nd Street Theatre, New York. *American Mercury*, May 1927.

———. Review of *Processional*, Theatre Guild, Garrick Theater, New York. *American Mercury*, March 1925.

"New Playwrights Abandon Productions." *New York Times*, 26 April 1929.

Notice. *New Masses*, June 1926.

Oates, Stephen. *Biography as History*. Waco, TX: Markham Press, 1991.

Osborn, E. W. Review of *The International*, New Playwrights' Theatre, Cherry Lane Theatre, New York. *Evening World*, 16 January 1928.

Ottanelli, Fraser M. *The Communist Party of the United States: From the Depression to World War II*. New Brunswick: Rutgers University Press, 1991.

Pollack, Arthur. Review of *Marching Song*, Theatre Union, Bayes Theater, New York. *Brooklyn Eagle*, 18 February 1937.

———. Review of *Nirvana*, Noble, Ryan, and Livy, Greenwich Village Theater, New York. *Brooklyn Eagle*, 4 March 1926.

Preston, Peter, and Paul Simpson-Housley. *Writing the City: Literature and the Urban Experience*. New York: Routledge, 1994.

Pyros, John. *Mike Gold: Dean of American Proletarian Writers*. New York: Dramatika Press, 1979.

Randrianarivony-Koziol, Liliane Claire. "Techniques of Commitment in the Thirties: A Study of the Selected Plays of John Howard Lawson," PhD dissertation, Indiana University, 1982.

Rathburn, Steven. Review of *The International*, New Playwrights' Theatre, Cherry Lane Theatre, New York. *Brooklyn Eagle*, 16 January 1928.

Review of *Success Story*, Group Theatre, Maxine Elliott Theatre, New York. *Daily Worker*, 3 October 1932.

Reynolds, Clay. *Stage Left: The Development of the American Social Drama in the Thirties*. Troy, NY: Whitston, 1986.

Sammons, Jeffrey L. *Literary Sociology and Practical Criticism: An Inquiry*. Bloomington: Indiana University Press, 1977.

Seibel, George. Review of *The Pure in Heart*, Theatre Guild, Nixon Theatre, Pittsburgh. *Pittsburgh Sun-Telegraph*, 11 October 1932.

Seldes, Gilbert. Review of *Marching Song*, Theatre Union, Bayes Theater, New York. *Scribner's*, April 1937.

Smiley, Sam. *The Drama of Attack: Didactic Plays of the American Depression*. Columbia: University of Missouri Press, 1972.

Smith, Barbara Herrnstein. *Contingencies of Value: Alternative Perspectives for Critical Theory*. Cambridge, MA: Harvard University Press, 1988.

Smith, Bernard. "Machines and Mobs." *New Masses*, March 1928.

Spence, Jonathan D. *The Gate of Heavenly Peace: The Chinese and Their Revolution, 1895–1980*. New York: Penguin, 1982.

Statement on *Marching Song*. New York State Communist Party, State Organization—Education Committee, *Lawson Papers*, pkg. 1.

Taylor, Karen Malpede. *People's Theatre in Amerika*. New York: Drama Book Specialists, 1972.

Toller, Ernst. *Transfiguration*. In *Seven Plays*. London: John Lane the Bodley Head, 1935.

Trainer, Kathleen Malia. "The Dissident Character in American Drama of the 1930s," PhD dissertation, University of Notre Dame, 1983.

Twyning, John. *London Dispossessed: Literature and Social Space in the Early Modern City*. New York: St. Martin's Press, 1998.

Tzara, Tristan. "Dada Manifesto, 1918." In *Modernism: An Anthology of Sources and Documents*, edited by Vassiliki Kolocotroni, Jane Goodman, and Olga Taxidou. Chicago: University of Chicago Press, 1998.

Valgemae, Mardi, and Harry T. Moore. *Accelerated Grimace: Expressionism in the American Drama of the 1920s*. Carbondale: Southern Illinois University Press, 1972.

Van Dyke, Thomas. Review of *The International*, New Playwrights' Theatre, Cherry Lane Theatre, New York. *New York Telegraph*, 16 January 1928.

Vessar, H. Aram. Introduction to *The New Historicism*. New York: Routledge, 1989.

Wainscott, Ronald H. *The Emergence of the Modern American Theatre, 1914–1929*. New Haven: Yale University Press, 1997.

Wald, Alan. "Culture and Commitment: US Communist Writers Reconsidered." In *Writing from the Left: New Essays on Radical Culture and Politics*. London: Verso, 1994.

Waldorf, Wilella. Review of *Marching Song*, Theatre Union, Bayes Theater, New York. *New York Post*, 18 February 1937.

Walker, Julia. *Expressionism and Modernism in the American Theatre: Bodies, Voices, Words*. Cambridge: Cambridge University Press, 2005.

Watson, Bradlee, and Benfield Pressey, eds. Introduction to *Processional*. In *Contemporary Drama: European, English and Irish, American Play*. New York: Scribner's, 1961.

Watts, Jr., Richard. Review of *Marching Song*, Theatre Union, Bayes Theater, New York. *New York Tribune*, 18 February 1937.

Wilder, Thornton. "The Turn of the Year." *Theatre Arts Monthly*, March 1925.

Wilson, Edmund. "An Appeal to Progressives." *New Republic*, 14 January 1931.

———. *Axel's Castle: A Study in the Imaginative Literature of 1870–1930, 1931*. Reprint, New York: Charles Scribner's Sons, 1959.

———. "Notes on Babbitt and More." *New Republic*, 19 March 1930. Reprinted in Edmund Wilson, *A Literary Chronicle, 1920–1950*. New York: Doubleday Anchor Books, 1956.

Wilson, Garff B. *Three Hundred Years of American Drama and Theatre*. Englewood Cliffs, NJ: Prentice-Hall, 1982.

Wilson, Norman. *History in Crisis? Recent Directions in Historiography*. Englewood Cliffs, NJ: Prentice Hall, 1998.

Winchell, George. Review of *Loud Speaker*, New Playwrights' Theatre, 52nd Street Theatre, New York. *New York Evening Graphic*, 3 March 1927.

Wise, Caroline. Letter to the editor. *New York Call*, 23 March 1923.

Woollcott, Alexander. "Life Behind the Scenes—Elmer Rice on Processional." *New York Sun*, 19 January 1925.

———. Review of *Nirvana*, Noble, Ryan, and Livy, Greenwich Village Theater, New York. *The World*, 4 March 1926.

———. Review of *Processional*, Theatre Guild, Garrick Theater, New York. *New York Sun*, 13 January 1925.

———. Review of *The International*, New Playwrights' Theatre, Cherry Lane Theatre, New York. *The World*, 16 January 1928.

Young, Stark. "Forward Equity," Review of *Roger Bloomer*, Marguerite Barker, Greenwich Village Theatre, New York. *New Republic*, 21 March 1923.

———. Review of *Processional*, Theatre Guild, Garrick Theater, New York. *New York Times*, 13 January 1925.

———. Review of *Processional*, Theatre Guild, Garrick Theater, New York. *New York Times*, 18 January 1925.

Zimel, Heyman. "Messiah of the New Technique." *American Hebrew*, 25 March 1927.

Index

Abbott, George, 75, 226n. 73
activist expressionism, 42–43, 49–50
Actor's Equity, 238n. 56
Adam Solitaire (Basshe), 230n. 16
Adding Machine, The (Rice), 42
Adler, Luther, 237n. 43
Adler, Stella, 237n. 43, 242n. 24
Airways, Inc. (Dos Passos), 90, 231n. 26
Aldington, Richard, 121
Aldrich, Richard, 165
American exceptionalism, 129
American Federation of Labor (AFL), 146
American left. *See* leftist community
American Red Cross, 35
American Socialist Party (SP), 30–32. *See also* Communist Labor Party (CLP); Communist Party (CP)
American Writers' Congress, 150–53, 180, 201–2
anarchy movement, 82–85
Anderson, John, 112, 166, 172, 192
Anderson, Margaret, 120–21
Anderson, Maxwell, 3
anti-Fascism, 195. *See also* Popular Front
antihumanists, 151–53
art: audiences and, 154–55; politics and, 128–29, 148–49, 198
Artef (Workers Theatrical Alliance), 158
artistic rebels, 3
artist-rebel, JHL as, 21–22, 114, 123–24, 149–53, 215n. 37
Artokov, Alexander, 86
art theatre: Cheney and, 22–24, 26, 79–80; JHL and, 59, 81, 86–87, 116–17, 199; little theatre movement and, 22–23, 216n. 16
Ash Can exhibition, 216n. 10
Atkinson, Brooks: on *Gentlewoman,* 172; on JHL, 112; on *Loud Speaker,* 103; on *Marching Song,* 192; on *Nirvana,* 75; on *Pure in Heart,* 166; on *Success Story,* 140–41
audience response: interplay between art and, 154–55; to New Playwrights, 88–89; to *Roger Bloomer* and its critics, 48
Authors' League of America, 143–45, 147

automatic writing, 121
avant-garde, the, 18, 101, 120–24, 150. *See also* Dada; expressionism; surrealism

Babbitt, Irving, 150–53
Bandbox Theatre, 216n. 16
Barker, Marguerite, 46–47
Barnard, Rita, 13–14
Barnes, Djuna, 121
Basshe, Emanuel (Em Jo), 88–90, 136, 230n. 16, 231n. 26
Baty, Gaston, 109–10
Becque, Don O., 233n. 57
Bedacht, Max, 94
Behrman, S. N., 171
Beilenson, Lawrence, 143, 145
Bell, James, 241n. 14
Belt, The (Sifton), 89–90
Bennett, Tony, 9–11
Berkman, Alexander, 121
Bessie, Alvah, 226n. 73
blindness, in works of JHL, 102
Bloch, Beverle Rochelle, 7
Bloch, Ralph, 141, 143
Block, Anita, 49
Boda, Mike, 83–84
Bonn, John, 200
Boston State House, 239n. 93
"Bourgeois Hamlet in Our Time, A" (Gold), 175
bourgeois social and political system, 122
Brannigan, John, 10
Brecht, Bertolt, 92, 158
Bresci, Gaetano, 83
Breton, André, 53, 72–73
Bright, John, 142
Brooks, Van Wyck, 119, 219n. 46
Broun, Heywood, 65–66
Broussard, Louis, 222n. 17
Browder, Earl, 94, 129, 155, 177, 202, 245n. 8
Brown, Anthony, 191
Brown, John M., 191
Brown, Richard Peyron, 7
Browne, Earl, 89
Buchwald, Nathaniel, 193
Buhle, Paul, 128–29
business theatre, 18–19, 59

Calverton, V. F., 151
Cambridge structuralism, 36
Cannon, James P., 93–94, 155
capitalism, 110, 122, 128, 139
Carlyle, Thomas, 213n. 20
Carnovsky, Morris, 242n. 24
Caudwell, Christopher, 9, 214n. 27
Centuries, The (Basshe), 89–90
Cheney, Sheldon: and art theatre, 22–24, 26, 79–80; and JHL, 1, 87; views of, 32
Chiang Kai-shek, 104–6, 233n. 51
Chinese Communist Party (CCP), 104–5, 233n. 52
Chinese Nationalist Party (KMT), 104–5, 233n. 51
Chinese National Revolutionary Army, 104–5
Clark, Barrett H., 3–4
Clurman, Harold: on JHL, 1, 126–27, 171–72; JHL's correspondence with, 136–37; on *Pure in Heart,* 163; on *Success Story,* 141
Cohan, George M., 19
Cohen, Lester, 178
Cohn, Harry, 177–78
Cole, Lester, 141–42
Collins, Seward, 150–53
Columbia Pictures, 177–78, 202
Comintern (Communist International), 31–32, 92–94, 156, 240–41n. 4
commercial theatre, 18–19, 59
commitment dilemmas, in JHL's work, 189–90
Communism: Michael Gold on, 25–26; in *International,* 108–10; JHL and, 128, 137–40, 153, 196; and social fascism, 156; in US, 92–94
Communist International (Comintern), 31–32, 92–94, 156, 240–41n. 4

Communist Labor Party (CLP), 32, 92
Communist Party (CP), 32, 92
Communist Party of America (CPA), 93
Communist Party USA (CP-USA): Browder's expulsion from, 245n. 8; factionalism within, 155; JHL and, 180–81, 193, 202; leftward movement of, 129–30; Gold and, 231n. 21; origins of, 94; Popular Front and, 156–57, 240–41n. 4
Connelly, Marc, 145, 228–29n. 110
conscious will, JHL on, 181–82
constructivist movement, 90, 97
Coolidge, Calvin, 102
Corbin, John, 47–48
Cousins, Mark, 9–11
Cowley, Malcolm, 151
CP-USA. *See* Communist Party USA (CP-USA)
Crane, Hart, 121–22, 235n. 10
creative theatre. *See* art theatre
critical response to works of JHL, 1–2, 79. *See also under individual play titles*
criticism, paradigm shift in, 29–30
critics, progressive, 219n. 46
Cronaca Sovversiva (journal), 83
cult of the primitive, 36, 58, 63
Cultural Front, The (Denning), 95
cummings, e. e., 53, 121–22, 235n. 10
Cutler School, New York City, 16
Czolgosz, Leon, 83

Dada: JHL and, 53, 60–62, 226n. 68; in *Loud Speaker,* 96–97; in *Nirvana,* 72–73; *Roger Bloomer* and, 222n. 24
"Dada Manifesto, 1918" (Tzara), 60
Dale, Alan, 47, 64
Davis, Burton, 103, 144
Davis, Dave, 217n. 25
Death in an Office. See *Success Story* (Lawson)
death of God, 73–74
Deeter, Jasper, 86, 89
De Liagre, Alfred, Jr., 165
Dell, Floyd, 219n. 47
De Mille, Cecil B., 126
Denning, Michael, 95
Dexter, Charles E., 192–93
dialectical thought, 114–18, 149
Dies, Martin, 202, 245n. 9
Diggins, John P., 82, 85, 156
Donnelly, Dorothy, 19
Doomsday Circus (Basshe), 203n. 16
Dos Passos, John: *Airways, Inc.,* 90, 231n. 26; debate with Garlin, 117; and *International,* 113, 233n. 57; and JHL, 19–21, 53, 136, 217–18n. 27; and New Playwrights, 88; in Paris, 34–35; and *Roger Bloomer,* 50; Sacco and Vanzetti executions, 85
Drain, Kathryn (JHL's first wife), 35–36, 52, 225n. 58
dramatic criticism, paradigm shift in, 29–30
dramatic structure, JHL and: conventional, 171; episodic, 216n. 16; of *Marching Song,* 190; of *Processional,* 58; social content and, 180–81; of *Success Story,* 138
Dramatists Guild, 144
Duclos, Jacques, 245n. 8

Eagleton, Terry, 214n. 27
Earth (Basshe), 89–90
Edmund, Susan (JHL's second wife), 68
Einstein, Albert, 68–69, 74
electoral politics Communists, 93
episodic structure, 216n. 16
Equity Players, 36, 46, 79
Espionage Act of 1917, 31
expressionism: activist, 42–43, 49–50; German, 41–42; Louis Broussard on, 222n. 17; changes in mode of, 222n. 19; JHL and, 35–36, 41, 46, 49–50, 221n. 7; mystic, 41–42; passivity in, 222n. 25

Faragoh, Francis, 88–90, 230n. 16–17, 231n. 26

farce style, in *Loud Speaker,* 98
Fascism, 108–10, 155–57, 195
Federal Theatre Project, 200–201, 244–45n. 1, 245n. 9
film industry: Columbia Pictures, 177–78, 202; MGM Studios, 126, 141–49, 238n. 68; RKO Studio, 126; screenplays by JHL, 126, 201–3, 236n. 20, 245n. 5; Screen Writers' Guild, 141–43, 147–48, 158
Fine, Nathan, 86
Fletcher, Anne, 6
Flexner, Eleanor, 201
Forrest, Sam, 19
Foster, William, 93–94
France: JHL in, 34–35, 40, 52–53, 86, 220n. 5; and League of Nations, 156
Frank, Waldo, 125, 136, 219n. 46
Frazer, James G., 36
Freeman, Joseph, 113–14, 117, 153
Freudian theory, 35–36, 41, 45–46, 72, 227–28n. 97
Friderici, Blanche, 226n. 73

Gabriel, Gilbert, 1, 65–66, 76, 80, 140
Gallagher, Catherine, 10
Galleani, Luigi, 83
Gardner, Mary, 216n. 10
Gardner, Robert M., 7–8
Garland Fund, 231n. 25
Garlin, Sender, 113, 117
Garrett, Oliver, 141, 143
Gellert, Hugo, 86
Gentlewoman (Lawson), 159–77; critical response to, 4, 172–73, 195; JHL on, 170–71; productions of, 159, 209, 242n. 24; synopsis of, 166–70; thematic center of, 171–72
German expressionism, 41–42
Glaspell, Susan, 3
God, death of, 73–74
Gold, Michael: criticism of JHL, 175–77; and leftist politics, 25–26, 32, 155–56, 231n. 21; New Humanists and, 151–53; *New Masses* and, 231n. 25; New Playwrights and, 88–90, 218n. 34, 230n. 17, 231n. 26; on proletarian theatre, 24–25, 240n. 94; Worker's Drama League and, 86
Goldberg, Neal, 144, 217n. 25
Goldman, Emma, 21, 121
Gorelik, Mordecai, 64, 75, 226n. 73, 241n. 14, 242n. 24
Grattan, Hartley, 151
"great man" theory, 7–8, 213n. 20
Green, Howard, 142
Green, William, 146
Greenblatt, Stephen, 10, 12, 77–78
Greenfield, Thomas Allen, 6
Green Gang, 105
Greenwich Village Theatre, 46–47, 52, 75
Gribble, Harry W., 89
Group Theatre, 132, 158, 237n. 43, 242n. 24

Hall, Dorothy, 241n. 14
Halstead School, Yonkers, 16
Hamilton, Clayton, 219n. 46
Hammond, Percy, 64, 75, 103, 166, 172
Harris, Sam, 19
Haymarket Riots of 1886, 83
haystack epiphany, 21, 217n. 25
Hegel, Georg W., 181–82
Helburn, Theresa, 159
Held, Jennie, 173
Henderson, Archibald, 219n. 46
Herndon Defense Committee, 177
Hewitt, Barnard, 5
Hillyer, Robert, 220n. 1
History of North American Theatre, The (Londré and Watermeier), 5
Hitler, Adolf, 155–56
Hoboken Blues (Gold), 89–90
Hollywood, JHL in, 141–49, 201. *See also* film industry
Hollywood Independent Citizens Committee of Arts, Sciences, and Professions, 202
Hollywood Quarterly, 202
Hollywood Ten, 144, 203, 245n. 10
Hoover, J. Edgar, 82–83, 220n. 4

hopelessness. *See* pessimism
House Committee on Un-American Activities (HUAC), 1–2, 5, 149, 203, 245n. 9
Hughes, Rupert, 142
Hull, Shelley, 46–47, 79
Hyman, Colette A., 6

Ibsen, Henrik J., 180–82
Immigration Act of 1903, 83
Industrial Workers of the World (IWW), 30
International, The (Lawson), 104–14; critical response to, 1, 4, 112–13, 117; JHL's worldview and, 110–12, 125; New Playwrights and, 89–90; originating conditions for, 104–6; productions of, 209, 233n. 57; synopsis of, 106–11
Italy, JHL in, 35

Jameson, Fredric, 9–11, 114–16
jazz: in *International,* 109; JHL's use of, 96; in *Processional,* 54, 57–58; in *Pure in Heart,* 160, 163
Jeliffe, Smith E., 227–28n. 97
Jerome, V. J., 158
Johnson, Hugh S., 147–148
Joint Fact-Finding Committee on Un-American Activities of the California State Legislature, 202
Joyce, James, 128
Jung, Carl G., 35, 228n. 97

Kahn, Otto, 88, 230n. 17
Kaufman, George S., 158
Kerrigan, Ron, 235–36n. 20
Kirkpatrick, Mary, 18
KMT (Kuomintang), 104–5, 233n. 51
Krutch, Joseph W., 76, 140, 172–73, 194
Kuhn, Thomas S., 28, 219n. 42
Ku Klux Klan, 56–58
Kuomintang (KMT), 104–5, 233n. 51

labor unions. *See* trade unions
LaCapra, Dominick, 214n. 25
Lasky, Roberta Lynn, 6, 90
Lawson, John Howard: early interest in theatre, 17; exit from theatre, 205; family of, 15–16, 215n. 1, 225n. 58; internal struggles of, 95–96, 124–25, 136, 150, 159, 189–90; marriages of, 35–36, 52, 68, 225n. 58; metaphysical phase of, 21, 68–69, 77, 217–18n. 27; misreading of works by, 11–12; as political revolutionary, 149–53, 194, 196–205; response to critics by, 76, 176; theatrical vision of, 50–52, 58–61, 189–91, 197, 243n. 45; worldview of, 20–21, 119–20, 127–28, 177–78, 226n. 68. *See also under individual plays*
Lawson, John Howard, works by (books), 4, 159, 181–82, 196, 203
Lawson, John Howard, works by (essays): "Art for Cube's Sake," 18; "Communism in Relation to *Success Story,*" 137–40; "Crisis in the Theatre," 197–98; "Debunking the Art Theatre," 86–87, 116–17; "Inner Conflict and Proletarian Art," 176; "New Showmanship," 90–91, 116–17, 165; "Straight from the Shoulder," 179–81; "Technique and the Drama," 180; "Towards a Revolutionary Theatre," 178–79; "What Is a Workers' Theatre?", 91–92, 116–17
Lawson, John Howard, works by (plays). *See individual titles*
Lawson, John Howard, works by (screenplays), 126, 201–3, 236n. 20, 245n. 5
Lawson, John Howard, works by (unproduced scripts): *Hindoo Love Drama,* 18; *Humanlike,* 220n. 3; *Invisible Mob,* 97, 232n. 36; *Jazz Tragedy,* 96, 159, 232n. 36; *Mad Moon,* 68, 220n. 3; *New England Fantasy,* 220n. 3; *Red Square,* 128, 138, 150; *Saga Center,* 235n. 10; *Savitri,* 17; *Silver Cord,* 220n. 3; *Social Whirl,* 232n. 36; *Spice of Life,* 19, 216n. 18; *Thunder Morning,* 203; untitled working draft, 77; *X Plus Y,* 96–97, 232n. 36

League of Nations, 156
League of Worker's Theatres, 158
Le Baron, William, 126
leftist community: aesthetics of, 32; authors of, 2–3; dramatic theory of, 27–28; factionalism within, 78–79, 155–57; lyrical left, 27–33, 78, 121, 150, 199, 219n. 47; transformations of, 31, 92, 94–95. *See also* New Playwrights; Popular Front
left-wing, defined, 223–24n. 36
Leland, Gordon M., 1, 112–13
Lenin, Vladimir I., 32, 93, 128
Let 'Em Eat Cake (Kaufman and Ryskind), 158
Levenson, Michael, 218–19n. 40
Levine, Ira A., 6, 27–28, 157–58
Levy, Melvin, 173
Lewisohn, Irene and Alice, 230n. 16
Lewisohn, Ludwig, 48–49
literary criticism. *See* critical response to works of JHL
literary fascism, 151. *See also* New Humanists
literary Marxism, 150–53
Little Review, The (magazine), 120–21
little theatre movement, 22–23, 216n. 16. *See also* art theatre
Londré, Felicia Hardison, 5
Longacre Theatre, 165
Loud Speaker (Lawson), 96–104; characterizations in, 101–2; critical response to, 4, 89, 103; JHL on, 104, 125; JHL's work on, 53, 232n. 36; New Playwrights and, 90; originating conditions for, 96–97; productions of, 209; synopsis of, 97–101
Louise (Charpentier), 17, 216n. 10
Lovestone, Jay, 93–94, 129–30, 155
Lozowick, Louis, 86
lyrical left, 27–33, 78, 121, 150, 199, 219n. 47

Macgowan, Kenneth, 46–47
Macpherson, Jeanie, 126
Mainstream (journal), 202
Maltz, Albert, 158
Mankiewicz, Joseph, 143
Mantle, Burns, 64, 75, 192
Mao Tse-Tung, 105
Marching Song (Lawson), 177–94; critical response to, 191–94; JHL on, 191, 193–94; JHL's objective in, 183; JHL's worldview and, 189–90, 196–99; originating conditions for, 178–83; productions of, 159, 209; synopsis of, 184–89; thematic design of, 190
Marion, Frances, 143
Masses and Mainstream (journal), 202
Massey, Edward, 89, 231n. 21, 241n. 14
materialist aesthetics, defined, 157–58, 224n. 52
materialist methods of analysis, 8–10
Matisse, Henri, 36
Mayakovsky, Vladimir V., 92, 128
May Day Riots of 1919, 83
Mayer, Edwin J., 142
Mayer, Louis B., 142
McCreath, Harrison W., 213n. 22
McKinley, William, assassination of, 83
Meisner, Sanford, 226n. 73
Mencken, H. L., 29
Merrian, Frank, 177–78
metaphysics, post-Einstein, 68–69
Meyerhold, Vsevolod Y., 92, 97, 232n. 39
MGM studios, JHL and, 126, 141–49, 238n. 68
Mielziner, Jo, 241n. 14
Milestone, Lewis, 201
Millay, Edna St. Vincent, 3, 48, 66
Mingo County, West Virginia, 52
Minor, Robert, 94
modernism, 95, 150–53, 212n. 10, 218–19n. 40
modern theatre artists, 3
Moderwell, Hiram, 219n. 46
Moeller, Phillip, 64
Mooser, George, 19
Mordden, Ethan, 5
More, Paul E., 150–53
Morelli gang, 84

Morosco, Oliver, 19
Motion Picture Industry Code, 146–47
mystic expressionism, 41–42

Nanjing, China, 104–5, 233n. 51
Nathan, George J., 28–30, 32, 64–65, 79–80, 103
National Industrial Recovery Act (NIRA) hearings, 145–46
Nazism, rise of, 155–56
Neighborhood Playhouse, 90, 230n. 16
neo-Marxists' methods, 12–13
New Critical analysis, 7
New England Fantasy, A. See *Nirvana* (Lawson)
New Era American society, 35
New Historians, 10, 12–13
New Humanists, 150–53
New Playwrights: audience response to, 88–89; Gold and, 218n. 34, 230n. 17; JHL and, 90–92, 114, 126, 179, 199, 230–31n. 20; O'Neill and, 230n. 16; seasons of, 231n. 21, 231n. 26; theatre scholars on, 6, 232n. 39
Newsboy (Jerome), 158
new showmanship, the, 87, 90–91, 96, 116–17, 165
new theatre, 29
Nietzsche, Friedrich W., 73–74
nihilism, of late 1920s, 121–22
NIRA (National Industrial Recovery Act) hearings, 145–46
Nirvana (Lawson), 68–77; basis for, 220n. 3; characterizations in, 72–74; critical response to, 4, 75–76, 228–29n. 110; JHL on, 70–72, 125; JHL's personal history and, 227n. 92; JHL's work on, 53, 216n. 16; originating conditions for, 68–69; productions of, 209; synopsis of, 69–70
Noble, Robert P., 75
Noble, Ryan, and Livy, 75
Nolan, Lloyd, 242n. 24
noncommercial theatre community, 22–26, 78–81, 117–18, 219n. 40
nonreflexive mode of thinking, 114–18
Norton-Harjes Ambulance Corps, 19–20, 34, 217n. 25

Odets, Clifford, 6, 201
O'Neill, Eugene: expressionistic dramas of, 42; *Hairy Ape*, 226n. 68, 226n. 70; JHL on, 182; as modern theatre artist, 3; New Playwrights and, 230n. 16
optimism, in activist expressionism, 42
Ornitz, Samuel, 142
Osborn, E. W., 112

Palmer, A. Mitchell, 82–83, 220n. 4
Palmer raids, 82, 220n. 4
Parlor Magic (Lawson), 201, 203
Peace on Earth (Maltz and Sklar), 158, 178
people's revolution, 196–99
pessimism: of early 1930s, 119–20; in *International*, 109; in late 1920s, 120–22; in *Loud Speaker*, 102–3; mystic expressionism and, 42; in *Nirvana*, 73; in *Processional*, 53
Peters, Paul, 158
Picasso, Pablo, 36, 61
Pinwheel (Faragoh), 90, 230n. 16
Piscator, Erwin, 92, 109–10
politics, and art, 128–29, 148–49, 198
Pollack, Arthur, 75–76, 191
Popular Front: CP-USA and, 156–57, 240–41n. 4; factionalism in, 196; JHL's rejection of, 199; left-wing theatre and, 191; and social energy, 159, 194–95
Porter, Katherine Anne, 151
Processional (Lawson), 50–68; characterizations in, 53–54, 58, 61–63; compared to *Hairy Ape*, 226n. 70; critical response to, 1, 4, 7, 64–67, 175; drafts of, 50–52; formal achievements in, 80; JHL on, 60–61, 81, 125, 244–45n. 1; JHL's work on, 35, 224–25n. 57; JHL's worldview and, 50–51; productions of, 200–201, 209; sequel to, 159; synopsis of, 54–58

progressive democracy, 80, 153, 195, 197, 199
proletarian art, 24–25
"Proletarian Realism" (Gold), 240n. 94
Proletbuehne, 158
Provincetown Players, 36, 218n. 34, 230n. 16
psychology-or-physics schism, 68–69
Pure in Heart, The (Lawson), 159–77; characterizations in, 163; critical response to, 4, 132, 166, 195; dramatic techniques in, 160, 163–65; JHL on, 125; JHL's work on, 150, 232n. 36; productions of, 158–59, 209, 241n. 14; synopsis of, 159–63

radical, defined, 219n. 48
Randrianarivony-Koziol, Liliane Claire, 7
Rankin, John, 245n. 9
Rathburn, Steve, 112
Rauh, Ida, 86
reading formations, 10–11, 26–28, 32–33
realism, 87, 106–7, 240n. 94. *See also* socialist realism
religion, JHL and, 16–17, 74
Reuters, 18–19
revolutionary, defined, 219n. 48
revolutionary ideology, 78–80, 198–99
revolutionary theatre, 22–26, 165, 178–82
Rice, Elmer, 3, 6, 42, 67
RKO studio, 126, 239n. 75
Roger Bloomer (Lawson), 36–50; characterizations in, 41; compared with other works by JHL, 102–3, 163–66; conflation of playwright and protagonist in, 221n. 14; critical response to, 4, 46–49; drafts of, 35–36, 43–46; influence of German expressionism on, 42; inspirations for, 21, 217n. 25; JHL's worldview and, 50–51, 125, 139–40; productions of, 209; staying power of, 68; synopsis of, 36–39
Roosevelt, Franklin D., 142, 146–47, 156
Roosevelt, Theodore, 83
Rosenblatt, Sol, 148
Russian Revolution, 128
Ruthenberg, Charles, 93
Ryskind, Morrie, 158

Sacco, Nicola, 82–85, 229n. 2
Sacco and Vanzetti executions, 85–86, 116–17, 122, 124, 239n. 93
Salsedo, Andrea, 82–84
Sammons, Jeffrey L., 9
Schopenhauer, Arthur, 182
science, new religion of, 74
Scottsboro Boys case, 127, 177
Screen Writers' Guild, 141–43, 147–48, 158
Seibel, George, 132
Seldes, Gilbert, 191–92
Servant-Master-Lover (Lawson), 19, 216n. 18
Shanghai, China, 104–5
Shanghai General Labor Union, 105
Shock Troupe of the Workers' Laboratory Theatre, 158
Sifton, Paul, 89
Silcox, Louise, 145–46
Sinclair, Upton, 90, 178, 231n. 26
Singing Jailbirds (Sinclair), 90, 231n. 26
Sklar, George, 158
Smith, Barbara H., 154–55
Smith, Bernard, 103
social energy, 77–81, 94–96, 194–95, 197–98, 204, 213n. 24; Popular Front and, 159; of 1930s, 157–58
social fascism, 156
socialism, 30–32
socialist realism, 139–40, 182–83, 243n. 45
social melodramas, 28
social modernism, 95
Stalin, Joseph, 32, 94, 130, 202
Standards (Lawson), 19, 216n. 17
Steel (Wexley), 158
Stevedore (Sklar and Peters), 158, 178
stock market crash, 123–24
Strasberg, Lee, 226n. 73, 242n. 24

Stravinsky, Igor, 36, 63
Strike! (Gold), 88
structuralism, Cambridge, 36
structure. *See* dramatic structure
Success at Any Price (film), 239n. 75
Success Story (Lawson), 125–41; characterizations in, 136; Clurman on, 136–37; critical response to, 4, 140–41; film adaptation of, 239n. 75; JHL on, 124–25, 237n. 43; productions of, 209; social commentary in, 139–40; as social currency, 150; synopsis of, 132–36
Sunup to Sundown (Faragoh), 230n. 16
Sun Yat-sen, 233n. 51
surrealism, 34–35, 53, 72–73, 77
Surrealist Manifestos (Breton), 72
symbolic style, in *The International*, 107

Taylor, Karen M., 230n. 17
Tenney, Jack, 202
Thayer, Webster, 84–85
Theatre Guild: art theatre and, 87; and *Processional*, 52, 64–66, 79–80, 225n. 63; and *Pure in Heart*, 132, 159; rejection of *Nirvana* by, 74–75; rejection of *Roger Bloomer* by, 36; and social energy of 1930s, 158
theatre scholars, 3–8, 212n. 15, 232n. 39
Theatre Union, 158, 191
theory of relativity, 74
They Shall Not Die (Wexley), 158, 178
Third Period, in Soviet politics, 94, 130
Thompson, Woodman, 46
thought, dialectical versus nonreflexive mode, 114–18
Threepenny Opera (Brecht and Weill), 158
Tobacco Road (Kirkland/Caldwell), 158
Toller, Ernst, 43
"Towards Proletarian Art" (Gold), 24–25
Trade Union Educational League (TUEL), 93
trade unions: American Federation of Labor (AFL), 93, 146; legal contract approach to organizing, 238n. 56, 238n. 60; New Playwrights and, 88; in *Processional*, 52; Shanghai General Labor Union, 105; Theatre Union, 158, 191; Workers (Communist) Party and, 93
Transfiguration (Toller), 43
Tresca, Carlo, 83–84
Trotsky, Leon, 93–94
Trumbo, Dalton, 203
Tzara, Tristan, 53, 60

Umberto I, King of Italy, assassination of, 83
unions. *See* trade unions
US armed forces, in China, 104–5
USSR, and League of Nations, 156

Van Dyke, Thomas, 113
Vanzetti, Bartolomeo, 82–85, 229n. 2. *See also* Sacco and Vanzetti executions
vaudevillian method, in works by JHL, 58–62

Wagner, Walter, 201
Wald, Alan, 2–3
Waldorf, Wilella, 192
Walker, June, 226n. 73
Ward, Lem, 191, 200
Washington Square Players, 216n. 16
Watermeier, Donald, 5
Watts, Richard, Jr., 191
Weill, Kurt, 158
Weinstone, William, 94
Weitzenkorn, Louis, 141–42
Wexley, John, 158
White Legion Knights, 177
Wilder, Thornton, 66–67, 152
Williams College, JHL at, 18, 221n. 7
Wilson, Edmund, 129–31, 146, 151–53
Wilson, Garff B., 5
Winchell, George, 103
Wobblies. *See* Industrial Workers of the World (IWW)

Wood, John S., 245n. 9
Woollcott, Alexander, 64, 67, 75, 112
Workers (Communist) Party (WP or WCP), 93–94. *See also* Communist Party USA (CP-USA)
Workers' Drama League, 86, 88
World War II, Communist Party and, 240–41n. 4
Writers' Congress, 150–53, 180, 201–2

Young, Stark, 49, 65–66
"youngster going to the city" storyline, 40–41, 221n. 13

Ziman, Edward A., 233n. 57

Jonathan L. Chambers is an associate professor in the Department of Theatre and Film at Bowling Green State University, where he teaches courses in dramatic and performance theory and criticism, modernism, and acting. His essays have appeared in *Theatre Symposium*, *Theatre History Studies*, *Theatre Annual*, *New England Theatre Journal*, and *Journal of American Drama and Theatre*. He has also served as editor for the journal *Theatre Topics*.

THEATER IN THE AMERICAS

The goal of the series is to publish a wide range of scholarship on theater and performance, defining theater in its broadest terms and including subjects that encompass all of the Americas.

The series focuses on the performance and production of theater and theater artists and practitioners but welcomes studies of dramatic literature as well. Meant to be inclusive, the series invites studies of traditional, experimental, and ethnic forms of theater; celebrations, festivals, and rituals that perform culture; and acts of civil disobedience that are performative in nature. We publish studies of theater and performance activities of all cultural groups within the Americas, including biographies of individuals, histories of theater companies, studies of cultural traditions, and collections of plays.